Rosebud

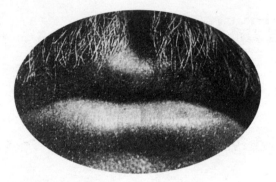

It was a miracle of rare device,
A sunny pleasure-dome with caves of ice!
　　—Samuel Taylor Coleridge, "Kubla Khan"

ROSEBUD

The Story of Orson Welles

DAVID THOMSON

LITTLE, BROWN AND COMPANY

A *Little, Brown* Book

First published in the United States in 1996
by Alfred A. Knopf, Inc.
First published in Great Britain in 1996
by Little, Brown and Company

A CIP catalogue record for this book
is available from the British Library.

ISBN 0 316 91437 1

Printed and bound in Great Britain
by Clays Ltd, St Ives plc

Little, Brown and Company (UK)
Brettenham House
Lancaster Place
London WC2E 7EN

for Rachel

CONTENTS

Part One

KENOSHA KID
1915-39

"That's a lot to try to get into a newsreel."

1

Not a Simple Man

H E   W A S   A L O N E the night of October 9–10, 1985, which is not
the same as lonely.

He was not well or strong: he was too heavy; he had diabetes; his heart
was exhausted. He had his own mother lode of disappointment, rejection
and failure. But that fragility is not the same as self-pity, or even melancholy. He had always been the most important person in his own drama.
His "failure" was a sustaining tragedy—his thing, his song. He was not a
possessive man in obvious ways, not with money or people. He let those
things slip through his hands. But some airs and attributes he kept—command, the magician's power, the rights on self-destruction.

He was uncommon in the lucidity with which he knew that, and acted
on it. He was not like others. They could not be like him. He was determined on that barrier. Why are there so few of you, he had taunted audiences, and so many of me?

He had known great friendships; he had left several people living in
his own rich shadow, whether they recognized the gloom or not. He had
moved people, men and women, with anecdotes, laughter, heady company, genius, beauty, the brightest heaven of invention. He had been
loved, admired, revered—yet something in him was resistant to giving up
loneness. Friendships never quite convinced, or satisfied, him. There was
something implacable in his soul that depended on being isolated, alone
in the house, whether it was Xanadu or a relatively modest place in the
Hollywood hills.

He died alone, that night, sitting in his chair, typing up script for

The days that we have seen.
—William Shakespeare, *Henry IV, Part Two;* 1979, at the funeral of Darryl F. Zanuck
(photo by Gary Franklin)

things he meant to film the next day. Let us say he died early in the morning of October 10—without nurse, companion, camera or recorder. Whatever he did or did not say to the silence of the house, there was the telephone. In the early hours, it seems, he called his friend Henry Jaglom, a film director born in the year *Citizen Kane* opened. His best friend? There were arguments over that. Some said that Jaglom had made a habit, for years, of recording his conversations with Welles. Some said Welles had never known about the recordings—he had been set up, bugged, like the character he played in *Touch of Evil*. Some said Welles had discovered this, late in the day, and felt betrayed.

Perhaps. But Welles was no stranger to ways of recording. And he knew Jaglom—he had had years to look into the face of a smart, talented, rich, insecure and very needy man. He saw how far he was a model and a father for Jaglom, a god who might grant him admiration or fellowship. And Welles was fascinated by neediness in others—he could see it from a distance, like a connoisseur. Moreover, Welles had been in the business of being betrayed all his life. He had used it as a way of always being right, superior and alone. But like people who complain of betrayal, he was sometimes feared by others as a savage betrayer himself.

He was not a simple man or a straightforward person, not necessarily a nice man—no one to sentimentalize. Still, he left a message on Jaglom's answering machine in the middle of the night: "This is your friend. Don't forget to tell me how your mother is."

When Jaglom woke up, the friend was dead—which surely adds to the magic or the infection of the message. There's no reason to think Welles intended the two sentences as last words. But he was a master, a manipulator, a ham, and sometimes fascinated by power. He had a habit of leaving words hanging in the air, pregnant yet not quite born—rosebuds, indeed. Put it this way: he talked like a man who was forever uttering grave last words and leaving us to wonder over them so that we could not be sure whether *rosebud* was the promise of color, sweetness and flowering or a knob of youthful hardness, a bullet that refuses to grow old or die. He had been wondrous and distant from birth, a prince and a devil, a genius and a forbidding master of solitude, someone whose voice could be so subtle, intimate and sly that it could appropriate your own mother.

He who had such mixed feelings about parents, those first examples of other people.

He was, truly, a director, someone who shaped everything, not least his failure and the legend of a rosebud that never quite bloomed, or withered. Thus, once upon a time, the cruel world, realizing the role that was written for it, looked the young prince in his wicked, shining eyes and told him, "No." And that was that.

It is likely that no one had ever given Orson Welles so large and irremovable a no before 1942, when he was twenty-seven, and he lost control of *The Magnificent Ambersons*. If that sounds fanciful, you will see, and judge for yourself. There were parents who adored him—perhaps *worshiped* is the better word, for it conveys an obligatory distance. Worship your child and you have surrendered some power or responsibility; there is no longer the usual need for warmth, or ordinary company. Worship can sometimes involve neglect; it may require blindness or bewilderment. And then both parents were gone before he was sixteen, the age at which common lives know terrible arguments and the hopeless defeats of family.

Maybe his parents did tell him now and then, "No, don't play in the snow in just that sarong," or "No, don't make up those ugly words to go with Verdi or Vivaldi," or "No, don't mock your brother's stutter," or even "No, don't bother to talk to your brother."

But there's no suggestion anywhere that either of them ever dreamed or dared to say, "No, Orson, you can't do that," or "No, Orson, that's not a marvelous drawing or a fine rendering of Edmund's 'Now, God stand up for bastards' speech." They never said, "No, you shall not go to Chicago or Shanghai." They never said, not those friends, not those books, not those ideas (this would begin to explain his large, yearning but oddly itinerant sense of all those things).

And they were parents whose brief, heightened, untidy lives were gifts to the boy's urge for fiction. He came away from family life with the blissful notion that he was not only brilliant, a genius even, but perhaps a changeling—*that* touch of magic.

Most biographies are built around a series of abiding questions. They are often the same questions, such as, Did you love her? or Were you happy? or Didn't he know that was a mistake? It is in their nature, and their beauty, that such questions can never be satisfied. There may be answers, but they are usually too many, or too terrific—"Rosebud" is one of those great answers that makes it harder to know the question.

The question here, or the first one, is Why did Orson call Dr. Bernstein "Dadda"?

The where was Kenosha, Wisconsin, a town fifty miles north of Chicago on the shore of Lake Michigan, the place where George Orson Welles was born on May 6, 1915. Maurice Bernstein was of Russian descent, a doctor from Chicago, an eager, quick, inquisitive man, with alert, fine features and dark, receding hair. He had set up his practice in Kenosha in 1911, and it was said that he had moved north because of trouble in Chicago caused by his hot temper. In Kenosha, he met the Welles family.

Richard Welles and Beatrice Ives had married in November 1903. He was thirty-one, and she was twenty-one. Her father had been in the coal-mining and fuel business in Chicago, important once and then broke. From her mother, Lucy, Beatrice had inherited musical talent. But from places no one could discover, she had also gained strength of will, strict-ness and an idealistic imagination. She was close to beautiful, and not far from fierce. She had been a concert pianist until family hardship made her take up typing. According to her son, she was also a champion shot, a skilled joker and a scholar of East Indian literature.

Richard Welles's mother put a curse on the union when her son married Beatrice. Perhaps she saw how little the couple had in common, though in those days such disharmonies were less remarked on. Richard Welles was an occasional inventor, a Sunday inventor, who specialized in the lights for automobiles—he must have seemed very up-to-date, for he was interested in flight, too. He was also a dandy—his son would remember spats that were white, dove gray or mauve—and a self-conscious man of the world. George Orson saw that his father "hoped to be mistaken for one of those he most admired: some sober figure in the world of high finance, and not the idle, hedonistic London clubman he despised—but so closely resembled." He was also a drunk, who had his own brand of cigars, and a gambler.

They had a son, Richard, born in 1904, who was already ten when Orson was born. At least one member of this family was less than an accomplished player of his part. The young Richard was clumsy; he had accidents. He was very shy, and he had a bad stutter.

The marriage did not fare well, and it was not helped by a less than attractive child. Beatrice did good works in Kenosha, helping immigrant families, campaigning for female suffrage and giving piano recitals. She was ill too often. She saw less and less of her husband. He traveled, and when he was in Kenosha he kept to male circles. Almost certainly he had mistresses. His drinking became a bigger problem. He took voyages, and he would often repair to a small hotel he owned in the country, in Grand Detour, Illinois.

When Dr. Bernstein arrived in Kenosha, he was a very lively newcomer in the gap of the Welles marriage. If for no other reason, he called on the Welles family at 463 Park Avenue to attend Lucy Ives, Beatrice's mother. She was living in her daughter's house, and she was unwell. By the time Orson was three, she died of cancer, screaming, it is said, when the drugs were wearing off. By then, Dr. Bernstein had a way of calling Orson

"Pookles"; in return, the boy called him "Dadda." Years later, Beatrice, herself unwell, would recite poetry to her son:

> *A lovely boy, stolen from an Indian king,*
> *Who ever had so sweet a changeling . . . ?*

What did she mean? he asked himself. "Was I, indeed, a changeling? (I have, in later years, been given certain hints. . . .)"

Magic and storytelling are the liar's parole. He never spelled out or explored those hints, for that left most room in his own mind. But the idea was potent and formative. The youth who was an orphan in fact at sixteen would create the Charles Foster Kane who simply *loses* his parents, or transcends them. Escapes them. Kane's orphanhood is one of the strangest states in that very ghostly film. But it shows a man whose early emotional life was such a failure, or such an emptiness, that he needed to believe in the magical advantage of a changeling.

An escape, a fancy. Welles is the man who once told an interviewer, "I don't want *any* description of me to be accurate; I want it to be flattering."

2

∽ *Tall Stories* ∾

IN *CITIZEN KANE*, as the three young men prepare to put out their newspaper—Charlie Kane, Bernstein and Kane's old chum Jed Leland—Kane makes up a Declaration of Principles to go on the front page. And Bernstein, in awe of Kane but shrewd and cautious warns, "You don't wanta make any promises, Mr. Kane, you don't wanta keep." Kane waves caution aside. "These'll be kept," he says, like someone wooing a lover.

Moments later in the film, but six years later in Kane's soaring career, there is a party in the newspaper office. Kane is going off on a trip, so Bernstein reminds him there are a lot of pictures and statues in Europe he hasn't bought yet. Kane promises to do his best. Bernstein thanks him and sits down. Then Kane calls out, "Mr. Bernstein," and the faithful Bernstein answers, "Yes?" (This stress on rhythm is not irrelevant: it is in the pacing of the film, and it comes from the dainty torture of magic acts, the small talk that traps.)

Kane then looks at Bernstein (full of the folly of adoration and destiny), and asks him, "You don't expect me to keep any of those promises, do you?"

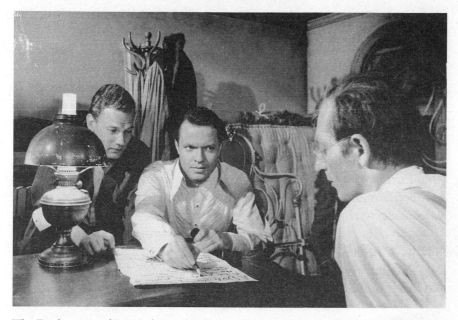

The Declaration of Principles: Leland (Joseph Cotten), Kane (Welles) and Bernstein (Everett Sloane)

Everyone roars with laughter: it is a party, after all, and there is no resisting the momentum of Kane's act. But it is a terrible moment. Not just because of dramatic premonitions that Kane plays fast and loose with truth or trust but because he exults in the performance. Lying is not simply his escape, his vacation; he thinks it is his passion, his strength and his charm. And he dares us all not to be charmed.

Orson Welles lied a lot; you will see. You may even decide that he lied all the time as the only available way of keeping patience with life. You have to decide when he knew he was lying, and when that clerical care was lost in the rush. And you have to wonder how much the difference matters.

At this early stage in his life, the lies or the fantasies can seem touching. For Welles was never happier than when looking back and seeing the lovely projection of his hopes. He could be so gentle and enticing a liar. There was often an air of nobility or blessing to it. The sexiest feeling one has with Welles the actor (or presence) is in being lied to, having the clothes of decent fact floated away, and not worrying. He was often awkward with women on-screen, but in his talking about the past he was a great lover.

He said that he had been conceived in Rio (he said Rio, not Rio de Janeiro), as his parents made an elaborate voyage. In fact, they took just a Caribbean cruise some time after Beatrice's pregnancy was known. He said his father had a cigar—the Dick Welles—named after a horse that had won the Kentucky Derby. Perhaps his father told him that nonsense. The photographs I've seen of Richard Welles are of an aging, heavy and depressive man, plausibly a drinker, ill at ease. How swell to have a wondrous child believe your stories. The boy said his father had created an airplane and broken the bank at Monte Carlo. He said that he himself, as a child, had been in the wings at the Chicago theater with his father where John Barrymore (Jack) was touring *Hamlet* and that he had held the bucket of champagne for the great actor. He would say, later, that on the opening night of *Citizen Kane* in Los Angeles—May 8, 1941—Jack arrived at the theater, in all the fuss and lights, to be seized by a radio interviewer who asked, "Are you a friend of Mr. Welles?"

"I'm not a friend," said Jack. "You might say I'm a relative."

"A relative?"

"Yes, I think it's time the public heard the truth—Orson is, in fact, the bastard son of Ethel and the Pope."

Previous biographers have struggled with such gems. There's no doubt that Jack Barrymore and Orson knew each other, and recognized each other's glory and self-destruction. The story is funny and harmless, and it helps build the palace of show business. There is no way of verifying the story, so it is easy for writers to conclude that such an exchange *could* have happened—indeed, *should* have happened.

But what do we do with a story Welles told Kenneth Tynan and *Playboy* in 1967? Tynan had been a Welles admirer for years—and Welles always preferred to talk to believers. He hated to be disliked. I say that to suggest how generous and leading Tynan's question was. He asked about Welles's travels as a youth, with his father. What places did Orson remember most vividly? Here is the answer, delivered, let us suppose, with a furrowed brow:

> Berlin had about three good years, from 1926 onwards,
> and so did Chicago about the same time. But the best
> cities were certainly Budapest and Peking. They had the
> best talk and the most action right up to the end. But I
> can't forget a party I attended somewhere in the Tyrol
> some time in the mid-Twenties. I was on a walking tour
> with several other little boys, and our tutor took us to
> eat at a big open-air beer garden. We sat at a long table
> with a lot of Nazis, who were then a little-known bunch
> of cranks, and I was placed next to a small man with a
> very dim personality. He made no impression on me at

the time, but later, when I saw his pictures, I realized that I had lunched with Adolf Hitler.

Well, why not? Fascists must eat, and after all, this was a man who had, in his way, mastered Hitler. In the superb, if hysterical obituary of Charles Foster Kane—the film stock deliberately scratched to mimic newsreel—he had stood as Kane, beside an extra dressed up as Hitler, while the commentary boomed away:

> No public man whom Kane himself did not support or denounce—often support, then denounce.

"At this point," Hemingway began Chapter Seven of *Death in the Afternoon*, "it is necessary that you see a bullfight." He was indicating a dotted line pathway so that the reader might step forward. In a few pages, the "old lady" was delivered, chatting to the author. Whenever Welles did magic tricks, he liked to summon someone from the audience, and he loved the challenging flirtation of making that person do and see what he wanted. I may try the same thing here, because—to be blunt—at this point it is necessary that you *listen* to Welles, that you let his voice fill your head. Perhaps my old lady should be my publisher, so that I can nag him about giving you a sound cassette with the book?

3

◦～ *The Voice of . . . Halloween?* ～◦

H E   H A D   A   V O I C E of magnificent appropriation, the deep, smooth, cultured sound of . . . chocolate pudding? . . . or of a barbarian masquerading as the world's most knowing insider. (Yes, this is an important point: he managed to sound like someone ineffably in the know, yet he had the piratical approach of an invader—not quite a hun, yet once people had seen him they saw the Mongol, the Tartar, the Genius Khan, and shivered. Oh, yes, he was always scary.)*

---

* In that remarkable picture *Heavenly Creatures* (1994), the two teenage girls in New Zealand in the 1950s dream passionately over the lustrous stills of movie stars. But those witches in the making somehow know that Welles is "the most hideous," and his glossy is floated away across a dark pond.

He came right in off the street and took over the words, and the world with them. In his heyday, in the late 1930s, he was forever rushing around Manhattan, going from the theater to the Columbia Broadcasting studios. He used taxis, but then he saw the extra potency of an ambulance. No law said an ambulance had to contain the sick. But when the ambulance bell rang, other traffic gave way. So he hired himself one of them, and he was there at the studio in the nick of time, rushed up in the elevator and set down with a script he had never seen before.

"Who am I this time?" he'd ask as he inhaled the steak dinner and the cheesecake dessert that secretaries had ordered in advance. There had to be meals there, hot, rich and ready. And he could eat a dinner as he scanned a script, fork in one hand, pencil in the other, reworking the lines. So, very often, he sounded like someone whose being was intensely involved in swallowing or digestion. Listeners often likened his voice to food or drink—not just chocolate pudding but fine brandy or rare caviar—when, really, *they* were being eaten, devoured.

And in those crucial years, in the late 1930s, it was the voice that America knew first—it was the voice that led and enchanted:

> We know now that in the early years of the twentieth
> century this world was being watched closely by intelli-
> gences greater than man's and yet as mortal as his own.
> We know now that as human beings busied themselves
> about their various concerns they were scrutinized and
> studied, perhaps almost as narrowly as a man with a
> microscope might scrutinize the transient creatures that
> swarm and multiply in a drop of water. With infinite
> complacence people went to and fro over the earth
> about their little affairs . . .

Look down there. Would you really feel any pity if one of those dots stopped moving for ever? If I said you can have twenty thousand pounds for every dot that stops. . . . Free of income tax, old man.

—Harry Lime in *The Third Man*

> . . . serene in the assurance of their dominion over this
> small spinning fragment of solar driftwood which by

Anton Karas records the zither theme tune during postproduction on *The Third Man*.

chance or design man has inherited out of the dark mystery of Time and Space. Yet across an immense ethereal gulf, minds that are to our minds as ours are to the beasts in the jungle, intellects vast, cool and unsympathetic, regarded this earth with envious eyes and slowly and surely drew their plans against us. In the twenty-eighth year of the twentieth century came the great disillusionment.

That was the introduction to the CBS *Mercury Theatre on the Air* dramatization of H. G. Wells's *The War of the Worlds*. The first draft of the script was written by Howard Koch, a young writer delighted but terrified at being on the Mercury staff. He was given six days to make a script out of the novel. It meant no sleep, endless drafts and rewrites, a night-

mare of pressure in which as he and the other writers felt themselves
shrinking, with no time to eat, the bulk of Welles seemed to grow. No one
felt Orson was ordinary or natural. And he gave those sad possibilities not
the least encouragement.

Koch's draft went to Welles and his partner John Houseman (at that
same time they were rehearsing *Danton's Death* for the stage—it opened
only three nights after *The War of the Worlds* broadcast). It came back with
orders for changes, with rewrites scrawled out in Orson's fat, galloping
hand. In the weeks before broadcast, the script heaved with change. I
stress this not just to indicate how clearly Welles grasped the concept of
that show but to mark how thoroughly he rewrote his own lines to his extraordinary, stealthy, seductive rhythms.

One of our abiding questions is going to be, Was Welles a writer?
What makes it so hard to answer is that he could so impregnate the ear
with the unwinding measure of speech that he seemed like a writer. Listen to him over the years—on radio, in film and in all the interviews—and
hear how seldom he sounded graceless. That was his pride, his dandyism,
his thinness even.

Now move forward, by decades, to a sound tape that came my way—
its provenance and date not certain. It is from a 1970s recording session
in England at which Welles was making a commercial, supplying the
voice-over for a few staple foods:

> OW (reading): "We know a remote farm in
> Lincolnshire where Mrs. Buckley lives. Every July peas
> grow there." [to the director] Do you really mean
> that? . . . Don't you really want to say "July" over the
> snow? Isn't that the fun of it?
>
> DIRECTOR: If you can make it almost when the shot
> disappears.
>
> OW: I think it's so nice that you see a snow-covered
> field and say, "Every July peas grow there." . . . We
> aren't even in the field, you see?
>
> DIRECTOR: Yeah, we aren't.
>
> OW: We're talking about them growing and she's
> picked 'em. I don't understand you. What must be over
> "July"?

DIRECTOR: When we get out of that snowy field.

OW: I *was* out. We were onto a can of peas. A big dish of peas. When I said "July."

DIRECTOR: I'm sorry, Orson.

OW: Yes. I'm always past that. . . .

The workingman. The decent, ordinary citizens know I'll do everything in my power to protect the underprivileged, the underpaid and the underfed. Well, I'd make my promises now if I weren't too busy arranging to keep them. But here's one promise I'll make, and Boss Jim Gettys knows I'll keep it. My first official act as governor of this state will be to appoint a special district attorney to arrange for the indictment, prosecution and conviction of Boss Jim W. Gettys.

—Charles Foster Kane

DIRECTOR: Could you say "In July"?

OW: Why? That doesn't make any sense. Sorry. There's no known way of saying an English sentence in which you begin with "In" and emphasize it. Get me a jury and show me how you can say "*In* July" and I'll go down on you. . . . Here, under protest, is Beefburger: "We know a little place in the American Far West where Charlie Briggs chops up the finest prairie-fed beef and tastes. . . ." This is a lot of shit, you know that?

DIRECTOR: Yes.

OW: You want one more?

DIRECTOR: You missed the first "beef." You were emphasizing "prairie-fed."

OW: You can't emphasize "beef." That's like his wanting me to emphasize "In" before "July." Come on fellows, you're losing your heads. I wouldn't direct any
living actor like this in Shakespeare. . . . I spend . . .
twenty times more for you people than any other
commercial I've ever made. You're such pests!

Somewhere along the way, we—you and I—are going to have to
think about those "we's." The "we" that knows now about the early years
of the century and the "we" that knows a farm in remote Lincolnshire.
What is there—
I noticed that.
Where did you come from?
*I sneaked in while that was playing. The way he said, "Such pests!" He
must have been a handful to work with on those things.*
But he stayed there. He didn't walk out.
The money, I suppose. Had to do it, to pay for all the better things.
I suppose. Like the way Kane insisted on staying in the election.
Had to do it.
Hmm. Are we a little premature, do you think?
He's talking before he's born? Back to the past.

4

⟶ *Lovely Boy* ⟵

HE WEIGHED ten pounds at birth, and began to grow. So his
prodigiousness in matters of the mind, learning and assertion was always
bound up in size and stature. There are pictures of him at two and three
in which he looks five or six. He wears billowy pajama suits; he is in bare
feet and sunburned, an infant giant enjoying himself in the yard. There is
such cheerfulness and self-satisfaction, one does not notice or ask about
fat beneath the loose garments. But the face is as broad and swelled as a
pumpkin. The cheeks go on all summer, and the long, ovoid eyes have
space to be reveled in. His forearms, jutting out of a loose shirt, seem
made for work or leverage. Kids his own age must have shuddered and
avoided George Orson.

Looking back, Welles said he hadn't really known about the George until later in life—until seven or so. Then his father told him they had dropped George because, after all, wasn't "every damned Pullman porter in the country" named George? But knowing kids in the neighborhood, older kids for sure, had heard a chant.

Georgie-Porgie, puddin' and pie,
Kissed the girls and made them cry!

You can imagine that six-year-old George Orson, all eighty pounds of him, leaning into a pretty eight-year-old girl, trying to shape his gorgeous parenthetic mouth for a kiss, and falling over.

For George Orson was a physical contradiction. Yes, he was big, burnished and even awesome. That mouth was already so daringly frilled and extended it might have come from Firbank or Beardsley. As for his hands, they were astonishingly large, long and delicate. He mesmerized people with his hands; it was the first gesture of conjuring before he had thought of tricks, black velvet or rabbits in his deep pockets. The hands seemed to know more even than George Orson's naughty mind.

But they were at war with his feet. Orson was no ordinary victim of flat feet—he was stricken. The larger and heavier he became, the more the strain on those vulnerable and stupid platforms. (And by the end of his life, he had difficulty moving or traveling if he had far to walk.) Maneuvering to kiss a little girl, he could have lost his balance and landed in a humiliated heap. He could not be athletic, only strong. The very thing that marked his mouth, his eyes and voice—the intimation of grace—was denied him in those essentials, feet. For all his life, he had back problems and the steady danger of falls in which he might fracture foot bones, ankles or legs. As an actor, he might be magnificent until he moved; then there was the threat of inadvertent clownishness. If ever he had to move fast, he looked like a wounded creature. So he sought advantageous positions, stillness and cloaks. He learned to loom over people. He became, in his own mind, enthroned.

No wonder he seemed no child: he could not really play with kids—he frightened those his own age (and he was known for lashing out at them as well as for eccentrically articulate rebukes), and he was afraid of their laughter. In later life, his capacious, preempting worldliness was a way of stopping anyone from having an advantage over him.

His odd education pushed him toward adulthood or the fearful isolation of infant genius. But no mere pushing can account for his powers. Orson Welles had little formal education. He was off on his own by the age of sixteen, and in the years before that a good deal of his education was done at home, by his mother, by Dadda Bernstein and even by his father. It is likely that he had very little experience of school that did not flatter and indulge him. He never met anyone who plainly knew more than he did.

And he *was* prodigious. In 1982, he delighted in scoffing at an inquiry as to whether he had really played *King Lear* at the age of ten—it was a very worldly groan, as if to ask, Whatever will they say next? But questions only remained because, years earlier, Welles had planted hints and stories when no one felt bold enough to scoff.

It might have been. As a very young child, he had been able to quote great stretches of poetry, about things children were not supposed to understand. His mother had taught him to read—at three?—using *A Midsummer Night's Dream* as a primer. Why fill a young and significant mind with the usual inanities of nursery literature? She took her son very seriously. Orson, that is. Richard, the older brother, was written off: he had no talents, he was backward, and he was as shy as anyone growing up in the shadow of an immense, demon younger brother.

Dadda Bernstein was more present than Orson's father. It was Dadda who bought Orson a puppet theater and who encouraged him in playacting and dressing up. Bernstein married, in 1917: his wife was Mina Elman, the sister of violinist Mischa Elman. The union lasted four months, until Mischa discovered that Bernstein was only interested in his sister's money (and in Beatrice and Orson Welles). When her mother died, Beatrice took Orson to Chicago, and Bernstein moved back with her. Richard Welles made the move, too, but as an extra—albeit the extra with money.

So Dick Welles traveled, while Beatrice set up her salon, with introductions from Dr. Bernstein. There is a group photograph, taken in 1921 or '22. Dick Welles and Dadda Bernstein are at opposite ends of the line, and the hulking Orson is holding Dadda's hands, his head halfway up to the doctor's necktie.

There were often musicians in the Welles home—Beatrice was a practicing pianist, and Bernstein obviously knew people in the business. Welles said that he could read scores by the age of seven, and that he would conduct with those sturdy arms waving. Dadda bought him a baton. For his mother's sake, he said later, the visiting musicians abided by the notion that the kid was more than a nuisance. And Beatrice had him taught piano and violin.

He said he learned both. He did not always enjoy music, but how could he be less than good at it? In later years, people seldom heard or saw Welles play a note. Peter Bogdanovich once found Welles trying out chords in an empty room. The younger man was surprised: he didn't think Welles played. "I don't," said Welles. "I stopped after my mother died. Never played another note." Do you believe that, or that he played badly—or that he knew the devoted and devout Bogdanovich was outside the room, listening for clues? Whatever the answer, Welles the filmmaker knew music.

One day, Welles's story went, he had been practicing scales with a teacher when the boy blew up.* He said he would kill himself, so he climbed out of the window and perched on some railings—magically, we discover that the building is the Ritz in Paris. The Welles family is cosmopolitan. He said he would jump.

There was silence within, as the teacher fetched his mother—they are in a larger suite at the Ritz. Then the boy heard Beatrice say, "Well, if he wants to jump, let him jump."

---

* He is the creator of maybe the most crazed music teacher in movies—Matisti (Fortunio Bonanova) in *Kane*.

No one ever said no. Welles supposed that she was bluffing, knowing how easily a plunge "would have appealed to me for its gaudy elements of melodrama and pathos." So he climbed back in and met his mother's "look." "Some of these could be quite terrible. I'd seen my father wither under them into a crisp, brown winter's leaf."

Only Beatrice's poor health, Welles thought, had gotten in the way of her career. They were in Chicago for his ninth birthday—May 6, 1924. There was some kind of a party for the boy, but he had the moment of his cake alone with his mother. She was ill, in bed, with hepatitis. She recited a little poetry to him, something about a changeling. She told him to blow out the candles and make a wish. He did as she said, but he was so struck by the dark that he never made the wish. She died four days later.

"Sometimes," he wrote nearly sixty years later—and now you must feel the voice and its resonance—"Sometimes, in the dead watches of the night, it strikes me that of all my mistakes, the greatest was on that birthday just before my mother died, when I forgot to make a wish."

It is one of the greatest scenes Welles ever made, on a snowbound Colorado prairie that is done in a studio, with just one isolated log cabin. A gold mine has come into the possession of the Kane parents. In response, the mother signs her boy, Charles, away to the care and guardianship of a Chicago bank and its head, Walter P. Thatcher.

Why? The question is never answered. The father may be a drunk and a bully. But he is nowhere near as strong as the mother (Agnes Moorehead). Is it her love sending the boy away for a better life? Or has she just sold him?

She goes to the window, raises it and calls out "Charles" to the boy who is playing in the snow. Her voice nearly breaks. We hear a mourning wind in the distance. We have Agnes Moorehead's great face—taut in the cold and the crisis. She seems desperate—at losing the boy? Then she says, quietly, to Thatcher: "I've got his trunk all packed. I've had it packed for a week now."

5

Grand Detour

AT NINE, he stood like a cadet linebacker between Dick and
Dadda. The wonder of this "son" brought the two men together; he may
have served to prevent them from violence. But for all Welles's knowingness in later life, he never made any public mention of whether Dadda had
had an affair with Beatrice, or of whether Dick had been cuckolded. Of
course, we may overrate his brilliance. Surely there were things he did not
notice or understand, or did not want to. But this is the first hint of something like backwardness, or chill, in Orson Welles concerning matters of
sex. His ability to recite poetry for hours on end does not mean he was
comfortable with matters of the heart. There is a kind of boy wonder who
talks so much, and so precociously, that people hear only "genius" or "for-
wardness." We still know too little about why so many children like that
flounder in adulthood.

It seems that Dr. Bernstein took Orson on a kind of European tour in the summer of 1924. The doctor liked to study the boy and tell stories about him to friends and journalists. The legend of young Orson had at least two artful promoters, Dadda and the boy. But Welles was not entirely taken with Bernstein. Later in life, he admitted that they had few tastes in common and that Bernstein could be an interfering fusspot. With Beatrice dead, Orson became more interested in his father.

He divided his time. Bernstein now lived in Highland Park, an affluent Chicago suburb. There were artists and musicians in his house, and Chicago then was a great center of business and the arts. Orson was taken to the theater, and he was the showpiece of Bernstein's salon, introduced to authors and journalists, always "on" and raised to hear the tough gossip of Chicago insiders who had a hard time seeing tenderness in the kid.

It is in Chicago that Kane builds an opera house for Susan Alexander to attempt *Salammbô*. But the real opera house in Chicago was run by the agricultural machinery tycoon Harold McCormick. He was married to Edith Rockefeller, but in 1920 he proposed to present his Polish mistress, Ganna Walska, there, in *Zaza*. In the event, the singer took fright—at the role or the social pressure—and fled the country. If only Susan Alexander had had a way out. By 1925, Welles would have known that story from smoke room talk. Around that time, too, he was observed to be smoking cigars—inhaling for real or keeping them stuck in his mouth so he could stay in the room.

> I have only to look at the sky, to see people in the streets, to see oceans, trees, roads, houses, to feel and smell snow and rain, and listen to wind—I have only to open my senses and I am again as I was in my boyhood—and in my Chicago time—delighted to be present.
>
> My years in Chicago were full of this mothlike avidity that kept me beating around the days as if they were shining lamps. When I look back to that time I see the city as I saw it then, all at once; no separate streets, neighborhoods or buildings, but a great gathering of life, an army encamped behind windows.
>
> —Ben Hecht, *A Child of the Century*

Orson had another home, and decades later he would look back on it as "a lost Eden." Dick Welles had plenty of money, and he was spending it. Though he was a great traveler, the most telling thing about him was that in the early 1920s he had bought that hotel, the Sheffield House, in Grand Detour. This had been done with no hope of profit, or even business. Grand Detour had its name because the railroad had passed it by. In the 1920s, the village and the hotel seemed to Welles to be still enjoying the 1870s. It was a little like the classic Wild West. His father deliberately kept the hotel old-fashioned. He would invite friends there for lengthy stays—providing home-cured meats and bootleg liquor—and never billing them. It was a way to help the money go, and to live in a precious past where men were not challenged.

If nowhere else, Orson seems to have had snatches of regular childhood in Grand Detour. He was known to other kids in the area; they resented him for his smarts, his loftiness, his size and his way of condescending to them as bumpkins. Orson once rigged up an amateur telescope and charged other kids to see the stars. They saw nothing, but then Orson thumped them in a way fit to bring on comic-book stars. He did magic tricks, and once when he was bored he sent his father to Chicago for toys. Dick Welles came back with a full clockwork train set. Orson played with it for hours.

Another summer, he got a crush on a little girl whose family was staying at the hotel. Together, the children ran away and were found only after a few days, traveling performers charging a penny a show.

It was at the hotel, Welles claimed, that he once met a friend of his father's, Booth Tarkington, the novelist who had published *The Magnificent Ambersons* in 1918.

Welles didn't get everything right about Grand Detour in later years: it isn't exactly where he remembered it; he got the facts of a fire at the hotel all haywire. But the world there stayed with him, no matter how briefly he had encountered it or how much he had inflated it in his imagination. In so many ways, Orson Welles seemed too superior for roots, ties and family. In later life, he sometimes seemed like an element in a conjuring trick—there for amazement, not necessarily subject to the laws of society or physics.

But Grand Detour gave him the fondness for his most resonant and daring work, the one film in which he risked being ordinary, *The Magnificent Ambersons*. And he believed that his father had invented this Grand Detour, holding it back willfully, so that Welles imagined there had been no electric light there as late as the 1920s. Here is the voice again; it is the voice that plainly loved to read the narrative in the film of *Ambersons*:

> . . . a completely anachronistic, old-fashioned, early
> Tarkington, rural kind of life, with a country store that

The end of the ball: *The Magnificent Ambersons*

> had above it a ballroom with an old dance floor—with
> springs in it, so that folks would feel light on their feet.
> When I was little, nobody had danced up there for
> many years, but I used to sneak up at night and dance
> by moonlight with the dust rising from the floor.

Dancing alone in the lovely splendor of the past's relics.

You can find passages in Tarkington that are as nostalgic, if not quite
as rhythmic. And the opening sequences of *Ambersons* are Welles's most
enchanting tribute to dark glories of the past. He sometimes called these
"Lost Edens" or "Merrie England," and he could convince himself as easily of the beguiling early life of Sir John Falstaff as that of Major Amberson. In Welles's life, the time spent in rural Illinois is one of those rare
instances when we feel and see the world around him. Maybe, for him,

there was the peace, for a moment, of not being a genius. Later, the memory settled as a version of happiness. But by then, he was bitter enough to wonder if he had made it all up.

6

━━━━❯ *Educating Orson* ❮━━━━

S O M E H O W the two rival fathers decided to get the boy into one proper school. Perhaps this was self-sacrifice; perhaps they were a little weary of his booming treble elocution. Hitherto, whatever he had learned had been determined by his own and his mother's tastes. He could read; he wrote—he typed; he knew acres of verse, including Shakespeare; he was musical; and he could draw—indeed, he had a puppyish way of leaving his cheeky cartoons all over the place. But of mathematics he knew and cared little. As to history and geography, his knowledge may have come from Shakespeare, his own travels and the overheard yarns of grown men. The sciences did not move him, beyond the simple mechanics of a train set and the optics that made folks suckers for magic.

In the fall of 1925, Dadda arranged for Orson to go to Madison, Wisconsin, where he would be examined and tested by a noted psychologist, Dr. Frederick Mueller. On the basis of that testing, Mueller would recommend a school—if one could be found worthy. That was the tone of the trip. Orson was being sent to perform, and it was up to doctors and schools to be his match.

Every story that survives has Orson triumphant, which may just mean that he and Dadda controlled the information. Dr. Mueller had a boys' club—called Camp Indianola—which Orson immediately took over. On principle, he never fitted in with others. He then adapted, directed and acted in the camp production of *Dr. Jekyll and Mr. Hyde*. If Mueller felt that choice signaled a disturbed child, he was entirely disarmed when his psychological testing began. Orson's answers were lengthy and dazzling; they gently corrected the feeble basis of some of the questions. He quoted Voltaire and Oscar Wilde.

The doctor was taken back, and then attracted. This ten-year-old so easily seemed more mature than his age; and while there was too much of him, he was, in exaggerated and poseur ways, very beautiful. The doctor came on to him, or so Orson said. This wasn't new to the boy: he was always sophisticated. Some artistic queens at his mother's musical salon had made advances. "From my earliest childhood," he said, "I was the Lillie Langtry of the older homosexual set. Everybody wanted me." But he didn't want to upset them, so he never quite said—at six or seven—that he wasn't homosexual. He said he had a headache: "I was like an eternal virgin." In real life, dull life, children are not always so smart, or so safe. But Orson is telling the story.

It was agreed that he would go to the Washington Grade School in Madison. On his first day there, a bully—some backward teenager raised on farms—set about him. Orson retreated to the bathroom and employed his pocket makeup kit (what *does* a boy keep in his pockets?) to make himself look bloodied and battered. The bully was amazed and upstaged. How could brute strength beat wizardry? Before long, young Welles was openly criticizing the methods of the school and playing Scrooge in *A Christmas Carol*. (He got his taste for grotesque old men long before he was twenty.)

No one apparently could find the height, angle or advantage to step on him properly. There was no comeuppance, though it seems that his dreadful arithmetic improved a good deal. In all other subjects, he excelled. He sometimes told stories to his schoolmates, providing illustrations as he talked. He was like the new animated movies.

Far from being subdued or chastened, he got his picture in the papers. There he was, fat faced, with a great lick of hair falling down his vast brow like India—a journalist said it was the face "of a young Grand Lama with large slanting eyes and an air of profound Mongolian wisdom." He also wore a black silk scarf around his neck. The picture went with a story, in the *Madison Journal*, about this cartoonist, actor and poet who was only ten and who held his new school in thrall.

Dick Welles made the next decision. Orson would be sent to the Todd School, in Woodstock, Illinois, the school that his older brother, Richard, had attended without success. Todd had been founded in 1848. It was modeled after English schools, and it was meant for exceptional boys. Orson would be there three years, the only concentrated formal schooling he ever had. And he loved it.

> *Excuse me, before we move on to Todd.*
> Yes?
> *The whole Madison episode is, as you say, like a story. But, just to look at the downside, this Dr. Mueller may have descendants, and we seem to be saying that he went after little boys.*
> That's what Welles reported.

And, am I right, did you mean to make us wonder whether Welles might have succumbed?

I only mean to suggest that being the Lillie Langtry of Chicago's homosexual set may not have been as funny or as comfortable as Welles makes it seem.

And he would have been only six or seven or so?

Yes.

Certainly in some of those pictures he is . . . lovely, I think one could say that.

I believe we have to recognize just how stunning he was as a youth—how fully he combined intellect and looks—and all in a nearly outrageous manner.

Like a grown person masquerading as a child?

Yes.

That could attract people.

Is there anything more alluring?

Yet I had been led to believe that Welles was also a ladies' man.

No doubt about it.

So, what you're saying—?

Is next to nothing yet, except that his work shows an exceptional interest in loyalty and betrayal among men who are friends.

My word, yes. What a subject that is.

Why was Welles happy at Todd? He was remembered there as a boy without friends, someone in closer contact with the great authors and savants than with his schoolmates. Once again, he dominated, though the competition at Todd was stiffer and standards higher. He made only one great friendship there, with Roger Hill, the son of Noble Hill, the owner and headmaster. Roger was a small, wiry and very active man in his midtwenties. He was in charge of athletics at Todd—something Orson was regularly excused from on the ground of delicacy. But Roger had a hand in theater, too, and in Orson's years there Todd became famous for its productions.

Roger was married, with children, and the rest of his family had to allow the large, authoritative new boy into their lives. He came to their quarters unannounced, and he would sometimes lie on the bed of the wife, Hortense, daring her to object. She believed Welles needed to be put down a peg, but no one had found the peg yet. And Roger did not just like Orson. The older man was entranced by the kid. He may even have felt he had found the raft on which he might sail away to bigger things.

One Welles biographer, Barbara Leaming, has described how later on

Welles teased Roger Hill that he might have been Roger's boy—in some amiable, sexual sense. There was a threat to the other Hills. Roger's own children were suspicious of Orson, and one of them married the second brightest boy at Todd then, Hascy Tarbox. The odd undertone here is that Hill seemed the innocent, chosen by Welles as his protector at Todd. The friendship would last until Welles's death, with Hill keeping an immense archive of Orson memorabilia. Hill always knew that he had met a marvel. But at first, at least, until affection took over and Todd became another "lost Eden," Welles may have been prepared to use Hill.

He used Todd like a repertory theater. Surely his general education was enriched—and there were stories of Orson arguing with teachers on their subjects. But it was at theater that he worked, learning to use the school's limited technical resources to great effect. It was at Todd that a style or attitude began to emerge, of making a lot out of a little. Thus the manner of *Citizen Kane* came not just from cameraman Gregg Toland's expertise and a studio's resources but out of amateur theater's necessary ingenuity.

In his first year at Todd, in plays or pageants, Orson impersonated the Virgin Mary, Christ and Judas. He helped put together musicals; he designed sets; and he played in versions of *Dr. Faustus*, *Everyman*, *Dr. Jekyll and Mr. Hyde* (again), *Richard III*, *Androcles and the Lion* and, most notably perhaps, with the Todd Troupers, competing against other schools, in a production of *Julius Caesar* which he adapted and directed, and in which he played both Cassius and Antony.

The contest was held at the Goodman Theatre in Chicago, and Todd lost for just one, or two, reasons. The school was disqualified for having two adult actors in the cast. The cup went to Senn High School. But then there were protests, and it was revealed, to the wonder of the judges, that one boy—not two adults—had played both Cassius and Antony.

Dadda Bernstein wrote to him about the disappointment. He called the fourteen-year-old Orson "Pookles dearest":

> Some day when you will be in the eyes of the world
> doing big things as I know you will, you will look back
> upon this disappointment as having been just a passing
> experience. We must learn to accept disappointments
> and profit by them. "Success is in the silence though
> fame is in the song." . . .
>   I love you more than all else
>
>   Dadda

It's a rather sickly note, reason to understand how far Orson was bored by Dadda. The cup had been no disappointment. Everyone went away talking about the misunderstanding and the boy who had seemed like both the Barrymores. In the *Chicago American*, Ashton Stevens, the city's most noted drama critic (and a friend of Dick Welles) made a remarkable prediction:

> Given as good an education as will adhere to him at a
> good college, young and not ill-looking Orson Welles is
> as likely as not to become my favorite actor. True, it will
> be four or five years before he has attained his majority
> and a degree, and I have yet to see him act. But I like
> the way he handles a difficult situation and to lay my
> plans long ahead. I am going to put a clipping of this
> paragraph in my betting book. If Orson is not at least a
> leading man by the time it has yellowed, I'll never make
> another prophecy.

One has to marvel at the splendid clouds of future glory that attended the boy. It may have seemed just and magnificent to him, but it was a kind of ruin, too. For what need had this marvel ever to work at his acting—or at anything? Some fans of Welles argue that his complete state of orphanhood was a kind of tragedy. But if being immune to parental warning is the key, he was an orphan already, a child not quite born of man.

7
The End of Family

WHILE ORSON WAS at Todd, in 1927, his brother Richard was certified as insane. Richard had been a failure wherever he had gone—at school and then later, in Montana, trying to get into the timber business. Dick Welles had given him money on several occasions, but the money had vanished. So, in 1927, Richard was identified as schizophrenic and sent to the Kankakee Institute, where he would remain for ten years. Dick rewrote his will, splitting his estate one-seventh to Richard and the rest to Orson "because of extraordinary advances" that had already gone to Richard.

Dr. Bernstein had helped in placing Richard, and he had the family responsibility for the young man's care. He neglected it and may have cheated the invalid on his one-seventh. But Orson let that happen. He never seemed to be a man who had a brother, or a skeleton in the closet. He had always behaved like an only child. Orson seldom saw Richard later on, but in the late 1930s, at least, he tried to keep the brother on a modest allowance.

He was growing. At Todd, he was famous for eating sweet things— pastries, dainties, strawberry shortcake. "You still eating?" Leland asks Kane, in mock despair, and the exultant Kane bellows back, "I'm still hungry." Then he calls for the waiter and admits, "I'm absolutely starving to death." There were people at Todd who warned him about stuffing, and who recommended fruits and vegetables. But he was encouraged by his growth. He shot up at Todd. By the age of fourteen, he was six feet and about 180 pounds. But that arrangement made him skinnier than when he had been a little boy. His face lost fat in the cheeks. He was handsome, a little sinister and so devilishly grown-up that fourteen seemed out of the question.

When Todd boys went to church in Woodstock, Orson's eyes ranged the congregation for conquests. There were girls in the town who blushed under his gaze, and he said that he had "affairs." In the summer of 1929, he went on another European tour, and on the boat coming back, a rather older girl took him in hand and introduced him to lovemaking. Yet Orson gilded the story, for he said he bribed the steward to let the hot kids have the use of an empty stateroom during the day. These girls never had names, and they never lasted past the moment. But you have only to look at the pictures to wonder whether full-grown women weren't after Orson, too.

He and his father made a strange couple in the summer of 1930, the boy ablaze with promise and so much taller and grander than the father, who was beating himself down with drink and unreachable sadness. Dick Welles had been to Todd to see his son act, and he was upset or afraid. Did he simply mistrust the theater, or was he shrewd enough to see how acting might encourage the most melodramatic streak in his son? Did he see that, beneath the wonder of it, Orson was a hollow actor?

The two of them talked on a long trip to the Far East in 1930. They stayed up late onboard ship drinking, and Orson often put his helpless father to bed. He liked his stories, and he said he loved him. But could they get close? While Dick slept off his drinks, Orson would live it up on the ship, charging everything. Then Dick found out and read him the riot act about financial irresponsibility.

They went ashore, as far as can be judged, in Hong Kong, Macao and Shanghai. They saw the Great Wall of China. Ever after, this was the basis for Orson's flamboyant knowledge of China and the East. I doubt the tour was much more than a simple seeing of things. But Orson knew the exotic when he sniffed it, and all his life people had been remarking on how "Oriental" he looked. Within a year or two, he was letting people believe that he had lived in China, spoken Chinese, wasted away his time in

MIKE (driving Elsa through Central Park at night):
Where does the princess come from?

ELSA: I don't know why she should tell you.
But . . . well, her parents were Russian, White Russians.
You never heard of the place where she comes from.

MIKE: Would Her Highness care to gamble?

ELSA: Gamble? She's done it for a living.

MIKE: I bet you a dollar I've been to the place where
you were born.

ELSA: Chifu.

MIKE: It's on the China coast. Chifu! It's the second
wickedest city in the world.

ELSA: What's the first?

MIKE: Macao, wouldn't you say?

ELSA: I would. I worked there.

MIKE: You worked in Macao?

ELSA: There's your dollar.

MIKE: How do you rate Shanghai?

ELSA: I worked there, too.

MIKE: As a gambler?

ELSA: Well . . .

MIKE: Hope you had more luck than tonight.

ELSA: You need more than luck in Shanghai.

—*The Lady from Shanghai*

opium dens and those quiet inner courtyards where whores waited in patient beauty. China was a film set for him, a place of the imagination.

Dick Welles came back from the trip and chose to live in the Bismarck Hotel in Chicago. Apparently alone, he died there on December 28, 1930, from heart failure and kidney disease. Father and son had not parted well, and Roger Hill had persuaded Orson to give Dick an ultimatum about his drinking. Dick had wanted a university one day for his son, whereas Orson was bored with school. So Orson felt guilt, and he embroidered. He said that Dick had killed himself, and he would say in a maudlin way that he, Orson, had been responsible. Yet observers had little doubt but that Dick's drinking would prove fatal, sooner or later. Orson was startled by the death, but that was only another instance of his not quite understanding things that his air of wisdom seemed to have mastered.

He said he felt terrible for not having been there, for having bowed to Hill's advice over the ultimatum. Yet had he ever been that close to his father? It is not so much that the young Welles simply manipulated people while claiming to feel for them. Rather, his principal energy was to turn everything into a story. So, ever afterward, he let the notion of suicide hang in the air, and he lamented the horror of his father's funeral when his grandmother Mary supposedly put a little witchcraft into the service. Did Orson really despise that smoke of magic—or did he envy her for adding it?

Years later, Welles wrote about it, shrugging off the funeral: "I was in no condition to interfere, being convinced—as I am now—that I had killed my father." Is that just romancing, or a sign of disturbance? Whatever else, it helps to show the slender chances people who knew Orson had of existing in their own right. His needs were so great, and so private, that they seemed very cold sometimes. With his parents dead, he could look back on them: Welles's warmth was confined to nostalgia. In life, they may have been not much more than bystanders, lucky extras.

There was money from his father's estate—about $37,000. The will also called for Orson to choose his own guardian. He was torn: he preferred Roger Hill, but he felt obliged to Dadda. He talked to Hill, and they agreed that he would nominate Bernstein. The single effect of this decision was to give Bernstein greater control of Dick Welles's money.

So what next, coming up on sixteen? Orson had advertised himself in *Billboard* as an actor—"Lots of pep, experience and ability." He said he would close one engagement in Chicago in early June (that was actually graduation from Todd) and then be ready. . . . Bernstein talked of Cornell; Hill preferred Harvard. Orson gave them both the slip. He wheedled a modest sum of money out of Dadda, and in the early summer of 1931, he was off. He was to take a painting tour in Ireland, he said. They let him go. The rest of the world has always left Ireland to fate.

8

∽ *Sometimes I'm Irish* ∽

LADIES AND GENTLEMEN, at this point in our story, I feel there is little choice but to enter into the record what we might call "an episode." If it sounds like a novelette or even a scheme for an entire motion picture, so be it—we are trying to deal here with a fellow who perceived himself as a series of ever more momentous and hilarious chapters, challenging destiny. If the hallowed tradition of biography sometimes appears to be jostled or pinched as we make our way—in other words, if unlikelihood casts a shadow on your pleasure—I ask you first to accept the idiotic and indecent fact that, on some day in August 1931, this hulk of a genius, alone, with a few clothes and paints, stepped ashore in Galway. There is no reasoning with such an entrance except according to the standards of flagrant adventure. Perhaps he fancied his own Irish accent and sought to practice it on a mass of fully credentialed Irish extras. Indeed, I would sooner believe that impulse than that he was drawn by a reading of Synge and an earnest wish to explore the Celtic twilight. Better the voice, the idea of liquor and Irish girls, and that unstoppable legend—advanced by the Irish themselves—that the country is a grand place for story, and its peddlers charming liars. For the rest of his life, Welles believed in his honorary citizenship of Ireland for the very reason that he reckoned you could get away with anything there.

So he stepped out of Galway, paints and easel on his back, walking until he found meadow or cottage to charm the eye. Now this may be a way of life for painters, but for a gentleman with dollars in his pocket, and for an actor cursed with flat feet, one day of solitary plodding will be enough. He accordingly converted some of his dollars—a few would do the trick—into a donkey and cart. You will yearn for a picture—of Orson carrying the donkey over rough patches (and getting kicked for his kindness); and then the cart! I know I prefer one of those tiny, curved-roof affairs—did gypsies use them, or just the gypsies in movies?—a kind of painted igloo, barely large enough to admit Orson. Would he, in Ireland, have invested in an uncovered cart, to store his canvases or shelter any roadside romance? But would there have been room for Orson, a girl *and* the bottles of Napoleon brandy? (There was no reason for the artist to stint himself.)

He wanders and he dreams, rejoicing in the relaxed Irish, trading his paintings for three-course breakfasts, and discovers the pubs, the dances and the impromptu storytelling. Then he hears that there is another American making a movie in the Aran Islands, and he takes a boat out there, ending on the isle of Inisheer, where Robert Flaherty is working on his documentary *Man of Aran.* He paints the wild shores, the empty valleys and perhaps even the sinewy fisherfolk. And he seems to get in trouble with some Aran women. There's a story of Orson approached by a local priest, who says to him, "Ah, well, Orson, I was after hearing confession this morning." (It is a role for Barry Fitzgerald.)

And the towering Orson nods, sympathetic to the hard ties of duty. The two men walk along in silence for a while until Father Fitzgerald sighs a couple of times and wonders, "Now, are you thinking of leaving soon, Orson?"

"On the next boat, Father," replies the suddenly devout teenager.

Biography might make its own journey to the Aran Islands, or to those parts of Connemara, Clare and Limerick that Orson frequented. Imagine the joys and curiosity of a summer spent searching for bold paintings on rough walls, or for eerily large and articulate Irish men and women who might have sprung from love's hurry.

> *Good Lord, you must! It would be terrific!*
> Terrific to imagine it, maybe.
> *But think what you might discover.*
> Think of the months I might spend—on your money, my good sir—inspecting watery landscapes and forlorn sixty-year-olds auditioning for the role of Orson's love child.
> *Still, it seems a golden chance to pass up. I mean, imagine a great-grandchild—a tall girl of seven or eight with blarney and magic, red hair and Chinese eyes.*
> I love to imagine it. And since you're so willing, I *will* give you one gem.
> *Yes?*
> Who do you think was born in Connemara in August 1932?
> *I've no idea.*

Imagine, say, the fruit of our Orson and some wondrous, tall, fair girl from thereabouts.

Yes?

Peter O'Toole. How do you like that?

Good Lord! That's remarkable. Why, he is . . .

Wellesian?

Wouldn't you say so?

I could see it.

Anyone could see it.

But we could never say that.

Oh, never. Never. The lawyers!

So, you see the great danger in going?

On the mainland once more, the painter's life was less appealing. Summer was gone. It rained. Sleeping in or out of the cart was no longer as pretty a prospect. So he moved eastward, by way of a barge on the Shannon and then bus. He came to Dublin itself, a place he called "the grand capital of eloquence," toward the end of September. Painting was reassessed as one more lost Eden, and one more thing that actually moved him more than whatever he was doing at the moment.

He sometimes said he was broke in Dublin. But he was an American tourist who could wire home to Dadda for more money. He could afford some kind of hotel and a ticket to the Gate Theatre, where he would see Micheál MacLiammóir in *The Government Inspector.* There were two great theaters in Dublin, the Abbey and the Gate. The Abbey was older, more prestigious and maybe more set in its ways—it had a reputation for Irish drama. The Gate had been set up only in 1928 through the partnership of two men who had met in Anew McMaster's touring company: Hilton Edwards, London born, an actor, but a director and a manager; and MacLiammóir, one of those actors so mellifluous, so eccentric in his timing, so gracious in his exaggeration that he was a reminder of the Victorian stage. They made a pair. They enjoyed a range of material far beyond that of the Gate, and they were—fit for Orson—vivid characters, forever in the limelight of that pretty, malicious and gossip-ridden city.

MacLiammóir was in the scene dock painting scenery—this was a theater where the bosses did mundane chores—when Edwards came to find him. "Somebody strange has arrived," he said. "Come take a look." So the two men assembled to see a phenomenon come in off the street, volunteering his services. As MacLiammóir would later write (despite Welles's tetchy observation that Micheál hadn't even been there that day):

A very tall young man with a chubby face, full powerful
lips, and disconcerting Chinese eyes. His hands were
enormous and very beautifully shaped, like so many
American hands; they were coloured like champagne
and moved with a sort of controlled abandon never seen
in a European. The voice, with its brazen transatlantic
sonority, was already that of a preacher, a leader, a man
of power; it bloomed and boomed its way through the
dusty air of the scene dock as though it would crash
down the little Georgian walls and rip up the floor; he
moved in a leisurely manner from foot to foot and surveyed us with magnificent patience as though here was
our chance to do something beautiful at last—yes, sir—
and were we going to take it?

Orson was sixteen,* smoking a cigar, fluttering American "notices"
under their noses too quickly to be read. He said he was eighteen and yes,
candidly, gentlemen, if they wouldn't make too much fuss about it, he was
the Orson Welles they had probably heard of. He maintained that he was
traveling, a touch bored, and free for a week or two. He lied like a maniac.
And he read for them as the Archduke in Lion Feuchtwanger's *Jew Süss*,
a part they were looking to cast.

They said later that, of course, they knew he was lying. What was
wrong with that? What better promise could one ask of an actor than
lying when managed with this boy's weary calm? They said he was pretty
awful as the Archduke but quite magnificent as himself. As the Archduke,
he threw chairs about, he slaughtered innocent scenery. They were sti-
fling their laughter while astonished by the "preposterous energy" that
pulsated through everything he did.

Later in life, Welles took credit for taking them in. He would also roll
his eyes a little to admit that they were ardent homosexuals while he was
startlingly lovely. But Edwards and MacLiammóir were experienced and
expert men of the theater, as well as connoisseurs of bullshit. That they
were amazed is beyond question; they may have been enchanted, and in
love. But show people can fall in and out of that sort of love without re-
linquishing their pitiless sense of what works.

They saw a marvel and a monster, a hollow actor and a helpless pre-
tender with uncanny gifts. They offered him the part, so long as Welles
would promise one thing.

---

* Years later, in anecdotage, he made it fifteen.

"Don't obey me blindly," said Edwards, "but listen to me. . . . You must see and hear what's good about yourself and what's lousy."

They gave him a little money and told him where to find lodgings. He would have to be ready for *Jew Süss* by October 13.

"Of course," he said.

"You're an extraordinary young man," said Edwards.

"I know," said Welles. But he always had to act as if he knew everything.

9

Or Spanish, Or ...

W E L L E S   W A S very nervous the first night of *Jew Süss:* this was the first time he had acted professionally, and there he was, playing a lead role with one of the more notable theatrical companies in Europe. He mangled a few lines, and at one moment there was a heckling cry from someone in the audience that threw him. It suggests that something in Welles intrigued or provoked the audience—the sheer presence, the cello voice and the outrageousness. The Archduke was meant to watch a pretty young woman (actress Betty Chancellor) exit and then say, "A bride fit for Solomon! And Solomon had a thousand wives, didn't he?" Whereupon a male voice in the audience cried out, "That's a black Protestant lie!" Welles had been walking on air, but now he felt himself falling. His Archduke was about to die, with the resounding line "Ring all the bells and fire the cannon." But the rattled sixteen-year-old reversed the line: "Ring the cannon and fire all the bells." In the shocked silence that followed, rather than execute the Archduke's designed death, slumping in his throne, Welles, without a word of warning, introduced a bit of business—a reckless back somersault down a flight of stairs—to let anyone know that he was still Orson, despite his fluff.

The audience surrendered. At the close of the performance, Hilton Edwards graciously arranged the curtain calls so as to display the newcomer from America. Micheál MacLiammóir was already fascinated—who knows what history of romance offered or rejected accompanied that? Still, he is the first observer in this story who is both thrilled and a little horrified. He watched Welles as the applause came down, and he saw the young man swell:

The chest expands, the head, thrown back upon the round, boyish neck, seems to broaden, the features swell and beam, the lips curling back from the teeth like dark tropical plants, twitched into a smile. Then the hands extend, palms open to the crowd, the shoulders thrust upwards, the feet at last are satisfied . . . and back goes the big head, and the laugh breaks out like a fire in the jungle, a white lightning shifts open across the sweating chubby cheeks, the brows knit in perplexity like a coolie's.

The fellow actor saw all the show of modesty and sharing, with a beast within, the lust for one extra curtain call, the will that can hear just a few people left clapping, and urge more, while the hesitant house breaks out again and "the unappeasable head" of the actor rears up once more as if to roar—"Me!" There are fine actors who go to pieces at curtain calls, as fatigue, modesty and shame combine in their longing for the whole thing to end. And there are actors who are most naked in the last rites of applause.

In *Citizen Kane*, the opening night of *Salammbô*, in Chicago. Bernstein is nodding off in his seat; Jed Leland has made origami of his program. The huge, frame-filling head of Kane hears a sotto voce joke. The last note falls. There is a routine round of polite applause, though Kane does not move—he has not really heard the music or Susan. Then the applause folds up and Kane tries to resuscitate it. He stands, looking at the camera, his hands beating, the pops and smacks hollow but resounding. Susan looks up: she hears his violence. But the applause dies, and the houselights come on, exposing Kane, his hands out. He draws back; he swallows in mortification. It is great acting.

Welles was seven months in Dublin, the winter season of 1931–32. He was in several other productions, though never in lead roles. For sure, he was well received; he had good notices in the Irish press, and a stringer got some feel of them into *The New York Times*. In later years, he ac-

Rehearsing the applause
scene: *Citizen Kane*

knowledged how lucky he had been: "Starting was too easy for me, so
nothing has ever been quite easy enough since." He was the character of
the season, but Edwards and MacLiammóir did not trust him with lead
parts. He played the Ghost and Fortinbras to MacLiammóir's *Hamlet;* as
the Grand Vizier in the Christmas play *Magii,* by Padraic Colum, he
adopted extravagant makeup and a large false nose of putty. He would not
be ordinary.

And he was a Dublin figure who liked to fill his time. He could be a
honey-bear of gregariousness, throwing generous parties, delighting in
the Irish talk, very flattering to his elders and seductive to either sex. With
wide eyes, he sought advice and promised to be reformed by it. After all,
he was a beginner with so much to learn. But under a pseudonym—
Knowles Noel Shane—he got an occasional newspaper column in which
he made a point of remarking on the downright wonder of this Mr. Orson
Welles from America.

That ploy could be no secret in Dublin, and Welles was more cunning
than secretive. He let few tricks pass unappreciated. MacLiammóir

watched him be the life and soul of so many parties, and felt alarmed. Welles went everywhere: to the music hall and to small, radical productions in lofts. He was sometimes seen—when the drink was on him—on his feet, lecturing others, pontificating when MacLiammóir felt an emptiness to his opinions. He would speak for the sake of being the center of attention.

"When the demon of showmanship was on him," said MacLiammóir, "he would be intolerable; something dark and brutal swept through him when a stupid audience surrounded him, and he would use them mercilessly, without shame or repulsion." MacLiammóir hated to see such demagoguery—of "Ariel borrowing the tatters of Caliban"—and this is the first account of something so vital in Kane: of charm, intelligence and humor turning on a word into a nearly fascist urge to dominate anyone and everyone. Welles had a face in which thunder could chase out sunshine while you were still congratulating yourself on being in his company. People called it temper, and some thought it was just acting. But it amounted to instability, for it allowed no plain, calm ground.

He quit Dublin for many reasons. He was bored, and spring was coming; there was no reason to put down roots. But also he was denied a lead role in the forthcoming Gate *Othello:* MacLiammóir was set for Iago, and Edwards cast himself instead of the American as the Moor.

Welles went to England and failed to get a permit that would let him work in the theater. According to the legend that sprang up later, he paid a call on George Bernard Shaw and chatted with him about Ireland and the theater. Then, as if in time for his seventeenth birthday, he went back to Todd. Throughout that winter, he had kept in touch with Roger Hill and with Dadda. He was not so independent that he didn't need to write home about his successes, and now he returned for the greeting worthy of a hero.

In Woodstock, he put on a production of *Twelfth Night* from Hill's adaptation of the play. The two men were already collaborating on a volume of Shakespeare plays, edited for acting, which they intended to have published. In addition, Welles and Hill planned a new play, to be written jointly, about the John Brown story. It was to be called *Marching Song.*

And then, apparently, he went back to Europe, reliant on loans or gifts from Bernstein and Hill, and probably playing the two benefactors against each other. That summer he passed in adventurous spirit in either Morocco or Spain—take your pick. He had somehow encountered a gaunt Moroccan nobleman—the pasha of Marrakesh—though no one ever saw these two men together. Morocco may have been only a day or two.

Spain is a little more credible, at least in outline. He went to the area of Seville, then inland and into the mountains, there to sit and think, there to write pulp thrillers and plays, and there to get *afición*. He said he lived in a nice apartment in a brothel, and on fifty dollars a week lived like Diamond Jim Brady.

Later in life, Welles was sometimes to be seen at Spanish bullrings as a spectator. He was even on the edges of that dangerous summer, celebrated by Ernest Hemingway, when Ordóñez and Dominguin fought a series of matches across Spain. And he would sometimes deliver magisterial opinions about the bulls. He said, much later, that in 1933 he had gone to the fights and subtly insinuated himself as a newcomer—"The American"—in real, if amateur, fights. He had bought bulls so that he could fight them. By 1960, Kenneth Tynan, a huge admirer of Welles and himself infatuated with bullfighting, wrote that in 1933 Welles "leapt in to challenge the bulls at every village *corrida* within striking distance of Seville." The two men talked of Ordóñez, and Welles revealed a few scars which, he said, came from those old ventures with the bulls. (This is the man whose occasional career as a fortune-teller was founded on the shrewd appreciation that nearly everyone alive has a scar on his or her knee.)

He was in Spain a couple of months at the very most, with some working going on. I'm sure he saw bullfights, and I'm sure he dreamed of leaping into the ring. Nor would I doubt that in a very foreshortened season he had, to his own satisfaction, understood the bulls so that he could pronounce upon them ever afterward. He had sat in the shade, without company, at small, provincial bullrings; he had been moved; and he had practiced veronicas in his room, cursing his slow feet. He may even have stepped into some tranquil meadow and waved his shirt at an innocent Ferdinand. And I am sure he loved that part of Spain, and treasured the safe summer. He would ask to have his remains scattered there.

While he was in southern Spain, he also wrote some of a play, *Bright Lucifer*, which gives more hint of how preoccupied and troubled he was about being Orson Welles. The play is a dreadful piece of cheap, psychological blood and thunder, and it was never produced. But its very rawness feels authentic and endearingly youthful in a person who was so largely successful at seeming older than his true age. The play suggests that Welles was observing himself with something like the mixed feelings of MacLiammóir.

The setting is a cabin in the woods where three people have come for vacation: Jack Flynn, a wreck of a Hollywood actor; his brother Bill, a newspaperman; and Bill's ward, a boy named Eldred Brand. Eldred is . . . an orphan. He suffers from hay fever, he smokes cigars and blows out Nietzschean smoke; he is a kind of devil. Jack calls him "a busy little bitch boy." He attacks Bill for having loved his mother; he manipulates everyone; he plays grotesque practical jokes; he brings about Bill's death and then provokes Jack into killing him. The play is unalarmed at suggesting that Eldred is a devil who seeks universal destruction. His destiny and huge energy set out to bring others down and to ensure his own disaster.

If the play was any better, its meanings would be more masked. But if the author had been more sophisticated, then it would never have been written. *Bright Lucifer* is only a play, but it is the first work of boastful, besotted confession from a very dangerous young man.

10

Mercutio in the Midwest

HE WAS ONLY eighteen in the summer of 1933, as he returned to America. It was frequently an opening remark of wonder as people reported on him that he was so young. Yet he gave off airs of mastery and experience that made eighteen seem absurd, or that raised suspicions of fraud or mistake—dislocation—in this large young man. He could sigh over tales of China, Spain and the North African desert. He was an experienced actor, not to say tried and tested in a hard school—if playing a winter in Dublin wasn't a hard school, then he didn't know what the term was supposed to mean. Bullfighting? Did someone mention bulls? (He had a rare, disarming and faintly insane ability to hear several background conversations going on in any room or ship's bar.) Well, since you mentioned it, yes, he did have a fair knowledge of the bulls, and later that night, when he would be a lot drunker, he was prepared to display his scars—if the young lady was bold enough to come to his cabin. Yes, he was a writer—wasn't that obvious from the way he talked?—and he had done a number of plays as well as pulp novels, which, you had to forgive him, he was too embarrassed to own up to specifically. When people fell silent in amazement, he might sneeze and catch the coins that fell from his nose, roaring with laughter at the public's fresh wonder.

At the same time, he was only eighteen, a kid in whom size and perpetual talk did not conceal so many marks of loneliness and terror. He was an orphan, with a brother in a mental hospital. He was an uncomfortable mix of giant and boy, with a bass voice and a baby face. He alarmed but mesmerized young women, and he had an undoubted attraction for homosexuals. But what was most disconcerting was the incongruity—the dislocation—between the booming assurance and the rootlessness, the lack of core or substance. So many attributes smacked of the bogus. Was he aficionado after one or two weekends? The scars, were they the welts of experience or merely makeup lines to aid seduction? There were those whose fascination with Welles grew out of their sense of his perilous masquerade—the feeling of an ordinary, innocent eighteen-year-old's vulnerability that was being so strenuously denied and lied about. When would he break?

So some people saw a great actor in embryo, while others saw the youngest ham they had ever met, who was using acting to avoid anything real or painful or commonplace. And anything that extraordinary can be so wearisome to onlookers that the marvel is forever kept from ordinary contact. People began to need revenge.

He went back to Woodstock and Chicago; he had to go somewhere, and he was still in the gravitational pull of those bickering father figures, Roger Hill and Dadda Bernstein. But in Chicago, at a cocktail party he was taken to by the Hills, Welles found himself standing beside Thornton Wilder, who was thirty-five and the author of *The Bridge of San Luis Rey*. Welles admitted that he was a writer himself, whereupon Wilder laughed and said he'd thought he was talking to Orson Welles. For Wilder had read of Welles's Dublin success in *The New York Times*, and he had had private word on Welles from his Dublin friends Frank and Elizabeth Longford. Wilder teased him and said, surely he *was* an actor. So Welles gave his good-fellow chuckle and agreed.

Wilder might have been warned or offended, but like so many he was intrigued. He wanted to help, so he said he would introduce Orson to the top New York theater critic, Alexander Woollcott. Welles should take the train to New York straightaway, and Wilder would phone ahead. It sounded so easy—why bother to be ordinary when fame, attractiveness and a theatrical manner worked like grease?

He went to New York, and Woollcott took him to dinner and studied him. The boy was dazzling, but badly dressed. So the very large Woollcott gave him a suit of his own clothes and bought him new shoes—the one item in Woollcott's wardrobe that did not fit Orson.

Thus Welles was passed along like a new, enigmatic sensation from one homosexual to another—from Wilder to Woollcott to Guthrie McClintic, director, theatrical manager and husband to the great actress Katharine Cornell. That is not to suggest that anything happened, only that there was something in Welles that was especially noticed by homosexuals—the mix of youth and worldliness, the profound voice and the naive face, that stormy eighteen.

McClintic, who was planning a nationwide repertory tour, thought Welles an "extraordinary-looking young man with a beautiful voice and speech." He had the recommendation of Woollcott, long an ally to McClintic and Cornell, and there were the reports from Dublin. Still, without so much as an audition, and without meeting Katharine Cornell, Welles was hired for important supporting roles—he would be Mercutio in *Romeo and Juliet*, Marchbanks in *Candida* and Elizabeth Barrett's shy brother in *The Barretts of Wimpole Street*.

The Cornell company had not previously played Shakespeare. Juliet would be the actress's debut—at the age of forty. Basil Rathbone would be her Romeo. It has been argued that Welles impressed McClintic because he could quote Shakespeare, and because he and Roger Hill had collaborated on actors' editions of three Shakespeare plays to be published . . . soon? But these books were only ever published by the Todd Press, and Welles at eighteen was hardly a credible scholar. No, the casting testifies to Welles's transfixing impact in person.

He spent time in New York that fall of 1933 as the company rehearsed. When Cornell arrived from Europe, she was not displeased. She rejoiced in Welles's voice and his "provocative acting" and believed in him as "a tremendously talented boy." Welles took voice lessons from Walter Huston's sister, Margaret Carrington, a singer who had lost her own voice and then specialized in teaching voice projection. Very often, Welles dined with Woollcott and was introduced around the town.

From late November 1933 to June 1934, the company toured the United States with three plays. They traveled by train, cast and technicians, with wagonloads of sets. There were more than 200 performances, from Buffalo to San Francisco, with stops at Kansas City, Cheyenne, San Antonio, New Orleans, Seattle, Salt Lake and Los Angeles. Wherever they went, Welles drew mixed attention—he was never quiet or placid, never simply one of the team. McClintic became exasperated with his shortcomings and his lack of discipline. Many people in the company found him overbearing, for he was forever describing to them the great future that was assuredly his. His was the voice that carried over all others. He was the actor most likely to be late for the train or a curtain. And when there were pranks, he was everyone's chief suspect

Yet he was frequently well received. One can only imagine this eighteen-year-old Mercutio being man of the world to Basil Rathbone's forty-one-year-old Romeo to think of daggers clutched at impulsively. But reviewers liked Orson. In Chicago—where he could have expected friendly fire—the *Tribune* found Rathbone cold, but as for Welles, he "swaggered out to prove that the critics of Dublin, who hailed him as a wonder boy, were not crazy. Welles is flamboyant, some will say—but so is Mercutio. Welles violated tradition by wearing a half-fledged beard— but it gives his boyish face a definite Tudor look. He reads the Queen Mab speech with nervy flourishes, and he plunges into the duel scene with a fine fury of swordsmanship."

He was good in *Candida*, too, if more bouncy than McClintic liked. But Cornell raised no evident objection, and Welles had the sense to lower his voice in the hushed awe of sincerity to make her speeches seem more vibrant. It was the brother in *Wimpole Street* that bored him: the fellow stuttered and had to have curled hair. It was a character part, whereas Welles was already more in his element as men unto themselves, masters of their own set pieces.

There were escapades that went down less well. He caused a scene in a San Francisco hotel restaurant once in front of Cornell and McClintic. He was in the habit of putting on funny voices and playing jokey parts. Sometimes on the train, or in the cities they passed through, he would become Mr. Swami, a fortune-teller, earning a little money by telling strangers they had scars on their knees or had likely had a great disappointment. The knack of observation is vital to magic, and Welles could bring to it the profundo voice of insight as well as the odd turban or two, and a discreetly sultry makeup.

He was an actor on the road and on the rails, and having a great time. If he could step so easily from Mercutio to the Swami, there was a lesson for any onlooker—that, as an actor, he was a show-off, a crowd pleaser, a barnstormer. He saw and felt no difference between the pinnacles of Shakespearean dramatic verse and the somber prediction of midwestern futures. Thus, he could sound like a tragedian or a seer in the fortune-teller's tent, and just a touch of the fraud onstage. The very heart of the matter in watching Welles was whether or not to fall for the act—and whether, indeed, the tremendous boy believed in what he was doing or was just surfing on attention.

11

~~~> *A Kind of Holiday* <~~~

THE CORNELL TOUR ended in June 1934 in Brooklyn—not on Broadway, as everyone had hoped. But, after the summer, there would be another chance. Until then, Welles was free. Whereupon, the nineteen-year-old embarked on a startling new venture. He would propose himself in theatrical management, having learned the ropes on one national tour. But it was an odd mixture of amateur and professional he had in mind, of adventuring and going home at the same time.

He persuaded Roger Hill to mount (and fund) a summer festival of drama at the Todd School. Students would be solicited for the summer program at $500 a head. That money, the box office and the rest from Hill or the school should suffice. As the featured attraction, Welles proposed to hire his recent masters. So, as the Cornell tour came to an end, he sent a cable to Edwards and MacLiammóir in Dublin:

> Would you both join me for summer season at campus
> in Woodstock Illinois three plays running a fortnight
> each. *Hamlet* for Micheál, *Tzar Paul* for Hilton, and
> something for me so far undecided. I am trying my
> hand at production. Lovely school to live in and small
> Victorian Theatre. Can pay your expenses of course and
> whatever is going. Now do say yes, it will be a kind of
> holiday and lots of fun. Love Orson

Edwards resisted. He was tired, and he looked forward to their normal holiday in Spain and North Africa. "It'll mean playing some little mid-Western town with Orson and a horde of stage-struck students," he warned. "It'll be like the small towns in this country without the charm."

But it would mean Orson, too—how had he grown in a year?—and "the boys" had never seen America. They persuaded themselves and sailed to New York, where Orson met them with Louise Prussing (a professional and Leslie Howard's mistress), whom he had hired as leading lady. MacLiammóir believed that Orson had acquired "a new habit of towering"—he felt that Welles's fond and rather patronizing smile was falling down on him from the top of a tall tree, like blossom or bird lime. The Irishmen were employees, put up for a few days at the Algonquin (the bill to Roger Hill) and slotted into Welles's program. They argued here and there, but what could they do in the face of his American energy? The Irish boys were given a white, wooden cottage in Woodstock. In the heat of the summer, they slept on the porch. And they agreed to Orson's casting.

One of the three plays was George du Maurier's *Trilby*, which Welles meant to direct himself. He would also play Svengali, that role model for unbridled directors. The Irish actors fell in with his plans, no matter that they felt themselves miscast. As MacLiammóir saw it, Orson's production was "disappointingly vague and indefinite," while his Svengali was a "lowering barbarian," without sufficient grace or humor. MacLiammóir reckoned Svengali was too subtle and European for Orson—the boy was more suited to the very American "preoccupation with ruthless grandeur and intoxication." That is a telling observation, as if in seeing Orson attempt to take charge, the Irish actor had felt the hot breath of Kane.

That urge to take over, to dominate, might be winning or ugly. It might also lead Welles astray from the art of acting. *Hamlet* on hot summer nights was evidently the event of the season. Edwards directed, MacLiammóir played the prince, and Welles was Claudius—one more example of his youth taking on an older character. Chicago critics came to Woodstock for that production, and they were perplexed by Welles's outright villainy as Claudius. He was physically unrecognizable: one critic called his makeup a cross between "an obscene old woman and the mask of lechery." Everyone was taken aback by the deviousness he brought to the role, the very theatrical wickedness, rather than flawed, human qualities. Of course, once Claudius is that evil, Hamlet's hesitation becomes less explicable.

Again, MacLiammóir's feeling was acute. In rehearsal, he thought that Welles's Claudius promised to be "outrageously exciting." But came the night, something bizarre happened—the pressure of a live audience "caused him to lose his head." He seemed like someone drunk or crazy. A melodramatic rawness in Welles would often lose control at the moment of exposure. Sometimes he would improvise beyond text or plan, seizing control from the proper line or meaning of a play. It was an unpredictable, headstrong energy, and it ruled out chances of depth or discipline.

It was a summer of unruly thrills. Later in life, MacLiammóir would say that he, Hilton and Orson had been in the Biograph Theater in Chicago, watching William Powell, Clark Gable and Myrna Loy in *Manhattan Melodrama*, when they heard shots outside. John Dillinger, on leaving the audience, had been shot to death. That would have been July 22. Maybe the sound of gunfire had to carry all the way to Woodstock, and into MacLiammóir's tremulous imagination. It is a story that Orson Welles himself seems never to have repeated. But, a few years later, as he looked for a movie subject, and an American life to portray, Dillinger was one of his candidates.

The Irish boys did not give too much time to the movies. They took it as their right and privilege to make homosexual plunder at the Todd School. Away from home, they did not fear scandal or retribution; and in the humid summer they chose to wear as little as possible. Welles was startled but amused, not least by Roger Hill's frantic efforts to police the stagestruck teenage boys at Todd. "They went through Woodstock like a withering flame," Welles would say later. "*Nobody* was safe. . . . It was a rich harvest there for both of them, and they knew no shame."

In that hotbed of affairs, Welles found a love of his own, the eighteen-year-old daughter of Chicago socialites. Her name was Virginia Nicholson. A close school friend of Roger Hill's daughter, she heard about the summer festival at Todd and persuaded her father, Leo, to enroll her. She was a slender, very pretty blond, whose audition became a formality once Orson set eyes on her. Virginia had been properly raised, but she had a youthful passion to be an actress. In the event, there was never the talent or the drive to make a career, but she had every urge to make a hero of Orson, above and beyond personal attraction. That set in very fast—there was a lot of undressing going on that summer—and Orson and Virginia were soon missing rehearsals. Roger Hill had another student to fret over, and this one was involved with the ostensible head of the program. By the end of the summer, Welles had proposed to her.

Why Virginia? It is hard to answer. Though the marriage produced a daughter, it had a short heyday. Welles never talked about, and he never really enthused over, the women in his life. Virginia had American class, and her parents were wealthy. She dressed well and was attractive. She admired him, and she was an undoubted asset. She also served as a vital diversion in what might have been a compromising summer. But no one could ever claim that it was a meeting of souls or a searching relationship. The Irish actors were snooty about Virginia. They said she was not worthy of Orson. But the young couple were caught up in the excitement of a grand creative season. Orson was the leader of the festival. He was effortlessly commanding. The wonder is that he had only one girl. As soon as Virginia was conquered, she began to appear as merely a consort or an appendage.

But Virginia was there that Sunday afternoon when Welles and a pal, William Vance, made his first movie. It was done silent on 16 mm, called *Hearts of Age*, and it was a frolic meant as a takeoff on European art films. It runs four minutes, and was apparently photographed by Vance, who went off with the single print. The film shows the encounter of an anxious old lady (Nicholson) and the rather sardonic figure of Death (Welles). Both actors wear heavy, comic makeup, and there are stylistic nods to American slapstick and German Expressionism. Several of the shots are very striking; the lighting is unusually good; and the whole thing shows some awareness of continental moviemaking. Not much more can be said. Later in life, Welles regarded *Hearts of Age* as a very minor piece of Wellesiana. The most useful point to make about the movie is its evocation of that summer—of smart kids being creative and finding that they were engaged to be married. But it is no more a love story than anything else Welles would ever make.

The summer ended; the Irishmen went home. In the fall, Welles and Virginia went to see her parents, who were not happy about their daughter marrying this explosive young man. But they gave their consent, and the marriage took place. They were living together in New York, and there was some gossip at the hotel, so on November 14 (with just the Hills present), they got married. Orson would say later that neither of them took it very seriously. A little later in the year there was a formal marriage for the family in West Orange, New Jersey.

The wedding had to be fitted around a major but troubled event. The Cornell production of *Romeo and Juliet* was revived for an opening in New York on December 21 at the Martin Beck Theater. But something had gone amiss in Orson's unimpeded progress. So that Brian Aherne would accept the role of Robert Browning in *Wimpole Street*, he was given the part of Mercutio. As recompense, Welles was offered two parts—Tybalt and the Chorus.

He could not refuse, or be seen to complain. Tybalt was a good role, and the Chorus was made for his enchanting voice. But he was furious, and when Mercutio and Tybalt fought their first duel, Aherne felt violence in the young actor. Twice, Mercutio's sword was snapped off at the hilt. To make matters worse, Welles was largely overlooked in the favorable reviews.

But one person in the audience noticed him. John Houseman was thirty-two, making his way in the New York theater as a director and producer. He noticed only Tybalt, and years later he remembered the experience as violent and altering:

. . . death, in scarlet and black, in the form of a monstrous
boy—flat-footed and graceless, yet swift and agile; soft as
jelly one moment and uncoiled, the next, in a spring of
such furious energy that, once released, it could be
checked by no human intervention. What made this figure so obscene and terrible was the pale, striking child's
face under the unnatural growth of dark beard, from
which there issued a voice of such clarity and power that
it tore like a high wind through the genteel, modulated
voices of the well-trained professionals around him.
"Peace! I hate the word as I hate Hell!" cried the sick
boy, as he shuffled along, driven by some irresistible interior violence to kill and soon himself, inevitably, to die.

This seems to describe one of the great Broadway debuts, yet the critics found Orson Welles only passable. Houseman admitted that perhaps
one needed to be sensitive or allergic to Welles. He went backstage but
could not find Tybalt. Still, he could not get the young actor out of his
head—"in much the same way as a man nurtures his sense of excited anticipation over a woman the sight of whom has deeply disturbed him and
of whom he feels quite certain that there will one day be something between them." No matter that this Welles seemed too lethal and so much
a harbinger of death.

12

Panic or Pleasure

I'M NOT INTERRUPTING?
My dear fellow. I had sat down with very little idea of what to say.
You come as rescue, so be provocative, be entertaining.
*Very well, here is the thing that's occurred to me. At the outset you said
something to the effect that no one had ever denied Orson Welles until the loss of*
The Magnificent Ambersons?
Yes.
*Yet here he is being demoted from Mercutio to Tybalt, and seeming to be
very upset. Is this not a denial?*

Well, you are a good, close reader. I admire that in a publisher.
We like to do our bit.

And you have a point. I don't want you to run away with the idea
that there were not occasions in Orson Welles's youth when, say, the lobster Newburg was off the menu by the time he sat down to dinner; when
a girl he saw walking over the Golden Gate Bridge didn't prefer to keep
walking rather than have her evening made secure in the best room the
Mark Hopkins could provide at short notice. There must have been buses
missed, picnics spoiled by a sudden rain—
You are making fun of me.

Not for worlds. What I mean to say, most gently, most respect-
fully, is that, until we reach the pivot of *Ambersons*, you may not know how
ruinous or fulfilling denial can be.
Well—

Further, Tybalt was not simply a reverse. Mercutio, I think you
will agree, is not a flat-footed fellow.
Not at all!

Very well. Did you notice that what John Houseman noticed—
and his noticing here is crucial, the way ahead—was the extraordinary,
bullish, trapped rage in Tybalt—
As if Orson had learned something from watching bullfights?

Oh, very good. That ponderousness tied to a mercurial imagination. And from being thwarted.
So Tybalt may have been a stroke of good fortune?

Or better casting.
Yes, I do see that. One small thing extra, however.

By all means.
The Golden Gate Bridge, I believe, was not yet opened in 1934.

Ah, sir, I know I am going to like you. Shall we replace it then
with the Staten Island Ferry?
Touché. May I add one thing further?

Quickly, quickly, we are impatient to get on.
*Mr. Houseman was truly infatuated with Mr. Welles? Are we talking
about involvement, relationship . . . ?*

We are pondering the deepest reasons for people noticing beauty,
sir—nothing less.

Houseman had a rare, masked ambition and acute practical intelligence: he was the best man Orson Welles would ever meet and endure for
a matter of years and for work of value. At that moment Houseman was

seeking to produce a play so uncommercial and so difficult that no one else would attempt it. This was a verse drama, *Panic*, by Archibald MacLeish. Its central figure is a man named McGafferty, a Wall Street giant in his late fifties who is overtaken by cataclysmic economic disaster, the Crash. As Houseman saw it, McGafferty must convey "the despairing fear a man feels at the sudden, inexplicable collapse of a world of which he, himself, had been a secure and confident part."

He thought of Welles. This tells us something so important about Welles the actor. Houseman had seen only his Tybalt; he must have known that Welles was very young—despite that voice reaching across the distance of a theater and Welles's dark makeup for the role. Houseman may have been moved personally by Welles—and surely there was something very physical in that—but he did not seek to cast Welles to type. He wanted to use his voice and his force. He had heard a voice ready for complex verse, and he had felt some power beyond youth. He had been thinking of Edward G. Robinson or Paul Muni—actors twenty years older—for the part before he saw Welles.

So Houseman returned to *Romeo and Juliet* and took himself backstage before the play was over. He found Welles in a tiny upstairs dressing room, naked to the waist, with Tybalt's sweat-soaked tunic tossed on a chair. As he waited for the curtain call, Welles was working on a play—it was almost certainly *Bright Lucifer* still—and Houseman saw gruesome drawings of devilish characters here and there in the handwritten text. They introduced themselves and agreed to meet in a bar after the curtain.

The Welles who appeared then was transformed. Without makeup, in a dark suit, he was scarcely recognizable, until Houseman spied the flat-footed walk. Then Houseman studied "the pale pudding face with the violent black eyes, the button nose with the wen to one side of it and the deep runnel meeting the well-sloped mouth over the astonishingly small teeth." This is not necessarily an attractive portrait; there is even something cruel being perceived. But that possibility was swept away by the voice—which seemed to vibrate in the bar—and the extraordinary hands: pale, long, tapering and so tenderly expressive.

By noon the next day, Welles called to say he would do *Panic*, quitting the Cornell company if necessary. He came to an audition with Virginia, and MacLeish was taken aback by his youth—could a kid play the poet's great character? But he was utterly convinced by the reading, and Houseman remembered one passage in which McGafferty talks about the power of fate behind the Crash. Houseman had no way of knowing then, but the politics of the play were fortuitously attuned to Welles's lifelong weakness for such things as destiny and magic. Ahead of time, the shadow knew:

You think this creeping ruin is a shadow!
You think it's chance the banks go one by one
Closing the veins as cold does—killing secretly—
The Country dying of it—towns dead—land dead—
Hunger limping every road—you think it's
Chance that does it? You think! So did I!
I do not think so now. I think they wish it.
We cannot see them but they're there: they loom.

James Light was hired to direct. Martha Graham handled and de-signed the movements of the large crowds. The cast included Houseman's ex-wife, the Hollywood actress Zita Johann. Despite reports of irrespon-sibility from the Cornell company, Welles behaved beautifully: he was on time, gracious and helpful to everyone. He was also superb as McGafferty, for Orson was one of those people whose natural speech seemed always to be edging into verse.

Panic opened at the Imperial Theater on March 15, 1935, and ran for three performances. The press was very mixed, though Welles was praised. The left was mystified by a play that explained the Crash in terms of malign fate. But MacLeish was in raptures, and the team of Houseman and Welles had been forged in a kind of bliss.

Orson and Virginia moved down from Bronxville to a one-room apartment on Riverside Drive. The two men planned other ventures, and now it was clear almost without saying that they were partners. House-man was older and more experienced in professional theater, but he felt he had so much to learn from Welles's instantaneous sense of what worked as drama. Houseman was a man of considerable formal polite-ness; indeed, there was something of the professional diplomat (or refugee) about him; as yet, it smothered his own creative urges—he would not have dreamed of acting himself then. He had been born in Bucharest to a French father and an English mother, and he had traveled a lot as a young man. In New York, he had to work to seem American. He was also innately more reserved than Welles—it was surely Orson's emotional un-inhibitedness that excited Houseman. So they threw off ideas, many of which were forgotten the next day. The team they were making would be well-named Mercury, for nothing was ever mulled over much.

They decided that they would put on a production of John Ford's *'Tis Pity She's a Whore*. By now, it was evident that Welles would be the direc-tor, with Houseman as his producer making life easier for him. Already Welles's timetable was becoming complicated by his need to dart off and do something for radio. A friend of Orson, Francis Carpenter, had promised that he could get the necessary $10,000 for the production from his mistress. The play was cast, and sets were done. But then the mistress changed her mind: the $10,000 was available but only for restoration at the Bijou, the theater where they had planned to open. In effect, *'Tis Pity* was ruined. It speaks to the mood of friendship that Welles did nothing but roar with laughter at the bad news. Houseman had expected a more dire show of temper. But maybe already behind the violent eyes there was some inkling of absurdity.

13

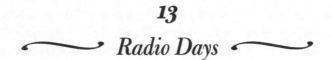

Radio Days

T H E   B E S T   P H O T O G R A P H S of Orson Welles in the 1930s— and maybe the best ever, the most natural and attractive, the ones in which he is endearing because he does not seek to be—have him with a microphone. No one is flat-footed, fat faced or overweight on the radio. In those pictures it is impossible to miss a few things that the man of the world Welles contrived to forget and obscure: he was a kid, he was raw, wild and abandoned; he had extraordinary fun, and he loved to float away on his magic carpet of a voice into adventure, romance and flat-out nonsense. Radio was his party.

That he got there so quickly and so often was testament to the essential conclusion that anyone made about him as an actor. He was at his best if you closed your eyes. All too often, to look at Welles was to miss the character he was meant to be playing. Instead, you saw the topology of makeup; the eerie misalliance of his own youth and the invariably older and grotesque man he was trying to be; and sometimes—if you were lucky, or if you were John Houseman watching Tybalt—you saw the thunder and brimstone of his rampant devil.

Whenever he played the large roles from classical theater or the grand monsters—Claudius or Svengali—well-wishers told him about his voice. That reputation spread. By early 1934, in New York, Welles was beginning to haunt the radio studios, looking for an hour's work and a check, ready to be anyone. The actor Paul Stewart made the right introductions for him. He had Welles meet Knowles Entrikin at CBS: he was the leading radio director at that network, responsible for many shows. That's where Welles met another young actor (though nearly thirty already!), Joseph Cotten, a smooth, handsome Virginian. They took to each other, and in the course of a friendly conversation Welles knocked his pipe out in the wastepaper basket and set the whole thing on fire. That's how Entrikin noticed him.

The director assigned them both to the *School of the Air of the Americas*, an educational service that played chiefly for schools. The actors in those shows were not named, and they made only $18.50 a show. They had to be ready to sound fluent and authoritative on any subject, the group of players gathered around a microphone, all in a polite dance of stepping aside as any one actor had to speak. As Cotten remembered, one show described the rubber industry in Asia. One actor—Ray Collins— had to deliver the line "Barrels and barrels of pith." But Welles and Cotten had naughty enough ears to mishear the line, and they ruined rehearsals with fits of giggling. In the end, Collins was a helpless heap of laughter on the floor while the boys stood above him like proud parents. (The company at the Amberson dinner table was assembled already— when their real day came, the actors would have a shared past.)

In only a few years, Collins would be Jim Gettys, Cotten Jed Leland and Paul Stewart Raymond, the Xanadu butler, in a show called *Citizen Kane*, which is, among so many other things, a great piece of radio. Within another year of meeting Cotten, in New York recording studios, Welles had also met and worked with Agnes Moorehead and Everett Sloane, as well as the composer Bernard Herrmann.

There were other shows that took him on—*Cavalcade of America*, at NBC, which told stories from American history; and, at NBC again, *The March of Time*, a dramatized newsreel in which current events called for actors to be politicians and celebrities of the day. There were also soap operas and opportunities to read verse. Within the space of a year, radio became the staple of Welles's income and an incentive to manic versatility. There is no way of making up a voice, but Welles had a better than average skill with accents and daring such that he took on anything. Forever afterward he was ready to dub in the voices of other actors on his films. No movie director knew better than he how the sound and picture tracks were separate, leaving room for deception, economy and comedy.

There were commercials, too, either product endorsements or promos for shows. He especially relished those voices of authority, the stamp of the network, the soft tones of wisdom and sincere recommendation— "We know a remote farm in . . ." or even "Who knows what evil lurks in the hearts of men?"

Welles began to play the Shadow for the Mutual Broadcasting System in the early spring of 1937. The series came from the comic-book char-

The Ambersons' dining table: Uncle Jack (Ray Collins), Eugene Morgan (Joseph Cotten), Major Amberson (Richard Bennett) and George (Tim Holt)

acter, created by Walter B. Gibson, in which Lamont Cranston was "a man of wealth, a student of sciences and master of other people's minds." His trick was the ability to turn invisible and exist like a radio wave. Indeed, in one episode, his unique story-making form of mental telepathy was called "the oldest wireless in the world." Cranston *was* radio, thus Welles luxuriated in the man's supreme power, his educated voice sorting out the affairs of gangsters and mysteries of the Orient with equal ease and shamelessly uttering lines such as "In the Orient, Margot, many strange things happen" and "Many fear the Shadow because they cannot see him."

The only confidant to the Shadow was Margot Lane—a role sometimes played by Agnes Moorehead. In thirty minutes at a time, for two years, to the accompaniment of warning organ chords, and with a sinister chuckle that did not quite match his treatment of Cranston but that was a schoolboy game all over the country, Welles reveled in the innocent foolishness of the Shadow. The show did not an atom of harm (beyond endorsing every melodramatic stereotype), unless it was to Welles himself. For he was the least critical boy involved with the show, not just happy to lend his smooth voice to it but yielding happily to the hokum. Here is the first instance in his career to say that Welles did the show not just to make a living but because he was suited to it, because the meretricious Lamont Cranston appealed to him. At the microphone, he was untidy, tousled, a little sweaty and carried away.

Onstage, Welles had been rather less than a success. Once the people in charge saw enough of him, they tended to reduce the size and influence of his parts. There was that headiness with an audience that worried producers, and an immersion in melodrama that had threatened to turn Claudius into just a leering, wicked uncle. But on radio, there was no challenge to Welles. He preferred reading lines to learning them. He felt freer, and he quickly got himself into real money—$185 for every Shadow episode, and by the end of the thirties, he said, $1,500 a week. He delighted in the fun and tension of live radio, the putting together of sound effects and the kick of grabbing a huge crowd of strangers then and there without having them see you or know you.

Years later, conversing with Peter Bogdanovich, Welles could not keep the excitement out of his recollections or his voice as he talked about *The March of Time:*

> I began as an occasional performer, because they had a
> regular stock company, and then I was finally let in—
> one of the inner circle. And then I had the greatest thrill
> of my life—I don't know why it thrilled me (it does still,
> to think of it now), I guess because I thought *The March
> of Time* was such a great thing to be on. One day they
> did as a news item on *March of Time* the opening of my
> production of the black *Macbeth*, and I played myself in
> it. And that to me was the apotheosis of my career—that
> I was on *March of Time* acting *and* as a news item. I've
> never felt since that I've had it made as much as I did
> that one afternoon.

We are coming to the *Macbeth*, which was a sensational event, the first in a series that made Welles known nationally, as opposed to within the theater. But how telling it is that he was at the same moment still an anonymous voice on a staple radio show, available to play this other

Orson Welles. It speaks to the rapidity of his rise and the way in which life added to his pleasure in trickery and the absurd. At the same time, it accounts for the development of a kind of superior fraudulence in his voice.

There were those who detected this rising bogusness. In the spring of 1937, Welles was the first choice to read the narration for the documentary movie *This Spanish Earth*, which Joris Ivens had made to assist the cause of the Republic in the Spanish Civil War. The narration had been written by Ernest Hemingway, who claimed that he had no desire to read it himself—until he heard Welles's voice. Then he objected and said he *would* do it himself. "Every time Orson said the word *infantry*," he said, "it was like a cocksucker swallowing."

14

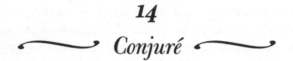

Conjuré

FOR THE REST of his life, Welles said that the Harlem *Macbeth* was the greatest or most vivid success of his life. In an interview with BBC television only a few years before his death, there was no mistaking his emotion at recalling the occasion: "On opening night for five blocks all traffic was stopped. There were so many curtain calls that they left the curtain open and the audience came up onstage to congratulate the actors. That was magical!" Those words seem important, for they pick on not a particular interpretation of Shakespeare or this triumph for black actors (though those things *were* important to Welles) so much as the public sensation, the living theater. He was there on the stage himself at the end, the director letting himself be dragged "on" by joyous, proud actors. Woe betide them if they hadn't claimed him. There would never be anything warmer or more overwhelming than *Macbeth*. This was a man who adored innocent audiences—and later cut himself off from them too much.

In the summer of 1935, Orson and Virginia went back to Woodstock. They were part of a relaxed production of *Uncle Tom's Cabin* with the Todd troupers, but they lazed away a lot of the days in a cabin on the shore of Lake Geneva. It was the last quiet time the married couple would have. Meanwhile, in New York, John Houseman was getting actively involved with the Negro Theatre Project, a branch of the Federal Theatre, one of the sweepingly idealistic schemes promoted by the Works Progress Administration (WPA). This was not so much the dream of bringing theater to the people as a way of putting people to work. With the black actress Rose McLendon, Houseman became joint head of the Negro Theatre (no matter that he was at the time an illegal alien living under a fake name—he was still legally Jacques Haussmann).

There had been riots in Harlem in the spring of 1935. The area was beset by crime. This sounds familiar. Yet Harlem in 1935 had a larger white presence than it does today, and it was not the "forbidden" or "impossible" place it is supposed to be now for white visitors. Whites ran Harlem, and exploited the blacks. The active forces opposing this situation were Communist and religious, and the riots had focused on the cry "Don't buy where you can't work," for whites ran many businesses and generally discriminated against black workers. The Negro Theatre was thrust into that world, and though it used and celebrated black talent, it was run by two whites—John Houseman and Orson Welles.

For when the Welleses returned to the city, and took a basement apartment on West Fourteenth Street, Houseman called on them and offered partnership. Welles accepted on the spot and leaped at the idea of doing Shakespeare with and for blacks. His experience with the Cornell company was that Shakespeare was too genteel in most prominent productions. At two the next morning, Welles telephoned Houseman with an idea of Virginia's—they should do *Macbeth* set in Haiti in an atmosphere of voodoo. It was a knockout scheme such as only bright white kids could have conjured up.

Macbeth was set in motion, with Welles adapting the text and devising a design scheme. But Houseman reckoned that the Negro Theatre should establish itself with some authentic black material. There was also a rush to be the first Federal Theatre project actually produced. And so, two black plays were packed into the Lafayette Theater (on Seventh Avenue between 132nd and 133rd streets) ahead of *Macbeth*—*Walk Together Chillun!* and *Conjuré Man Dies*. The latter was directed by Joseph Losey, who kept a very interested eye on Welles. As well he might have: Losey was six years older than Welles, and from Wisconsin, but he was already definitely behind Welles. Losey had seen Welles in *Candida*, and he had a poor opinion of him as an actor. But as a director, Welles was something else—unerringly brilliant, yet conventional and even old-fashioned. Losey had visited the Soviet Union in 1934. The things he had seen there—by Meyerhold and Okhlopkov—were the true avant-garde. From the outset in New York, there were those who, while admiring Welles, regarded him as something of a throwback, a private dead end of magnificent invention. Losey was of the left, and he knew theater history. In those lights, Welles was rather suspect: his ideology seemed confined to dazzling people and working longer hours than anyone had ever managed.

Well before its actual opening, *Macbeth* was taken over by the frenzy of work and expectation. Because of his radio calls, Welles did much of the stage rehearsal at night. That only added to the glamour and the nocturnal atmosphere of the production. And gradually it drew attention to Welles's apparent neglect of sleep. Those close to him observed his trick of catnaps, collapsing for twenty minutes, then surging ahead. But for most people, his labor was phenomenal and supernatural, fueled by great meals eaten at rehearsal and the steady consumption of liquor and barbiturates. Large and young, he began to take on the aura usually reserved for extraordinary athletes, of having a force or stamina that was not quite human.

Welles and Houseman picked their cast. For Macbeth, they would use Jack Carter, a tall, light-skinned man, who had played Crown in *Porgy*, who had done jail time for murder and who was rumored to have underworld ties in Harlem. Carter was insecure, and even unstable; he was inclined to drink. Welles took him on. He took the actor out boozing. They went to the best dives in Harlem. And still Orson seemed larger than life. Carter became the white boy's loyal disciple, and the rest of the cast followed suit. Call it calculation or inspired example, Welles knew how far with that show he had to dominate. He loved the challenge as he began to fall in love with the exuberance and directness of black people. Not least black women.

Edna Thomas was Lady Macbeth, and the rest of the cast included Maurice Ellis and Canada Lee. Abe Feder was in charge of the lighting, and Virgil Thomson did the music, though he left the Haitian drumming to a troupe of African drummers led by Asadata Dafora Horton. Thomson regarded Welles initially as a bluffer and intimidator. There were clashes, and Houseman was at his best as a go-between. Welles was so definite, and so unready to tolerate argument. Thomson was nearly twenty years Welles's senior, with much music to his credit. He felt challenged *and* overawed. He was too proud or fearful to write new music for Welles, but he produced every effect that was called for. A relationship developed, wary but admiring, and Thomson taught Orson to drink wine instead of whiskey at rehearsal.

Publicity mounted, and there was talk in Harlem that blacks were being exploited or set up. The left was angry, the churches were alarmed, the WPA was anxious about their own new venture. The company was over 130 people, and the drummers were truly from a world of superstition. There was a witch doctor in the group as well as a chief. There were fights and scenes, and sometimes Welles and Houseman trained the disparate energies for the stage. Imagine such an attempt today and you may realize the daring, the commitment and the innocence of those in charge. Houseman did wonders of diplomacy (and probably felt he got too little thanks). Welles bullied, flattered, tricked, seduced and never stopped. He told people to shut up and follow him and forget about being tired.

It all worked. By opening night, April 14, *Macbeth* had become an event. The streets were blocked because so many people were coming to see the show, and so many more were interested to see who was coming. The set was a jungle with a crazy nineteenth-century palace. The costumes were as bright as kids' dress-up, and they were augmented with masks. The music pounded away. The inherent melodrama of *Macbeth* was played to the hilt, and if the actors were not always at ease with the verse, they had energy. Welles's version of the text made the shortest of Shakespeare's tragedies even more economical. So it was fine that the curtain went up over half an hour late—time for the air in the Lafayette to get hotter and thicker.

Nothing remains but still photographs and memories. I cannot help but think Welles's feeling for the production was enhanced by that absence of record. Though a man of film in so many ways, he always seemed encumbered and frustrated by film's fixed record. He would come to be a maker of incomplete movies. He was also in love with theater's momentariness and the miracle that vanishes in the beaten air of applause. The great old men in Welles's work are such devout rememberers, and *Macbeth* was left to that fragile, uncertain faculty.

It hardly mattered what critics said in the hubbub. But the reviewers were swept away, too, even if some criticized the speaking and the lack of poetry. As if they had witnessed a great game in which the scores remained absurdly tied as the melodrama went into overtime, reviewers seem to have felt lucky to have been there. In *The New York Times*, Brooks Atkinson listed stunning moments and effects and concluded, "As an experiment in Afro-American showmanship, *Macbeth* merited the excitement that fairly rocked the Lafayette Theatre last night." The black press were flattered. Nearly everyone recollected the color, the music, the feeling of a dread carnival. Martha Gellhorn felt an "impression . . . of hot richness that I have almost never seen in the theatre or anywhere else." Jean Cocteau was in New York, and he fell in love with the "strange and wonderful spectacle."

One critic demurred. In the New York *Herald Tribune*, Percy Hammond called it "de luxe boondoggling," whereupon the voodooists in the company put a spell on him. The poor complainer died of pneumonia in a week!

The Lafayette sold out for sixty-four performances, then the show moved downtown to the Adelphi. The actors were hugely affected by the success—blacks then were not prepared for so much attention. The play went on tour in the early fall, by which time Jack Carter was drinking heavily. He had a passion for Virginia Welles. Maurice Ellis took over the lead role, but in Indianapolis Ellis too fell ill, so Orson put on makeup and himself played Macbeth in blackface.

The frenzy passed. Harlem remained much the same. The place of blacks in America and entertainment did not alter. A few years later, when *Gone With the Wind* opened in Atlanta, that city expressed its hope that the black actress Hattie McDaniel would not attend the premiere. She kept away. But then she won the supporting actress Oscar, sitting with her husband at a table for two in a corner of the banquet room.

"Orson Welles" is what people remembered. Yes, he had used blacks, and he may have raised some hopes too high. That *Macbeth* was a showman's dream, conjured up in the early hours of the morning. On the other hand, Welles found great fun and fellowship with blacks in the experience. It was something he would never lose, and something that would bring trouble for him one day.

15

Orson Eats Everything

WELLES HAD HAD his twenty-first birthday during the run of *Macbeth*, presiding for a moment not just over a company of black actors but over Harlem itself. He had played Shakespeare's verse above the pulse of African drums. Birnam Wood had moved on the stage like a samba of jungle fronds. No matter that the government had paid for it, or that Houseman had kept the unruly production together, Welles had managed it. And Welles did seem a little like Macbeth, for he had surely done all of this for his own glory, challenging the regular order of things and consorting with supernatural forces so as to be a king. Nothing worked better in this production than the reappraisal of the Scottish witches as voodoo practitioners. Houseman noted that Welles himself— the master of all things—was profoundly and naively superstitious. Welles was moved by the production, the discovery of black culture and his own ascent—and those three strains were hopelessly mixed in his exultation. The Welles of those years is not explicable or possible without that intense, self-dramatizing belief. The great tale of the boy wonder was coming true—childhood's legend was being fulfilled. He was not like other men.

Houseman knew that the Negro Theatre would never hold Welles. For that matter, it was a dead end to his own ambitions. The WPA itself was anxious that this star attraction not be lost, yet, to the commercial theater. Houseman could feel the way ambition and boredom made it impossible for Welles to face a level of excellence and maintain it: the sense of some very rapid, spectacular arc was already guessed at by others. Who knew whether Welles had foreseen it?

There were friends warning themselves that Orson was headstrong, dangerous and unprincipled. The considerably vain Houseman had reason to feel that his contribution had been neglected. Equally, Welles resented the steady administrative hand in Houseman that he relied on. So they were vital to each other, just as they were surely headed for some sort of ugly clash. There was too much mutual understanding, and fascination, to avoid terrible damage. So Houseman yielded, for the moment. He accepted to himself that Welles was the more active, more dynamic and more tempestuous. He would do as much as anyone could hope to keep the ship riding in its storm—even if eventually he was damned for being the fool on the bridge. He was curious, too, to see how Welles's evident self destructiveness would assert itself. Meanwhile, Welles responded to Houseman's presence and his necessary virtues with greater confusion. This was a relationship worthy of Shakespeare, with brotherhood and betrayal in such a tangle.

Houseman was a builder. He understood about the closeness of a company that might last and grow, and might even use the WPA's support to become a kind of national theater. Welles could speak wonderfully well of the company—just as he could about the Spanish republic, or even the American—but most onlookers shuddered a little to see how easily he let that rhetoric blind him to the naked truth: that any company involving Welles was subordinate, and vulnerable, to him, to his being Orson. He could speak the enthralling speech to the company about sacrifice and the group and its purpose. But all who heard that voice heard the truth of his glory and knew that offstage as well as on they were creatures in his drama.

So Houseman went to Hallie Flanagan, the head of the Federal Theatre, to gain escape from the Negro Theatre. She consented, so long as he and Welles could ensure a proper succession in Harlem. Those new appointments were made, and Welles and Houseman drove south, to the Maxine Elliott Theater at Thirty-ninth Street and Broadway, their new base. At the Lafayette, nothing was ever as exciting again, and Harlem lost its status of fashionable colony. Very soon it became a place where, famously, white people did not go.

But as if to stress their thorough dedication to the New Deal, Welles and Houseman called the new arrangement Project 891, using the designated WPA work number. They announced that their first productions would be Eugène Labiche's *Italian Straw Hat* and Marlowe's *Doctor Faustus*, for it was their official duty to present "classical" theater—thus a farce and a drama, centuries apart.

René Clair had made a delightful movie of *The Italian Straw Hat* in 1927. Virgil Thomson remembered it and recommended the play. He also proposed that his friend, the poet, critic and dancer Edwin Denby, might work the Labiche text into something viable for the New York stage. Denby had lived in Paris, and he brought a flavor of the French avant-garde of the 1920s, of surrealism and Dada. But Welles worked with him on the adaptation, pumping in the more robust strains of vaudeville, of anything worth doing because it had never been done before and of raw Orson Welles. Magically, it worked. Though, as Welles saw it, the success of what became *Horse Eats Hat* owed a great deal to Houseman's absence. The producer had to be in Canada, working on his American citizenship, and he had also promised himself as director on Leslie Howard's dream of doing *Hamlet*. For Welles, that was indelible (if inane) proof of treachery—so the furious knockabout of *Horse Eats Hat* represented an escape from Houseman so liberating and merry that Welles needed hardly notice he had no great role in the farce.

The complicated, seven-door set was designed by Nat Karson. Bil Baird made ingenious furniture that would "break up" in the riot of action. The set also had a chandelier and a fountain that worked—if not always when expected: in one rehearsal, Joseph Cotten was swinging from the chandelier and the fountain came on to soak him. It was chaos, but so funny that the effect was straightaway incorporated. Thomson thought it was all like a wonderful, intimate circus. He was helping Paul Bowles with the music—Bowles was the composer but he needed Thomson to assist with the orchestration. And there was so much music—not just the pit orchestra but pianos that played automatically and musicians in one of the boxes closest to the stage.

As Welles directed the play, the workings of the farce were meant to show: stagecraft mingled with, and got into comic mix-ups with, the demented action of the farce. Not for the last time with Welles, audiences were delighted by the mystery of wondering what was play and what was real. Where did the show cross over into life? There was a zest for mischief in Welles, an exuberance and a love of showing off, that was tickled by showing the machine while still having it function. It was, maybe, the influence of conjuring, and it was something that would be most fulfilled in moviemaking. Yet in movies, when Welles looked up, there was none of the warmth, smell or noise of an audience. He would be alone.

Horse Eats Hat was an audience show, and it reminds us on how very few occasions Orson Welles played anything strictly for laughs. Yet he himself believed it was "the best" of his stage productions of the 1930s. The play was frivolous and mechanical—coming after *Macbeth*, that proved his versatility. But it was a really entertaining evening. Even so steady a critic of Welles as Joe Losey thought it "imaginative, vigorous and delightful." Indeed, Losey wrote a long letter of congratulation, which Welles never responded to: he feared that the severe Losey was only setting him up. Orson was still a boy.

It was a cast of friends. Joseph Cotten was the central figure, Freddy, the bridegroom, who is kept from his own altar when his horse munches the hat of a married woman who had been with her lover; Virginia played the bride; Hiram Sherman was a cousin; Welles sometimes had the small role of the bride's forbidding father; and the cast also included Arlene Francis and Paula Laurence, an exotic-looking beauty from Brooklyn. It was also observed that Ms. Laurence actually moved in with Orson and Virginia during the production—not that anyone had much time to be at home.

Horse Eats Hat opened on September 26 and ran until early December. Some reviewers were baffled by the elaborate flimsiness of the show—so much effort and artifice going into so trivial a piece. There were even complaints that government money should not be devoted to so minor a play. *The New York Times* said, "Probably it is bad, certainly it is not good in the usually accepted sense of the theatre, but it *is* the only one of its kind." The critic Stark Young called it "not so much vigorous as unnecessary." But audiences came, and the play picked up a camp following just because of its indifference to the conscientious social realism of the time. Some people went back to see it several times, and a few—like Losey—saw a carefree approach that was close to surreal experiment.

As the run of *Horse Eats Hat* proceeded, Welles was replaced in his small role (by the far shorter Edgerton Paul) so that he could honor a commitment to act on Broadway in Sidney Kingsley's play *Ten Million Ghosts*. This was exactly the kind of play *Horse Eats Hat* was not—a solemn antiwar sermon, based on the character of munitions dealer Basil Zaharoff. Kingsley was directing and paying for the production, with Welles as the young poet hero (playing his own age for a change) and George Coulouris as the tycoon. Taking the part amid so many other things to do may have been a rude gesture to Houseman or sheer bravado. In the event, the play was a flop: it ran only a week, and at times Welles was observed (or pretended to be) asleep onstage. So he did the Kingsley play for a rest. And then returned happily to his farce at the Maxine Elliott.

By then, plans were under way for the second 891 production, *Doctor Faustus*. Here Welles was set not just as director but as lead actor—as such, it would be his first major acting job in New York. And here the play was much more than a directing spectacle or trifle. For anyone close to Welles, it was evident that *Doctor Faustus* had elements of self-portrait. He rose to the challenge, but in doing so he became more embattled with Houseman than ever before. (Houseman was sometimes heard to murmur that if Welles was Faust, he was also his own Mephistopheles.)

Houseman had recognized and indulged Welles's neurotic hope that the producer keep away from rehearsals. Despite his air of authority, Welles was insecure: how often the bully acts to preempt his own victimization. Like most directors, Welles believed in the evolution of productions, and he feared that other eyes would misunderstand early errors—and feel bound to make useful suggestions that had to be accepted. Welles was intent on his vision. Houseman was pledged to helping him. He believed a producer should both protect the director and give him what he needed in the way of people and material. But there were budgets to observe, and sometimes a producer could be more clever if he knew what was going on. Above all, Houseman saw the need to guard Welles from exhaustion, and his tendency to fuss over details whenever he was uncertain.

Such difficulties were intensified when Welles was acting a big role as well as directing. And Houseman had not had that experience before. He had to be more present. Welles needed opinions, and he valued no one's as much as Jack's. But he hated to admit that, and he hated to have anyone as cool and smart as Houseman watching him become Faustus: "At such times," wrote Houseman, "I became not merely the hated figure of authority, to be defied and outwitted as I refused further delays and escapes, but the first hostile witness to the ghastly struggle between narcissism and self-loathing that characterized Orson's approach to a part."

It was in watching *Faustus* come to life that Houseman saw how truly Welles believed in the Devil. This was more than the atmosphere of magic and voodoo. Houseman fancied that Welles was living in a conscious state of doom, a precocious talent who had a date with devils. It was a remarkable observation (tender yet critical) of an extraordinary condition. For Welles, in so many ways, seemed beyond conscience or fate. He was unbridled in so many things: in roaring at people; in eating; in work, women and his own genius. He was as free as anyone in America, and exultant. Yet, as Houseman observed, "in his most creative, manic moments, in his wildest transports of love or on the topmost peak of his precocious victories, he was rarely free from a sense of sin and a fear of retribution so intense and immediate that it drove him through long nights of panic to seek refuge in debauchery or work." Houseman was one of the first to see depression as part of the ebullient boy wonder.

What provoked that? Was Orson guilty at the loss of his parents, or the institutionalization of his brother? Because older men had used him, or because he had flirted with them? Because already he was unfaithful to Virginia? Because he knew how much he lied? No one answer seems adequate, or irrelevant. Maybe Houseman was close to the truth in seeing the passion and torment of narcissism and self-loathing. Orson was a monstrous egotist, not simply vain and ambitious but incapable of grasping anything except in his own terms. And he was smart enough to use that—and despise it. So he was bound to soar and to require his own downfall. Consider also that, in cool measure, he reckoned he was the equal of Faustus in genius, learning and mastery of the world. The dread took an odd form, as Houseman saw it: it left Welles afraid to sleep, driven on to do more.

16

The Light

M A C B E T H had had tropical color; *Horse Eats Hat* was pretty and pastel. With *Doctor Faustus* there would be another look. Welles declared that the only good reason for doing a play as old as *Faustus* (or as disjointed as drama) was "to rouse the same magical feeling [as felt in the sixteenth century], but we use modern methods." The policy of 891 might be to revive the classics, but Welles had little interest in anything that did not excite him *now*. And he had utter confidence that he could make the audience share the thrill.

Faustus moved *him:* for here was a model of knowledge, enlightenment and eloquence who would not deny himself more—Faust wants greater powers, dark magic, the chance to be exalted for twenty-four years, all in return for the bargain with the Devil that guarantees destruction. But wasn't Faust anyone in New York having a good life as the world sought to steer its way between economic depression and war? Wasn't Faust any one of the new leaders in the world—Hitler, Stalin or Roosevelt—those huge personalities intent on mastering history? *Doctor Faustus* is the first of those works in which Welles meant to dramatize the struggle between enlightenment and darkness in the late 1930s.

He was one of those people who saw just one test in the theater when dealing with classic material—will today's audience be thrilled, delighted or terrified, as if . . . as if they were at a movie? So he took Marlowe's text and drastically cut it. Welles loathed the intervals in regular plays. All that happened then was that people had a drink, relaxed and talked to friends about the market or the Yankees. They might even elect to go to dinner early. Turning on the houselights was so feeble and defeatist a measure. Audiences were to be shaped and enslaved by darkness and the light on the stage. So he loved to turn his plays into single acts in which scenes shifted on very rapid blackouts. One may say that this was a conscious cinematic influence already. But it was also the magician's method, and an unconscious insight—that audiences had discovered a delicious, dangerous servitude at the movies. It follows that Welles was an astute editor of texts aiming for that kind of theatrical domination. His theater companies were very little concerned with commissioning new plays, and Welles seems never to have dreamed of doing one of his own plays. But surely his vision in *Bright Lucifer* was translated into the savage economy and fatal, phantom look of *Doctor Faustus*.

He made *Faustus* into a one-act play of less than ninety minutes, in which the darkness rose in waves against imperiled shafts of light. There was a silent movie of *Faustus*, made in Germany in 1926 by F. W. Murnau, with Emil Jannings as Faust—but there is no suggestion that Welles had seen it. Rather, his *Faustus* seems to have been influenced by the entire expressionistic experience of cinema, of darkness and light in harmony and conflict. More than that, Welles employed several techniques familiar to stage magicians, chiefly the way light and black velvet backing and surrounds could be used to make things disappear and reappear. He constructed cylinders of black velvet, open at the front and only to the height of a figure, with strong lights at the top of each cylinder pointing down. Precise control of light cues could take any character in and out of existence—like ghosts, or cuts in movies. Abe Feder did the work and ran the lights, and the electrical crew had to master a scheme of lighting changes far more extensive than Broadway was used to. But the concept belonged to Welles, and the intent was to have audiences feel they were in some cockpit more fluid and threatening than a normal theater.

Naturalism was the more fully abandoned when Welles turned to sound. He had not been wasting his time in radio. Instead, he had studied the enchantment of sound effects, no matter how humble or foolish: coconut shells knocked together to make the sound of galloping horses, or breathing to convey menace. He filled the play (and its patches of darkness) with sound; for radio, if it works well, always brings us closer to blindness. There were echo effects, and sometimes voices were augmented or distorted by microphones. The music, by Paul Bowles, was all in haunting woodwind. And as in any great black-and-white movie—as in *Citizen Kane*—Welles sought a unity in which the audience felt that the mix of sounds, voices and music was entirely blended with the picture. There was nothing left to chance or nature. The very dictatorial beauty of the medium was being stressed. Faust's bargain was no longer a quaint idea; it was a choice in which the spectators were involved.

The people who knew Welles were persuaded by *Doctor Faustus*. Being close to a boy wonder exposed them to his cunning, his lies and the act of precociousness. Being his companion left wounds. But *Doctor Faustus* was a work of genius in which all the people and all the desires were poured into an inescapable drama. John Houseman saw the tricks assembled—the cylinders, the trapdoors, the small explosions, the puppets for the Seven Deadly Sins, the magic fraudulence—and knew that "at the center of the production, there was deep personal identification which, across a gulf of three and a half centuries, led [Welles] to the heart of the work and to its vivid re-creation on a contemporary American stage."

Welles played Faustus in a floor-length robe and a long, dark wig—he was somewhere between Christ and Rasputin, and his own face is livid, sensual and very scary in the photographs that survive. For his Mephistopheles, he went back to Jack Carter, sober again, his head shaved, and directed to play the part cold, quiet and patient. Houseman was especially thrilled by their scenes together, for they were like perverted love scenes, enriched by a vital complicity. Here was a model for Welles, not just of black and white men together but of a nobleman and a devil who require each other for life to begin. Helen of Troy was Paula Laurence, the archetypal beautiful woman always there to beguile and be abandoned, and silent.

Hallie Flanagan attended a rehearsal and left a wonderful account of what it felt like to see this drama coming to life:

Going into the Maxine Elliott during rehearsals was like
going into the pit of hell: total darkness punctuated by
stabs of light, trapdoors opening and closing to reveal
bewildered stagehands or actors going up, down, and
around in circles; explosions; properties disappearing in a
clap of thunder; and on stage Orson, muttering the
mighty lines and interspersing them with fierce adjura-
tions to the invisible but omnipotent Feder. The only
point of equilibrium in those midnight seances was Jack
Carter, omnipresent, quiet, slightly amused, probably the
only actor who ever played Mephisto without raising his
voice. More subtle than the red flares and necromancy
was the emphasis on an element of tragedy more in keeping with our age than that of a man being snatched away
by the devil—that is, the search to lay hold on reality.

The curtain did not rise until 9:00 p.m. on January 8, 1937. With the
play's length, it was possible to begin later—and then Orson could keep
his date at a radio studio, with a live audience. But he had to do the radio
show wearing his makeup—truly this Faust spanned worlds and media
that night.

The reviews were outstanding. Brooks Atkinson in *The New York
Times* was very impressed that a hitherto forbidding classic had been made
"grim and terrible" on a modern stage, and he was convinced that lighting in the theater had undergone a revolution:

> The modern switchboard is so incredibly ingenious that
> stage lighting has become an art in its own right. The
> points and shafts of light and crepuscular effects commu-
> nicate the unearthly atmosphere of *Doctor Faustus* with-
> out diminishing the primary importance of the acting.

Not only the production was praised. There was tremendous respect
for Welles as an actor. Stark Young had been particularly taken by the
blend of sound and music, and he said that

> Marlowe's play is spoken far above the average by Mr.
> Orson Welles, who has a beautiful even voice, perfectly
> placed, and has, too, a remarkable sense of timing. He
> possesses also both naturally and by study a notable gift
> for projection.

As Faust

Doctor Faustus ran until May 9. Nearly every night was sold out, and on many evenings there were people standing at the back of the theater.

Enter the publisher, applauding, like one of the audience.
Well, thank you.
I find myself very frustrated.
Yes?
I want to have been there, all the better if standing. In these last few chapters my sense of loss has been mounting.
You wouldn't want me to make the shows seem plainer?
Of course not! But does nothing remain?
Only a few photographs.
How tormenting! I feel like someone from Cleveland or Dallas just about to undertake a theater weekend in New York. I long to see Macbeth, Horse Eats Hat *and* Doctor Faustus. *To think that New Yorkers could have seen all three in the space of, what—?*
Nine months. And there is more to come.
Don't tell me!
Of course, it is especially frustrating in the career of a man whose later work—or much of it—lives there, endlessly available. There is nothing like live theater—I know, that sounds like a homily—but it is true, and Welles did wonders.
God, yes!
Or so you feel, having read the work of an author who was not alive when the plays were produced.
I trust your reports, but I would want to see for myself. To think that the grandeur of Faustus, *the playfulness of the farce and the music of* Macbeth *are all quite gone. Vanished!*
Doesn't it make them especially poignant and lovely?
It does!
Whereas, the movies—if I may say so—their beauty is too available.
How's that?
There was a time of my life, the 1970s, when I regularly taught *Citizen Kane*, going through it in a class, in detail, looking at the film over and over again. I probably saw it ten times a year.
And?
I wearied of it. I had to stop seeing it. It became only its tricks, do you understand? It lost its life. Welles felt the same, I think. Consider how many times he saw every detail in the editing, how he labored over its

grace. He reached a point where he could not see it ever again. It made him feel . . . futile, cynical even, empty. Films can do that.

　　But a play.

　　Ah yes. I think nearly every day of plays I've seen, or even plays I directed. Nothing remains of them. Or much of them. I have Sondheim's *Into the Woods* on video in a filmed performance. And I like to see that. But it does not match what I felt that Sunday matinee at the Martin Beck Theatre—the marvel and danger of it, the cries of the audience, the passion of being there.

　　And Welles gave that up. That's what you're saying?

　　I fear so.

　　His Faustian bargain?

17
No One at All

NINETEEN-THIRTY-SEVEN, John Houseman would recognize later, with survivor's hindsight, was "the most confused and disturbed of those difficult years—a time of transition between the end of the Great Depression and the beginning of the slowly gathering industrial boom that accompanied our preparations for World War II." Some things were getting better—which only left those still in hardship feeling more resentful and more violent. There is a moment in recovering from disaster that is more dangerous than the disaster itself—if, deep down, you believe in order. For it is then that energy and courage are renewed and may hurl anger and bitterness into action. It is often as things get better that revolutions occur. And not every bursting young person in political theater wants that, for revolution is one of the few things that can stop your show going on.

　　So, in 1937, it was not just possible for some but a test of faith to look on the black side: there were 12 million unemployed in the United States; for those with eyes to see, there were the scars of poverty all over America—in 1937, Dorothea Lange was in and around California's San Joaquin Valley photographing the tense patience in those waiting for work or relief checks or trying to beg; there were dramatic strikes in the American heartland, with police firing on strikers and demonstrators; there were those who had visited Soviet Russia and seen a bright new way ahead and who had not quite digested the meaning of the trials there. In 1937 there was civil war in Spain, Germany would begin to take unto itself the body of Czechoslovakia and Italy would quit the League of Nations.

It all depended on what you wanted to see. Sincere people in America rejoiced to see the Depression ending, and some now determined to shut down those subsidized artistic projects—that "featherbedding." In 1937, Hollywood made *A Star is Born, The Awful Truth, Swing High, Swing Low* and *A Damsel in Distress*, as well as *Dead End, You Only Live Once* and *The Life of Emile Zola*. "Nice Work If You Can Get It," Astaire sang in *A Damsel in Distress*, and Orson Welles was having a terrific time getting to be twenty-two.

It was in that birthday spring of 1937 that he began to broadcast *The Shadow* for the Mutual Broadcasting System, using voice, unflappable courage and Lamont Cranston's advantage to right any wrongs—wooing not just the public but underprivileged radicals in the true cause of reform. Someone who worked in small parts on *The Shadow* that spring was Elia Kazan, actor and director from the Group Theater and from a wing of the radical movement that believed itself less spoiled than Orson Welles. Such people smelled the showman and the show-off in Orson; they knew he was doing it all for glory, but they envied his helpless ease and talent. Kazan was six years older than Welles, and he watched in awe, too much in love with theater to resist:

> I remember [Welles] arriving for rehearsal one morn-
> ing; he'd been up all night carousing but looked little
> the worse for it and was full of continuing excitement. A
> valet-secretary met him at the side of the stage with a
> small valise containing fresh linen and the toilet articles
> he needed. The rehearsal was never interrupted—
> Orson had unflagging energy and recuperative powers
> at that time—and he soon looked as good as new. There
> was no swagger of aesthetic guilt there; *The Shadow* was
> not patronized, only slightly kidded, and this affection-
> ately. . . . Seldom have I been near a man so abundantly
> talented or one with a greater zest for life.

That "been near" seems very important. Kazan was himself all his life an intensely physical animal (I had to interview him once, in Boston on a warm day, and he led us out of the hotel to stretch out on the Common, gazing at girls). In Kazan's movies, people hold and struggle with each other in vital, heady ways, and there is Kazan, decades after the event, remembering "being near" Orson. I think Welles shone and stank with glory and fleshy magnificence. He drew people to him and made them want to touch him. And he had greedy eyes to watch their temptation. I have said that he knew how to play homosexuals amazed at his eerie beauty. And surely he took women by the score. But his fascination was more extensive than that; it was some kind of universal, seductive yet sexless, physical command—it was a way of letting himself be seen that spread the rapturous condition of "audience" everywhere he went. Or wherever he was heard—for Welles relished the Shadow's power, to move without having to be anywhere. That was not just conjuring; it was the height of modernism. Moreover, it was in radio that Orson began to see how one might be handsome, heroic, beautiful as well as . . . overweight, unkempt or in scandalous company. And it was by radio every week that Welles reached millions, not just those in New York's know.

Faustus ran at the Maxine Elliott Theater until early May—long enough for Welles to grow bored. *The Shadow* came along to pick up his spirits, and there were other ventures. It was in the spring of 1937 that he did his reading of the Hemingway commentary for *This Spanish Earth*, only to be declined. At the Henry Street Settlement, Welles helped mount *The Second Hurricane*, an operetta for children by Aaron Copland and Edwin Denby. (It was there that he first met William Alland, a notable recruit.) He was also the narrator for a radio play, *The Fall of the City*, by Archibald MacLeish.

Though only thirty minutes long, this was a momentous occasion that affected Orson's future. *The Fall of the City* was meant to inaugurate a series, and MacLeish had been asked to write a play in verse specifically for radio. Its subject was the way in which some unnamed modern city succumbed to fascism: it sounded like a Czech tragedy written for the age of Adolf Hitler. Irving Reis directed the show and experimented with mixing different sound tracks. Welles did all his work from a soundproof booth, looking out on a crowd that was the people of the city—200 college students. Listeners said that the different levels of sound were like music—and compellingly close to the real sounds of totalitarian oratory and crowd response currently available on radio from Italy and Germany. MacLeish wrote in English, but the aural context was that of 1937 newsreels.

The historian of broadcasting Erik Barnouw would say of the show and its radio audience, "They heard something that, by the very texture of its sound, gripped the attention and chilled the marrow. Orson Welles, its principal voice, established himself as one of the great performers of radio."

The announcer he played was at the same time a version of 1930s radio's ubiquitous commercial *and* the poet himself—and Welles would not have failed MacLeish's verse. He made listeners see the scene:

> *We are here in the central plaza.*
> *We are well off to the eastward edge.*
> *There is a kind of terrace over the crowd here.*
> *It is precisely four minutes to twelve.*
> *The crowd is enormous; there might be ten thousand;*
> *There might be more; the whole square is faces.*

This is gripping radio, but it is also the seed of Welles the filmmaker. For he was deeply moved by the offering of witness and the voice and mood of a man urging you to see. This is, I think, the innate politics of Welles's art, and it is as dictatorial as it is poetic. Though he feared tyrants, he was fascinated by them. Shut your eyes, he seems to say on radio, and when you open them the world will be new. There has never been a moviemaker who was more shaped and driven by radio—nor a director who had so mined his own ambiguous soul in radio first.

In the play, the fascist conqueror comes to the city. The people's fear and anticipation have been so great that they amount to a dread that *needs* such a tyrant. "The city of masterless men/Will take a master." The new leader is an armored figure—listeners heard the noise of the metal. And then MacLeish's genius taught Welles something, the very pit of magic, the absolute emptiness at the heart of great conjuring. The announcer looks into the tyrant's open visor for the radio audience, and reports,

> *There is no one.*
> *No one at all.*
> *No one.*
> *The helmet is hollow.*
> *The metal is empty.*
> *The armor is empty.*
> *I tell you there is no*
> *One at all there.*

And here, as early as 1937, Orson Welles—a genius who always needed to acquire, borrow, beg or steal; for he was not a very original thinker—had found his lasting theme. Here is the enigma of Kane becoming somehow less the more we know about him. Here is the emptiness that sustains mystery in so many of the films. And here is even the horror in which a tremendous egotist apprehended his own absence—if only he could believe in his own tricks. My God, this is nearly religion, not to mention politics at the end of the twentieth century. This is how Ronald Reagan became president, and that is why—out of sight, so to speak, in Buenos Aires, in 1941—Jorge Luis Borges would say of *Citizen Kane:*

> In one of Chesterton's stories—"The Head of Caesar," I think—the hero observes that nothing is so frightening as a labyrinth with no center. This film is precisely that labyrinth.

18

⟵ *Cradle* ⟶

WHAT NEXT onstage? As *Faustus* continued its run, Welles and Houseman considered other possibilities—*The Duchess of Malfi*, Ben Jonson's *The Silent Woman* and, even then, *Julius Caesar*. But nothing took hold of them, and there was already talk that the Federal Theatre's budget was being reappraised as times "improved." For many people, subsidized art was emergency treatment only. Once it could be claimed that America was on the mend, the dangerous medicine was to be locked away.

Yet Welles did have a notion, and it may have been one that he was reluctant to share with Houseman. Their partnership thrived on suspicions and maneuver. In the fall of 1936, at the time of *Horse Eats Hat* (through Virgil Thomson's introduction), Orson had met Marc Blitzstein, the son of a wealthy Philadelphia banker who happened also to be a socialist. Marc, ten years older than Welles, had grown up to be a modern composer, a very busy radical and a rich man—this was a mixture not uncommon in the 1930s, and it appealed to Welles, who always liked his revolutionaries to be sophisticated and well-heeled. Blitzstein's wife had just died, and the two men got on famously. Houseman called it "love at first sight" and admitted to a degree of jealousy. No working relationship for Welles was ever simply professional: associates had to be won; he had to be adored.

Houseman felt Blitzstein was entranced. Furthermore, the composer had an intriguing project, *The Cradle Will Rock*. This had begun as a sketch about prostitution. But, on the advice of Bertolt Brecht, it had grown into a vast play with music, set in Steeltown, USA, about labor, strikes, the prostitution of all kinds of integrity and about that enormous romantic aspiration for vague but large change in brilliant, rich kids.

This was Welles's most politically radical venture. There were some close to Blitzstein and committed to the left who warned the composer that Welles was erratically frivolous, that he would turn the political material into one more of his own dazzling shows. For *The Cradle Will Rock* had been promised first to hard-core activists, like the Actors' Repertory Company. Welles had been trying to woo it away, and Blitzstein had been tempted—for where Orson went, attention followed. Welles later confessed that he had had to make himself rather redder for Blitzstein than was really the case. Of course, he *sympathized* with the play's cause, but, he said in retrospect, "I was only radical because I was showing off. I've never been anything more than a progressive. I allowed myself to be thought of as farther to the left than I was because I didn't want to lose his friendship."

By March 1937, the Actors' Repertory Company had backed out: they lacked the funds to mount the show, or to compete with Welles's vision of it. Houseman was at last allowed to hear the score, sung and played by Blitzstein himself. Then, soon afterward, Hallie Flanagan of the Federal Theatre was invited to dinner at the apartment Houseman shared with Virgil Thomson, and she was won over. "It took no wizardry," she wrote, "to see that this was not just a play set to music, nor music illustrated by actors. This was in its percussive as well as its verbal beat Steeltown USA—America 1937."

Flanagan gave her official approval, no matter that there were many promptings from Washington to cut back on the Federal Theatre program. Houseman felt that she had backed *Cradle* very deliberately, courting some kind of confrontation. But controversy was never just over funding the arts. Steel was an industry in torment. As *Cradle* was rehearsed, there were strikes at major auto plants. At the end of May, there were serious riots at a Republic Steel mill in Chicago. Police fired on strikers and demonstrators, and ten were killed, some of them shot in the back. Johnstown, Ohio, had to be placed under martial law. The CIO was making intense efforts to unionize the steel industry. There were problems in the fabric of American society, headlines every day or so, making for violence and death, and things far beyond the guile of Lamont Cranston.

But Welles was conjuring up his Steeltown, and he was devoted to the genius of his new friend and composer. The play had many scenes, and it moved quickly from one to another. To serve that journalistic urgency,

Welles called for moving scenery—glass-bottomed platforms loaded with scenery and props that slid in and out, all in a scheme of pastels. Houseman was required to get the scheme to work (it was a small factory of moving parts), and he played an important role in the mechanics of the production so that Welles could concentrate on the music, the orchestra, singers and actors, to say nothing of *Faustus* every night and the regular routine of radio shows. Rehearsals for *Cradle* frequently occupied the early morning hours.

Then an announcement was made in Washington that the WPA faced significant reduction in size. June 30, the end of the budgetary year, loomed as the moment of decision. But *Cradle* was set to open at the Maxine Elliott Theater on June 16. In Washington, there were rumors that an incendiary play about steel could hardly come at a worse time. Someone was sent to New York to observe a run-through, and rumors mounted that the play was a threat to order and stability. Virginia Welles was counseling her husband to get out of the production and take no risk: after all, she said, he did not actually believe in its sentiments. Virginia was unashamedly loyal to a certain view of capitalism, order and conservatism. Orson found himself at a loss—what did he believe? He himself? In all the drama of the birth of *The Cradle Will Rock*, he played an oddly shy role. Yes, he was the director of the show. But Houseman ran it, and Blitzstein was its author. Ever afterward, Welles was inclined to give *Cradle* scant attention in his history of what he had done. There is no shame in this, and no thought of denying what *Cradle* owed to him. But, as never before in his life, circumstances had conspired to make the meaning of a show all-significant, so Welles was less comfortable than usual.

Rehearsals were chaotic, but that was the norm, and this was a very elaborate production. Advance sales were very good— 18,000 tickets—yet nothing could still the talk that the show was doomed. As late as June 11, Hallie Flanagan was given the order that no new WPA show could open before the end of the financial year. That blatant maneuver was aimed at *Cradle* and nothing else, and it is plain that a conspiracy of censorship had been mounted. Welles now was trapped in the role of hero.

He gave a special preview on June 14. The next day the WPA sent guards, who padlocked the theater and occupied the premises. There followed thirty-six hours of living drama, enough to make *The Cradle Will Rock* famous for all time.

The company got into the theater and made a council office in the basement. The magnificent, complex scenery had been confiscated. All members of the cast who were dependent on the government for their wages were threatened by embargo. Even the theatrical unions were restricted from being helpful. There was no theater, no sets and maybe no performers or orchestra. Still, Houseman told the press that the first public preview—set for the night of June 16—*would* take place.

Houseman and Welles agreed to mount the show as their own independent venture. Blitzstein signed an emergency contract with them. At the eleventh hour, at seven o'clock in the evening of the sixteenth, the Venice Theatre (at Seventh Avenue and Fifty-ninth Street) was proposed and agreed to. A piano had been hired, and it was taken to the Venice in the truck that had been driving around waiting for the emergency relocation. Ticket holders for the preview, gathered outside the Maxine Elliott, were asked to walk the twenty-one blocks to the Venice. All of this on a hot June night, with dark falling.

At ten to eight, Houseman and Welles drove up to the new theater with Archibald MacLeish, who had been making frantic efforts to change minds for them in Washington. The Venice stage had an old Italian backdrop from a forgotten production. The lighting board blew out. But the audience began to arrive. The piano was set up: Blitzstein would himself play and be the orchestra and he would sing whatever roles he had to. All of them? It was unclear in the chaos how many of the cast actors and singers would ignore their union orders.

At five past nine in a theater nearly full, with Abe Feder operating one spotlight, Orson Welles and John Houseman walked onto the stage to explain the situation. There was that rush of joy and applause that is only provoked by outrage, by the sense of galvanic improvisation and by the certainty that the audience was about to see something rarer than it had ever seen before. Think of all that Orson would ever do and never forget the excitement of this ramshackle evening.

Houseman explained the WPA and its crisis. Welles thanked people for coming, he sketched out the play to cover for so many elements that had been sacrificed, and then he said, "We have the honor to present— with the composer at the piano—*The Cradle Will Rock!*"

There was Blitzstein, in shirt and suspenders, exhausted before he began, the composer but not a singer, in front of a ludicrous backdrop of the Bay of Naples. The guys in charge knew that some of the actors and singers had arrived—but how many? The first cue called for the whore Moll to sing—Olive Stanton was cast in the role. In the darkness, her shaking voice sang out. Feder searched for her with the spotlight, and there she was standing up in the audience to sing.

There is nothing like theater, and nothing like its danger. And if you are not reading this with your hair on end, then never go near any place called a theater.

They got through that night, and when it came to its end there was Larry (played by Howard Da Silva) roaring out at the audience and the world:

> *When you can't climb down, and you can't sit still;*
> *That's a storm that's going to last until*
> *The final wind blows . . . and when the wind blows . . .*
> *The cradle will rock!*

The curtain dropped. There was silence, shock, and then, as Houseman said, "all hell broke loose." There is nothing quite like moving people to the depths of their being: it justifies so much that is sad, ugly and dull. The evening was both an accident and a conspiracy of fate, for the WPA and everyone afraid of the opera had made a piece of living theater so that no one would forget. Maybe the excitement of being there eclipsed the drama or the meaning of the show. Things were getting better: and how could America be ruined if plays and their audiences could find such unity? The show belonged to no one in particular, and if there was an individual, it was the haggard, ecstatic Blitzstein. Welles had done it, and been trapped. But he was as romantic and as moved as everyone by the demonstration of defiance. For if nothingness was his theme, defiance was his vibrato and flourish.

19

Something Deathless and Dangerous

THE CRADLE WILL ROCK played on at the Venice for another two weeks, its first night of uncertainty becoming a more mannered attempt at preserving the impromptu. Crowds came, for the opening had been reported as an event even if the show was not reviewed. It was broadcast on the radio, and one Sunday the company went to the Pennsylvania steel country, to Bethlehem itself, to play to the workers. A miserable 200 showed up—the bulk of the labor force had opted for a company picnic arranged to compete with the opera. The Manhattan intelligentsia might have fallen in love with a strike to music, but workers preferred sunshine and beer. Welles was the more certain that the show had never been quite his thing.

Meanwhile, the Federal Theatre was shrinking every day. Over 1,500 people got pink slips. Theater leases were terminated. The *Federal Theatre Magazine* was closed down. Welles submitted his official resignation. His summer was given over to a seven-part adaptation of *Les Misérables* for Mutual, with himself as the hounded Jean Valjean and Martin Gabel as the pursuer Javert. This romantic, rhetorical cry for liberty was much closer to Orson's heart, and his voice dominated the show, for he had elected to make the radio drama turn on Valjean's first-person narrative. Lamont Cranston had had his inner voice that was the core to *The Shadow* programs. Something in Welles reveled in the chance to take unknown millions into his confidence, to be a zealous voice colonizing the darkness. Time and again, in so many media, his ego and his art combined in the exultant, yet sometimes treacherous claim to be telling a vital, desperate story.

Welles and Houseman had seemingly never been closer than at that moment when they strode onto the Venice stage together to let that wild game commence. But in anticlimax, they had not lost their wariness of each other. As Houseman saw it, "Our immediate emotional response to the success of *The Cradle Will Rock* was the usual need, on both our parts, to prove that each of us could exist without the other."

Welles was approached by the venerable producer Arthur Hopkins to put on *King Lear.* Houseman was told by Hallie Flanagan that he was fired. But she had better news. Her own service at the WPA had left Vassar without a head for its drama department. She offered Houseman the job. He went up to Vassar to meet the college president, and he was thinking it over very seriously. But then things fell out between Welles and Hopkins. Welles claimed the older man didn't actually have the money for *Lear.* Some countered that Welles had been too free in interviews proclaiming what *he* was going to do with the play, forgetting to mention Hopkins. So the producer had changed his mind.

It was mid-August when Houseman went to see Orson and Virginia for the weekend at their house in Sneden's Landing. The couple seemed very happy; they were pregnant—the baby was due the following March. The two men became friendlier on the summer evening after supper.

"Why the hell don't we start a theater of our own?" said Welles.

And Houseman answered, "Why don't we?"

They wondered what to call themselves, and saw the name of an old magazine in the fireplace: the Mercury Theatre it would be. Houseman would be president, Welles vice president, and Augusta Weissberger secretary. They started with capital of one hundred dollars. They found an empty theater, the Comedy, at Broadway and Forty-first Street, and took out a magnificent three-year lease on it.

Houseman went to see Brooks Atkinson, a friend to their venture. As a result, on Sunday, August 29, the *Times* ran a lengthy article titled "Plans for a New Theatre." It was really a declaration of principles before that term had been thought of. Houseman was the author of this manifesto, but clearly he spoke for Welles, too. He listed the desires of an audience identified in the production of *Macbeth* and *Doctor Faustus*. Theirs was not "the regular Broadway crowd" but people who were discovering, or rediscovering, theater and who craved classical plays in exciting new productions. Audience surveys made during *Faustus* provided a theoretic statistical proof of these claims. But, in fact, Houseman and Welles were hoping for a crowd ready to see what they wanted to do.

In that respect, the manifesto firmly distanced itself from the mood of *The Cradle Will Rock*. "While a socially unconscious theatre would be intolerable," they now said, "there will be no substitution of social consciousness for drama." They reckoned on doing four or five plays a season, in repertory, and they promised several old favorites—*Julius Caesar, The Duchess of Malfi, The Silent Woman*—along with William Gillette's comedy *Too Much Johnson* and Shaw's *Heartbreak House*. Not everything worked out as promised, but the manifesto is an accurate portrait of Welles's view of drama. He trusted proven plays, and he felt most free at giving them his own stamp and slant. "New plays and new ideas may turn up any day," they said. But Mercury would only ever find one major, original work—*Citizen Kane*. It was a part of Welles's confidence that he could best address the modern audience by having them see *Julius Caesar*, say, in a contemporary light. It was a director's theater he wanted, with himself as director. In so many ways, he was still the brilliant schoolboy amazing people with his drastic reappraisals of Shakespeare.

The Monday after the *Times* article, Welles was on the air for CBS in his adaptation of *Twelfth Night*. Cedric Hardwicke was Malvolio, he was Orsino and Tallulah Bankhead played Viola. Then, as Houseman took on the infinite tasks of recruitment and administration, Welles retreated to a hotel in New Hampshire to edit a version of *Julius Caesar*, their first production, scheduled for November 11. He came back not just with a text but with lighting plans, music cues and a model for the set.

In legend, the production that was to come is known as one without sets or costumes—in other words, a stripped-down parable in which

Shakespeare's Rome was made to illuminate the fascistic Europe of 1937. That was the thrust of the Mercury production, and that is why New York audiences were so taken with it. But no one in the show believed in it as just a bare-bones production. Welles's "empty" stage was actually a series of carefully graded ramps and platforms. There were many hiding places within this set for spotlights, for Welles wanted to imitate the light effects achieved at Nazi rallies, themselves the fruit of expressionist theater. These sets would cost twice the allocated budget, and they were the cause of intricate technical problems.

Where Welles saved was in costumes and by cutting out most of the battle scenes. Even the forum crowd was to be relatively modest in size but enlarged by the "radio" of many more voices. The show was done in modern dress, with military uniforms (dyed dark green) supplying the air of the fascist state.

But Welles had extracted and highlighted the story of Brutus and Cassius. His *Caesar* was the debate as to what could be done to keep the state from magnificent tyranny: Cassius was bitter, envious, resentful, while Brutus was intended to be a noble liberal. But the two were shown as friends who differ in outlook and sense of necessary action. Then, in their argument or hesitation, they are outflanked by a simple demagogue, Antony, who wins the crowd and becomes a more ruthless fascist than ever Caesar could have made.

I stress this interpretation for several reasons: because meaning is sometimes lost in the bold look of the Mercury *Julius Caesar;* this Brutus was the Welles who had been so confused over *The Cradle Will Rock*— whether to act, how to act, when does a liberal become a radical, and are there times when the best liberal is left stranded? But also because Welles was in his element as dramatist when exploring the unease behind male friendship. Brutus and Cassius were a match and an argument that would be returned to in Kane and Jed Leland; in Quinlan and Vargas in *Touch of Evil;* Hal and Falstaff, and in so many of the failed friendships in Welles's own life—not least that with Houseman.

The show's simple effect was a nightmare of labor and correction. Welles had commissioned a score from Marc Blitzstein, but over at CBS he had also been making a complex sound track—the voices of the crowd—that required a new speaker system at the Comedy Theater. The money ran out. Houseman was compelled to go looking for more: one notable coup was securing $2,500 from Henry and Clare Luce. Still, the income from ticket sales was gone before the show opened. It was the pattern of the company that Welles would invent fresh desires and expenses for a show, then gaze at Houseman, daring the producer to fail and betray

Caesar: Brutus (Welles) confronts Antony (George Coulouris).

him. But whenever Houseman left the theater to find more money, Welles was likely to throw a tantrum. He liked to have Houseman *there*, to take notes and get small things done.

Houseman was used and abused, and he got little of the glory. He took it all because he believed in Welles:

> Orson Welles was a prodigious, if somewhat erratic, worker. This time he was fanatical in his preparation. Between the personal scenes, which he continued to rehearse long after they seemed to be ready, the crowd scenes which he drilled and repeated endlessly, the setting of lights and the balancing of Marc's musical background, he was spending between sixteen and twenty hours a day in the theatre and making scenes if I wasn't by his side for most of the time.

The rehearsals went very badly. George Coulouris (Antony) was saying that the Mercury would fold a few days after its opening. Every technical area was a list of problems. Norman Lloyd couldn't "get" the part of Cinna the Poet: Welles considered eliminating the character. Then in a series of furious rehearsals, close to madness and violence, he and Lloyd arrived at what was one of the show's most arresting scenes.

John Mason Brown, the influential critic of the New York *Post*, begged to come to a preview. Houseman was horrified—the show didn't seem ready. But he took the risk, and in that preview the chaos of rehearsal was magicked into a whole drama. Brown came backstage afterward to meet Welles, and he hailed genius.

In the *Post*, a few days later, the reviewer raved:

> The astonishing all-impressive virtue of Mr. Welles's production is that, magnificent as it is as theatre, it is far larger than its medium. Something deathless and dangerous in the world sweeps past you down the darkened aisles of the Mercury and takes possession of the proud, gaunt stage. It is something fearful and turbulent which distends the drama to include the life of nations as well as of men.

The reviews were uniform and sensational. The show sold out until the end of the year—the Comedy had close to 650 seats, and the Mercury policy had been to price many of them at a dollar. Houseman agreed to manager George Zorn's suggestion that they hold off other plays for a while and just run *Caesar* in order to build up funds. So Houseman talked to Welles: it was Cassius and Brutus again, and Welles had had enormous praise for his Brutus. In *The New Republic*, Stark Young had said, "Brutus as Mr. Welles understands him is the prototype of a bewildered liberal, a great man with all the faults and virtues of liberalism."

So, what do we do? asked Houseman. Make a killing or stick to repertory (*The Shoemaker's Holiday* was already being prepared). Welles laughed and said he'd die of boredom if he had to play Brutus for more than a couple of months. No, they would do more, not less. Champagne and glory were all the fuel he needed. And now that the company was more solvent, Zorn could hardly play the sourpuss whenever Welles raided his own box office for dining money.

20

Naked in the Dark

O R S O N W E L L E S was the age of someone graduating from college, and he was expecting his first child. He was copartner in, and the bold public face of, a new company, the Mercury Theatre, that had begun life with a revelatory production of *Julius Caesar*, a critical sensation and a box-office success. His prior production, *The Cradle Will Rock*, was revived in December 1937 in the version that had been originally intended. On the first day of 1938, the Mercury opened its next show, directed by Welles—a seventy-minute playing of Thomas Dekker's *The Shoemaker's Holiday*. It, too, found success.

Welles had cut the Elizabethan comedy down to make a very brisk entertainment. The sets depicted street scenes and interiors—all very bright and lively—and the costumes were fit for pantomime, with special, fond attention given to codpieces for the men. The lighting was high and uniform, which allowed for a simpler rehearsal period.

Thus, like magic, as the curtains fell on the sold-out Christmas Day performance of *Julius Caesar*, Welles/Brutus stepped out onstage and asked if the audience would stay awhile for a special Christmas present, a preview of *The Shoemaker's Holiday*.

"Ladies and gentlemen," he must have said—he loved those moments and their power—"before your very eyes the Roman forum becomes Olde England." In half an hour, with most of the audience happy to see this inside stuff, the stage was transformed and the new show played. It was irresistible, and no one has ever had a better way of taking classics, trimming and pinching them, so they work for a modern audience.

He was also the Shadow still. He was regularly a voice on *The March of Time*, and in early 1939 he played parts ranging from Haile Selassie to Sigmund Freud and Fiorello La Guardia. He and Houseman had prevailed upon George Bernard Shaw to let the Mercury put on a production of *Heartbreak House*. Welles would direct and play Captain Shotover. Shaw had been dubious. Despite Welles's claims of having met the writer in England, the irritated Shaw sent the boy wonder a cable asking, "Who are you?" He would not allow the play to be cut, a further arrow in Welles's flank, for he prided himself as an improver of other people's plays. Shaw demanded tough terms but then sent the letter to the wrong address. As a result, despite phone calls to discuss the play, the Mercury *Heartbreak House* opened, on April 29, without a signed contract with the author.

Rehearsals in New York and radio assignments had to be fitted in with the March opening in Chicago of a touring *Caesar* (its cast included Edmond O'Brien as Antony). Welles was eager to go back "home" for such a triumph, so he had to travel, too. And March had another date to be attended to: the birth of his child. The Chicago papers gave amused reports of Welles's general frantic breathlessness at the time. His expectant father was a fine comic act, but it did not stop him giving lectures to throngs of Chicago children or doing an interview with his old friend Ashton Stevens, who confessed of Welles, "He is a restlessly constructive fellow who just won't leave the stage where he found it. I'm afraid he is a genius; but mighty good company nonetheless."

Welles was there, at the Harkness Pavilion in New York, on March 27, for the birth of a daughter. He sent out a cable, "Christopher, she is born," and for the rest of her life the daughter wondered if her odd naming had not been for the sake of an arresting telegram. Observers noted that Welles had no notion of how to deal with a baby. He looked at her in bewilderment, for how can an infant begin to grasp the nature of audience?

Still, in March and April of 1938, we could easily offer the portrait of a contented, and fearsomely busy man. But consider the dismay of Virginia giving birth, wondering whether Orson would be there, or whether his being there would be useful. And remember the old adage that the very busy man is as he is because of some dread of concentrating on just one thing—which means that, however busy, he is ready for more.

When every day is eighteen or maybe twenty hours of activity, and when being Orson Welles at twenty-two is racing with the shadow of rumor and report, there is so easily more. Nor is this a book that makes any pretense to say the entire story has been told. Welles at this time of his life lived by the minute. He spoke and acted for immediate effect. Much in the company of homosexuals, he had picked up languid manners, hardly knowing how much he was teasing them, colored by their company or intrigued by that behavior. And he was fucking around—why not? He was twenty-two, sonorous, tall, handsome and empowered with jobs, ideas and opportunities. People had to work hard to resolve to dislike Orson Welles; otherwise they were seduced.

In January 1938, the ballerina Vera Zorina accompanied George Balanchine to see *The Shoemaker's Holiday*. Balanchine was her mentor, her maestro and he had been her lover. After the show, they went to a party Cecil Beaton was giving for the cast at the Waldorf. Beaton was hoping to be employed by Welles as a costume designer; they were talking already about some version of the Falstaff story. Zorina was smitten: she saw Welles as Byronic, "with one quizzical eyebrow slightly raised, and often laughing in a special throaty way."

They began to be seen together. Zorina was "totally bedazzled," and Welles let it be known that he had discovered with delight the extraordinary litheness and stamina of ballerinas. They would dine at "21," and, she said, she had "never enjoyed anything more. If I never see him again, I shall always remember it. How we talked and understood each other. He is wonderful and for the first time since Léonide [Massine] I felt my heart pounding and hands trembling."

But Zorina said decades later that she had only the symptoms of being in love. The attraction, she said, remained "platonic and short-lived." She knew he was married with problems; she loved him for his imagination.

It may have been the imagination that improved Welles's stories about fucking Zorina. He said she was phenomenal—which hardly left himself as a slouch. The legend was out that Welles was a demon lover, a hand-to-mouth genius. Well, he'd say, you can't take a kid to Macao without him picking up a few tricks. He told a great story about smuggling Zorina back to his tiny New York apartment and being on the point of taking her when the radio boomed forth with "The Shadow knows!" so that he was made temporarily impotent! (On February 6, *The Shadow* had an episode called "The Phantom Voice." That rare evening, Welles addressed a meeting on behalf of the magazine *New Masses*, and Zorina later described being moved by a political speech she heard him deliver: "He made a strong point and said acceptance rather than tolerance was what we should strive for.")

Was he also at almost the same time infatuated with the Irish actress Geraldine Fitzgerald, whom he had hired to play Ellie Dunn in *Heartbreak House*? Fitzgerald was dark, very animated and very young—by which I mean to say she was only a few years older than Welles. He had known her at the Gate—but how well? In London, the actress had cast a spell over the playwright Patrick Hamilton, who would use her as the basis for the character Netta in his 1941 novel, *Hangover Square*. Fitzgerald was married already, with a husband in Europe. Sometimes one affair is employed to cover another. There was another ballet dancer, too: Tamara Toumanova. But maybe in his hurry and his great glory Welles was taking any human dish he saw. After all, he was dieting at the time, and good boys reckon they deserve rewards.

There were more important intrigues under way. If only as an actor, Welles was beginning to receive offers from Hollywood. He had also met David Selznick in New York, and that newly independent producer had sought to hire Welles as an overall chief of screenplay adaptation. Selznick and Welles had one thing in common: a taste for taking classics and making them work anew. Welles had gently declined the offer—he could be very courteous—because he was set on directing and acting. Instead, he had proposed his partner, John Houseman, for the job, always interested in being rid of him.

Since that first approach, Welles's reputation had only grown. The public circus of *The Cradle Will Rock*, the total impact of *Caesar* and the great reviews for *Heartbreak House* had put Welles—a week away from his twenty-third birthday—on the cover of *Time* in his Shotover makeup. The Selznick organization made another approach—would Welles play Beethoven? Kay Brown, Selznick's New York representative, had lunch with Welles in July. She found him pompous, youthful, but extremely pleasant. He had not yet made up his mind about the role, but he agreed to make a test, and he promised that he would be available by March 15, 1939. This is an intriguing glimpse of how surely he was thinking ahead, whatever the long-term plans of the Mercury Theatre. Moreover, only a few weeks earlier, he had spoken to a convention of teachers and told them that theater was a vastly inferior entertainment—compared with movies.

In the event, he chose not to do *Beethoven*, for that would have meant putting up with Selznick as producer, and with Selznick's director—and Selznick was about to make *Gone With the Wind*. But in the same month of July, Welles and Houseman took the decision that would determine the direction of Welles's career. They made an agreement with CBS whereby the Mercury Theatre would do a series of weekly dramas to replace *The Lux Radio Theater* during the summer. *The Mercury Theatre on the Air* would last longer, and it would produce the greatest outrage of Welles's career.

I put it this way to suggest how far the Mercury radio shows were intended, by Welles, as a way of going west. There is further proof of how his mind was working. For in the summer of 1938 he made a kind of movie that would serve as an introduction to Mercury's next stage show, the Gillette farce *Too Much Johnson*. It was a fairly amateur short, done up in Yonkers, with assistants having to hold up the flimsy scenery against the wind. Jack Berry was one of those kids, happy to be doing anything for Orson Welles.

Berry and a few others held on to the sets for hours of rehearsal and shooting. Then the truck arrived bringing lunch, and Welles and the others set to eating. Berry watched for a while, hungry, then gave up the ghost. The scenery fell down, and Welles jumped up in horror. "What's going on?" he asked, and Berry, a street kid, had to admit the pangs of hunger. Whereupon, Welles put on a lovely act of contrition. Berry recalled, "He said, 'You haven't been fed? You must take my seat.' He said, 'You must!' Of course, we all went back and continued to hold up the fucking sets. Orson did that all the time—operate, manipulate, function."

Berry helped Welles and Houseman edit the footage at a suite in the Waldorf—a setting that showed Welles's respect for editing and kept him close to good room service. He was always pouring his own radio money into these theater productions, and ordering everything for energy to keep going.

The film was never used because the summer theater where *Too Much Johnson* opened, and flopped—in Stony Creek, Connecticut—was too small for the projection's throw. The dismay was sudden and savage. William Alland had by then become a secret agent for Welles, not just actor and stage manager but someone employed to rent love nest apartments for the dancer of the month. One day that summer, Alland was called in by Welles to the St. Regis Hotel, where he was staying temporarily. The hotel had air-conditioning, and Welles was inclined to be asthmatic in the heat.

Alland was taken aback. Welles was stretched out stark naked on the bed with the blinds down. There was no modesty, and at first Alland wondered if the bisexual rumors were true. Then he realized that Welles was in a crushing depression. He talked for hours, about failures and uncertainty, and about the riddle of Jack Houseman: resenting the way he needed him, feeling the urge to do away with him. But, then, how would he manage?

The lament went on and on; the gloom was heavy. Alland had never dreamed of this capacity for melancholy. Three years later, he would play the attentive reporter in *Citizen Kane*. Of course, in the summer of 1938, *Kane* was unimagined. But as that day came, Welles could remember that Alland had been trusted with a glimpse of the wounded beast of loneliness.

21

⟶ *A Little Foolish* ⟶

E X C U S E M E , *before you begin, there is something I must say.*

Well, be quick then, there is so much to cover hereabouts, and I am eager to do it before I forget.

Of course. Really, all I wanted to say was that these reports of Welles as an amorous . . . as a—

The sex?

Exactly. They are most encouraging.

You are encouraged?

These are the little things that catch a reader's interest. They are the fruit in the cake.

The sunshine? The moonlight? The bites? The book clubs and the paperback?

I was wondering—is there more?

In the future? Ample.

Not just that—not that that's not good and very exciting. I meant, I think, is there more of this here and now?

You mean the Misses Zorina and Fitzgerald, not to mention any others we might round up?

Yes. You don't quite say whether they—

The ladies are alive, and they don't quite say.

They don't?

They deny it.

Ah.

In very charming ways.

Ah, yes.

You know, I have been through this before.

You have?

Publishers do believe they want the "here and now," the smell of sex, the abandon of unmade beds, cries in the night—until you deliver it. Whereupon the publishers have other things to do. They put you in touch with their lawyers, who underline "problematic passages" and want to be reassured that there is no "danger."

I see. Because the ladies are still alive?

Would you more happily tell brazen lies about them when they're dead?

It is easier. But, of course, we don't want lies. We only want the truth.

The plaintive request of scoundrels. The truth, I propose, is this. That George Orson Welles at this time was tall, dark, satanically handsome, touched by the romance of thunder and the legend of genius.

Yes!

He was so extraordinarily attractive that his profound self-love and his chronic trickery could be overlooked. He was also twenty-two and twenty-three and at least averagely susceptible to, shall we say, soft, fragrant hair somewhere around the color of blood, copper and chestnut; to legs and thighs that are as taut, and yet as soft, as youth and training can make them; to those variously convex and concave curves in the white of a woman's body between the knees and the throat; to taking every and any lovely young thing, like banknotes fluttering in the wind, and to delighting in the promise of fucking any sweet creature who found him glorious, lovable and powerful. Shall we say that?

I think we should.

Let me add this—I am not persuaded that young Welles ever loved a young woman.

Really?

Not compared with lovemaking's blunt rapture. Not compared with the use of power and opportunity. Not compared with the way in which all those hollows and hills were like glass, a mirror for seeing himself. Not compared with the chance to do something.

To do something?

He was so busy, so dementedly occupied, and so proud of being that able, so anxious to seem in charge. So an affair is a way of cramming one thing more in—*that* is the real penetration—of rising above the chaos of too much to do.

But he was a genius?

Or someone possessed by genius. It is not always the same. He was also spoiled, self-indulgent, greedy, a little cruel and maybe fuck-happy. He *was* a kid. Let him be that boy—for now, at least. He took women as a way of not having to be involved with them. Remember the work—remember to notice as we come to the films: he hardly knew women, and was seldom interested in them.

The Mercury Theatre had been the talk of the town—yet it was always on the brink of collapse. As if without thinking too much about it, the company had chosen in *Julius Caesar* and *The Shoemaker's Holiday* two plays with large casts. In addition, Welles had elected to have very elaborate, technical productions with complex, moving sets and lighting schemes that called for constant change—indeed, they altered like the intensity of the light on a movie screen. Then he made further changes in his own plans. Such changes were vital to the air of frenzy that attended Mercury rehearsals, and they were a keynote of Welles's reputation for genius. That the changes eventually worked onstage never alleviated the expense. By habit, Welles made things up as he went along. He was at his best then because he was most excited and most driven by danger.

Despite its modest ticket prices, the Mercury had sold-out business only in *Caesar*'s first flush of success. Their shows were very well attended, in general, but in 1938 the New York theater was not flourishing. In the week ending April 23, 1938, for instance, with *Caesar* and *The Shoemaker's Holiday* playing, the box-office income was $6,166. Against that, the salaries for actors, social security taxes and normal box-office costs amounted to $5,400. On top of that there had to be some salary for Houseman and Welles, as well as the development costs of other productions. Someone had to pay for the dinners Welles ordered in from restaurants—double steaks and sundaes, with brandy and cigars—meals he put away as if they were fast food.

It's clear that Welles picked up many bills himself. His own salary from the Mercury was $200 a week plus 2.5 percent of the box-office gross if it exceeded $8,000. (George Coulouris, the nearest to a star the Mercury had, made more than Welles.) But Welles had his radio income, too: the amount is not known, but it was enough to permit largesse and generosity. Among the many things Welles was not bothered with, money was the most notable.

That same attitude made him a poor fund-raiser. The search for new stockholders, and the servicing of existing patrons, was a steady part of Mercury business for Houseman and Welles. Houseman said that they both regarded those angels in the way that teenagers do parents. And Welles was so rebellious as to be a handicap. In the Mercury's best moments, he treated the stockholders as leeches and hangers-on. When the company was in great need, he was guilty and resentful. So Houseman had to do what he could to keep the extravagant but neurotic giant of the company from its possible benefactors. Here was a sign of how far a Welles might depend on someone as tactful as Houseman. For Welles had a wayward, romantic refusal to deal with financing which he expected to have imitated by those who did believe in money. In an American moviemaker, it is the kiss of death.

To have been businesslike would have offended him. Here is a small but telling example of his urge to make a game out of dry things. In the summer of 1938, Welles himself fixed a deal with CBS for a season of *Mercury Theatre on the Air.* This was a coup, meaning more money for the Mercury, though it committed them to an hourlong show every Sunday for ten weeks. It was a huge extra load, yet Welles saw it merely as an opportunity. Once it was announced, the Mercury had many requests from people eager to be a studio audience. Welles never wanted any kind of audience at his radio dramas. He could not welcome strangers seeing how totally and how crudely he dominated the proceedings. Instead, he cherished the notion of an intimate and tense gathering of conspirators, tip-toeing, signaling under the red light, urging the exquisite sounds of story down the wires. Radio for Welles was a covert enterprise in which he was the more able to be ridiculous, intolerable and superb because he was not seen. To have admitted the public would have been like a magician opening the doors to his rehearsals.

But the begging letters came in, and he could not resist being coy. The polite refusal was a secretarial chore, but Welles insisted on doing the letter himself and made it an occasion for charming fascination, indecision and mockery of ordinary affairs. Here is the voice of the Kane to come, too exuberant to be sober or straightforward, turning down a supplicant, a Miss Eleanor Goldsmith of New York. "This is flat, this is final," he said. She had to understand. The Mercury people were out of their minds with work and worry. Choosing a studio audience would be one more problem. So "thank you" he said, "and you Mr. Flinkinirons, the vice president of CBS, and you Mrs. SomebodywhowillnevercometoseeanotherMercuryplayagain. . . ." But *no*—and for God's and Orson Welles's sake, *understand!*

There is a gaiety in that unnecessary note, a zest for comedy, that might have been offered on a Mercury stage. As a rule, Welles cast himself grandly and solemnly, but imagine that voice in a comedy of manners—the young Kane is not a million miles away from the Cary Grant of *The Awful Truth, His Girl Friday* or even *Bringing Up Baby*. Of course, Orson was so famously so many things—yet he might have been more.

So he was Captain Shotover in *Heartbreak House*, a play that involved royalties to an author (the Mercury's first) but a small cast and a resolutely plain, naturalistic production. *Heartbreak House* was a disappointment: it found an audience, but the reviews were not generally good. The play was called "interminable," "garrulous, unfelt and tiresome." Yet Shaw's play was, among other things, a warning about war and the end of civilization well suited to the anxieties of 1938. That's why the Mercury had chosen it. That's one reason why, it would be said, *The War of the Worlds* worked so powerfully on radio. The cast in *Heartbreak House* were praised (except for Welles himself), though Houseman felt that Welles had rather neglected Geraldine Fitzgerald's performance. But he had not triumphed in the straightforward rendering of a substantial text. If theater worked for Welles, he had to have that chance of a radical reworking of the text. The Mercury players were used to his retreats, from which he would arrive with a new version of the classic, a text that depended on his plan for directing it.

Still, *Heartbreak House* was respectable. In June, in *The New York Times*, as the Mercury ended its first season, Houseman reflected on promises largely kept and on the difficulties of making repertory pay. He reckoned they had played to 250,000 people, a third of whom were teachers and students.

> To sum up—we've produced a lot of plays. We've
> played to a lot of people. We've enjoyed it. We have
> plans—some definite, some still to be worked out. And
> we'll see you again in September.

In fact, the Mercury would not be back on the New York stage until early November. And by then the public's sense of what "Mercury" meant had changed.

22

We Know Now

I SAID THAT the regretful letter—flat, final, yet probably foolish—refusing an audience at the radio broadcasts was something a secretary should have handled. To which a mocking Welles might have replied, "Certainly, if only *the* secretary had been free. If only she had not been at Mr. John Houseman's side night and day hashing out a script for our first radio production, *Treasure Island*." For the tickets letter was sent out just six days before the debut of *Mercury Theatre on the Air*, with *Treasure Island*. And then our imagined Welles might have grinned and said, "Well, no, but they had to start on *Treasure Island*, didn't they, before I changed the first production to *Dracula*. Then we had the Stevenson ready for week two. Just because a man is deprived of a secretary doesn't mean he has lost his wits."

The summer of 1938 was a new kind of chaos. It was in this very July that the Mercury people were to be seen around New York, in and out of Central Park, attempting to make the movie episodes for *Too Much Johnson*, with the film piling up in Welles's hotel room. It was that summer they were supposed to have a vacation, while Welles was intended to repair his marriage and get acquainted with his new daughter. If he could disentangle himself from the affair with Vera Zorina—if it *was* an affair. But, at the last moment, it became, thanks to the Columbia Broadcasting System, the start of a frantic two-week period to get the first show on the air. The programs were to be called *First Person Singular*, written, directed, produced and performed by Orson Welles—if he could be persuaded to attend.

Treasure Island had been settled on as the first show, with Welles doing the narration as the adult Jim Hawkins while playing Long John Silver

within the story itself. Houseman took on the task of furnishing a script, assisted by that secretary, Augusta Weissberger. He was making progress—sixteen or so hours a day will do that—when Welles knocked on the door to say, No, *Dracula* instead. There was a week to go; it was the assertion of authorship and authority by way of emergency fiat. He gave Houseman a quick tour of the Bram Stoker novel, outlining favorite scenes, and vanished. A day later he was back to see what progress had been made. Then the three of them sat down at Perkin's restaurant, and as the meals, the customers, the night and the dawn passed, they produced a script. In the morning, Welles celebrated with eggs and bacon, kippered herring, coffee and juice. It was no accident that the labor had been done in a restaurant, for as always the pages and the shows were the result of raw food energy.

Dracula went on as scheduled. It was what it had always been, a late Victorian melodrama (Stoker had been the manager of the great actor Henry Irving), with groaning doors and fluttering wings, and the baronial, utterly Transylvanian voice—the chocolate that was Orson—as Dracula himself. There were also all the skills and facilities of CBS and its best-equipped sound studio, as well as the twenty-three-piece house orchestra, led by a brilliant young man, Bernard Herrmann. This was a vital association for Welles, a man who had hobnobbed with Manhattan's musical avant-garde—Copland, Thomson, Blitzstein—but who immediately seized upon the far greater dramatic acuity in Herrmann. As a "serious" composer, Herrmann was pretentious and derivative. But as a musicalizer of dramatic moods—from *Kane* to *Psycho* and *Taxi Driver*—he was unsurpassed. He was also a man who made drama—prickly, temperamental, passionately quarrelsome. He began by crying out that Welles was impossible. Whereupon Welles seduced him by saying, Of course, aren't we both? until the young Herrmann found nothing less than his soul and his future working for Welles. No small gift. You might fuck pretty actresses and dancers, but a grander, hands-off wooing is required for the more complicated business of winning real talent to your side.

First Person Singular was a success, though it had only about 10 percent of the listening audience that heard the Edgar Bergen–Charlie McCarthy show on the NBC network. *Treasure Island* was week two, and it was followed with *A Tale of Two Cities* (with Welles as Sydney Carton and Dr. Manette, and with the *sound* of the guillotine), John Buchan's *Thirty-Nine Steps* (in which he played Richard Hannay), a life of Lincoln, Arthur Schnitzler's *The Affairs of Anatol*, *The Count of Monte Cristo* (with Welles as Edmond Dantès), a particularly favorite novel of Welles,

G. K. Chesterton's *The Man Who Was Thursday* (a story that must have affected *Mr. Arkadin*, seventeen years later), a return to *Julius Caesar*, *Jane Eyre* and a *Sherlock Holmes* in which Welles was the Shadow of Baker Street.

These shows never threatened the Edgar Bergen audience. But their dash and energy entertained an audience not always sure how far the modes of nineteenth-century theater were being kidded or played straight. It's central to Welles himself that he never bothered to decide. He would have admitted how broad his John Silver was; no one could have denied the desperate haste with which the shows were "written," or the mischievous use of music and lurid sound effects to paper over the cracks. But Welles had no shame about it. He took it as seriously as he did Shakespeare or Shaw—and he was convinced that a radio show as much as a play relied upon his magic heat and pressured improvisation making it all work. Bernard Herrmann described this intense focusing on Welles and his decisions, the thrill of a brilliant boy's theater:

> Welles' radio quality, like Sir Thomas Beecham's in
> music, was essentially one of spontaneity. At the start of
> every broadcast Orson was an unknown quantity. As he
> went along his mood would assert itself and the temper-
> ature would start to increase till the point of incandes-
> cence. . . . Even when his shows weren't good they were
> better than other people's successes. He inspired us
> all—the musicians, the actors, the sound-effects men
> and the engineers. They'd all tell you they never
> worked on shows like Welles'. Horses' hooves are
> horses' hooves—yet they felt different with Orson—
> why? I think it had to do with the element of the un-
> known, the surprise and the uncomfortable excitement
> of improvisation.

The radio show's contract was extended into the fall. *Too Much Johnson* had its disastrous opening at the Summer Theatre in Connecticut. The Mercury Theatre's promised fall return was delayed—*Too Much Johnson* was postponed; it would be replaced by *Danton's Death*, an epic drama about the French Revolution, written by Georg Büchner. This would prove in many ways the most troubled of the Mercury productions, and enough to conclude their stage life in New York. For the moment, it is enough to say that Welles was furiously occupied with the Büchner play. He could not be especially aware of what was coming on radio. *The War of the Worlds* was not a wicked, premeditated plan.

Mercury Theatre on the Air, despite all the glories of spontaneity, had settled into a routine. Welles and Houseman picked the book or the play to be adapted several weeks in advance, then they passed the work of adaptation on to Howard Koch, a lawyer turned playwright who needed hard work to support his family. Koch was "young," and a beginner. He had his career ahead of him. But he was thirteen years older than Welles—a reminder of Welles's astounding precociousness.

Welles and Houseman proposed H. G. Wells's *The War of the Worlds.* There was the similarity of names; and it was clear that the Wells show would play the night before Halloween. Still, Houseman felt nothing ominous or loaded in the plan: neither man had more than a vague memory of the book, or any idea how it would be adapted. But when Houseman talked to Koch, he did suggest employing a format of news bulletins: this was October 1938, in an America that had been fixed on live radio reports tracing the recent Munich crisis. More than many people in show business, Houseman and Welles were cosmopolitan, well aware of world events. Koch, as usual, had a week to deliver a script of maybe sixty pages.

He read the Wells novella and found little except the original situation that could be used. So he shifted the action from England to . . . rural New Jersey, where he happened to be at the time. He saw the name Grovers Mill on the map, realized that Princeton was nearby and got a rough idea. But it was heavy going. He called Houseman and asked him for a different subject. Houseman and Welles told him to get on with it. The only other script ready was an adaptation of *Lorna Doone* that impressed no one. Houseman agreed to help Koch and his assistant, Ann Froelich. By the time he arrived they were already having fun with the show. By the close of Wednesday, there was a script—the fruit of three days' brainstorming. So much for deliberation.

On the Thursday, a rough cast read through the script. A recording was made and played for Welles and Houseman. They listened and found it boring: it had to be made more immediate, with more sense of the documentary. Koch, Froelich, Houseman and Paul Stewart (who had directed the rehearsal) stayed up Thursday night to improve the script. On the Friday, CBS saw it and gave their approval, on condition that several real names were changed. On the Saturday, Stewart rehearsed and selected some effects. Orson Welles did not meet with the script, the cast and the plan for the show until the Sunday itself, broadcast day, October

30. The general feeling was that this would not be one of the better Mercury evenings.

With the best will in the world, auteurists can say that Welles had chosen the material and called for the quality of radio newsreel. Then he had pushed for it when the script seemed unresolved. But Koch and Houseman had done the writing. Stewart had overseen the show. Herrmann and the CBS orchestra had managed to become Ramon Raquello and his orchestra in the Meridian Room of the Park Plaza Hotel in New York City. Welles simply turned up and directed the show on air in the way that a conductor leads an orchestra. He was the narrator (as always), and he was Professor Pierson at the Princeton Observatory. So the sensation simply happened, by happy or unhappy coincidence of radio's power and the available idiocy of several thousand people.

On the other hand, Welles *had* made it all possible. He had got the deal with CBS. He had Houseman and Koch, Herrmann and Stewart, and he had their faith. He also loved Halloween in the spirit of a prankster who will never completely grow up. And he had conceived of a kind of radio drama that came into the ear, like a potion and a rumor. Still, he was as astounded as anyone by what happened. But more moved. Grant that he meant to goose the audience. Allow that he had merry mischief in mind. Still, the result was so far beyond his imagining that it was as if—at least for once, confirming the yearning shut-eye*—magic *had* happened. Something in the air over America had descended on the ears of citizens to make Orson Welles notorious forever.

The show ran from 8:00 p.m. eastern time, for an hour. The announcer presented Orson Welles and the *Mercury Theatre on the Air* in *The War of the Worlds* by H. G. Wells. Herrmann plunged the CBS orchestra into the opening of Tchaikovsky's first piano concerto, the Mercury theme music. As the music subsided, the announcer introduced "the director of the Mercury Theatre and star of these broadcasts, Orson Welles."

Welles then delivered the opening speech of the narrator. This had been written by Koch, rewritten by the group, and Welles had surveyed it before he read it. Let everyone have some credit, and let it be agreed that the speech could have been portentous and hokey without the rich, heady self-belief and fraud of Welles. This is classic melodrama, it is great radio, pure Orson and one of the highest peaks of late 1930s demagoguery (a competitive field):

---

* Shut-eye: a magician who believes in his own magic.

We know now that in the early years of the twentieth century this world was being watched closely by intelligences greater than man's and yet as mortal as his own. We know now that as human beings busied themselves about their various concerns they were scrutinized and studied, perhaps almost as narrowly as a man with a microscope might scrutinize the transient creatures that swarm and multiply in a drop of water. With infinite complacence people went to and fro over the earth about their little affairs, serene in the assurance of their dominion over this small spinning fragment of solar driftwood which by chance or design man has inherited out of the dark mystery of Time and Space. Yet across an immense ethereal gulf, minds that are to our mind as ours are to the beasts in the jungle, intellects vast, cool and unsympathetic, regarded this earth with envious eyes and slowly and surely drew their plans against us. In the thirty-eighth year of the twentieth century came the great disillusionment.

It was the end of October. Business was better. The war scare was over. More men were back at work. Sales were picking up. On this particular evening, October 30, the Crossley service estimated that 32 million people were listening in on radios.

They were enjoying Charlie McCarthy. But about ten minutes into that concurrent show, a less than compelling singer had the air. A certain number of listeners switched stations . . . and came upon the very artfully done business of an interrupted program, of word that Martians had landed and were bent on mayhem.

There were many responses: the majority were amused and held by the blatant fabrication; many went back to Charlie McCarthy; some recognized nonsense; and a few believed. They listened. They became afraid. Some telephoned CBS. Some took to the streets. There was and is not one recorded instance of anyone dying, being seriously hurt or doing damage. That doesn't matter. A "sensation" was occurring, and a new kind of American appetite had been formally declared open. As soon as he realized that, Orson Welles was in charge. For, like any confidence man, he could feel belief as if it was a matter of temperature and pressure.

23

The Dummies

W E L L E S W O U L D say later, in interviews, that before *The War of the Worlds* show was over, the studio was packed with cops. No one else saw any of them. But the CBS supervisor of the series did come to the control room to report that the studio switchboard was jammed with calls. He wanted to interrupt the show with some reassurance. This was the halfway point in a program which began slowly and then moved very fast. By then the Martians were supposedly in Manhattan. The announcer himself had been silenced by their advance—the announcer was Ray Collins:

> Smoke comes out . . . black smoke, drifting over the
> city. People in the streets see it now. They're running
> towards the East River . . . thousands of them, dropping
> like rats. Now the smoke's spreading faster. It's reached
> Times Square. People trying to run away from it, but
> it's no use. They're falling like flies. Now the smoke's
> crossing Sixth Avenue . . . Fifth Avenue . . . one hundred
> yards away . . . it's fifty feet . . .

Then silence, broken only by the plaintive call of a ham radio operator searching for life: "Isn't there anyone on the air? Isn't there anyone?" Here was the bleak vision that had ended *The Fall of the City* a year and a half earlier. The link was chance, perhaps, except that this was the logical, melodramatic conclusion of Welles's sweeping urge to be an omniscient wizard. Sometimes an artist recognizes what he is doing only when he hears or sees the work, or when the echo it makes comes back from the world. *The War of the Worlds* had that sinister grace with which familiar and comforting things are made to disappear.

There was a station break in which the CBS announcer reiterated that this was a show, an Orson Welles Mercury presentation. In the second half of the program, a surviving figure begins to rebuild the world. To this day, it is possible never to have heard of that second part. Those in panic or flight were not listening. Those who did listen took it more or less for granted. At the very end of the show, the attentive, sardonic voice of Welles was back with a speech that had been in the script. Still, his delivery must have been sharpened by some knowledge of the effects he had had. So he sounded more thrilled and wicked than ever:

> This is Orson Welles, ladies and gentlemen, out of character to assure you that *The War of the Worlds* has no further significance than as the holiday offering it was intended to be. The Mercury Theatre's own radio version of dressing up in a sheet and jumping out of a bush and saying Boo! Starting now, we couldn't soap all your windows and steal all your garden gates by tomorrow night . . . so we did the next best thing. We annihilated the world before your very ears, and utterly destroyed the Columbia Broadcasting System. You will be relieved, I hope, to learn that we didn't mean it, and that both institutions are still open for business. So good-bye, everybody, and remember, please, for the next day or so, the terrible lesson you learned tonight. That grinning, glowing, globular invader of your living room is an inhabitant of the pumpkin patch, and if your doorbell rings and nobody's there, that was no Martian . . . it's Halloween.

What should be said about what really happened? Is there anything as substantial as "history" connected with such a legendary occasion? The show is preserved; we can hear now how clever and vivid it was. There are newspapers from the day after—looming headlines and columns of accounting. The New York *Daily News* said, FAKE RADIO "WAR" STIRS TERROR THROUGH U.S. *The New York Times* said, RADIO LISTENERS IN PANIC, TAKING WAR DRAMA AS FACT. The *Times* switchboard counted 875 calls. Many police stations in New York and New Jersey had inquiries. People went up on their rooftops and saw . . . smoke over New York City—some concluded that the show's stories of poison gas were correct. Some people took to their cars to escape. There were stories of traffic jams. Some people declared they believed they were going to have heart attacks. Reporters had no difficulty in finding citizens prepared to gabble away about believing the world was ending. This *was* America. There is reason to believe that in the alarm one woman fell and broke her arm. But suits were threatened against CBS. Lawyers were woken from their tranquil sleep.

And people with a chance of getting in the papers said with shocked conviction that it was a disgrace for CBS and that Orson Welles to be thinking of such things.

The network denied malice: they pointed to the several disclaimers. Reached at the theater, where he had gone to get on with *Danton's Death*, Welles spread his hands, widened his eyes and consented to pose in front of a low light so that his shadow loomed on the wall behind him. "I had no idea," he said, looking like a very unreliable young man. He said he had actually hesitated over presenting the show for fear that "people might be bored or annoyed at hearing a tale so improbable."

In fact, Welles's manner that night was insolent and provocative. The first stories had reported deaths galore, and the fear of legal retaliation was intense for a few hours. There had even been talk of arrests: a few policemen did turn up long after the show. It was in the aftermath that Welles appropriated the show and the joke: he was uttering denials, but everything in his bearing whispered, "Suckers!" There was a press conference the next day at which his hammy, unshaven contrition and surprise were close to insulting. As he emerged from the grilling, he winked and flashed an OK sign to Mercury colleagues. He wasn't taking that great a risk—for in twenty-four hours most reports of panic had dissolved—but he could not conceal his nature or his jubilation.

The sensation wilted. So few details of the great story were substantiated. There were suits, but even lawyers knew they were dreams. CBS adopted the restrained regret of any network that has dominated the front pages with its show. The Federal Communications Commission promised an inquiry. And more intelligent commentary took over, fixing on the gullibility of Americans, the real prospects of war and the impish genius of Mr. Welles. Heywood Broun admitted that Welles had "put too much curdle on the radio waves," but he welcomed the lesson in keeping news rigidly separate from other genres, and he warned that censorship was a greater danger than anything Mars might offer. Dorothy Thompson said that "unwittingly" Welles and the Mercury had done everyone a great favor:

> They have cast a brilliant and cruel light upon the failure of popular education.
> They have shown up the incredible stupidity, lack of nerve and ignorance of thousands.
> They have proved how easy it is to start a mass delusion. . . .

> Mr. Welles went all the politicians one better. He
> made the scare to end scares, the menace to end men-
> aces, the unreason to end unreason, the perfect demon-
> stration that the danger is not from Mars but from the
> theatrical demagogue.

Yet no one could claim, then or now, that Welles and the Mercury had done the show to awaken America. Years later, Welles would claim that he had "merrily anticipated" the kind of response, while being astonished by its intensity. That is credible, though Welles became the master of any event once it had happened. The regular magician *is* a professional cynic: he bases his work on the way people's beliefs can be calculated. Moreover, *The War of the Worlds* brought him a new kind of power. He had never had such widespread attention, the clearest proof that boldness is rewarded with fame. He had discovered the potential in an artful mix of fiction and documentary. He had, at last, done or made an entirely contemporary work. And he had gotten away with it.

The proof of that came quickly. For a moment, for a week, CBS voiced some doubts about continuing the Mercury broadcasts. Does any-one believe those doubts were real, or a way of improving their deal? Im-provement came when the Campbell Soup Company agreed to sponsor all future Mercury broadcasts at CBS. Quite naturally, the Mercury audi-ence jumped after the *War of the Worlds* show. Now they had major cor-porate backing.

But most important in the long run was the fact that Hollywood now perceived Welles not just as a man of the theater but as the author of sen-sations. Forever afterward, Welles would tell any interviewer that the one clearest result of the panic broadcast was that he got to Hollywood. He needed somewhere else to go, for the real and original Mercury—the theater company—was coming to an end.

So measure the effect of the broadcast on the arrogance of Mr. Welles. Not just his movie opportunity sprang from the show. So much of the ideology of *Citizen Kane* is embodied in the chutzpah of the show, the cool, mischievous teasing of the public. For years, Welles kept a cable sent to him immediately after the radio show by Alexander Woollcott, who observed the odd way in which Welles had upstaged the Charlie McCarthy show:

> THIS ONLY GOES TO PROVE, MY BEAMISH BOY, THAT THE INTELLIGENT
> PEOPLE WERE ALL LISTENING TO A DUMMY, AND ALL THE DUMMIES WERE
> LISTENING TO YOU.

Press conference, the day after *The War of the Worlds*

The shock wave wore off, but the show has never been forgotten.
When I began teaching American students, in 1971, *The War of the Worlds*
(not *Citizen Kane*) was the one thing they all associated with Orson
Welles. But the man himself was not always so secure about the broadcast.

In the spring of 1940, by which time Welles was in Los Angeles, he
heard that Hadley Cantril was preparing a book about the *War of the
Worlds* broadcast, to be published by Princeton University Press. The
publisher asked Welles to give a promotional quotation. He was willing,
but on looking into the book he had found "an error so grave, and in my
opinion so detrimental to my own reputation that I cannot in all fairness
speak well of it until some reparation is made." Cantril was saying that
Howard Koch had written the script for the radio show. Welles allowed
that Koch had worked on the show, but so had John Houseman, Paul
Stewart, the engineer John Dietz and Bernard Herrmann. "The idea for
the *War of the Worlds* broadcast and the major portion of its execution
was mine. Howard Koch was very helpful in the second portion of the
script and did some work on the first, most of which it was necessary to
revise."

Welles had approved the Wells novel. He had recommended the newsreel approach. He may have done a good deal of revision on the day of the broadcast. Cantril's book made it clear in every way that the program would never have taken place but for Welles. So it seemed ungenerous to undermine Koch, who had done the final, complete draft under intense pressure. Cantril wanted no grievance, so he proposed this amended credit for his book's second edition:

> Script idea and development by Orson Welles assisted
> by John Houseman and Mercury Theatre staff and writ-
> ten by Howard Koch under direction of Mr. Welles.

Welles would not be persuaded. He wired Cantril, marveling at the man's stubbornness and reiterating that the show had been "my conception," but also, according to any propriety, "my creation." It was a little like a god taking credit for every party and committee meeting he had attended.

Professor Cantril, of the Psychology Department at Princeton, was now perturbed. He did further research. Koch reiterated that he had dictated the script to Ann Froelich and that he had a contract giving him copyright. Affidavits were offered. And anyway, said Cantril, every reviewer continued to refer to "the Orson Welles broadcast."

Welles was furious. He said that Ms. Froelich had once been Houseman's secretary and was now working for Koch, who had a play that Houseman was planning to produce on Broadway (all this came after the inevitable break between Welles and Houseman). Such people were not to be trusted. *He* could produce affidavits, too. It was not credit he was after, he said now, but accuracy: "*Mr. Howard Koch did not do the actual writing on* The War of the Worlds. *He only did some of it.*" This came from a man who was already pondering whether or not to give screen credit to Herman J. Mankiewicz for writing *Citizen Kane*.

Years later, when CBS did a program about the 1938 show, Welles threatened suit for $375,000 to have his due as author. He lost. Altogether, it is a distressing sidebar. The best contemporary accounting I can manage suggests only that Welles had the germ of the idea, which he focused on the day of the production. Yet "everyone" credits him with the whole enterprise. He could do so much . . . but he wanted everything. It feels greedy and mean-spirited, but it helps us see a man who was a brilliant, inspired adapter and not quite original. That small failing rankled in him, and sometimes it killed his charm.

24

Danton's Death

THERE WAS ALSO a theater to play to, the original purpose of the Mercury. The second season was supposed to be *Too Much Johnson*, *Danton's Death* (proposed by the actor Martin Gabel—with himself as Danton) and *Five Kings*, Welles's own adaptation of the Falstaff story. But when *Too Much Johnson* was put off as a New York production, *Danton's Death* became the opening play of the Mercury's new season—albeit very late. As Welles imagined it, he would make "a drama of lonely souls and the mob" out of the French Revolutionary epic. Houseman urged that the mob be heard rather than seen, to save money. The ever-watchful colleague also saw a director who never quite found this play: "He brought to it, as he could not fail to do, intermittent genius, spasmodic energy and an occasional flash of vision, but none of that impregnable personal conviction that had carried him irresistibly through his first seven productions." Just because Welles was superhuman, why should he not be tiring? There were occasions when he was seen to be using Benzedrine to keep going, along with as much as two bottles of spirits a day.

He conceived of a nightmarish set: a curved wall filled with heads— at that time of year, Halloween masks served—the bounty of the guillotine and an ambience to haunt the characters. The masks were painted and stuck to the cyclorama, and then they had to be lit. But it was difficult keeping every head free from shadows. Welles recollected that there were over 350 lighting cues in the show—yet he was always changing them in rehearsal. There was also a pit and an elevator that never worked reliably. The stage was as perilous a place as any the Mercury had mounted. Moreover, the play was constructed in a series of brief scenes—it *was* movielike—and the actors were having a hard time finding their characters or momentum in the drama. Some felt that Welles was less than his usual obsessive self. He neglected Gabel—perhaps because he never got over the feeling that he was himself a natural Danton. The Robespierre, Vladimir Sokoloff, had played the role, in German, for Max Reinhardt in 1927, and Welles asked him just to repeat that performance.

To add to the problem, the music had been assigned to Marc Blitzstein. His work was beyond reproach, but as he listened to the play his Communist principles were offended. The analogy of Danton and Robespierre to Trotsky and Stalin was too obvious. He foresaw difficulties, and the Mercury could not afford to alienate the leftist audience. So, grudgingly, a few changes were made to accommodate the composer.

October was a ghastly month of rehearsal in which nothing went right. Relations between Welles and Houseman became more strained than ever. John Berry was one of Welles's assistants, and he saw something like madness building on Welles's uncertainty:

> Orson needed someone like Houseman, but Orson
> could never trust anybody. You had to be prepared to
> take such an enormous amount of guff and madness
> from him. I remember one day, at rehearsal, he accused
> Houseman of trying to poison him. He asked for tea or
> something. Houseman brought him his drink. All of a
> sudden Orson threw this big number—aaggh!—accus-
> ing Houseman of poisoning his drink. Total nonsense.

They were always facing crises in the early hours of the morning. At one point, Welles turned to Berry and said, "Chalk. I need chalk."

"I don't know where to get you chalk at two o'clock in the morning," said an exhausted Berry.

Welles turned on him with somber glee. "Why? Must you betray me, too, booby?"

So Berry went down to a basement room and hacked some white plaster out of a wall.

One week ahead of previews, Welles declared he was dissatisfied with the script. He assembled the cast around 11:00 p.m. and ordered everyone to come back at ten the next morning, when he would deliver a saving text. This was his grand retreat, but one left desperately late. Then, next morning he did not show up. William Alland was with him at the hotel. Inquiring telephone calls from the theater were greeted by Alland's whisper that Orson was not quite ready yet. Late in the day, he sent word that the rehearsals would resume at noon the next day. He came in at 1:30 p.m. in a heavy overcoat. As he took off the coat, he discovered that the new, improved script had apparently fallen out in the taxi! It was never found. There was no salvation.

One preview had to be canceled. There was at last an accident with the elevator: the actor Erskine Sanford broke a leg. And this was the week in which *The War of the Worlds* was, if not written, composed for the air. It would be understandable if Welles was more amused by *The War of the*

Worlds. Houseman now believed that his colleague was more stimulated in the recording studio than in a live theater. The radio show rehearsal time—usually from noon to eight—was a storm of tantrums, violence, hurled scripts and building tension. "Sweating, howling, disheveled, and singlehanded he wrestled with chaos and time—always conveying an effect of being alone, traduced by his collaborators, surrounded by treachery, ignorance, sloth, indifference, incompetence and—more often than not—downright sabotage."

This was genius turned pathological, and it could do great damage to people who adored and revered Orson. For all the past triumphs, despite the famous spirit of the Mercury group, Welles had insisted on a solitude not far from tyranny. He had the greatest helper he would ever find in Houseman, yet as many saw it he was forcing the urbane, polite Houseman to withdraw. He was a hopeless muddle, veering from one venture to another, from one week to another, dragging his finances into ever greater chaos, making so many alterations in the complex *Danton's Death* that its budget was out of control. And like many egoists in chaos, he was angry with the world, nearly ready for vengeance. For he saw treachery and plots everywhere. In that dark light, the antisocial naughtiness of *The War of the Worlds* may have been emotionally very satisfying for him.

Danton's Death was the Mercury's greatest failure. Many critics found the production both showy and old-fashioned. The play ran for only twenty-one performances, and the production put the Mercury in debt by as much as $50,000. Yet this was in the immediate aftermath of *The War of the Worlds*. On radio, Welles's stock had soared. But there was no sign of that public going to his theater. Rather, many people felt he had betrayed that cause with the sensationalism of the Martian program. Welles had done so little to temper his genius to ordinary talents. He had made many enemies, few allies. He had been brusque, cavalier, insulting, reckless, extravagant. There were many who were waiting for his comeuppance.

No one at the Mercury was strong enough to prevent disaster. There would be an attempt at *Five Kings*, but the hints of closure were plain to see. The great idea for a new theater would not last out two full seasons. Houseman felt the loss of morale, and he made no special effort now to go out in the world and find rescue. Welles had done so much to create the notion that salvation was his alone to give. And he had lost his gang. Houseman wrote,

> The truth is we were no longer interested. In the
> grandiose and reckless scheme of our lives, the Mercury
> had fulfilled its purpose. It had brought us success and

fame; it had put Welles on the cover of *Time* and our
radio show on the front page of every newspaper in the
country. Inevitably, any day now, the offers from Hollywood would start arriving. It was too late to turn back
and we did not really want to.

Welles needed a rest. Hollywood, in a curious way, provided that.
And once the chaos had passed, and the theater had learned to get on with
its life, there was not a lot more to be said than that a twenty-three-year-
old had done *Macbeth, Faustus, Horse Eats Hat, Caesar, The Cradle Will
Rock, Heartbreak House, The Shoemaker's Holiday,* the radio and *The War of
the Worlds.* He had done whatever he wanted, and everything except put
down roots, deal with people or grow up.

25

Going Hollywood?

IN HINDSIGHT, everyone attached to the Mercury company
decided that Hollywood had become inevitable sometime around 8:30
p.m. on October 30, 1938 — once that providential outrage was unmistak-
able. The stage productions had signaled a filmmaker in waiting, if any
Hollywood executives saw the shows. But the radio show promised someone who could grab America by the balls while tickling it under the chin.
Hollywood understood that mixture of rape and allure.

Yet John Houseman noted that the crucial talks with RKO did not
begin until the following May. Which may be a sign of how unimportant
Houseman was in such dealings. Nothing had dogged or depressed
Welles more in the history of the Mercury Theatre than his own reliance
on Houseman. He had failed abysmally and repeatedly at the tactful and
self-effacing process of sucking up to the wealthy to get a little of their
money. He scorned Houseman because of his skill at such things. He
longed to make some dramatic deal of his own as a way of showing Jack
how boldly geniuses handled the world. So he shut him out of the Hollywood dealing.

By the time *Danton's Death* closed—in early December—Houseman
was noting the lack of will to persevere with the theater company. That

can only mean a feeling that Welles was less than wholehearted about such a future, for the life and momentum of the company had always been driven by his mood. One of the problems in *Danton's Death* had been that Welles had never properly learned his lines in the supporting role of Saint-Just. That had always cursed him as an actor. It was as if something resisted the discipline of sitting down, quietly and alone, for hours on end, studying a part. Time and again, his rolling eloquence and his memory from childhood for so much Shakespeare by the yard prompted him into reckless improvisation whenever he lacked the lines. Connoisseurs noted a Shakespeare medley in some of his roles, a "gift" of the gab and an indifference to the real text. But the problem had been most acute with *Danton*, as if his sense of purpose was already weakened.

Uneasy with the text and always self-conscious when moving onstage, Welles did prefer radio as an actor. He was so much more adventurous and mercurial with the script in his hand and the lovely mercy of invisibility. Several people in the Mercury Company compared his strain as Shotover and Saint-Just with his abandon during *The War of the Worlds* and the radio shows that followed it. There was a version of Conrad's *Heart of Darkness* in which Welles played both the narrator and Kurtz. He did Mr. Jingle and Serjeant Buzfuz in *The Pickwick Papers*.

But the radio show was taken up by Campbell's. They would sponsor *The Campbell Playhouse*. That meant more money, better productions and a more competitive time slot. The show now played on Fridays, and it had guest stars—real Hollywood names. In addition, the Mercury people had to deal with Campbell's advertising agency, Ward Wheelock, in the person of Diana Bourbon, to secure stars, contracts and Campbell's approval. By its first contract, Mercury signed on for thirteen shows at $5,000 a show—vital income at so difficult a time.

The Campbell's debut, on December 9, was a production of Daphne du Maurier's *Rebecca*, first published only a few months earlier and a bestseller: it sold 200,000 copies in three months and had been purchased for a movie by Selznick. Welles played Maxim de Winter in the radio show, and Margaret Sullavan was the young woman who becomes his second wife (this was enough to put Sullavan in contention for the role in the movie). In addition, the Campbell show included a telephone interview with Ms. du Maurier in London.

In the following weeks, Beatrice Lillie and Jane Wyatt appeared with a Mercury cast in an adaptation of Dodie Smith's *Call It a Day*; there was *A Christmas Carol* with Welles as Scrooge when Lionel Barrymore was too sick to appear; a striking pairing of Welles and Katharine Hepburn as the lovers in Hemingway's *Farewell to Arms*; and Aline MacMahon in Elmer

Rice's *Counselor-at-Law*. The work of adaptation was still carried out by Howard Koch and Houseman, but Virginia Welles joined them for a rewriting of *Mutiny on the Bounty* in which Welles played Bligh with Joseph Cotten as Fletcher Christian. At the end of January 1939, *The Campbell Playhouse* did a version of another hit novel from 1938—*I Lost My Girlish Laughter*, a very funny take-off on the movie business, co-written by Silvia Lardner, who had worked for Selznick as a secretary. In that production, Welles played Sidney Brandt, an arrogant, memo-mad, oversexed producer cheerfully based on Selznick himself.

In some Hollywood circles, both the novel and the show of *I Lost My Girlish Laughter* were regarded as betrayals and attacks. In pinching the nose of one of his Hollywood friends, Welles was adhering to that streak of cocksure rebelliousness that would prove so dangerous.

But there was one last piece of theater for the Mercury, not just the most grandiose and disastrous but the one closest to Welles's heart. For a year, the Mercury had been talking about *Five Kings*, Welles's own adaptation of the two parts of *Henry IV*, as well as *Henry V*, with several other bits of Shakespeare's histories thrown in. This was always the most expensive of the Mercury schemes: even with some doubling up, it meant a huge cast and many costumes. But as the Mercury faced ruin, Houseman had struck a deal with the Theatre Guild whereby they would put up three-quarters (or $30,000) of its budget and make it a part of the Guild subscription series.

A tour was envisioned—Boston, Washington and Philadelphia—before a New York opening in the spring. Welles would play Falstaff, Burgess Meredith would be Prince Hal and Henry V (thus Hal was an actor seven years older than the one playing Falstaff). Meredith was persuaded to do the part by a weekend of entertainment at the Welles place in Sneden's Landing, for which Orson laid on a lovely French girl for the actor. It's unclear whether Virginia and Christopher were still in residence.

Nothing less than a revolving stage would do for Welles's concept—brilliant—of a lazy Susan of different sets for the various scenes. As Houseman saw it, they were operating on a fifth of the budget they needed, and most of that was Theatre Guild money. The costumes were never fully paid for. There was no adequate plan to rehearse the elaborate show. All of which made it harder to recognize that this *Five Kings* was looming up as a four-and-a-half-hour evening, for Welles still believed that the story should include all the martial action of *Henry V.* He had not yet perceived the natural dramatic beauty of the story of Hal and Falstaff. Indeed, as Houseman observed the attempts at rehearsal, Welles was going on memory of the plays alone. He had little notion of the dramatic properties of the text he had adapted himself.

But things had never been worse between Welles and Houseman. The older man reckoned that the wonder boy was close to a breakdown. The drinking was worse, and indecision was mounting with it. Houseman was concentrating on the radio shows so that Welles could do *Five Kings*. But time and again, Welles missed his own rehearsals, and when he appeared he wanted to do nothing but tell prolonged, half-insane stories to explain his absence. Once he said he was on the run from the Mob because he had been seduced by one of their ladies. Another time he went to Chicago—for yet another ballerina, everyone knew—and on his way back, he said, he had to take over the controls of the plane from a pilot terrified by a storm. Those who once had been seduced or so impressed by his talent that they would take anything were now becoming embarrassed.

The play opened in Boston at the Colonial Theater on February 27 with a company of forty-two. There was music by Aaron Copland, but the composer had never been able to talk to Welles long enough to find out what was required. The turntable did not always work. Actors were injured in the battle scenes—Agincourt was to take place on a revolving turntable like an unwinding frieze; Meredith called it a movie dolly shot. There was never a complete rehearsal. On opening night, the curtain went up one hour late—the show did not end until one in the morning. Welles was still trying to cut scenes.

As they began, in the wings, Meredith turned to Welles: "How'd we get ourselves into this frigging nightmare?"

"Don't worry," said Welles. "There is a thing called magic—theater magic—it's here—wait and see! Now take this pill. It's potent. It's called Benzedrine."

But what kept the audiences going? Often enough, the magic did work. Wrapped up in foam rubber so that he sweated puddles, Welles was at his best as Falstaff. He loved that old man and the excuse for grotesque makeup. He was so hidden as Falstaff, and he so loved the dreamy old England that character presented. The reviews were tolerant and amused, and sometimes impressed. Meredith was called a great Hal. But he was worn out and demoralized as everything went wrong.

"You can blame Orson," he wrote, "only in the sense that he should have demanded the kind of help he needed." Houseman was around, and Meredith could not understand why he was not trusted more. "The confusion threw us all—befogged everyone who was in it. We will always remember it as a towering drama that almost came to pass, but that finally turned into a nightmare. It was a brilliant concept of a great man, but the mechanical problems were never solved. None of us came up to the vision, because of fatigue, logistics, and time."

The show closed in Philadelphia late in March, in theory because Meredith wanted out. But it had lost money that was no longer the Mercury's to lose, and it had been a wearying scene of chaos for those involved. Houseman left in disgust, ready to take up other offers and letting Welles hear of them in the papers. Copland wrote to Virgil Thomson, "Orson's stock is very low at the moment. Last year's hero arouses very little sympathy."

Loyal followers felt let down by Welles. He could see Houseman as a traitor. Years later, he could rebuke Meredith by saying that the *only* reason they ever closed *Five Kings* was because their Hal deserted. Whereas, it was a dream that was nowhere near ready for the public. But *Five Kings* is a play about the end of friendship and the pathos of betrayal. And he who knows he has been betrayed is still master of the drama.

26

To Kill the Prompter

I DREAMED of Welles last night.

Isn't that the author's special insomnia?

I'm sure there's enough of him to go around. But I was struck that he had so entered my fantasies. It made me realize what has surprised and moved me most so far . . .

Please.

Somehow, in advance, I saw him as magisterial, large—of course—and always supremely knowing. Never at a loss.

Like a stage magician?

Well, yes, but like a genius, too, a seer—"My name is Orson Welles!" The reassurance of it. Yet now I see that he was so turbulent, so neurotic, so much of a mess, even. That point about not being able to learn lines. That struck me.

It has so many possible meanings. To learn a part is to be alone—even on a bus or in a crowded greenroom. It means giving up the crowd—

that can be terrible for anyone whose great dread is loneliness. Then there is the discipline, the going over lines, time and again. That can be torture for someone constitutionally averse to discipline. And in both of those things, we may begin to smell Welles's terrible rebelliousness.

Not just resistance to authority?

Not at all: resistance to order, to fate, to death. Here is an actor who longed to believe the show was unique, original, spontaneous—that it had occurred, like life. That is why, I think, as several people have said, he had such difficulty in repeating a performance. He had to be different every time, had to believe he was new and fresh. It is a very romantic urging.

And, as you said, he was a magician who wanted to believe there were no tricks. It is tragic, as well as yearning.

He was always and only a boy, and the child he had not managed to be. He sometimes spoke of innocence—with desperate reverence—yet so often he seemed heavy with experience, the knowledge you spoke of. He was innocent only when he laughed.

Really?

And actors, you know, are famously uneasy when their characters have to laugh. Laughing is the hardest thing to do without showing the actor's real person.

He is so torn—I had not expected this.

I was told this story by William Alland, who prompted for *Danton's Death.* Welles was playing Saint-Just and going up on his lines—time and again. The prompter kept whispering. Welles was becoming more and more angry. Finally he strode off the stage, picked up the prompter by the neck and punched him against the wall. "God damn you!" he told Alland.

He wanted to murder the prompter?

Or the idea of the script.

You feel the terror in his temper.

It was unforgivable, yet so many forgave him.

And this finale to Mercury—what a time of crisis, of fear and hope, and betrayal. But we are getting to Hollywood?

You want to be there?

Doesn't everyone?

Five Kings was such a calamity, with depression anew. Welles responded by claiming that Paul Stewart had been stealing the radio show away from him—no matter that Stewart had looked after the show only to give *Five Kings* a better chance of success. So there was a tantrum, and

Stewart was fired. Then Welles was contrite again and begged the valued assistant to stay on. Stewart would be Raymond, the butler in *Citizen Kane*, the man who knows where the bodies are buried at Xanadu. And there were ways by then in which those very loyal, supporting actors— like Stewart and Bill Alland—were closer to Welles than John Houseman.

The radio shows went on. Mary Astor was guest star for *Royal Regiment*. They did *The Glass Key*, from Dashiell Hammett. In *Beau Geste*, Welles was Beau while Laurence Olivier was his brother John. In *Twentieth Century*, by Ben Hecht and Charles MacArthur, he played the great ham actor Oscar Jaffe—John Barrymore's role in the movie—with Elissa Landi as the female lead. For *Show Boat*, they had Margaret Sullavan, Helen Morgan and Edna Ferber herself in the cast, with Welles as Captain Andy. He now was Javert in *Les Misérables*, with Walter Huston as Valjean. He did a *Private Lives* opposite Gertrude Lawrence, and a *Victoria Regina* in which he played Albert to Helen Hayes's Queen.

No one was making more than vague noises about more Mercury on the stage. Welles had lost some of his stamina, and the Mercury lived up to the verdict of Harold Clurman, a leader of the Group Theater: "It was sensational but not controversial." Several newspapers saw the opportunity to write the company's obituary. In the New York *World-Telegram*, Sidney Whipple said,

> Genius unchecked by practical considerations is its own
> worst enemy. Mercury, succeeding by Mr. Welles' great
> genius, may well fall by the same means. Genius is
> sometimes a direct denial of common sense, and the
> present situation calls for the exercise of a lot of the
> latter commodity.

Welles wrote back, world-weary and conciliatory. He also fashioned a credo that would prove prophetic. Anyone making a show, he said, should be prepared to fail—"nothing is worthwhile doing if it isn't worth doing badly." Only time would show how close that could come to a defense of the slapdash as a sign of character.

This was not exactly what RKO or anyone in Hollywood would have wanted to hear. By the spring of 1939, still in New York, Welles was talking to RKO, and principally to George Schaefer, who had become head of the troubled studio late in 1938. There were other reasons to be attracted by California beyond the thought of making a movie. The debts in New York were heavy. Costume companies plagued the relics of the Mercury organization, and Welles was slowly paying back a personal obligation of $13,000. He had radio income in addition to the Campbell's series still. But the outlay! The apartments, beyond the one he shared with Virginia. The hotel rooms, the meals, the transport whenever he wanted it. Not that far ahead, he foresaw the burden of alimony and child support. Going west would be the effective end to his marriage.

Yet, we should be careful not to present him as a thoroughly calculating person. Escape is always emotional. The rise and fall of the Mercury Theatre had left Welles deeply confused. Years later, John Houseman admitted that while he and others had given up trying to advise or steer Welles, they had real doubts about how he would end up: "We . . . always supposed that having started so early, he must also end early. We assumed that he would be carried off in middle age by some ghastly glandular disturbance, or else disappear on a freighter and turn up as a missionary on some obscure South Sea island." The arc of his life was so fierce, no one anticipated stability.

There's little doubt that Welles had made up his mind about RKO. He was privately determined on California—if nothing else proves that, consider the insane position he found himself in of living in Los Angeles while having to commute to New York once a week to do the Campbell's radio show. But he approached the negotiations in a deliberately insolent, or haughty, manner: whatever they offered, he would ask for more; he would push them to show that he was not to be had or controlled.

In fact, Schaefer had been seeking several new talents on productions for RKO. But no deal he made was as generous as the one with Welles and Mercury. Not that Welles wanted money: indeed, he might have made his own life easier if he had simply settled for that. But Welles never sought money; he only spent it. The most aggressive, or offensive, thing he could ask for was liberty. He wanted to make his films, his way, no matter that he had no idea as yet what that might be.

Agreement was reached early in July, though the full contract was not signed until August, by which time Welles was resident in Los Angeles. RKO would hire him to write, produce, direct and act in two films. He had the right to cast these films, to hire technical personnel, to see the daily footage privately, to cut and complete the films. RKO reserved the right to approve the project and its story line, and they could veto any budget that exceeded $500,000. For the first picture, Welles was to receive $100,000 and 20 percent of the profits; on the second, his terms rose to $125,000 and 25 percent of the profits.

History (and Welles) called that contract unprecedented, and "carte blanche." That is not quite accurate. Erich von Stroheim had once done everything on film that Welles was hired to do—and he was ruined by his own arrogance and excess. But several of the great screen clowns—most notably Chaplin—had had similar liberty. Chaplin had thrived and made a fortune. On *City Lights*, made in 1931 under more complete control than Welles dreamed of, Chaplin had earned over $5 million. I do not mean to imprison Welles in a comparison with Chaplin. We can look elsewhere: in 1937, Shirley Temple earned over $305,000; to make *Gone With the Wind*, Clark Gable was paid about $121,000. The first director of that film, George Cukor, was paid at the rate of $4,000 a week. Five hundred thousand dollars was not an especially high budget for a movie. Most "big" pictures cost over a million. B pictures were generally made for under $200,000. RKO was never well endowed, or extravagant. If we look at the studio's greatest successes of the late thirties—the Astaire-Rogers musicals—we see that they cost as follows: *Top Hat*, $609,000; *Swing Time*, $886,000; *Carefree*, $1,253,000. *Kitty Foyle*, made at RKO in 1940, cost $738,000.

Of course, Welles didn't know how much or how little he could do for half a million. He knew that Houseman had dreamed of having $200,000 for *Five Kings*. One hundred thousand dollars a movie struck him as plenty, and enough to absorb his uncertain understanding of his debts. Welles would have been so much better respected in Hollywood if he had held out for a lot of money—for $250,000, say, modest enough income for anyone serving his four roles on a picture. Nor did he quite under-stand how shocking his liberty was. Only prisoners know that feeling. So the movie community was stung by the rapidly circulating rumor that a kid, a smart-ass, a novice had got the right to shoot his script, with his people, and cut it how he liked. That was impossible freedom for, say, George Cukor, Ernst Lubitsch, Howard Hawks, Frank Capra, John Ford or any of the other worthy filmmakers who had to be ready to fight for every foot and cent of what they wanted. So Welles broke two rules: he scorned money and he was given astonishing privilege. More than he could guess, he was blackballed as a careerist.

But no one had yet accused him of being that steadfast. He told the Mercury people there would be jobs for all of them—there was a separate contract between RKO and Mercury—and he asked Houseman to come along. That is remarkable and touching. Welles had done the deed in a way that left Houseman in the dark. The terms of the contract made his old partner his assistant. Yet still he asked Houseman, as if some part of him knew how vulnerable he was, or wanted the company.

They went by way of Chicago, where Welles put on a shortened version of the melodrama *The Green Goddess* on the RKO vaudeville circuit. Houseman was horrified: it was the rawest he had seen from Welles, in beard and turban, sometimes with John Barrymore in tow, and with one more lovely young woman to admire him.

On July 20, they arrived by plane in Los Angeles. Welles was twenty-four, and he noticed that he hated the place.

Part Two

CARTE BLANCHE
1939 – 42

"People are going to know who's responsible."

1

The Jungle

IN THE NEXT three years and one month, from July 1939 to August 1942, Orson Welles detached himself irreparably from ordinary life and common fame. He made an exemplary inversion of Hollywood, and a tactless, eternally incriminating assault on the notion of the proper ways things were done there. He achieved glory, but he ruined himself; the one was not possible without the other. His greatness had to reveal how hollow and trivial everything else was. He had no real thought of reforming Hollywood (he was never that hopeful, or political); rather he dreamed of having it disappear in a puff of smoke. If that hope failed, then he would vanish himself.

In that thirty-seven months, as well as establish the intractable chaos of his personal life—in a way that terminated or shelved it—he undertook a lavish, disastrous adventure, an exquisite trip; he made a second movie, and made it broken and bleeding, a picture that approaches the pitch of great tragedy but settles finally for being one of Welles's most characteristic inventions—the lost film; and he made the greatest movie that ever has been or will be made, the work that sums up the entire medium and holds in reserve for those prepared to look and consider the ultimate desolation of the thing called cinema.

But in those three years, he also went from being what Hollywood saw as the naughtiest boy, deserving of rebuke and comeuppance, to being the most lastingly influential of American filmmakers. For in his willful stress on genius, independence and mercurial ungraspability, he offered a treacherous beacon to generations of young people seeking to make more movies. He was as merry and cruel in this as a Santa with an empty sack, for he knew that no one would surpass or match what he had done. He had hijacked a vital part of America and its twentieth century and taken it down a dead end.

Even as the RKO contract was being drawn up, Welles had proposed Conrad's *Heart of Darkness* as his first picture. He was thinking about it on the flight to Los Angeles, recollecting the radio adaptation from the previous November and deciding that he was made for Conrad—the tragedy, the terror and the foreboding mood. Wasn't the story a parable of the failure of civilization, and hadn't Welles on radio been both the voice of Kurtz, the tyrant up the river and the narrator who tells his story? He thought he saw a way of doing it as a movie whereby the first-person singularity of the radio show could be translated into camera terms. The camera would *be* Marlow, the young man going in search of Kurtz. Its tracking forward over water and into the dark would be the physical motif of the movie. And as the inquiring eye of the film moved inward, Marlow would become the narrator, accommodating much of Conrad. From the outset, Welles wanted to keep the real language of Conrad's psychological narrative.

Of course, we are talking about the material that would one day become *Apocalypse Now*, Francis Ford Coppola's movie of 1979. *Apocalypse* became a famous ordeal for Coppola, and for everyone else on the picture. It ran over schedule and over budget; it involved something like a breakdown for Coppola as he faced the exigencies of weather, money and the Philippines, as well as the elusiveness of Conrad's story and the limits to his own talent. Beyond the journey and the quest, Conrad's story does not have much action. There is talk of "horror," of infinite collapse or decay in human purpose. There is a creeping sense of entropy and disillusion. But it is in the nature of those things that little happens. And movies are uneasy about that absence. So Coppola speculated over different conclusions and tried in vain to draw his Kurtz (Marlon Brando) into improvised scenes that might make Conrad's moral atmosphere concrete.

Welles never faced such critical, soul-destroying tests. He never went up the river himself; *Heart of Darkness* would be his first unmade or unfinished film. Yet there is some reason to heed his own claim that he never prepared any picture so thoroughly. In other words, he learned from it things about the medium and about himself.

He made an adaptation of the novella in the only way he knew. Pages of the book were stuck on blank script pages, then cut and amended to show what parts of the original were to be used and highlighted. Then with the aid of an RKO employee, Amalia Kent—a woman Welles liked and trusted—this "scrapbook" was turned into something that resembled a script. She told him how shots were described. Of course, he had known what a shot was, but he had not known the terminology or the rather stilted discipline of a screenplay, that hybrid of literature and a skeletal plan for making a film. He learned in the process, and he was studying movies when he had the time—especially John Ford's *Stagecoach*, he said, which had opened in March 1939. So he saw what the technical terms meant on the screen—and he perceived what a ridiculous and unreadable form the standard script was. He recognized that it existed so that the factory system could think of itself as builders putting together something as solid and useful as a house.

But at the outset, Welles saw that the "house" would be irrelevant and useless if it was not haunted. He fastened upon the realization that movies are . . . atmosphere, séances or dreams. Theater may never have moved Welles very much—I see no great evidence that it did—but he loved the secretive passion of radio, the way the listener constructed not just a story and a world but an intimacy with the story's heartbeat, by having all his senses concentrated in the ear. What Welles saw in movies was a spell-making that had to do more with radio than with theater. He saw a way in which authorial power delivered a state of wonder and emotion.

As far as *Heart of Darkness* was concerned, the emotion, the magic, the meaning lay in this simple ploy: Welles would play Marlow *and* Kurtz. (In terms of *Apocalypse Now*, he would be both Martin Sheen and Marlon Brando.) In the heat and swelter of the jungle, and in the brooding closeness of the novella's sense of decay, Marlow the inquirer would discover that he *was* Kurtz. Naturally, Welles as Marlow would be the twenty-four-year-old, whereas Welles as Kurtz could be some Falstaff bloated and disfigured by fever, debauchery and self-hatred. Welles had discovered a vital principle of *Citizen Kane*—that the personality of the inquirer and the life being tracked might be the same. He may never have known this intellectually, but its emotional truth possessed him. He would be talking about himself, shutting his eyes in radio's conspiratorial dark, to become something mighty and eternal—himself at the end of the river, on the brink of death.

I have spoken already about the pattern in so much of Welles's work of an older, relatively powerful figure and a younger, more critical observer who first admires and then sees fault in the larger man. It can be seen in *Lucifer Rising*, that early play, in Faust and Mephistopheles, in Falstaff and Hal. We will see it later in Kane and Leland, Arkadin and Van Stratten, Quinlan and Vargas, and again in Falstaff and Hal. But what emerges here is the way the pattern aspires to some unity, to two halves of one being.

In the late summer and fall of 1939, Welles went to school on the movies and *Heart of Darkness*. Not that his labor was concentrated. The already exhausted and hounded creator had provided himself with demented problems in Hollywood. He could not do just one thing. Still, by November, there was a script for *Heart of Darkness*. It was 200 pages long, and it was like a testament. In addition, Welles had made thousands of drawings to show what the film would look and feel like. Models had been built, and there was even a day's test shooting in which a vessel moves up a model river, past jungles, viscous liquid, going deeper toward Kurtz's jungle lair. "This is a place where the jungle has crawled to in order to die." Emotionally, this sequence can hardly be distinguished from the opening of *Citizen Kane*, in which the camera moves in through the defenses of Xanadu to the chamber where the beast is ready to expire.

Heart of Darkness was measured out on paper and in his mind's eye amid comic upheaval. On landing in Los Angeles, Welles and Houseman had taken up residence at the Chateau Marmont, a famous hotel for movie people on Sunset Boulevard. But as more Mercury people came west—and Welles was eager to have them around him—he rented a property in Brentwood, 426 Rockingham Drive, where most of them could stay, even if that meant bedding down in the changing room next to the pool.

Hollywood was not kindly disposed toward the boy wonder or his remarkable contract. There were plenty of people ready to sneer. The trade papers were hostile and suspicious. In a restaurant one night, the actor Ward Bond sliced off the end of Welles's tie. Bond—a John Ford stalwart—was probably responding to the Hollywood rumor that Rockingham Drive and its male entourage was a bed of New York homosexuals. If only to get better press, Welles set about earning a solid heterosexual reputation in his new town. He did it the old-fashioned way.

There was also, at last, a war in Europe, which gave George Schaefer fresh reasons for wondering whether he had done the right thing. Schaefer was in Europe in September, surveying the effects on business. In a state of alarm, and well aware of the mixed reception his star was getting in Hollywood, Schaefer cabled:

> PEOPLE ARE HESITANT TO CONGREGATE IN THEATRES BOTH IN FRANCE AND ENGLAND. ALL THIS SEVERE BLOW AS YOU OF COURSE KNOW AND PUTS US IN POSITION WHERE I MUST MAKE PERSONAL PLEA TO YOU TO ELIMINATE EVERY DOLLAR AND FOR THAT MATTER EVERY NICKEL POSSIBLE FOR *HEART OF DARKNESS* SCRIPT AND YET DO EVERYTHING SAVE ENTERTAINMENT VALUE.

It wasn't exactly what a kid in the process of self-education wanted to hear. But RKO back talk was already warning Schaefer of extravagance.

Welles cabled back that the boss had nothing to worry about. He would weight every penny of expenditure. He would deny himself every "luxury" and would subordinate all things and everyone to the "potency of story." Pass the brandy.

The script Welles arrived at was for a three-hour film, with jungle or the best that a studio tank, models and effects could provide. The reaction at RKO was not overwhelming. Schaefer thought it very talky and long, though promising and unusual. The budget analysis declared that the picture would cost at least $1 million. Five days later, on December 10, it was effectively agreed that *Heart of Darkness* was off. Some said it was simply postponed. Years later, Welles claimed it was only $50,000 over budget, though it is $500,000 more than the contract figure. So the pressure grew: by then he had Mercury actors in Los Angeles, on the payroll; he had also built up six months of expectation, with all that entailed in anticipatory derision. Some said he was a fraud. The system, and all those who had abided by its rules, was banking on his failure. The great cruelty in Welles's contract—the certain trap—was to make him the object of envy, fear and loathing. For if Orson Welles turned out right, then Hollywood had always been wrong.

2

⟶ *Somewhat Arbitrary* ⟵

WELLES HAD BEEN in Los Angeles only a week when he received a concerned letter from the Ward Wheelock Company. They were beginning to read press accounts of the commitment Welles was making to RKO in terms of time—and place of residence. The contract with Campbell's had insisted on New York as the studio site for the new radio shows, and it had stressed the use of Broadway people: "There was never any talk or consideration of starting our series on the West Coast." Yet Welles had arbitrarily signed a picture contract that depended on his being in Los Angeles, and he had failed to consult with Ward Wheelock. They felt they were being deceived and sought to restrain their young star: "This is not only a mess—but a needless, useless one—from all angles."

There was only one solution, and it added terribly to Welles's problems of concentration. Every week, he had to make the coast-to-coast flight back to New York. In those days, the flying time was at least twice what it is today, so that Welles gave up his Thursday to flying east. On Friday, he rehearsed and did the show. And on Saturday he returned. That pattern lasted until November, and it means that a lot of the *Heart of Darkness* work was done on airplanes.

The only person who welcomed the arrangement was John Houseman. He had never felt at ease with Welles in Los Angeles; it was plain that he was no longer as trusted, or allowed a role in the development of the movie project. So Houseman said he would go back to New York. He had some other theater ventures there, and he would continue to oversee the writing of the radio scripts and the coordination of players and studio. Houseman usually took Welles to the airport after the show, and sometimes their talk was so intense that Houseman found himself swept along on the flight.

But Houseman was no longer responsible for looking after Orson's organization. That task was now shared among the publicist Herbert Drake, Richard Baer—near enough his manager—his ex-agent, Albert Schneider, and the lawyer Arnold Weissberger (Augusta's brother). They had plenty to occupy them. The RKO contract was complicated, because it involved not just Welles personally but the Mercury entity. The radio dealings with Campbell's and Ward Wheelock had been undermined by mistrust. And then there was the matter of Welles's own finances, for once arrived in Hollywood he began to throw money around in the serene confidence that there would be more to replace it.

In Los Angeles, Welles courted his own unpopularity with a grin and a teasing refusal to take the locals as gravely as they were accustomed. At one party, late in July, Welles had gotten into a drunken spat with one of his few genuine admirers, David Selznick—no matter that Welles had lampooned the producer in one of his radio shows. Selznick wrote to apologize for any offensiveness: "And second, my offer to be of help if you see fit to call on me. This was on the level, and still goes." Welles sent a thank-you letter in response, and he spoke that early about his situation being a "Gethsemane and very possibly, my Waterloo." But he couldn't resist a barb. He offered Selznick best wishes on *Rebecca:* "It is almost certainly going to be the best movie you ever made." But in August 1939, Selznick was agonizing over the editing of *Gone With the Wind*, which had to be the best picture anyone had ever made.

That old, cheeky rebelliousness was something Welles could never smother. The flights to New York began in September, and the weekly shows were *Peter Ibbetson*, with Helen Hayes; O'Neill's *Ah, Wilderness!*;

What Every Woman Knows, with Hayes once more; *The Count of Monte Cristo*, in which Welles played Edmond Dantès; and then, on October 8, a version of *Algiers*. And here again, Welles began to break the rules.

Algiers was a departure in that it was produced in Los Angeles. It was also a radio adaptation of the 1938 movie, a very successful Walter Wanger production that had starred Charles Boyer and Hedy Lamarr, and that was itself a remake of the French film *Pépé le Moko*. Wanger had agreed to the adaptation, and to a set amount of dialogue from his film being reproduced. But Welles had turned experimental with sound effects. The day after the broadcast, Diana Bourbon (of Ward Wheelock) wrote angrily to Ernest Chappell, the agency's man at the studio. First of all, Welles had altered the introductory announcement so that a "Campbell's Playhouse Presentation" became an "Orson Welles Production." Far more alarming was the show itself—"one of the worst we have done—entirely due to overproduction." In Ms. Bourbon's view, Welles had sacrificed and omitted much of the story for sound effects:

> At my home, I had a hard time being allowed to keep
> the radio going. Finally (in that *long* stretch of sound

Welles on the air, with John Barrymore and Rudy Vallee, January 1941

effects with nothing happening—when Pepe was supposed to be coming out of the Casbah) my guests got up
in a body and went and sat in my bedroom where they
couldn't hear the radio. . . . Now I know the Casbah—
(probably better than Orson!)—and I check with him
that this noise and music was absolutely authentic. The
atmosphere was stunning in its perfection—but there
was too damn much of it.

Welles had hired native musicians and an Arabic girl singer—none of
them on budget. Who had paid for them? How had it happened? As Ms.
Bourbon saw it, Chappell had been the victim of Welles's charm:

> Orson is a very fascinating personality. He sings a siren
> song to anybody who listens to him. Keep your feet on
> the ground, a firm grasp on your common sense, and
> *don't let him hypnotize you!!!*
>   I'm not saying this behind his back because I'm
> sending him a copy of this letter. But remember—he's
> dangerous!

The letter is shrewd enough to have felt its own victimization. Perhaps Ms. Bourbon had succumbed to Welles. Her sparring letters to
him are all full of affection—and he wrote back an eight-page letter,
signed "with eternal love." He repudiated every criticism and fiercely
objected to sniping. "Any 'siren song' I've sung in New York you can lay
down to my very real affection for you. I'm not a wheedler or charmer.
My fault as a personality, as you must know, is that I am somewhat arbitrary by inclination and often unreasonable." She did not back off an
inch but told him, "You hypnotize in spite of yourself. You can't help
it. It's part of your value to us." There are few other examples of people who worked with him telling Welles off so surely or with such
insight.

Rather similar concerns about waywardness were being voiced by
those looking after Welles's affairs. He was beginning to spend his RKO
salary, and spend it fast. His living expenses in Brentwood were running
at $800 a week. He had even proposed purchasing an airplane so that he
could fly to New York at his own convenience. It was only the $20,000
price tag that had stopped him. But still, some New York trips ran up bills
of $2,000.

To warnings from Weissberger, Welles had referred to his trust fund—the inheritance from his father, due in May 1940, when he reached the age of twenty-five. Weissberger looked into it and found that the fund was $33,438, but Welles had incurred loans from banks for $15,000. He owed Dadda Bernstein more than $1,200. And there had to be an income tax provision in the range of $12,000. When all the sums were done, Welles could expect only $2,692 from the fund. Added to which, a divorce from Virginia was clearly in the offing, with burdens of alimony and child support.

Everything was further aggravated by the "delay" in getting a movie going. Welles had taken it for granted that he would be shooting before the end of the fall—when more money could be paid to him. As Weissberger took charge of Welles's financing, he found more and more liabilities and a recklessness in the man himself. He wrote to Richard Baer,

> As you know, most large money earners in Hollywood,
> who have persons like myself in charge of their affairs,
> are kept on fairly stringent budgets and are told what
> they may and may not spend. Orson does not like to
> conduct his affairs in that way.

The lack of a clear movie plan only increased his uncertainty, and the restaurant bills. It could seem generous in Welles to pick up such checks, but the grand gestures were a way of masking doubt. The trips east were especially costly, but they kept up and led to Campbell productions of Galsworthy's *The Escape* (in which Welles costarred with Wendy Barrie), Molnar's *Liliom* (in which he played the doomed hero, with Helen Hayes as his wife) and, on October 29, a production of Booth Tarkington's *The Magnificent Ambersons*, in which Walter Huston played Eugene Morgan, with his wife, Nan Sunderland, as Isabel Amberson. This version omitted Aunt Fannie entirely. Welles himself was credited with the adaptation—and he took the role of George Amberson Minafer. There was also a dramatization of *The Hurricane* in which Mary Astor was Welles's costar.

But in November there was some relief. Campbell's agreed to relocate the series to Los Angeles. The first show done from there was Agatha Christie's *The Murder of Roger Ackroyd*—all the more appealing in that Welles was cast as both the detective and the murderer. Seek thyself! The writer who adapted the novel that way was Herman J.

Mankiewicz, perhaps the most fruitful acquaintance Welles had found on the West Coast. At that moment, Mankiewicz—who was forty-two —was also a reject of the system. He had been a top screenwriter, with more than fifty credits by 1930. He had worked on *Laughter, The Royal Family of Broadway, Horse Feathers, Million Dollar Legs* and *Dinner at Eight.* But by the midthirties he was in a slump, largely propelled by liquor and his own contempt for what he was doing. Scott Fitzgerald called him "a ruined man who hasn't written ten feet of continuity in ten years." However, Mankiewicz was famous for his acid, self-mocking wit, and he and Welles were fascinated by each other. In a strange and lovely way, each one was the weapon the other was waiting for. History has them as opponents, but only because at first they were such allies.

When the radio show moved west, John Houseman came back to Los Angeles. So he was there to observe the collapse of *Heart of Darkness,* the mounting financial disarray and the embarrassment of so many radio actors brought out in the expectation of doing the Conrad film. There was glib talk of replacing *Heart of Darkness* with an English thriller, Nicholas Blake's *The Smiler with a Knife.* And Welles kept saying that the Conrad was only postponed.

A week before Christmas 1939, there was a Mercury dinner in a private room upstairs at Chasen's. Along with Welles and Houseman, the company included Albert Schneider, Herb Drake, Richard Baer, William Alland, Richard Wilson (another loyalist assistant) and a secretary. The awkward reason for the meeting was word from RKO that, come December 31, they would stop salary payments unless and until a new script was presented. So who would pay the actors?

Welles said *he* would, out of his own pocket, but then he was told there was no money. Whereupon, he declared he was being betrayed—"I work myself to the bone for this money and you sons-of-bitches piss it away!"

Houseman decided he had had enough of this dishonesty. So he asked Welles what *he* was going to do.

"What would *you* do?" said Welles, his temper building. He had been needling Houseman all evening.

"Tell them the truth for once."

Welles roared at Houseman: "I don't lie to actors. I've never lied to an actor in my life! You're the one who lies! That's why they hate you! You're a crook and they know it!"

Houseman got up and prepared to leave. But before he could exit,

"Sing Sing, Gettys!" Kane and Gettys (Ray Collins)

Welles began hurling dish heaters at him. They missed, but a curtain caught fire. Onlookers had no doubts: Welles had instigated the scene to make up for frustration. Houseman left Chasen's, and the next day he got in a car to drive east. The most noted creative bond in Welles's life was over—or nearly over—and touched by a need for vengeance.

3

⟿ *Rosebuddies* ⟿

A S C R E E N P L A Y was composed for *The Smiler with a Knife*. No
one seems disposed to argue that it was the work of anyone except Welles
and Amalia Kent—though the screenwriter Gene Towne apparently gave
some useful advice. The script shifted the book's action from Britain to
America but kept the essential situation of a well-to-do young woman
who has to penetrate a fascist movement. For the leader of that movement, Welles turned the novel's English aristocrat into a young aviation
tycoon, a figure evidently based on Howard Hughes, with whom Welles
alleged some acquaintance.

No one at RKO was much impressed with a script that seemed influenced by the comedy-thriller tone of Alfred Hitchcock's recent English
films (*The Thirty-Nine Steps, The Lady Vanishes*). The studio offered it to
Carole Lombard, who declined. Welles preferred a young RKO contract
player, Lucille Ball, but the studio said she was not bankable enough. So
much for casting control. But not even Welles seemed persuaded that this
script was sufficiently important—the more time passed, the greater the
need for his debut to be extraordinary.

On January 8, 1940, *The Hollywood Reporter* gloated over Welles's
dilemma and what might be a humiliating conclusion:

> They are laying bets over on the RKO lot that the
> Orson Welles deal will end up without Orson ever
> doing a picture there. The whole thing seems to be so
> mixed up no one can unravel it. You can get better odds
> that the original Welles announcement, *Heart of Dark-
> ness*, won't ever be done, and can get 50–1 that neither
> Dita Parlo nor Lucille Ball will ever go into the second
> announced picture, *Smiler with a Knife*.

This prodigiously talented man was now at a loss, and embarrassed.
He was very late on his RKO deal; he was sorely pressed for money; he
had become an object of ridicule in a film community that studied the

huge advance publicity and gossiped about everything. He had not plucked a great, knockout idea from out of the air.

It was in this crisis that Welles met with Mankiewicz, who proposed telling the life story of a great man, beginning immediately after his death, and working from the several points of view of people who had survived him. It's clear that, in his enforced alcoholic idleness as a Hollywood outcast, Mankiewicz had been playing with such a scheme for some time. He had thought of John Dillinger and Aimee Semple McPherson as possible models. But as he talked to Welles, he suggested William Randolph Hearst.

In time, each man would say it had been *his* idea alone, and the followers of each would join battle on their hero's behalf. So let us make two basic points: Welles and Mankiewicz were both very talented, mischievous men, and in the making of movies it is the movie that is the marriage and the script that makes a prenuptial agreement. But fifty or sixty years later, a man and a woman may look back on decades of bliss or disaster and know that nothing would have happened if, say, a young woman once seen on the Staten Island ferry hadn't been talked to, and smiled in the right light.

Welles and Mankiewicz were under no rule or obligation to live and work as separate entities. Collaboration and competition were natural. They talked often, and often when there was no one else there. They were grand rapid talkers, masters of interruption, one-upmanship and cutting jokes. Later on, John Houseman imagined the two of them together— "magicians and highbinders at work on each other, vying with each other in wit and savoir-faire and mutual appreciation. Both came away enchanted and convinced that, between them, they were the two most dashing and gallantly intelligent men in the Western world."

They schemed and dreamed together—they surely often talked at the same time. And they could both of them have known privately, "I'm rescuing him," which is not quite the same as knowing, "He's rescuing me." There was a frenzy of collaboration about which no one's colder, later memory was reliable. There is also the likelihood that, in listening to and watching each other, they were excited and inspired. By which I mean to suggest that, at the outset, Mankiewicz beheld Welles and was moved and amazed, overwhelmed but suspicious. After all, it would be Mankiewicz who not long afterward said of Welles—without much effort to be discreet—"There, but for the grace of God, goes God!" Dillinger and Hearst were all very well, celebrities sure enough. But Orson Welles was riveting: it was eat or be eaten.

Something profound and decisive in the idea of the film came from Mankiewicz alone—yet it was a better notion for a movie than he ever had before or later. On the other hand, for years Welles had been preoccupied with the allure of greatness in a man and that great man's dread of the abyss, of nothingness; he had made several dramas that vitally confused fiction and the real world—most notably *The War of the Worlds; Lucifer Rising* and *The Fall of the City* anticipate the mood of *Kane*. There are also small, precise origins: Robert Carringer has noted that as early as 1936 in a *March of Time* broadcast on the death of Sir Basil Zaharoff, Welles had done scenes of a great house with papers being burned and the dying Zaharoff wheeled out into the garden to expire, beside a rosebush.

Still, in every dispute that followed, Welles made it clear that the "Rosebud" idea came from Mankiewicz—he was the happier to pass it off, he said, because he always thought it a rather hokey device. But there had to be something, one last word, to inspire the film's inquiring process. To demonstrate its artificiality, one writer on the movie once speculated over a Kane who chose a word at random—the third word of the seventh line on the ninety-second page of the third book from the left on the top shelf of the library. That search comes up with "Rosebud," so that is what Kane says as he dies. More amazingly, as late as 1989, Gore Vidal declared that "Rosebud" was actually William Randolph Hearst's pet name for Marion Davies's clitoris. When pressed on that matter, he said that the information had come from Charles Lederer. This Lederer, a screenwriter himself, was a nephew of Davies, a frequent guest at Hearst's California home, San Simeon, and a good friend of Mankiewicz's. He was also, early in 1940, paying such court to Virginia Welles that she was about to become his wife. Suppose, instead, that "rosebud" was some part of Orson Welles's sexual fancy.

So Welles and Mankiewicz talked, and then Welles called Houseman in New York. This was a curious step, for their quarrel had not been settled. Still, Welles flew to New York and insisted that Houseman have lunch with him. At "21," Welles mentioned the Mankiewicz idea, and he asked Houseman to consider serving as editor, companion, whatever, as Mankiewicz did the writing. Houseman suggested that Welles do this himself, but Welles refused—it would be better this way, he said, if Houseman was willing. So Houseman went to California and liked the idea. He also, quickly, became an admirer of Mankiewicz. A deal was done.

As of February 19, Mankiewicz went under contract to Mercury (but was paid by RKO) to do a script for Welles. He would get $1,000 a week, with a bonus of $5,000 when the script was delivered. One clause of the agreement read as follows:

> All material composed, submitted, added or interpo-
> lated by you under this employment agreement, and all
> results and proceeds of all services rendered or to be
> rendered by you under this employment agreement, are
> now and shall forever be the property of Mercury Pro-
> ductions, Inc., who, for this purpose, shall be deemed
> the author and creator thereof, you having acted en-
> tirely as its employee.

In other words, there was no guarantee of a credit for Mankiewicz. This was, essentially, the deal that Mercury gave to its radio writers, and it was meant to conform with Welles's overall contract with RKO, in which he was hired to be everything on the film—actor, director, producer and writer. A boy wonder must do everything.

Why did Welles need Houseman now—especially when he no longer had much reason to expect warmth or reliability from his lost friend? One answer is that the Mercury years had taught Welles the value of House-man as an editor, and as a guide to the writing process. Was Welles also shrewd enough to foresee that, in tandem, he and Mankiewicz might eas-ily lapse into destructive competition, eating and boozing the days away? Mankiewicz needed to be kept on the wagon if the work was going to get done. His wife, Sara, recommended that Herman be bodily removed from home, Los Angeles and temptation. So it was agreed that Houseman would go off with Mankiewicz and a secretary to the Campbell Ranch, near Victorville, a small town on the edge of the Mojave Desert.

Mankiewicz had a nurse, too, for he had a badly broken leg as a result of an automobile accident. So the two men led a very simple, hardwork-ing life, eating the ranch meals, with Mankiewicz allowed one drink a night. Houseman kept vigil for illicit bottles, smuggled in, like the cigars Jed Leland keeps begging for in *Citizen Kane*. The secretary took dicta-tion from Mankiewicz, and Houseman was there to observe, to comment, to throw in his five cents. Time flew by:

> With no family to make him feel guilty, no employer to
> hate and no one to compete with except an incompre-
> hensible, cultivated, half-gentile hybrid with a British
> upper-class accent, the mental and emotional energy
> which had been squandered for years in self-generated
> conflicts and neurotic disorders was now concentrated
> on the single task of creating our script. After so many
> fallow years his fertility was amazing.

Houseman was self-effacing in his account of those weeks in Victorville. He was just doing whatever he could to help. In the process he observed how thoroughly Hearst was at least one model for Charles Foster Kane. But Houseman was really the co-writer (or enabler) on the film because he was smart enough to get on with Mankiewicz, because he was a very good editor and because he knew Welles better than anyone. For some other resemblance developed behind the showy but superficial kinship of Kane and Hearst. In emotion and energy, Kane was based on Welles. No one was better equipped to guide that resemblance than Houseman. And so I have to wonder whether that wasn't why Welles ate enough humble pie to beg his insulted friend back—for a very special blend of betrayal and glorification was in hand, and Welles sensed it. It was a matter of Welles's rare grace and cunning that Houseman went to Victorville.

4

The Mythical Hero

A N D S O , after eight weeks, Mankiewicz and Houseman came down from the desert with a script called *American*. It was—

> *Excuse me, it amounts to a conspiracy between the two of them up there in Victorville to tell a story that is a portrait of Orson Welles?*

If you mean by conspiracy the clear, premeditated determination on a plan that is then faithfully executed—no, nothing so plain.

> *I ask because I am troubled—our readers, I think, are expecting the Hearst story. They know that story; they look forward to it.*

Do not trouble yourself about Hearst being overlooked. There is plenty of Hearst—more than enough to ensure that, as time goes by, *Citizen Kane* becomes the world's chief reason for remembering both Hearst and Marion Davies. So, if they are interested in the vagaries of history, then the shades of Hearst and Davies should be grateful to *Kane*. It is the broken glass ball that reminds us of them.

> *But* Kane *lasts longer, and more vividly, than Hearst?*

Fiction is the great virus waiting to do away with fact—that is one of the most ominous meanings of the film. "Nothing else remains—but the wondering."

> *Still, as professionals involved in biography we have our duties—*

Of course we do. And that is exactly why I asked you and our readers to notice the oddity of Houseman being assigned to Victorville.

Yes, that is curious.

Consider also that, shortly after the delivery of the first draft of the screenplay, Houseman returned to New York.

He was not present for the filming?

He said he no longer felt a part of the enterprise.

He had been used?

Perhaps. But he was too subtle a man for only that. I think he was a user and a prompter, too.

The conspiracy?

Except that it's not that simple. Consider those two men, Houseman and Mankiewicz—springtime in the desert. They begin to get along. They have a pleasant routine. Mankiewicz sleeps late. Then they settle down together, arguing out the story. There was apparently a great deal of laughter and shouting.

I can imagine it.

To tell you the truth, I have often thought of it as a play—a radio play, I think. The writing, the editing, their going off to a cowboys' bar, the Green Spot, for that one drink and dinner. Occasional visits to the only movie house in Victorville. Mankiewicz playing cribbage with his secretary. The acting out of certain scenes. The high spirits of good work being done. The desert sunsets. Not to mention the special angles of two uncommon men.

How do you mean?

Mankiewicz was brilliant, yet by then he was a failure. He had grown up loving newspapers and theater, and he had become a Hollywood drunk. He was a man of real intelligence, fascinated by politics. Someone who knew he could have been so much more. And here he has a rare chance—to work with a new force and a great talent, and to tell a story he could never sell elsewhere. So Mankiewicz at the outset, at least, is full of the thought of making a commentary on Hearst. He had known Hearst; he had suffered and bitten his lip at San Simeon, trying to scrounge drinks.

And Houseman?

Houseman was someone who had felt love for Orson Welles, and an admiration that overcame his own inherent skepticism. Then he had seen the bully, the wayward egotist, the helpless self-destructive, the boy incapable of growing up. And he had felt betrayed: he loved the talent; he envied it; and he was mortified to see it wasted. So he came close to being vengeful—and he had been abused at Chasen's, in front of others, treated as badly as Welles could treat anyone.

Their love? Was it ever enacted?

I don't think so. Yet I suspect both men entertained the thought, and smiled loftily at each other sometimes to signal the awareness. They were sometimes reckoned as lovers by their colleagues—they were both theatrical enough to play up to that. And their play may have been a way of masking, or diverting, the real feeling.

Houseman felt love?

Have I not managed to convey just how lovable Welles was? And never forget his extraordinary physical being—that air of the Mongol prince. Ravishing—

But frightening!

Exactly. And so constantly fearful of being betrayed that he gave others ideas. And magicked them into the postures of treachery.

He needed to be betrayed?

Counted on it.

So he sends Houseman to the desert?

It is never clear-cut, never anything that anyone can count on.

Houseman, otherwise, was not needed there?

At the time there was a good excuse—Mankiewicz was unreliable. Yet in the event Mankiewicz worked with a will and a focus he had seldom known before. This was the best opportunity he had ever had—redemption. Perhaps he could have done a script without Houseman.

But Houseman talked to him about Welles?

Must have. Those desert evenings. . . . "Tell me more about Orson," Mankiewicz asks, and he begins to see how mixed Houseman's feelings are. He hears the stories of prodigy and profligacy, creativity and cruelty. And this Welles will *be* his hero on-screen. Writers cannot help but be affected when they know who will play a part.

My God, it is *a play. Did Welles ever telephone or visit?*

There were calls. William Alland sometimes drove up for pages, and once a chauffeur took Welles out on a visit. Half a day. He looked at a hundred pages of script and was evidently encouraged.

How so?

At about that time, the production took shape. He told the RKO people it was going to be all right. He began to imagine the film. He had seen enough to be excited.

But he could not know yet that it was about him?

Not know it, no. I daresay he never absolutely, coldly, knew it till the day he died. But, remember, he reckoned everything existed as some version or reflection of himself.

What did Welles do in those weeks, the Victorville weeks?

There were the radio shows. *It Happened One Night*, with two guest stars—William Powell and Miriam Hopkins; *Mr. Deeds Goes to Town*—in which his sultry, enchanter's voice tried to be Deeds; *Dinner at Eight; Only Angels Have Wings*, with Joan Blondell; *Craig's Wife*, with Ann Harding; *Huckleberry Finn*, adapted by Mankiewicz; *Jane Eyre*, with himself and Madeleine Carroll.

He went on a lecture tour—making money—talking about what he called "the New Actor." He delivered this speech in April at Pasadena, Kansas City, Spokane, Portland, Tacoma and Wenatchee. He was all the time scrambling to get his finances in order, yet going off on money-raising ventures that incurred heavy expenses. With his divorce finalized, he had to see to making payments to Virginia for Christopher. And he was fucking around with Dolores Del Rio.

There's a reason to miss the desert. He's in love!

It may have helped keep him in town. There is something charming about the Del Rio romance. He had seen the Mexican actress as a kid: it would have been in 1932, just after Ireland, when he was seventeen (and she was twenty-seven), and he saw her, apparently naked, swimming underwater, rescuing a wounded sailor, Joel McCrea, with kisses in *Bird of Paradise*. He later rhapsodized, "She was as *undressed* as anyone I'd ever seen on the screen, and *maddeningly* beautiful! I had some young lady in the back row with whom I was fumbling. It changed my life!"

He believed the movie was silent, yet it must have been *Bird of Paradise* (a Selznick picture at RKO—one Welles may have rerun as he became entangled with the nymph herself). But the frail memory gives one glimpse of a Welles not blessed with precocity. Whatever he had learned in the brothels of Macao, there he was at seventeen, fumbling with a girl in the dark of the movies. It is suspiciously like normalcy.

Del Rio was a famous beauty and exotic. She never seemed less than a scrupulously graven image—a sometime actress, and dancer, and married in 1930 to Cedric Gibbons, the head of design at MGM. By 1939, that marriage had foundered. Yet Welles went to lengths to be secretive. He got William Alland to find a small house in the hills which he rented as his hideaway for Dolores. He reveled in her. He thrilled to the endless variety of her lingerie—he was now in the boudoir of a conscientious movie star. Not for the last time, he was attracted to a certain kind of spectacular, if rather unoccupied, beauty. He was crazy about her. He was fascinated, scarcely able to believe the meeting of fantasy and reality—but in love? No one who knew Welles in those days could ever believe that he was in love with any of the women. That potential in them was hardly noticed compared with the legend they offered as consort and

With Dolores Del Rio

bedmate. He would attend the opening night of *Citizen Kane* with the wide eyes, the arched eyebrows and the sheer epitome of fashion of Del Rio on his arm.

So perhaps it was simply erotic chance that kept him from Victorville?

You are so determined to be *practical* about this.

I like the commonsense answers: he was horny, so he stayed in town.

You resist the magical logic that I have offered you—that some gentle, underground gravity was at work in fashioning *Citizen Kane*.

I don't entirely. I am tempted by it—though it's largely a matter of atmosphere. But you are so set on having me see Kane as Welles, and I am nostalgic for Hearst.

Very well, then. This is the moment.

The moment?

Before I take another step, you must watch the movie.

I've seen it. Many times.

But now you must see it with this very question in mind. We should also give instructions to our readers—

We cannot dictate to them.

Don't be defeatist. We can do nothing more seductive to them than order them about. No one is supposing that this book is self-sufficient. It is a book about a filmmaker, and his films, and very much about this one film, *Citizen Kane.* So we will give orders to our readers to see it *now*—before the next chapter will proceed.

With any special instructions?

To ponder the matter of whether Hearst or Welles most colors Charles Foster Kane.

But I know too little about the real Hearst.

Enough, apparently, to suppose he is Kane?

Even so, can you help?

Hearst was rich. He owned newspapers. He had had political ambitions. He built a palace for himself on the California shore, San Simeon. He had a wife in New York and a mistress in California, a blond, Marion Davies, an actress who liked to do jigsaw puzzles. For all I know he did talk to her clitoris. Mankiewicz had been a guest at San Simeon. He set out with Hearst as his target. There, you have all that on your side, along with the incontrovertible fact that the Hearst forces acted as if he *had* been the target once the film was released. Hearst *was* a target. He was also a pretext. Remember, the film is profound because of its emotion. Yet Orson Welles never mustered much more than a passing interest in anyone except himself.

As the room darkens, let me give you Houseman's realization, written thirty years later, that he and Mankiewicz, up there on the high desert, were "creating a vehicle suited to the personality and creative energy of a man who, at twenty-four, was himself only slightly less fabulous than the mythical hero he would be portraying."

5

⸻ *A Damned Man* ⸻

THE FIRST SCRIPT to emerge from Victorville—it was called *American* (or sometimes *Orson Welles #3*)—was 268 pages long. That is nearly enough for a four-and-a-half-hour film. In later years, Welles would sometimes say there were actually two scripts on the boil—the

Mankiewicz-Houseman one and his own, done simultaneously in Los Angeles, while lecturing on the road or in the Del Rio love nest. Nothing of that second script has ever been found, nor is there any reason to believe Welles even *knew* the whole story. He understood just the idea and the approach before Mankiewicz left for the desert. Beyond that, Mank was candid (and self-protective) about making it up as he went along, and as Houseman reacted to the work.

That doesn't mean Welles gave no thought to the idea, especially after he had seen work in progress on his visit to Victorville. He knew the central role was not just his but him; eventually, any script would have to bow to how he, Welles, moved, spoke, waited and watched. And he began to make drawings of what the movie might look like. At the time of the script's delivery, he was already in early conversations with a cameraman, Gregg Toland. So, as Welles's best script work—its editing—began, he was driven forward by wondering what *American* would feel like *on the screen.*

He read the script, and he reacted. We do not have the response itself, but there are stories that he groaned over many of the scenes and deplored the excessive length. That does not take away from the evident fact that *American* gripped him. Here, at last, was the picture he would make. Whatever its faults and digressions, *American* is a groundbreaking script, the unequivocal basis for an original picture. It uses a great man's death and the rather contrived dissatisfaction of newsreel men with their first obituary to launch a more searching inquiry. Thus a reporter tracks down people who knew Kane. They tell stories about him—though not necessarily in chronological order—so that the film builds toward a final confrontation with its self-appointed mystery. The structure is very intricate; the dialogue is brilliant; the overall view of America and its functioning is ironic; and the mood is pessimistic—not just in wondering whether this man was happy or fulfilled but in its suspicion that meaning itself, and human purpose, is a vain hope. The script's role and originality can never be denied, for *Kane* is nearly the only movie to suspect that power, wealth, prowess and ambition are forlorn engines, the noise of which tries to hide silence and emptiness. There is something of Dreiser in *Citizen Kane.*

Mankiewicz had never written anything like this before, reason on the one hand to appreciate his inspiration and the seized opportunity to speak out at last. But he had been a writer of comedies, and usually a co-writer: he did jokes, scenes, bits and pieces, without often addressing the entire structure of a script, let alone one as complex as *American.* His mode was satiric, deflating, urbane—he had shown no taste for or faith in psychological drama. He had never dared to be so adventurous.

Welles gave him that opportunity: it is not too hard to conceive of urges in Mankiewicz that had been held back by failure, the conventions of the picture business and his own reputation for being just a wit. So he was one of many people who were freed from Hollywood's industrial grind by Orson Welles. But Welles was also an example to the writer, a spectacularly divided soul, a tragedy as well as a prodigy. And, with Houseman's assistance, Mank saw that—and so repaid Welles's gift of freedom.

No one saw Mankiewicz's predicament in Hollywood better than Welles:

> The big-studio system often made writers feel like
> second-class citizens, no matter how good the money
> was. They laughed it off, of course, and provided a good
> deal of the best fun—when Hollywood, you understand,
> was still a funny place. But basically, you know, a lot of
> them were pretty bitter and miserable. And nobody was
> *more* miserable, *more* bitter, and funnier than Mank . . . a
> perfect monument of self-destruction.

After Welles's first response, there was a serious bout of cutting, done by Mankiewicz and Houseman. Then, as the writing team came back from Victorville, and as Houseman returned to New York, Welles took over the task of making the script into a picture. From mid-April to mid-July, the script came down to 172 pages. Many episodes were abandoned—for example, Kane's honeymoon with his first wife, Emily; a later meeting between Kane and his father, when the older man is remarried to a "young tart"; Kane's son's involvement in a fascist movement; a good deal of political byplay with an oil scandal; scenes in Rome, when Thatcher goes to visit Kane; an affair Susan Kane has with a younger man at Xanadu. These deletions make *Kane* simpler to follow—and we should realize that nothing hurt it more on first release than its difficulty. In addition, Welles strengthened the line of dramatic consequence—the way Kane's career hinges upon the exposure of the love nest during the electoral battle with Jim Gettys, and the way Susan's nightmare career breaks the bond between Kane and Leland.

Mankiewicz's *American* is a dazzling chronicle that needed discipline and dramatic focus. It is a medley of great scenes but without sufficient line. Welles always doubted that "Rosebud" held Mank's story in place for an audience. So he rewrote a tragedy out of the original script. But I cannot believe he would have known how to do that, or felt the impetus, without Mankiewicz's groundwork. Welles had seen something of himself in the script, just as Mankiewicz and his "junior writer" (Welles's phrase) had been mindful of the personality of the man they were working for. Mankiewicz's real creative torture, his very mixed feelings about America and his proclivity for self-destructiveness, had found expression in Welles's rebelliousness. For as Welles would say of Kane, "he doesn't believe in anything. He's a damned man, you know. He's one of those damned people that I like to play and make movies about."

Hearst never created that impression—so few people in real life seem to come close to damnation, or glory. This was part of the rare, comic theatricality in being Orson Welles. Hearst was born rich; he was raised spoiled; he had ups and downs; he was thwarted in many things; yet he had a good time. So many rich people do. He *was* like Kane in some local respects: he had been thrown out of college; he had been given a rather moribund newspaper (the San Francisco *Examiner*) to play with; he took an actress as his mistress; he collected artwork that he hardly bothered to look at; he had his own version of Xanadu. But he was not very interesting as a dramatic figure.

How important it is to the tragedy in *Citizen Kane* that Kane becomes wealthy by strange chance—the kind of good luck that makes a mockery of the American dream of merit rewarded. From that comes the ironic wistfulness of Kane's remark "You know, Mr. Bernstein, if I hadn't been very rich, I might have been a really great man."

And greatness preoccupies Kane, not just in terms of wealth and power but in the Shakespearean reaching for heroic grandeur. There, above all, Kane is Welles. And therein lies the chance of tragedy. For Kane *is* possessed of genius. In that exhilarating part of the movie when he takes over the *Inquirer*, remakes it and bestrides the world, still eating because he's still hungry—there we see the dynamic, the leadership, the handsomeness still, the radiant glory of the young Welles. The *Inquirer* is Mercury. The adoration of Bernstein and Jed Leland is the loving regard felt by such men as William Alland, Joseph Cotten and even John Houseman.

But the movie also contains the darker, disappointed view of Houseman, and there are warning signs in even the halcyon days. Kane is magnificent and compelling, but he is prey to gestures that reveal his divided nature. He *is* a chronic actor who actually believes in very little. When he writes the *Inquirer*'s Declaration of Principles (so closely related to the Mercury's plan in *The New York Times* in 1937), he says he wants to make the paper as important as the gaslights to the city—and then he turns out those lights. Welles understood the flamboyant hypocrisy of Kane at that moment, and his all-powerful need to make Leland and Bernstein his slaves, his audience.

No one who knew or has written about Hearst has ever reported such complex depths, such an air of the damned. But there is a magnificent scene in *Kane* in which the young man exults in the contradictions in his own nature. Here is the basis for Kane's seeming both communist *and* fascist to his fellow Americans, and for Welles being both a genius and a charlatan to those who knew him. The moment comes as Thatcher (his guardian and banker) rebukes Kane for attacking companies in which he is himself invested. The speech is Mankiewicz's, but it comes to us on-screen as one of Welles's greatest pieces of acting—forthright, and hopelessly ruined:

> The truth is, you don't realize you're talking to two
> people. As Charles Foster Kane, who owns eighty-two
> thousand, three hundred and sixty-four shares of Public
> Transit Preferred—you see, I do have a general idea of
> my holdings—I sympathize with you. Charles Foster
> Kane is a scoundrel, his paper should be run out of
> town, a committee should be formed to boycott him.
> You may, if you can form such a committee, put me
> down for a contribution of one thousand dollars. On the
> other hand, I am also the publisher of the *Inquirer*. As
> such, it is my duty—I'll let you in on a secret—it is also
> my pleasure—to see to it that the decent, hardworking
> people of this community aren't robbed blind by a pack
> of money-mad pirates just because they haven't anybody
> to look after their interests. I'll let you in on another
> little secret, Mr. Thatcher. I think I'm the man to do it.
> You see, I have money and property. If I don't look after
> the interests of the underprivileged maybe somebody
> else will—maybe somebody without any money or
> property.

As the drama of *Citizen Kane* unfolds, we see this contradiction destroying the man. Hearst at times had been deeply in love with his wife, Millicent, and with Marion Davies. Kane takes his first wife, Emily, as a path to the White House, and his second, Susan, as a way of reforging his bond with the public, the audience. Susan's "career" is but a version of his own role on the public stage. There is nothing in the film to make us feel he loves either woman, and that, sadly, reflects what many of his friends felt about Welles. Kane never thinks about the son he left, who was killed in a car crash. Welles, too, was an unthinking parent, bewildered by the needs of his infant daughter.

Welles's heady resistance to authority and public compromise is dramatized in Kane's refusal to accept the political compromise offered by Boss Jim Gettys. He will not live to fight another day. Rather, he drags down his career and his family in the dire inability to eat humble pie. Kane has so much of Welles's love of reckless gesture—he treats money as something to be spent; he delights in being a spellbinder and in putting people under his sway; he is a stirring public speaker, so long as no one expects him to keep the promises he is uttering; he can create bright new enterprises, then give them up; and he seeks out challenging friendships for what they offer eventually in the way of betrayal.

The deepest relationships in Kane's life—in the movie—are with his mother and Leland. Hearst was happy enough with his parents. Why not? They adored and indulged him. Kane's parents are astonishing—they sell the boy, leaving a lasting wound, an inexplicable betrayal. With Houseman's help, Mankiewicz had made a remarkable dramatic version of such a wound in the scene on the prairie when Kane is about to be taken away by Thatcher. There is an overpowering, unresolved emotion in Agnes Moorehead's mother—seeming so pained at losing the boy, yet why does she need to lose him? and why has she had his trunk packed for a week?— that stands for Welles's refusal to admit to any deprivation he had known as a child. "Rosebud" may have been a hokey device. But it has always seemed to me that its load, that of ruined, lost childhood, works wonderfully well. Kane has never had a chance to be whole: on a cut, he goes from abandoned boy to huge kid.

And so he longs for Leland's friendship, just as he must destroy it. Leland is the movie's version of Houseman—a friend on the hero's level, admiring, moved, very understanding, yet unable to throw off skepticism and fear even. What a superb piece of drama and film it is that Kane seizes the moment and gesture to complete the damning review of Susan's opera debut when Leland is too drunk to finish it. The triumph, the zest, the anger and dread with which Welles's Kane types that notice—beats it into the paper—it is like a scorpion stinging himself. Character!

6

~~~~ *Credit Stealer* ~~~~

B A C K   F R O M   T H E   D E S E R T, Houseman detected a confidence in Welles that he had not observed since the early days of the Mercury company. Welles was editing the script, and doing so with the expert advice of a technical crew that now included Gregg Toland. Houseman also noticed that Welles's name began to appear alongside Mankiewicz's as author of the screenplay.

Toland was thirty-six, a cinematographer since 1931, an employee of the Goldwyn organization and easily the most inventive and artistic cameraman in Hollywood. On the one hand, he was an industrial stalwart, securely placed at Goldwyn with his own camera crew and with the opportunity to make experiments in the development of lenses and lens coatings. But he was confined to Goldwyn's product, and thus he had lavished his attention on many mediocre pictures—*Roman Scandals, We Live Again, The Wedding Night, These Three, Dead End, The Cowboy and the Lady.* He had won the Oscar for black-and-white cinematography on *Wuthering Heights,* and in 1940—on loan out—he had shot two films for John Ford, *The Grapes of Wrath* and *The Long Voyage Home.*

The Grapes of Wrath opened on March 15, 1940; its famous "harsh reality" is actually offset by a markedly pictorial, even epic, striving that is true to Ford but that also shows Toland at liberty. What I am trying to suggest is that Toland was like many Hollywood technicians: aware that much of what he was doing was second-rate and wasteful of real talent, but lacking the creative will or independence to determine a way to go. Great cameramen do not make great films, unless they have the right director to serve. That said, *The Grapes of Wrath* shows an ability with black and white, and a yearning for tough emotional content in the imagery that a Welles would have understood.

Toland was unusual among movie cameramen in that he liked to talk to directors; he was also a master of his craft intent on using wider-angle lenses and extending the image's depth of field. And he wanted some higher work than had ever come his way. That shows, rather painfully, on *The Long Voyage Home,* completed by the spring of 1940 but not opened until October. Taken from several short plays by Eugene O'Neill, *Voyage*

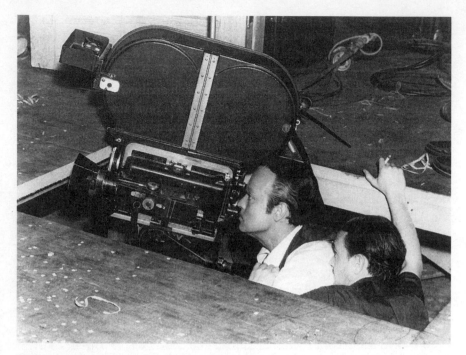

Welles and Gregg Toland lining up a shot

is a movie in which the artistic photography is out of control. Moody lighting, emphatic composition, the sense of tropical nights, the depth in the imagery—these things are so poetic that the film is watchable only as a curiosity. Ford's presence is far less evident than in *The Grapes of Wrath*. We begin to see how precious a film Toland might have made on his own. But in the tonal range of *The Long Voyage Home* there is something Hollywood had never achieved before—a kind of fevered, hallucinatory texture in skin and darkness—that is vital to *Citizen Kane*. The clearest clue to the subtle nature of cinematography is that the same effects are arty in *Voyage* and sensual in *Kane*.

Toland approached Welles: that's how the director put it, and it is very likely, for Toland was doing all he could to get away from Goldwyn's control, and he was sophisticated enough to know what plays like *Caesar*, *Faustus* and *Macbeth* had looked like. There's no evidence that he had seen those productions, however, and every reason to suspect that he regarded Welles as a great outsider, a rebel, a man of new vision—that's exactly how Welles described himself. By early June an agreement was made whereby Toland, his Goldwyn crew *and* his personal equipment—camera, lenses, filters—were all hired for *Kane*.

It's not so much that Welles and Toland became friends—the basic material for personality didn't exist for that—but they quickly found a trusting, collaborative relationship. Welles saw not just that Toland was the best cameraman in town but that he was leaning toward work that had a personal, as opposed to a house, style. From Toland's point of view, Welles was ready to learn, and free from industrial orthodoxies about how things ought to be shot. There is an excitement in the look of *Citizen Kane* that has to do with Welles discovering a medium, and finding it far richer, far more playful and far more personal than Hollywood liked to think. Toland was the teacher in this process, and he was without ego or vanity because he felt fulfilled, not threatened.

Mankiewicz, on the other hand, was suspicious and combative just because *American* was his great work—and a project which, under normal circumstances, no studio in Hollywood would have produced. Mankiewicz, too, had been given carte blanche, but he understood that rare gift better than Welles did. And sometimes the trained cynic, the famous wise guy, can turn especially angry when he is given Christmas and then has its bounty compromised.

Writers are dramatists, and they are inherently closer to the creative force than cameramen. Mankiewicz knew what this project was about: he saw it as a satire on American greatness, a slap in the face to Hearst and a pinch for Orson's bottom. He also understood how far *American* on-screen would depart from American narrative structures in film. We should not miss the cynic's pride in what he had done. He suddenly had so much to lose, and here was a brilliant kid (unaccustomed to failure) appropriating *his* story.

That greed was in Welles's nature. It was also in his contract. He could only do his great work if he believed he had become, for a moment, Shakespeare, Marlowe or Herman Mankiewicz. This was tyrannical ego, if you like, but it was genius, too, the heartfelt magic of metamorphosis. And Welles, as a rule, did not find himself in characters he played. He was aroused by the notions of creative control and originality. He had to be master of ceremonies.

So there are two sides to what happened: Mankiewicz felt tricked and robbed; Welles came into his own. If we watch the movie—and in the end it is *the* American film to watch—we have to honor Welles's imperialism, and admit that Mankiewicz could never have *made Kane*. Moreover, in movies it is one thing (and not a small thing) to raise an idea and quite another to make it into a film. Nothing else Mankiewicz ever did has a whiff of *Kane*. Everything Welles did breathed its air—even if sometimes it got drunk on it.

That said, Welles acted like a pirate . . . like Kane, who made the *In-quirer* his own by remaking the front page so many times everyone else was exhausted and servile. Mankiewicz was kept onboard in the rewriting, still at $1,000 a week. He was not terminated until August 3, a few weeks into the shooting.

We don't know how far, or whether, he fought the cuts and changes Welles made. So often, the writer finds no voice in the archive, and in such disputes Welles's voice was inescapably final. I suspect that Mankiewicz was smart enough to know that the shooting script was an improvement on *American*, not to mention a practically filmable piece with an actual start date. But as shooting went on, Welles gave interviews in which he sometimes admitted, airily, that he had written *Citizen Kane*. Mankiewicz sent a message to Welles, calling him a "juvenile delinquent credit stealer beginning with the Mars broadcast and carrying on with tremendous consistency." He threatened reprisals—not legal ones; he had no grounds there—but by going public and getting friends like Ben Hecht to write the "true story."

A little later, Mankiewicz made his point clearer. He knew that Welles's horning in on credit was inevitable, but he could not tolerate Welles telling the world that he had written *Citizen Kane*. Arnold Weissberger talked to the RKO legal department and established that Welles and Mercury were in the right—if they wanted to be: the Mankiewicz contract allowed for the writer getting no credit. In part, this was a case of people unused to movies trying to gauge the weather. But Welles was beginning to see that, according to Screen Writers' Guild rules, the writer of an original draft that was important to a picture did usually get a credit.

It is not a pretty story. Welles certainly contemplated taking credit, or using some formula that made clear his paramount role. That was unjust in every sense. The later career of Orson Welles makes plainer than anything the value of Mankiewicz in creating a story for *Citizen Kane*. Without *American*, Welles could not have been seized by the definitive, practical energy of an editor and adapter.

Still, by October 1, Arnold Weissberger was proposing a kind of tactical withdrawal to Welles. For it had come to the lawyer's attention that the matter might be raised for arbitration before the Screen Writers' Guild. The balancing of options was plain and cold-blooded. "It would be unwise to deny Mankiewicz credit on the screen," wrote Weissberger, "and have him get credit therefor through the press by publicizing his complaint."

Ironically, the question of credit would never die. But it remains a most Wellesian paradox that Orson struggled to drop Mankiewicz just at the time when he was volunteering the unprecedented generosity of sharing a credit with Gregg Toland. For, on the final film, the last credit reads:

ORSON WELLES
Direction—Production
GREGG TOLAND A.S.C.
Photography

But Weissberger had other problems in the summer of 1940, as Welles took on the greatest work of his life. Virginia had been complaining with increasing bitterness about her divorce agreement with Orson. She had been endearingly loyal at the time of the divorce itself, in Reno in February 1940. She said that it was a simple, sad matter: Orson was a genius and that left him no time to be concerned with his daughter. But there was a strain. She suffered a nervous illness which, she said, was due to Orson's cruelty. He, for his part, had been hard-pressed financially. So he had sought a reduction in his alimony payment to her, in return for which he said he would cover her hospital bills. According to Virginia, this was agreed in a telephone call. But, later, he had reneged on those payments.

In the summer, Virginia remarried, and thus her new husband, Charles Lederer, joined the battle on her behalf. It extended to money for Christopher's education as well as rights of ownership in the New York apartment and its furniture. Through the years of marriage, Virginia had stood by Welles. But it shocked her to see how he lied and how completely he sought to disown his past. Here is a frightening glimpse of Welles's ruthlessness, and the cold feelings left in others when charm had passed by: "If because of my decision to send for my furniture and personal belongings, I am to be deprived of Christopher's support, I shall sue. I have already consulted a lawyer, who informs me that . . . a child's parents cannot relieve themselves of their obligations to support their children."

So, as Welles sought ways to claim ownership of the script of *Citizen Kane*, he was cutting himself free from his young daughter. Put like that, perhaps the point is unfair. But I make it to help indicate the affinities between Welles and Charles Foster Kane, who never seems to think of the son he first abandons and then loses, and who sees emotional ties as the projection of his own glory. Remember also that Hearst and Davies stayed close and loyal until his death. When he faced hard times, she sold jewelry to help him out. Hearst was a very wealthy and powerful man who often behaved badly. But he was a softy, a rather vague, mystical fellow who tried to do well by people. Welles had no grasp of money, but he was a capitalist where power was concerned.

In 1940–41, Welles made a film that unkindly drew attention to Hearst and mocked the brave Marion Davies. At the same time, William Randolph Hearst, among his other concerns, agonized over this poem (which is not quite Kane's sort of thing):

> *The snow melts on the mountain*
> *And the water runs down to the spring,*
> *And the spring in a turbulent fountain,*
> *With a song of youth to sing,*
> *Runs down to the riotous river,*
> *And the river flows to the sea,*
> *And the water again*
> *Goes back in rain*
> *To the hills where it used to be.*
> *And I wonder if Life's deep mystery*
> *Isn't much like the rain and the snow*
> *Returning through all eternity*
> *To the places it used to know.*

Hearst believed in so much, and had such childlike ways of expressing it. Welles was something like a genius, but he was already besieged by the loneliness that can only believe in itself.

7

⟶ *Toland & Co.* ⟵

I N T H E E A R L Y summer of 1940, Welles had budgetary crises at home and at the studio. He attended only to the latter. By then, "home" was a more than usually nebulous concept. He had taken on a cheaper rental, at 8545 Franklin Avenue, but he lived at the RKO offices on Gower Street. Anyone trying to find him, with bills, advice or simple correspondence, was directed there.

In the matter of personal finances, Richard Baer was the West Coast guardian of the purse, who reported back—usually in defeat—to Arnold Weissberger in New York. The two men had intended to put Welles on an allowance, while holding back portions of his income for taxes and for alimony and child support. It was a fine theory, but it never worked. Baer found that Welles eluded or challenged the scheme by undertaking sudden and quite considerable purchases. He only ate out at expensive places. He bought things whenever temptation arose.

By Hollywood standards, Welles was not well paid—he never would be for movies. But he was keeping high company: taking Dolores Del Rio *and* Marlene Dietrich on the town, with Dietrich as a kind of chaperone. (Their friendship would easily outlast the passion for Del Rio.) He was running up gasoline bills on his car of nearly $150 a week—enough for at least 200 miles a day—but he was letting Mercury people use the car. There were also creative undertakings that Weissberger only heard about when the bills came in—rights to books and plays bought here and there but never exploited. Something like $500 to $750 a month in cash vanished into the warm Los Angeles air. And when he was broke, Welles simply asked for more, as if he deserved the miracle of ease.

"When you say that it is a question of how a business manager would operate with Orson," Weissberger wrote to Herb Drake, "you . . . place your finger on the difficulty. Orson is not a person who wants a manager to guide or direct him." No matter that he begged Weissberger to manage him, he then behaved like an irrepressible rebel, doing it all his own way before turning to the woeful manager and asking for the simple restoration of order. His greatest concentration in working was the assumption that everyone else was there to execute his wishes. Yet he never seemed an unworldly person. So was the behavior an act, daring refusal? Was it some deep-seated aversion to money and calculation? Or did it have an element of gambling self-destructiveness, a provocation to the staid, balanced world?

There was no way of escaping some discipline at RKO. By mid-June, the studio costing people warned that the production would exceed $1 million. This put the movie in jeopardy. With speed and purpose, Welles sought ways to reach a compromise. The cutting down of the script continued, and Mankiewicz was put back on the payroll to facilitate this—he had been away, at MGM, working uncredited on *Comrade X*. So, whoever had written what, the two men cut and enhanced together, with the script changing several times a day in small ways—the way a fetus moves and kicks in the womb, getting ready for the radically different adventure of being born.

The crisis in late June and early July was in getting the studio to give the green light on a project at last known as *Citizen Kane*. No matter that Welles had been invited to Gower Street under such privileged circumstances, he had engineered the situation he needed emotionally—of himself against "them." In Welles's own mind, this tight spot brought out the best in him. Others, however, reckoned that it only played into his greatest handicap: for he could not be the genius without becoming the impossible rebel. In a factory system that viewed him as outrageously spoiled, he had found his own most precious ground, that of feeling besieged and opposed. We may note in passing that the Charles Foster Kane who is steadily reported as being one of the richest and most powerful men in the world has the rather bitter hunches and the teeming self-pity of someone who feels thwarted and misunderstood. Hurt ego is at the poetic core of the movie.

In so many ways, the making of *Kane* was like a conspiracy or a plot. Welles was answerable to no studio executive other than George Schaefer himself. And Schaefer would only lose face and authority if he elected to abandon the Welles adventure without anything to show. By breaking his own rules, Schaefer had trapped himself. Though he argued down the budget for *Kane*, it still ended up at close to 150 percent of the contracted figure. In the whole story of *Citizen Kane*, it is often overlooked how valiantly George Schaefer kept to the contract he had permitted. Yet eventually Welles would make a villain and a spoilsport out of him.

Virtually all the players would be new to film, and loyal in advance to Welles: Joseph Cotten as Leland; George Coulouris as Thatcher; Everett Sloane as Bernstein; Bill Alland as the shadowed reporter, Thompson; Agnes Moorehead, Erskine Sanford, Paul Stewart, Gus Schilling, Ray Collins—these were Mercury veterans making their screen debuts. Only Kane's wives required "professional" players, but the Mercury had kept few actresses on its books for long, and the wives were and are external lights that fall upon the closed, dark male world of Kane. So Welles found Ruth Warrick for Emily, the first Mrs. Kane, and he flattered and indulged her as befitted a president's niece (and maybe one day a president's wife). He bedded her, too, with something like the absentminded athleticism with which the young Kane made love to Emily.

As for Susan Alexander, he chose someone he saw as a waif: Dorothy Comingore, a pretty, instinctive actress of no great career record and no assured talent. She was a small-part player on the RKO lot with a history of B Westerns and Three Stooges movies. Comingore was made to read several times for the role. She was kept waiting, and then there was a reading for Welles and Mankiewicz. "What do you think?" Welles asked his fellow writer in front of the actress, and Mank answered, "Yes, she looks precisely like the image of a kitten we've been looking for."

Comingore was cast, but she was always treated as the sort of woman men discussed openly in her presence. Welles was hard on her: he said it was the only way to treat her, for he was working toward the look of crushed hatred that Susan must have for Kane, and he reckoned that Comingore was not a good enough actress to pretend. She had to feel it. No one knows or recalls, or noticed, but it would have been in keeping if Welles had seduced Comingore once, brutally, and then dropped her. There is no feeling of conventional sexual infatuation in the movie between the older tycoon and the would-be singer. Rather, she is his instrument, the display of his power, his cruel creation. Dorothy Comingore is let us say perfect in *Kane*, but her career went nowhere afterward. The huge predictive authority in the way she was used came to pass.

More vital still to the feeling of pact or entourage was the way Welles had acquired his camera team, his way of seeing. Gregg Toland brought a corps of experts onto the lot capable of overriding the knowledge and habit of RKO's methods. Virtually all of *Kane* was shot in the studio, under lights. A movie studio in those days was ordered like a factory, with lights fixed in the rafters of the soundstages and standing sets there waiting to be photographed. Look at enough studio films of the thirties—from MGM, Paramount or Warners—and you may *feel* the house style and an attitude of mind that went with it. Thus most MGM films were more optimistic than most Warners films: this was in the light, and in the slowly forming habit of how to film things—it did not have to be something pondered and decided on. And it was in the way the electricians and stagehands expected to work. Many a movie director found that his dream was subtly appropriated by all the ways contract employers took their job and his art for granted. They lit things their way. They did certain shots in the house manner.

On *Kane*, Toland's presence, and the unquestioned eminence of his team, shattered that orthodoxy. Welles was always generous about Toland's contribution to the film, yet not necessarily understanding. He would say that, as filming began, he simply assumed it was *his* job to set the lights—after all, wasn't that how he had worked in the theater for the Mercury? No, it wasn't; people like Abe Feder had placed the lights there. But in New York Welles had picked up a reputation—deserved—for stage productions that were uncommonly cinematic in their lighting schemes.

But, as Welles told the story, Toland tactfully indulged that vanity, while quietly making adjustments behind the director's back to ensure that his wishes were fulfilled. (There is a sweet implication in this story that Welles and Toland were silently of one mind. There was never a clash.) Then one day, early on, this game had to end. Some incident let Welles recognize his own ignorance and Toland's well-mannered loyalty. There was a brief hiatus in which, according to Welles, Toland said he could teach Welles all there was worth knowing in two or three hours. He may have said that; it would have been the perfect way of flattering Welles and the process of education he was undergoing. Whatever was said, the talk was oil for the film: Welles now trusted Toland completely, Toland was free, while Welles believed himself in charge of an elaborate technology which "they" had employed to make him feel stupid and intimidated.

In truth, there was more going on in the photography of *Kane* than Welles grasped in a lifetime. It *is* a very technical film, the swan song of an inventor who evidently despaired of most of Hollywood's old habits, even if he had little notion of how to liberate fresh looks in terms of story. Toland used *Kane* as a test case for many cinematic developments in the late thirties. The first was unusually wide-angle lenses that allowed a greater depth of focus than was common. Such lenses risked distortion: the image easily began to warp or curve at its edges. They also made for a dramatic but rather queasy stretching of space. Nor were they well suited to close-up photography, that staple of movie factory glamour. In the classic close-up, the face feels natural and is lifted out of a blurred background by backlighting. So we are helped to fix on and feel for the lovely emotions in the face. A close-up from a wide-angle lens can quickly make the face seem bloated and rubbery, and it gives you the background as sharp as the face, which may detract from the romantic emphasis of the standard close-up.

The second asset used by Toland, and pioneered by him at the maker's request on *Wuthering Heights*, was the new blimped Mitchell camera. Its novelty was a relative lightness that allowed it to be moved more easily. Thus, the chance of extending depth with the wide-angle lenses was boosted by the first mobility of the blimped camera.

Super XX film had become available, four times faster than prior stocks—thus more susceptible to depth of field. In addition, Technicolor—first used in 1935—had required the development of more powerful lamps. Toland himself had also been a leader in lens coating (painting a lens surface with magnesium fluoride), which captured more light for the film emulsion.

In concert, these opportunities permitted a kind of deep-focus cinematography in which everything seems in focus (and thus relevant), no matter that the overall image might contain a great deal of shadow and darkness. Simultaneously, Toland could deliver a new degree of realism allied to all those brooding feelings that accompany low-key, or very contrasty, photography. He could do something that was unique to *Kane* in 1941—make us believe we are seeing the entire world while feeling the anxieties and hopes of the inner mind.

Of course, that capacity is not magic in itself. *The Long Voyage Home* had shown that it could be nothing but ponderous artiness. But Welles as an artist had remarkable need of the two reaches—outward and inward. There is no suggestion that he and Toland talked this out. It is not clear that either man could have described what was happening in those terms. But happy chance had presented a technology in which Welles could discover himself. And it felt like a private game, something RKO could never puzzle out. For here, with amazing completeness, Welles and Toland were delivering a film that took the expressive force of movies deeper than Hollywood had ever contemplated.

8

A Radio Picture

GRANTED CARTE BLANCHE BY RKO, Welles began to look for darker designs. He maintained that there were informants planted in his unit, men or women who were reporting back to the executives. Of course there were—where did he think he was? His paranoia showed a belligerent naïveté about the way any studio—or any serious corporation—functions. There was a lot of studio loyalty in Hollywood in those days, and many people took it for granted that Welles should be grateful to RKO as a uniquely generous employer. But one searches long and hard to find a Welles who was amiable with superiors. As a rule, he stayed suspicious—because he was stimulated by an atmosphere of intrigue. Time and again, he solicited crew members who would count as "his" rather than "theirs." That built up a furtive camaraderie, but there were veterans in Hollywood who could have told Welles that a subtler managerial style was necessary for prolonged careers. Perhaps he never meant to be there that long.

Welles was fascinated with the opportunity in *Kane* of going from a man of twenty-five to one of seventy. He had always done his own makeup, but stage makeup is seen from a distance. In movies, the requirements are so much more intimate. Welles could have gone to Mel

Berns, the head of makeup at RKO. Instead, he saw and then courted an eccentric young Russian, Maurice Seiderman, who was only an assistant in the hairdressing department.

But Seiderman was an obsessive who did things on his own—experiments with noses and hairpieces. He had a little corner where he practiced. Welles was drawn there, and Seiderman was pleased to be noticed and talked to. Another pact was formed, brilliant in execution, and far more detailed and realistic than any makeup transformation in American pictures to that point.

One reason for such care was Welles's exceptional interest in old age and his excitement in anticipating his own. Makeup was a Faustian experiment with mortality, one of his most emotional subjects. We should not underestimate this in measuring the restrained passion of Welles's acting in *Citizen Kane*—nor the glimpse it allowed him of his own future. In so many ways, *Citizen Kane* loomed over Orson Welles as he grew older, not just as an achievement beyond equal but as an underground presaging of his own destiny. The final loneliness of Kane is made eloquent by the weight he takes on, the near baldness, the despair in his face and the hunched sitting position. In all his movies, Welles was more interested in—if more horrified by—his own body than in those conventional carnal objects, the actresses. If a dreadful, ruined narcissism is vital to *Kane*, the makeup was a precious glimpse of the future. Seiderman was the personal servant Welles needed, a familiar as much as a technician.

The music would be done by Bernard Herrmann from the Mercury Theatre. It was the industrial practice in Hollywood then to have composers on contract who were assigned to pictures only as the editing progressed. Then they laid in a conventional score at the producer's instruction. Invariably, the score sounded like others—the genre of movie music was as codified and predictable as the piano accompaniment for silent pictures. Welles employed Herrmann in a quite novel way. The composer was on the film from the start. He talked to Welles in advance: they had a musical concept as well as particular plans for the opera in which Susan Alexander would fail. The work was done over a stretch of fourteen weeks—not the four or five weeks that most Hollywood composers could expect. Even so, Herrmann had been planning long before going on the payroll in October. This privilege was not widely admired. Herrmann was warned off in Hollywood: "I was told by the heads of many music departments that there was no room for people like me there. They had a tight little corporation going."

His brilliance would soon overcome that antagonism, but the comment speaks to the way Mercury people were regarded. Moreover, Herr-

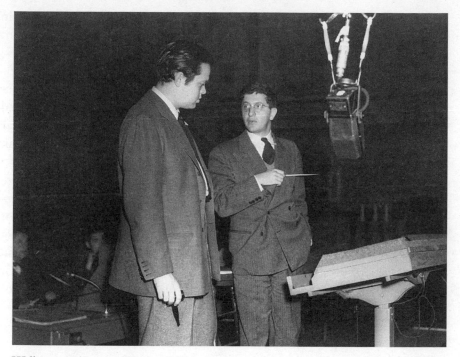

Welles consulting with Bernard Herrmann

mann was writing a score for *Kane* that defied the fixed limits of movie music. It has many moods and functions, as befits a story told from several points of view and one with a good deal of incidental music—from the opera through the newspaper party to the forlorn blues heard in the distance during the Xanadu picnic excursion. But the most remarkable thing about the score is its romantic and psychological quality, and its rapport with the film's deep space. This is potent, symphonic music—ranging from brooding to hopeful—that befits a large imagination, and a tragic hero. Though independent, quarrelsome and generally resolved to work on his own, Herrmann always admitted that Welles was the most sophisticated director he ever worked with, as well as "a man of great musical culture." So it seems reasonable to suppose that Welles's talk, along with the film itself, inspired Herrmann's aching music, so full of aspirations and mortification. It is a yearning score, sounding sometimes like the accompaniment to a horror movie, sometimes like that to a love story; how well it would match a version of *Beauty and the Beast* in which the monster is not just the source of feeling but the urge to tell the story.

What the music indicates is how the complex enterprise of the movie is held together by the feelings, the hope and the scrutiny—albeit the

dying scrutiny—of some large tragic figure that can only be Kane. And
Welles. The astute Herrmann also said that Welles was the most romantic director he ever met or worked with. That awareness shows in his
music—so another pact in the making of *Kane* helped to illuminate the
solitude of narcissism and genius.

Even when Welles was obligated to use RKO talent, he took steps to
establish a very personal alliance. For his editor, he chose the "young"
Robert Wise (Wise was a year older than Welles). But this was only after
Welles had met and rejected one of the more senior RKO editors—an act
that underlined the director's authority and awed the young replacement.
Most other directors had to take the editors assigned them, and often they
were not allowed to attend the editing themselves. By contrast, Welles
had a contractual right to keep the daily footage for his own eyes, or for
his editor only. The film could not be spied upon in the regular way,
which only put more strains of loyalty on Wise, an ambitious but junior
studio employee. That strain might tell one day.

Wise admired Welles and carried out the director's wishes happily
enough. But he was a careful, conscientious man, far from Welles in tem-
perament and well aware of the great man's calculated volatility:

> Working with him was never very long on an even keel.
> It was either up or down, marvelously exciting, stimu-
> lating, maddening, frustrating. He could one moment
> be guilty of a piece of behavior that was so outrageous
> as to make you want to tell him to go to hell and walk
> off the picture. And before you could do it, he would
> come up with some idea so brilliant it would literally
> have your mouth gaping open. So you never walked,
> you stayed.

There was no such ambivalence in James G. Stewart, in charge of
postproduction sound at RKO. Stewart, like most movie soundmen, had
been trained in radio. So he knew how timid the movies' use of sound was,
and he knew how much of Welles's genius came from radio. Sound in
movies in those days was a matter of achieving functional clarity: could
the dialogue be heard in even the worst projection systems where the picture would play? Were the sound effects synchronized? And was the
music track properly integrated with the speech and effects? Sound people seldom met the "creative" forces on movies. They were not deemed
much more important than the anonymous technicians who processed
the film. Very few movies had begun to exploit the atmosphere of sound,

to use sound as a narrative motor, to bring qualities of feeling and timbre to sound—let alone to have people talking at the same time. As a radio man, Welles took such powers for granted. He wanted to meet Stewart, to be able to trust him, to assure him. Stewart was delighted, and he quickly felt blessed to be learning so much.

It is an arresting experience to listen to *Kane* in the dark—without the picture. Apply the same deprived attention to other films of the period, and the sound is notably uniform, "realistic" (granted that mood music is as yet missing from nature) and rational. The level of the track does not vary much; the things that are to be heard for story point are very plainly indicated; the play on the ears is sensible and undemanding. With *Kane*, though, a quite different energy is at work. As if listening to radio, we are asked to see and imagine because of what we hear—an odd illusion is achieved: we feel the thing itself, the picture, is running inside our heads (close to our ears).

The level of voices is dynamic and varied, from "Rosebud," the essential inner-ear line, to "The Union forever," shouted by the boy Kane, playing outside in the snow, as his parents sign the documents that break up his family.* So many sounds are "placed" physically: very far away or very close. The variety of sound levels is always illustrating and fleshing out the visual depth of field. Sounds are emotional: they are intimate or remote. Many voices are edged with echo: Xanadu is a sound chamber where lines are theatrical or furtive, rarely level or normal. There are odd, intruding noises—the screech of a cockatoo, the dying flutter of a voice as heard on a Moviola—and always there is an emotional impairment of "clear" sound. This is one reason why *Kane* didn't "play" for mainstream audiences in 1941. They were not accustomed to listening that intently. So they felt they were missing things—and a movie then was a show where the audience was meant to feel they could *get* everything the first time. *Kane* was the first American movie so dense that it needed to be seen more than once.

Another skill from radio is pitching the level of talk so that we may gauge the size of the room where the characters are. Film often neglected that fineness: the talk always sounds like voices in the same studio. But in *Kane*, the track boldly distinguishes cabin, car, small room, great hall and auditorium. The famous ceilings that *Kane* supposedly pioneered in its sets are usually just muslin scrims (or later mattes). But we *hear* ceilings in

---

* That poignant line, a throwaway, is often inaudible in poor projection conditions. Moreover, the line was never in Mankiewicz's script—or even in the cutting continuity.

the confined density of sound. It is part of the picture's unique claustrophobia—the threat that no matter how wide the angles, or how vast the perspectives, still those outer limits are inching in, like death.

But here we have reached the most important technical matter after photography: that of design. It has been unfairly neglected, as if photography and the places to be filmed could ever be separated. As it was, the daily battle to make the picture involved a trio: Welles, Toland and the RKO designer Perry Ferguson. He was a company man, an engineer and a manager more than a creative personality. His job was vital because the designer in turn saw to the building of sets, their availability and their practicality for shooting. Welles had to learn the way movies used only those fragments and pieces of sets that need to be seen. It is likely that he could not have handled Ferguson so easily without Toland. But it is just as clear that Ferguson was as essential to the look and style of *Kane* as was the photographer.

In early drafts, the script had called for well over a hundred sets. Even as made, it had far more sets than was common. Yet nothing was sacrificed more than the sets in taking 25 percent off the budget. And as shooting went on, money was saved on building with camera tricks: matte shots, painting on glass, models and even black velvet shots, in which different strips of film were combined. Toland made Ferguson's task easier by contributing concealment in the decor: shadow or darkness, areas left to the imagination, solid and oppressive even in the image but actually empty—and thus cheap.

Kane used standing sets at RKO, sets waiting for other movies, with just a minimum of redecoration. It has many large sets—the political meetings, the exterior of the *Inquirer* building—that are flagrantly artificial. Sometimes the most telling dialogue scenes are played in corners with just a few props and a simple flat to shape them—granted the light is making so much more of a design. The challenge to make Kane's real world—from 1871 to 1941—from the cabin on the prairie to Xanadu itself was underlined by budgetary need. But it was a way of disciplining Toland's photographic genius just as it made the *Kane* crew into a band of pirates raiding the studio for what it could find.

Ferguson was a loyal assistant in that quest: he was saving the studio money and getting the picture made. Still, there is a pattern to the design, and a meaning, that can only have come from Welles. The picture is airless; daylight hardly obtrudes. But it is not simply an interior film in the sense of indoors. The sets make a psychological labyrinth, given tone by the lighting and enigma by the steadily searching, probing camera movements. The sets are emotional: large, rich, emblems of achievement, yet also confining, crushing and mocking possessions. The subtle stretching of real space, the closeness of the dark and the varieties of "fake," painted or fabricated settings all contribute to a dreamlike atmosphere in which that real world is like the outer bowl of a skull, pressing in on the imagination, held off only by life and hope. The snowball that breaks so early on is just one model of that pressure to be found within the film.

I do not mean to say that Welles calculated all this in advance, but he discovered or intuited it as the work went on. He found that movie decor was a model for Kane's life—so much accumulation, lovely for a moment when looked at but dross waiting to be burned. There is a special emotional charge in the final sequence in the great hall of Xanadu, when we see all the art, rubbish and things Kane has accumulated as they stand waiting to be burned. The scene is like a city of skyscrapers, but it resembles nothing so much as the props department of a movie studio—and that is exactly what was filmed. So as Xanadu begins to be destroyed, Welles is reflecting on all the dead apparatus of filmmaking. The close of *Kane* would not be as emotional as it is without this sense of the absurdity of all things and the futility of creation. That is the ultimate pitch of Welles's despair, that early in life, at the end of a masterpiece. And it is achieved principally through his insight into the nature of decor—living furniture that becomes dead leaves.

So Ferguson, Wise, Stewart, Seiderman, Toland and the actors—a band of compatriots, all given a unique opportunity, a moment against the grain of the factory system, a chance for rebellion and for showing what a movie could be. As word of that spirit got around, one may guess how dangerous Welles seemed. He was laying down the way to overthrow the system. And he was ungrateful. When George Schaefer and other RKO executives came by the set to say hello, to give good wishes, to see just a touch of the wonder at work, Welles shut down shop. He had given advance orders for all those involved to stop what they were doing. Instead, Welles engaged in conjuring tricks for the executives. They were hurt, bewildered and driven away. Welles was cutting himself adrift from his most valuable allies, the ones who had given him the train set to play with.

A few, like Wise, saw terrors in the man. Most were just happy to be there. Is it any wonder that the script had scenes that might be mirror images of Welles and his people taking over RKO as Kane and his fellows invaded newspapers? Of course, Mankiewicz could not have predicted that. But Welles must have felt the resemblance, and gone with it, thrilled at the discovery of self. There is such exhilaration in those early scenes at the *Inquirer*, such glorious panache in the exchange between the fuddy-duddy Thatcher and the rogue genius Kane:

THATCHER: Is that really your idea of how to run a newspaper?

KANE: I don't know how to run a newspaper, Mr. Thatcher. I just try everything I can think of.

For years afterward, Welles liked to suggest that was the mood he had done *Kane* in, a lively innocence that never knew enough to be cowed. It was such fun. But *Kane* is so rueful about any enterprise, whether running a paper or making a movie. Time and again, Welles laughed to ward off emptiness. Still, in *Kane* there are lovely passages of guys crazy for their work and in love with its compulsion. There is an idyllic portrait of the ordinary RKO technician in Solly, the *Inquirer*'s compositor. It is very late in Kane's first day at the paper. He has made the paper over four times in one night, searching for something fresh. Then he dreams up the Declaration of Principles:

Solly gets the message.

KANE: I'm going to print it. (*He rises, yells*) Solly!

SOLLY (appearing): Yes, Mr. Kane.

KANE: Here's an editorial, Solly. I want you to run it
in a box on the front page.

SOLLY: This morning's front page, Mr. Kane?

KANE: That's right, Solly. That means we'll have to
remake again, doesn't it, Solly?

SOLLY: Yes.

KANE: Better go down and tell them.

SOLLY: All right.

The look on the man's face is one of disbelief, fatigue, despair and
bliss. And there were people there who looked on Orson Welles with all
of that and more, and who tottered home happy to be worn-out, proud to
be lesser men.

9

— *In the Dark* —

I WONDER . . . ?
   Yes?
   *I was thinking of looking at a little of the film itself. I wondered if
you . . . ?*
   Join you? Why not? Though I have to warn you the picture may
give me the jitters.
   How so?
   As I wrote earlier in the book, I taught it regularly for ten years.
Stopping and starting it. Explaining the wonders. Seeing how it worked.
Until one day I had to stop.
   I can understand that.

Welles found something similar himself. He said that after all the time he'd spent on the picture, all the hundreds or thousands of times he'd worked scenes over in the editing—he could never look at it again.

Where did he say that?

On one of the chief confessionals of his later years, *The Merv Griffin Show.*

Perhaps you would rather not watch?

No, I think I would enjoy it—and it might prove useful. Anyway, I've never lost that mixture of hope and alarm that comes from sitting in the dark with another person.

It's rather apt, don't you think, that the picture begins with that old RKO image of the radio beacon?

My favorite among the old logos, not just because it was so often a reliable portent. But it reminds us to listen, and it actually matches some of the imagery from the obituary newsreel you are about to see. It *is* a part of the cunning subterfuge that what we are seeing is not just story but news, the facts, done in the best style of the day.

And then "A Mercury Production," with "by Orson Welles" added. Like a book.

And *not* like a film. Straightaway the audience is being warned. And now the title itself. What do you make of that?

Very simple. And large, filling the screen. It's claustrophobic.

Emotional?

Yes! It makes you realize how far titles today are elegant and tasteful. And then the movie, nothing else. No extra credits. We're plunged in.

You have to see how assertive that opening was in 1941, how violently it went against the grain. It still feels threatening, as if we should be ready for some uncommonly direct confrontation, without the fuss of show business. Now, as it begins—what do you feel?

The music has the ominous chords of . . . a horror picture, or something supernatural.

And it is night, but not a real night—a night of the mind and of movie soundstage. We see the sign "No Trespassing," and the camera climbs up the wire fence on which it hangs. Then a dissolve takes us deeper in. The energy of the film here is all music, movement and dissolves: it's teaching us how to know it. Those are keys to *Kane* no one should abandon or forget. And they are stylistic things, of the medium. We are being told to watch film itself and its motors. What do you see in this night?

A huge K on the gate and the shape of a castle on the mountain beyond.

What do you think of?

Kafka! The Castle. *Did Welles know them, then, in 1941?*

I don't know. Perhaps he only knew their mood. What else do you feel?

Dracula's castle in the mountains.

A creature who cannot die?

Yes, and the brooding quality. It's sinister.

Is there a bad man in the castle?

There must be. But not simply "bad." Wounded, too.

We are approaching him? How?

We are drawn in. The music inhales us.

The ominous music?

Yes!

What else do we see?

Part of a zoo. The prows of gondolas on a still pool. An abandoned golf course—this feels very fake.

Not a real golf course?

The wreck of one—as if a wrecked one had been built purposefully.

Such sadness.

The music alters. The notes are high, now, but shrill and feverish.

They match the small, bright light we have seen in an upper window of the castle. Do you notice how we have been drawn in through night or a nightlike state toward a burning light?

Yes?

It is like us here, sitting in the dark, trying to be part of the screen. And now the light goes out.

And the music shuts off—as if terminated. But it comes back on.

What was that? Wasn't that action?

I don't know. Now—we're dissolving all the time—

Right. There have been no cuts, always the slippage from one thing to another. We see a form on a bed.

It's like a tomb.

Is someone dead already? Now, describe what you see.

A snowstorm. It's the storm in a glass ball, with a house in it and snow thick on the roof. Now we see the hand holding the ball. And—oh—a huge mouth, crusted with mustache (like snow on the roof), straight on—like the title—and it says, "Rosebud." The voice echoes and resonates.

You were startled by the mouth.

It was so sudden.

Where does the voice come from?

From that mouth.

Why the echo then?

Because . . . because the voice came from the dark, from the house, from inside my head. We see no eyes as it speaks. It makes us feel we are speaking.

Go on.

The ball falls from the hand. It rolls down steps. It breaks. Through the broken glass and the wreck of the snowstorm we see a door open—the door to the room—and a nurse comes in. She folds the arms on the body on the bed. Draws the coverlet over the face.

Someone has died?

Yes.

In the house of the undead? Now! "News on the March!"

Oh, the shock! It's like a great "boo!" in our faces. But we're having such fun.

How? Isn't this an obituary?

But it's so confident, so loud and snazzy. It's just like the old March of Time.

Much better.

I suppose so. It's so rich. The voice!

William Alland—the same actor who will play the humble inquiring reporter.

And Xanadu is plainly modeled on San Simeon.

Yes, the visuals in the newsreels are the most flagrant thing about that comparison.

And "Kubla Khan" reminds me of the K again.

Welles will one day play khans as well as Kafka.

I love that line—"the loot of the world"—to describe all the things in Xanadu.

It makes us think of piracy, but somehow a useless piracy: all the things taken and stolen to be forgotten or burned. There's an undertone of despair already.

The divided soul—the communist and the fascist.

Reconciled in his emotional assertion, "I am an American."

And the newsreel gives us so many elements of the story that we can return to.

Yet this was not really helpful, I think. This is so crammed and quick a sequence. It still makes many viewers feel they can't keep up—can't follow so much so fast.

The obituary is so rich. The fun they must have had with it.

They poured sand on the film stock to scratch it—so it would look like old archive footage.

And Hitler on the balcony!

A waiter Welles found in town and nagged to come to the studio for the shot. It's still eerie, I think, and in 1941 it must have felt alarming.

Welles is so good as the old man.

Isn't he? The stoop, the narrowed eyes, the repressed anger. We do not see him at all in the obituary as a really young man. That splendid figure is kept for the movie itself, for the story (if it ever comes), so it has an extra sensual shock.

And the opera house in Chicago.

That's not Hearst. Very plainly, that is Harold McCormick, who married the soprano Ganna Walska, and Samuel Insull, who actually built the Chicago Civic Opera House.

And the candid camera shots, through the trelliswork, of Kane in a wheelchair in the garden at Xanadu.

I doubt there had ever been such shots in a movie before. See how they shake, from being handheld. There is an extraordinary understanding of the media and how they function in the newsreel—it's loving and proud, it relishes the detail.

Would Welles have felt that?

Kane might have. Kane loved the media. He helped create them. And do you see how we are several minutes into this film and there is no story, no one really to identify with—unless we are expected to cling to a dead man—and no sense of where we are. It may be exciting and fun, but no American film took such chances with entertainment's ground rules. Movies tell us what kind of story they are—

But, as you said, this one asks us to study movie itself.

Exactly. But it risked a loss of support. It allows the audience to feel neglected and overawed. There is so little appeal or charm for the crowd. But now, see what happens.

The weird atmosphere of the sound dying. The violent removal to a screening room where the obituary has been shown.

This was actually a screening room at RKO, packed with people, cameras and lights. No set. Everything is shaped by the light in what is one of the more abstract scenes in the picture.

We see no faces.

A good thing, too, for Joseph Cotten is one of the men in the crowd.

Why?

A joke, a piece of daring, a way of mocking the thing called continuity, a trick under the audience's nose. And maybe because the scene was announced as only a test. Welles told RKO they were doing tests, but really they had begun filming, despite the hold-off on budget.

So that was a trick, too?

But I'm sure Toland was testing lights as well—this is so pure and aggressive a scene visually, just patterns of shadow, defying recognition. Here at last the movie comes to ground: real people in the present—but you can't see their faces.

And because they're all talking at once you can hardly hear them.

The audience feels more lost than ever. And in that confusion, a great but necessary trick is put over.

What's that?

Wasn't the obituary a piece of work?

Brilliant.

Fun, excitement, crammed? The best you ever saw. And larger than *The March of Time* ever dared. But now the boss claims it's not enough. He says it doesn't *explain* the man—the nerve! As if such things ever sought to explain anyone!

Well, that is a convenience to launch the rest of the movie.

Or is it a media-mad personality given the medium at its best but still craving some secret insight?

Kane?

Saying, "Understand me." Don't you think that any real network given this show would have moved on to other things?

Of course.

So what more intimate request is being lodged? Who wants to know what this word meant?

"Rosebud dead or alive."

That's what the boss says. That famous last word. "Rosebud." Who heard him say that?

Well . . .

Do you remember?

A nurse came into the room.

After he died. After he said it.

There were others in the room.

You saw them?

No.

Then they hardly exist in this movie.*

The nurse heard him cry out from the other side of the door.

---

* Later, the publisher discovers that Raymond, the butler at Xanadu, says he was there to hear the word. But Raymond is so shifty, so proprietorial. He's like a man who just saw the dailies.

But you said the sound of the word seemed to be inside *your* head. Our head. The lips spoke to . . .?

To us.

We are moving on.

I'd like to think about that—

No time. Look at *this:* the El Rancho in Atlantic City. The roof. And see the camera moving forward—movement again. We are back with the camera style that began the film.

We go through the sign.

It was made in pieces to fly away.

We go through the skylight?

A dissolve on the flash of lightning. And we sink down to the floor of El Rancho. And here is the beginning of a visual pattern that runs all through the film: a diagonal from front right to rear left, shaped by a cone of bright light surrounded by dark. And the light *is* Susan's fallen blond head. As Thompson comes to talk to her.

The inquirer. Always seen over the shoulder. A dark figure. A man without a face.

The first row of the audience.

Yes!

Susan Alexander (Dorothy Comingore) and Thompson (William Alland)

The man sitting just in front of us. See how feeble Susan is. She says, "Who told you you could sit down here?" And he sits down nevertheless.

The defeated look, whipped even, in Dorothy Comingore's face.

And then an even more glorious diagonal composition with Thompson in the phone booth, in the dark, and Susan away in the distance in the light. Like a fire. Notice the space as the waiter steps forward—a lovely little performance by Gus Schilling, by the way. What happens?

It's hard to describe.

This is a wide-angle-lens shot. Space is distorted. In just three or four steps a character can seem to move from far away to very close. That midground has been stretched.

And there is a claustrophobia because of it. But more—an enchanted air. The composition is sublime.

That way of watching the light from the dark—do you see how it resembles our situation?

I'm exhausted already. I need a break.

A pity. I was beginning to get interested again.

10

The Best Showmanship

ONE YEAR AFTER Welles's arrival in Los Angeles, shooting began on July 22 (under the guise of tests). It would last until October 23. There were problems, of course. As they filmed the sequence in which Kane charges down the staircase of the "love nest," at 185 West Seventy-fourth Street, pursuing Boss Jim Gettys with roars of defiance—"Sing Sing, Gettys"—that are a grisly warning of Susan's assault on Kane's ears, Welles either sprained his ankle or chipped the bone. That compelled changes in the schedule. Joseph Cotten had to come in early for his first Leland sequence. He was to be the old man in the wheelchair, and he found that his director was similarly equipped. The two friends—jokers and gigglers—played dodgem cars in their wheelchairs before getting down to work. Then there were problems with Cotten's makeup as the old man, with racing around town to get new wigs and finally the filming of Cotten on the second day, done and wrapped before lunch—the whole mournful soliloquy of the old man, the best friend, begging Thompson for a cigar and summoning up enough love and pity to give an epitaph for Kane in Xanadu: "He was disappointed in the world, so he built one of his own, an absolute monarchy."

Filming was Welles's kingdom. He faced all the problems of a determinedly innovative production. Like any director, he had to know when to use seduction, comradeship, bullying, lies and naked deception, and he had to keep the whole thing in his head. He had to see the bills and disasters of his other life, the allegedly real one. He had to fend off the bitter pleas of Virginia and the altogether more beguiling ones of Dolores Del Rio. He had to handle the press and the studio, all greedy to know what the hell was being put on film.

Early in August, the columnist Louella Parsons visited Welles on the set. This was a necessary formality for a new director with so much hype behind him. But Parsons had another mission: to explore rumors that this film might make reference to her boss, William Randolph Hearst. So many people have to see the script for a film; there are so many ways information can leak. And it is likely that Mankiewicz himself had made a few incriminating boasts. Virginia's second husband, Charles Lederer, may have carried word back to Hearst. So Parsons had lunch with Welles and asked him to tell her the truth. The picture dealt with a dead man, Welles emphasized—"When a man dies, there is a great difference of opinion about his character. I have everyone voice his side, and no two descriptions are alike." Louella was satisfied for the moment—or so she said. She wrote a very favorable story in which she quoted Welles to the effect that he had written *Citizen Kane*.

Herman Mankiewicz took umbrage at that, for the credit battle was continuing, and Welles was acting on the principle that it was within his own gift and generosity to let Mankiewicz have some mention. The writer also saw some of the footage at the end of August. He was impressed but startled: he had not imagined this kind of photography. He thought it was "magnificent" aesthetically, but he did wonder if the public would understand it. Mankiewicz had never supposed they were embarked on anything other than a mainstream picture—no one in Hollywood ever fell into that heresy. But no one from RKO was yet entitled to see the rushes or make the same observation.

Welles was tired, of course, but incapable of yielding to fatigue. In September, after a day's shooting, he and Del Rio entertained Fay Wray and Clifford Odets for dinner. Odets was nine years older than Welles; he was an established playwright; he was a famously brilliant young man—

and he felt overwhelmed by this weary Welles. Odets saw someone not just articulate, but glib. "He is a sort of biological sport, stemming out of Lord Byron through Oscar Wilde, I should say. But he has a peculiarly American audacity." Odets could easily have taken offense: the young man was too much, too scornful of others and too flattering towards Odets. But then the wonder confessed, "I have a touch of rhinestones in my blood," and Odets was won over. He disagreed with everything Welles had said, yet he liked this "very octopus of ego." It is a pretty picture of Welles the impossible and Orson the seducer.

Many people remarked on the intensity of Welles's concentration during the shooting. He worked very long days—some of the filming took place at night. He was like the young Kane, driving the enterprise forward, and for Orson Welles he was singularly undistracted by other things. Once finished, he had a bizarre vacation.

For no other reason than the shortage of money, he had been booked for another lecture tour. On October 25, two days after the last wrap, he was at the Cornhusker Hotel in Lincoln, Nebraska, to speak on "the New Actor" for $1,250. The tour went through Toledo, Fort Worth, Dallas, San Antonio, Houston, Oklahoma City, Tulsa, Detroit and Des Moines, where it concluded on November 9. In theory, he was supposed to pocket about $12,500. But things went wrong. He canceled the Oklahoma dates. On several occasions, Welles bought late-change air tickets more expensive than those prebooked. He ran up large telephone bills, talking to the people he had left behind on *Kane*. Whatever the pecuniary need, he also longed to see the film falling into place. Thus the young man who was making perhaps the greatest movie ever in America found himself at 8:30 p.m. on a Saturday at the Shrine Auditorium in Des Moines, Iowa, where he had settled for 65 percent of the gross receipts on the assumption that the teachers in town for a convention would happily stay for the great man's thoughts on acting. But the teachers decided they were weary and had had enough of the Shrine Auditorium. Most of them elected to sample the nightlife of Des Moines, leaving a handful and a pittance (or 65 percent of a pittance) for the frustrated lecturer.

He had decided on the spur of the moment against Oklahoma City and Tulsa because Gregg Toland and Perry Ferguson agreed to meet him for a few days in the Southwest to look at locations for an intriguing project. Welles had taken it into his head to do a life of Christ set in the classic locales of the Western. Just as Renaissance painters had depicted the Gospel story against fifteenth-century Italian backgrounds, he would use the real and recent West. There are a few things to be said about this: that Welles and Toland had evidently concluded *Kane* on excellent and hopeful terms; that the Christ project was never done—though Welles tried to resuscitate it in the 1950s; and that this was an extraordinary man, not in any way devout yet capable of seeing how an old story might be adapted and made to live again. It is still a great idea.

So by mid-November, he was back at RKO, able to supervise the postproduction. Robert Wise has agreed that the editing had been fairly straightforward because the structure of the shooting script was adhered to. But Welles had time to weigh the timing of the opticals—especially the dissolves that meld together the different time periods—as well as the shock cuts. Herrmann's music was recorded. A singer was found who could convey Susan Alexander's forlorn attempt at *Salammbô*. The tricks were accomplished wherever photography alone had been inadequate. By the end of the year, the cut ran only a few minutes longer than the version that would be released. Welles spent Christmas with Dolores Del Rio. They had visitors: Dadda Bernstein and his new wife. Oddly, the group got on, and Welles took pleasure in making the festive decorations. At some time that December, Welles sneaked into an empty movie theater in Los Angeles and ran the cut print for himself. It was his way of okaying it, watching it in a solitude akin to Kane's at Xanadu. Thereafter, he claimed, he never saw the movie again.

And early in the New Year, reality began to intrude on that splendor. The movie was set to open in New York at Radio City Music Hall on February 19. A screening was arranged for writers whose magazines had long lead times—*Life, Look* and *Redbook*—on January 3. Hedda Hopper heard about this in advance and begged to get in—for Welles had apparently once promised her that she would be the first to see the picture. Hopper was especially anxious to be ahead of her rival, Louella Parsons—for reasons no one knows, Parsons seems never to have heard of the January 3 screening.

Hopper spoke about it, on the telephone: she let it be known that the picture was corny, the photography old-fashioned and the whole thing "a vicious and irresponsible attack on a great man." By January 7, issues were available of the magazine *Friday*, which contained a detailed comparison of the movie and Hearst's life. The sources for this article have never been pinned down, but it is likely that RKO released some material ill-advisedly and possible that some of the actors and crew had talked. The worst thing in the *Friday* article was a mischievous Welles quoted as saying, of Louella Parsons, "Wait until the woman finds out that the picture's about her boss." Welles claimed he had never said it, and *Friday* seemed ready to print a retraction. Yet it's just the thing he would have said, without judging the company he was in.

Louella Parsons was by now angry, demanding to be shown *Kane*. It is plain that she had talked to Hearst, or his lieutenants, for when she arrived at RKO on January 9, she was accompanied by two lawyers. She stormed out of the show before it had ended and began telephoning George Schaefer's office with threats of "the most beautiful lawsuit" if the film was released. On the tenth, it was said that Hearst papers were banning any mention of RKO product. At this point, Schaefer gave orders that there should be no further screenings, and no press comment from anyone.

There were those at RKO ready to say this crisis was the result of carte blanche, and proof of how misguided it had been. With more scrutiny of the script and the rushes, they said, the problem could have been avoided. Why was there any reason to offend a man as powerful as Hearst—except out of incorrigible cheek? Certainly, it is not too hard to imagine a picture as impressive as *Kane* that did not court such hostility.

All the more reason, therefore, to honor the steadfast George Schaefer, who consistently defended *Kane* and assured everyone that Hearst's threats would blow over. In outline, Hearst seems to have been saying, Abandon the film or face legal suit. But the studio and Arnold Weissberger were of the opinion that such an action would be very hard to win. Without delay, Weissberger sought independent opinions on Welles's standing on two scores: whether Hearst had a case for libel or invasion of privacy, and what Welles's rights were if RKO caved in to pressure and shelved the picture.

At the time, and in the aftermath, Welles put on his most innocent face in denying any intention of besmirching Hearst. Much later, he admitted he had known the danger all along, and had expected trouble earlier. Which only compels one to wonder what he had been thinking of. For is there not something ingenuous and self-destructive in making a film so powerful and original, with unnecessary attachments that put it in jeopardy? This is not just rebellion against power and those who hold it, it is biting the hand that feeds, and it is a way of putting one's own film in jeopardy.

Welles trusted no one. Though Schaefer behaved like a friend and a gentleman, Welles and Weissberger were immediately considering whether to rely on him in what might become a suit against RKO. On the one hand, they calculated that Schaefer had no option but to defend his protégé; on the other, they envisaged ways of betraying him in dealing with the RKO board. Much later, Welles claimed that he offered to buy the picture outright from the studio—just as Louis B. Mayer proposed refunding the negative costs if RKO would destroy it. Welles also urged on

Schaefer something like a nationwide, barnstorming, tent-show release of the picture, trading on the Hearst embargo and making a virtue of it:

> The mistake that Schaefer made was not to believe me when I made the best showmanship suggestion I've ever made, which was that *Citizen Kane* should be run in tents all over America, advertised as "This is the picture that can't run in your local movie house." If we'd done that, we could have made $5 million with it. But he couldn't—I can see why not. Still, I *know* that I would be a rich man today if they'd listened to me.

11

~ *All Packed* ~

JUST AS HISTORY fixed on the quarter truth, that Charles Foster Kane was William Randolph Hearst, so it is the conventional wisdom in film culture that *Citizen Kane* was crushed by Hearst's retaliation. This is at best a half-truth. Hearst did retaliate: he made life harder for the movie, and for RKO. But that is the uninteresting half of the truth. What is far more instructive about *Kane*'s failure with the first audiences is the number of ways in which Welles had cut himself off from success. Here was a filmmaker who seemed not just disappointed with the world but too lofty to beseech or woo an audience. So he made his picture into another world, his own.

I have tried to stress the ways in which the opening sequences of the picture intimidated audiences of 1941. (Their effect is not that different today—for if the common viewer now has heard in advance that *Kane* is a masterpiece, still he or she is less accustomed to following quick, complex narratives on the screen.) But narrative is steadily denied or evaded by *Kane*, especially in its opening. The convention of giving the audience necessary information is ignored; the moods of the first few sequences are deliberately jarring; there are no characters to identify with.

To take just the last point: many movies of 1941 would have made Thompson the hero or a kind of detective who, in pursuing the mystery of Kane, resolves some problems in his own life. To speculate for a moment: Joseph Cotten might have been Thompson; he could have been photographed in a way that would make him known and appealing; he might have found a person in the search who came into his own life— Kane's granddaughter, perhaps. They could have fallen in love so that as Thompson proceeded he found a dark secret to Kane's life that threatened the granddaughter, and the love affair. This is not a wild fancy: it is the skeleton for a picture called *Mr. Arkadin*, or *Confidential Report*, which Welles would make in 1955.

But in 1941, the reporter was seen under cover of darkness, or as a back bent toward the light. He has no substance, much less appeal. There is no personal, or emotional, link between the inquiry and its alleged mystery. In other words, Thompson has been sent on an absurd chase, a task for which he feels no passion.

Kane has no relatives to care. His first wife and his young son were killed in a motor accident a couple of years after the divorce.* His second wife was never fit company for the man; she was only his instrument or his possession. There are old men left—Bernstein and Leland—who knew Kane very well. The one is simply adoring, and the other abidingly skeptical. But they are too old or too simpleminded to believe in a mystery to Kane worth solving. They regard him as dead and finished. There is no mention in the film of an estate, an inheritance or a will that might be fought over. Indeed, the "estate" seems to be destined for the furnace, as if death wanted to draw away every possession, every thing, down to its own abyss and darkness. There is no museum planned for Kane—everything is to be burned.

In which case, why is *Citizen Kane* so emotional a film, or one so much about feeling? Not that that richness helped it in 1941, a moment when emotion on the American screen was best demonstrated in *How Green Was My Valley*, *Sergeant York*, *Penny Serenade*, *The Little Foxes*, *Back Street* and *Meet John Doe*. In their different ways, these are very emotional pictures: a haze of sentiment or sentimentality rises off them; we are encouraged to weep; we are negotiating the stories by identifying with characters—and their travails and joys enlist the energy of our fantasies.

An audience happy (or fruitfully unhappy) with those films does not get the emotion in *Kane*. Indeed, they probably find Welles's film obscure,

---

* Automobiles usually bring trouble in Welles's work: *The Magnificent Ambersons* sees them as a virus; in *Touch of Evil*, a car blows up; and Harry Lime's first death is blamed on a car.

intellectual, overly complex, gloomy or cold. But that is because *Kane* does not meekly adopt the scheme of realized fantasy and narrative momentum that American films still use. It is only if one considers the force of emotion latent in, say, a Mahler symphony, a Bonnard painting, in Tolstoy or a real landscape that one may begin to gain access to the power in *Kane*. And I do not employ these comparisons to stress the throb of music, the beauty of composition or the loveliness of nature. These things are all present and active in *Kane*, but they are less important than the structure, the tone, the ambivalence and our sense of the source—where the film is coming from. Similarly, the narrative is never offered in *Kane* as reliable rails for our vehicle to run on. Rather, it is a series of possibilities that are seldom clear or resolved. In other words, it is not easy always to say what has happened in a sequence—for contrary moods or feelings have been created. And here is the real nature of feeling in *Kane:* it absorbs opposites and ambiguities.

Let me talk about one sequence: the scene of the prairie cabin in Colorado in 1871 in which Thatcher arrives to take charge of the boy Kane. That is what happens, and it is—if you like such pivots—a turning point in Kane's life. But as we watch the film, so much more happens.

The scene is dominated by the mother, played by Agnes Moorehead. Her decisive forward motion drives the camera back on its tracks. It is her decision that is sending the boy away to Chicago, to education, society and the proper arena for wealth. The father protests, but he is feeble: "It's going to be done exactly the way I've told Mr. Thatcher," the mother says. Moorehead looks like a madonna, but a cold, imperious, adamantine one—she has the eyes of a saint, yet she could play Miss Murdstone in *David Copperfield* or Mrs. Danvers in *Rebecca*. Her appearance and her playing—her presence in the film—amount to a disturbing ambiguity.* This mother is sending her only child away. There is a sense of absolute finality. She will never see the boy again. She does not abandon or deposit the weak father and go off with the boy and the money that is hers. She sells him—that is what it amounts to. Yet she acts under the assumption that she is doing this for the boy's good.

Then consider the exquisite moment at which the mother goes to the window, raises it and calls out "Charles!" across the snow to where he is playing. We hear the wind on the prairie, the music rises, and there is a note of buried agony in Moorehead's voice—she has only this one scene

---

* Welles revered Moorehead more than any actress he worked with. In a trailer made for *Kane*, he called her "one of the best actresses in the world." Nothing happened between them: Moorehead was not heterosexual.

in the picture, but it is enough to place her among the most mysterious mothers in film. Thatcher says they should be going, and the mother assents on this line, said . . . well, how is it said? How do you *hear* it?

> I've got his trunk all packed. I've had it packed for a
> week, now.

In the shooting script, the line reads:

> I've got his trunk all packed—(*She chokes a little*) I've had
> it packed for a couple of weeks—(*She can't say any more*)

There is nothing as blatant as choking in the film, no settling on one exclusive meaning. We are left to reconcile the mother's grief with the psychological riddle of her apparent eagerness. Wouldn't a mother reluctant to lose her son put off packing? Yet would a loving mother send a son away? The sequence ends with an extraordinary close-up in which the camera moves down from her face to his as she holds him—the black and white seems engraved; the pose is nearly religious, the short but emphatic camera movement has bound them together—this couple who are parting. The sequence ends on the boy's intransigent possessiveness—in a regular Hollywood movie that last shot would lead to the son and mother going on together. As it is, the whole movie betrays the resolve, making for irony, tragedy and something more total—the disbelief in possessions, in bonds and even in pictures.

The episode from the prairie is what Thompson reads in Thatcher's journal, but nothing about the brusque, unfeeling banker (he *is* a Dickensian stereotype) finds him capable of such subtle perception. No, there is only one way to read and measure the scene—and that is through Kane's troubled feelings: what did my mother do, and why? Of course, this cabin in Colorado is the original of the house in the snow ball, the last thing Kane holds. As a rule, his dying word, "Rosebud," is interpreted as an answer—albeit a rather glib one—to the mystery Thompson is trying to settle. But if one attends closely to the Colorado scene, "Rosebud" hardly supplies an answer; it refers much more to a question that haunted Kane and that hung over his relationships with his mother and every other bond in his life. Far from being a play upon lost innocence and parents, "Rosebud" refers to the possibility that there never was real love, that solitude is the only reliable condition and that love—that big thing—is no more or less than what Kane toasts as he parts from his best friend, Jed Leland: "A toast, Jedediah, to love on my terms. Those are the only terms anybody ever knows, his own."

It is at moments like this that even William Randolph Hearst might have watched the film with compassion. *Kane* is not a barb that might have wounded Hearst; it is a cold, candid self-assessment by a solipsist. Perhaps Mankiewicz conceived the character and wrote the lines. But Welles delivered them as if they were his own death sentence, without flinching and without the swagger that marred so much of his acting. His performance as Charles Foster Kane is the simplest, most direct and best he ever gave, whether he was being the beautiful young master of the world, the middle-aged cynic or the old man. All his life, Welles was a rhetorical actor, someone who chose to kid silly roles and worse dialogue. But as Kane he permitted so little fuss or diversion. With justice, people remark on the scene in which he destroys Susan's room and the entire passage in which he takes over the *Inquirer.* But look, too, at the middle scenes, especially the long talks with Leland. They are superb, and they are naked, for they show a young man's premature capacity for being wearied and sickened by the loneliness of his magnificence.

In this light, I want to propose a way of reading the whole of *Citizen Kane* which is not simply aesthetic—though it helps pinpoint the film's tragedy—but biographical. When Kane dies, no one in the film hears the word "Rosebud." But *we* hear it. Similarly, at the close, Thompson and all the newsreel men have given up on finding any answer or equivalence for "Rosebud." "I don't think any word can explain a man's life," says Thompson. They depart, leaving us and the camera with the few men who are preparing to consign the loot of the world to the furnace. It is at that point that the camera is carried in its last forward searching with a sled and into the fire's bright light. The workman does not stop to see the thing that bubbles away as soon as we have seen it—the trademark "Rosebud" on the sled. Just as only we heard "Rosebud," we are the only people who get anything close to an answer.

Not that it is a comfort, or even a means of closure. If we have watched the film closely, it leads us only to painful enigma. And if we felt eager to offer the bare understanding to Kane, he is gone, he has always been gone. The only coherent way to explain the form of the film is as the dying Kane's reverie. It was Welles's way later in life to say that, early on with *Kane*, they had played with a *Rashomon*-like idea—that of different versions of one central fact, leaving us uncertain of what happened. But they let that go gradually, and it was replaced with the overall perspective of all the reports being voices in Kane's head—characters in his

play. Like a newsreel man, he has rerun his own life, with the hope that there may have been some mystery, some romance and hence some meaning to the solitude surrounded by possessions, by power and a kind of genius.

Here is another reason why so few Americans could like the film—for it maintains that the pursuit of happiness and the search for meaning are futile. Biographically, *Kane* is a metaphor about extraordinary talent, charm and power that have no faith in themselves. The film talks about Kane's need for the love of the people in two arenas—politics and theater—and it is Leland's harshest attack on Kane that "you just want to persuade people that you love them so much that they ought to love you back." Orson Welles had been so deeply admired since birth, so praised, so spoiled, that he had never been able to muster faith in love. So he went into a career that sought the love of strangers. No one in film has ever had such talent, such energy, such innate depth. But he had made a film that ensured his career's end, and he had done it all so that the film's grim portrait of solitude would be fulfilled.

12

⟵ *It's Terrific* ⟶

THE CRISIS OVER *Citizen Kane* would have daunted lesser men, or anyone who saw his own future only in terms of Hollywood. But Welles was galvanized, amused and encouraged—there is no better proof of how far his aversion to the establishment or to the powers of others stimulated his own genius. Without any public weakening, he dared the hostility of Hearst and his allies, and even the possibility that RKO would cave in. He and Arnold Weissberger mulled over the question of how to handle RKO—whether to threaten legal action early or trust the reassurances George Schaefer was giving. They believed that, in the end, Hearst had no legal grounds. The lawyer Morris Ernst had confirmed Weissberger's feeling that "where a man's career or incidents in his career are known to the public, have been publicized by himself and have been written about, the man's career can be made the subject of a fictional narrative. . . . Would a man be allowed in effect to copyright the story of his life?" As in so many areas, Welles's provocative invention was decades ahead of its time.

Schaefer and Weissberger were reassuring—and there were rumors of other schemes to release the film, involving direct purchase by other parties, notably Hearst's rival, Henry Luce, if RKO weakened. Still, the threats had an edge to them. Early in 1941, Welles went on yet another lecture tour, in the East, to bolster funds. He told the story ever afterward—though sometimes it was set in Buffalo and sometimes in Pittsburgh—how as he finished one lecture he was tipped off that "they" had loaded his hotel room with an underage girl and photographers at the ready in an effort to smear the name of Welles. There were also threats about revealing his relationship with Dolores Del Rio, and possibly other ties.

His response was predictable, from *Kane:* he found another hotel in Buffalo, or Pittsburgh, but as to "legitimate love-nests," publish and be damned! He told great stories about the predicament. There was that proposal from Louis B. Mayer and other studio heads to pay for the film's destruction. Schaefer believed then that controversy would guarantee the film's success, but still he didn't communicate the Mayer offer to the RKO board, and he was always asking for a few days more when Welles called. The original February 14 opening in New York was postponed. According to Welles, there was a screening in Los Angeles for Joseph Breen, the Roman Catholic director of the Production Code. His decision was being sought on whether the picture should be banned. It was "nip and tuck," Welles said, but he saved the day by inadvertently dropping a rosary under Breen's nose, saying, "Oh, excuse me," and then reverently picking it up.

Despite the little business with religious props, the decision was not made clear. Welles was on the phone twice a day with Schaefer, and he was refraining from direct threats, but he did not enjoy being told to be patient. In that hiatus, John Houseman reappeared. He was in Hollywood to discuss a job with David Selznick—and Selznick was one of the many Hollywood celebrities at this time invited to special screenings of *Kane*. In general, those screenings impressed people a lot, and Hollywood insiders relished the early chance to see the supposed attack on Hearst. From Schaefer's point of view, those screenings were also helping to deflate the Hearst threats.

Houseman had one commitment before joining Selznick. He owned the theater rights to Richard Wright's novel *Native Son*, and he had worked with Wright and Paul Green to get a play out of the story of a young black man accused of killing a white woman. But he needed a director—so he said—and he felt wretched about his association with Welles having ended so badly. So he offered the job to Welles—who accepted! He needed the money, and being in New York would help take his mind off the *Kane* delay. So he went East, with Del Rio (and her mother), daring the scandalmongers.

The cast was headed by Canada Lee, as Bigger Thomas, Wright's hero, Evelyn Ellis and Anne Burr, but several Mercury players—Everett Sloane, Ray Collins, Paul Stewart and John Berry—were cast in supporting roles, and Welles was at his best again. Houseman found him "happy, overbearing but exciting to work with," and he did nothing to prevent Welles from adding an inexplicable prop that had no point in *Native Son*—a sled bearing the name "Rosebud." Welles also called for a stage with ten moving parts, requiring thirty-five stagehands. As expenses—including the Welles–Del Rio hotel bills—mounted, Orson coaxed $55,000 out of some Hollywood people who hoped to secure him for future projects.

Native Son was well received, despite being picketed by both the Urban League and a faction of the Communist Party. It opened on March 24 and got only more attention because of the *Kane* controversy. Welles was steadily followed by journalists wanting to know the fate of the film, and he claimed to be in receipt of letters from the general public begging him not to sell out. The play's reviews were very good. It was called "overwhelming," and Canada Lee was especially praised. Some critics welcomed Welles's return:

> *Native Son* also gains by the thunderous and lurid
> theatre methods of Mr. Welles. In my opinion, Mr.
> Welles is one of the best influences our theatre has, one
> of its most important forces. . . . This talent begins with
> the violent, the abundant and the inspired-obvious, all
> of which make for the life of the theatre-art as
> contrasted with the pussyfooting and the pseudo-
> intelligence and the feminism that has crept into this
> theatre of ours.

There were only a few grumbles. Some critics noted that Welles's flamboyant adoption of the black issue was perhaps a little too entertaining for the point to be properly absorbed. The strongest attack came from the Hearst press, the *Journal-American*, which said that the whole show smelled of Moscow's influence. Wright had had ties to the *Daily Worker* and *New Masses*, and Welles himself had supported causes and issues that were also promoted by Communists. The Hearst smear was stupid and ill founded, but it was attended to: for it was in the spring of 1941 that the FBI began to gather information on Orson Welles.

Welles was still telephoning Schaefer, though he found it harder to make contact. While rehearsing *Native Son*, he wrote to the studio head admitting that he suspected he was being soft-soaped. When Welles asked for reasons or dates, Schaefer failed to respond. He painted a picture of himself waiting patiently by the phone for some message. There were people in New York telling him to be ready for the worst, even studio treachery! Yet Orson could hardly believe this of an old friend. But what should he tell these people, and the press? What answer was there for the world that deserved *Citizen Kane*? It was a terrific letter, manly but insinuating, with a nice ironic finish:

> Don't tell me to get a good night's rest and keep my
> chin up. Don't bother to communicate if that's all you
> have to say. There's no more rest for me until I know
> something concrete, and as for my chin, I've been lead-
> ing with it for more than a year and a half.

Still, he did more in this tense time. The human rights activist James Boyd had been approached by the Department of Justice to develop radio programs to spell out the vital significance of American law and ideals in the time of crisis. The scheme was called *The Free Company*, and it made a deal with CBS for a series of radio plays or documentaries. Such a series was hardly conceivable then without something from Orson Welles, but in his other crisis how easily he might have been let off. Instead, as he finished off *Kane*, Welles wrote a play for the series, *His Honor—The Mayor*. It told the story of Bill Knaggs, mayor of a small town near the Mexican border. The life of the town is beset by a movement called the White Crusaders—racist, extreme right-wing and antilabor. But Knaggs is a steadfast believer in the right to free assembly and free speech, so he struggles to let the Crusaders have their say.

Welles wrote the play, directed it and played the role of narrator (one who often interrupts the actors) in the April 6 broadcast—the show went out on Sunday mornings. Ray Collins played Knaggs, and Agnes Moorehead was his wife. Coming so close on the heels of *Kane*, *His Honor* is remarkable for its plain decency, its didactic approach and its dramatic dullness. *Kane* is a far more credible study in the intricacy of politics and compromise. Yet Welles managed to fit in this play, at a time of great crisis, for next to nothing. It was as if he could side entirely with the part of Kane that worked to defend the decent, hardworking people of America, leaving behind the self-conscious manipulator. And it helps suggest that Welles was not easily able himself to make a script in which two sides of his character were together, and at war.

He got no great thanks for the play. Hearst's *Journal-American* noted how many left-wingers were employed by *The Free Company*, and it willfully distorted the point of the play by arguing that Welles had defended the right of an anti-American group to use City Hall for its meetings. Major publications came to.Welles's defense, remarking that those foolish and inaccurate attacks were part of Hearst's campaign to block or smear *Citizen Kane*.

Welles issued a statement that was printed by many papers:

> William Randolph Hearst is conducting a series of brutal attacks on me in his newspapers. It seems he doesn't like my picture *Citizen Kane*. I understand he hasn't seen it. I am sure he hasn't. If he had, I think he would agree with me that those who have advised him that "Kane" is Hearst have done us both an injustice. . . .
>
> The Hearst papers have repeatedly described me as

a Communist. I am not a Communist. I am grateful for
our constitutional form of government, and I rejoice in
our great American tradition of democracy. Needless to
say, it is not necessarily unpatriotic to disagree with Mr.
Hearst. On the contrary, it is a privilege guaranteed me
as an American citizen by the Bill of Rights. . . . As a
citizen I cherish my rights, and I'm not fearful of uncertainty. I only ask that I am judged by what I am and
what I do.

Hearst's actions on the public stage had made a fool of him in ways
unmatched by *Kane*. Perhaps the radio play was a provocation. Perhaps
Schaefer counted on time exposing the bombast and exaggeration in the
Hearst attacks. It surely made people more curious about *Citizen Kane*
itself.

So finally, on May 1, the picture opened. Radio City Music Hall had
declined to run it, possibly because the Hearst empire had threatened to
publish exposés on the Rockefeller family. Instead, the picture had its
world premiere at the RKO Palace at Broadway and Forty-seventh Street.
This was not a major opening venue, but RKO did what they could in a
hurry to smarten the place up. The front of the theater had the legend IT's
TERRIFIC above a series of images of the young Kane in a white shirt standing with his arms raised—this was the chief promotional motif for the
film, though it has no basis in the movie. For the opening, there was a lavish souvenir program, which stressed the genius and diligence of Welles,
but it said nothing about Hearst or his campaign against the film. The
promotion was earnest, well-intentioned and generous but not acute or
ruthless. It lacked showmanship, and it did not convey an easily grasped
notion of what to expect.

But how would you advertise *Kane*? What should the poster have
been? What is the image to build on? The studio's failure reflects the decisive complexity of the picture. Hearst did all he could to impede the
picture. His papers did not advertise it. He prevailed upon some theater
chains not to take the film; others took it but then refused to play it.
RKO had control of very few theaters and was therefore dependent on
others—that was one of the business conditions that had always kept the
studio small.

The reviews were extraordinary. In *The New York Times*, Bosley
Crowther said, " 'Citizen Kane' is far and away the most surprising and
cinematically exciting motion picture to be seen here in many a month.
As a matter of fact, it comes close to being the most sensational film ever

made in Hollywood." The New York *World-Telegram* said, "Staggering and belongs at once among the great screen achievements." In the New York *Post*, Archer Winston said, "Not since Chaplin's 'A Woman of Paris' has an American film struck an art and an industry with comparable force. Orson Welles with this one film establishes himself as the most exciting director now working." "The boldest free-hand stroke in major screen productions since Griffith and [cameraman Billy] Bitzer were running wild to unshackle the camera," proposed Otis Ferguson in *The New Republic*. What more could anyone ask, except not to be cast immediately in historical perspectives that few ordinary filmgoers understood? From the outset, the praise of *Citizen Kane*—in harking back to the history of the medium—gave ominous warning that only time would tell.

No one said, "This is the most moving picture ever made." No one knew to add, "Or ever will be."

No one noticed how little Welles cared. He had made a master-work—and he was intelligent enough to know it—but it was one in which achievement and understanding were cast in such a forlorn light. It had been "nip and tuck," Welles said later: *Kane* had nearly been burned. There's not much evidence of so close a danger. Welles was honored and protected by RKO. But in his own reckless being and hopeless search, he had been ready to lose the picture. Sooner or later, it was likely, a picture would burn or be lost. The most un-American thing about this friend to Communists was his failure to believe in what he was doing, in having and holding it in the way Americans kept a firm grip on property, persons and privates.

13
Already in the Bag

WELLES WENT to all the first openings, like a collector, and there were stories from all of them that indicated the many different rooms within the bulk of Orson Welles (he *had* put on weight in all the stress and activity of early 1941). In New York, he had been so presentable that he looked like a Eurasian ambassador, with Dolores Del Rio on his arm, all alight in white fluff, and George Schaefer at his side. She shone her dark-eyed smile into the camera, believing she was at a major event. He let her light shine, planning ways to get out of the dark to avoid seeing the film itself. Could he tempt her into the greenroom—if movie theaters had anything so civilized?—or into any other dark closet there to make autumn of her white fluff while Charles Foster Kane bestrode the screen? Anything to escape that flat-footed tyrant who would now plod after him all his life, like Javert!

In Chicago, on May 6 (his twenty-sixth birthday), he and Del Rio were greeted by Roger Hill and a choir of Todd boys, who sang a song Hill had prepared:

> *Happy birthday to you,*
> *Felicitations we strew*
> *On our dear friend in Orson*
> *From the boys old and new.*
> *Let the Hearst face turn blue,*

Shouting red bunk at you.
Those who know you, dear Orson,
Know you're white through and through.
If he thinks this Kane's like him,
It's his privilege and whim.

Two days later, in Los Angeles, at the El Capitan, John Barrymore was in Orson's entourage. On May 28, Welles was in San Francisco for the opening. There it was—he said often later, though sometimes the meeting was at the Fairmont and sometimes the Mark Hopkins—that he happened upon W. R. Hearst in an otherwise empty hotel elevator and offered the old boy good tickets for the opening. Hearst says nothing in the story, and Welles was left to reflect that Charles Foster Kane would have gone along for the show—and might have stood up at the end, defiant and alone, in applause?

There was little applause in theaters, and small audiences. The tiny crowd for the Chicago opening had been especially dismaying to Del Rio. *Kane* had a good first week in New York, but then, as everywhere, it fell off fast. This was at theaters in big cities, in the full flush of publicity and great reviews. As the picture made its way around the country, Hearst's boycott was more effective. But even in the smart cities, where it had the best chance, *Kane* did not do well. On its more general release, RKO shifted their emphasis. Beyond stressing Welles's work on all fronts, they cast the movie as a dark romance—"What made this cutie walk out on $60,000,000? A girl who never made more than $15 a week—wed to the world's wealthiest man! But neither she—nor any woman—could endure his kind of love!" Nothing worked. The public stayed away, and a year after its release, *Kane* was withdrawn and estimated to have lost $150,000.

Just as Welles had distanced the suspense before *Kane* by doing so many other things, he offset the disappointment afterward by the surfeit of projects. This was still a man who had too little time for all the tasks and stories that beckoned him, to say nothing of the meals, the conversations or the girls. He still had a commitment to RKO. The original contract, the "carte blanche," had been waived—because of the time it had taken Welles to complete one film. In its place was a more regular agreement, calling for two films but without the same liberties. So, already, he had been restricted and had had to abide by the change. Nearly every other American filmmaker, in the history of his dealings with the business of pictures, improved his deal; Welles could only go downward, because of his start and because of his inability to be circumspect.

Shortly before *Kane* opened, he had submitted a script—*Mexican Melodrama*—that was an earnest attempt to be popular and movielike. It was based loosely on a novel, *The Way to Santiago*, by Arthur Calder-Marshall, and it is one more Welles project that nearly swoons with its own tricky enterprise. As far as I can tell, *Mexican Melodrama* was drafted before the shooting of *Kane* and revised after it: that may account for its fascination with the media and with the sleight of hand possible in the way a movie is presented.

It begins with a man who tells the camera, "I don't know who I am." This man, to be played by Welles himself, is an amnesiac, in a Latin American country (or, as Gregg Toland was meant to show, a chiaroscuro realm). He then discovers that he closely resembles Linsay Kellar, an Englishman and a famous fascist of the airwaves, who has come to Mexico to make propaganda broadcasts to the United States. In the end, the Welles figure defeats the real Kellar only by taking over his radio station in the jungle and delivering a very melodramatic warning broadcast.

The studio refused the project: they feared protests from Mexico, and they disliked the heavy political tone. But what is so intriguing about the script is the way Welles the narrator and on-camera protagonist is a "lost" soul, somewhere between dreams and paranoia. It is a remarkable script—ripe for Toland's genius—but it does anticipate the odd mixture of garish melodrama and political philosophy which marks Welles's later works—*The Stranger, The Lady from Shanghai* and even *Touch of Evil*. Moreover, the script has a subtext of special relevance to Welles—that delicate uncertainty as to whether he was fascist or democrat, an artist dedicated to humanity or one gripped by the terrible manipulative magic of the medium.

In the light of Welles's overall career, *Mexican Melodrama* seems characteristic. But at the same time, he had plenty of other ideas: he thought of a version of *The Pickwick Papers* that would have had W. C. Fields and John Barrymore (presumably as Pickwick and Jingle)—why is the world so unfair or stupid as not to make such things? He became briefly infatuated with the story of Landru, the French wife killer, and Mercury registered several titles for the project. Then he thought how superb Chaplin would be in the part, and he wrote a script, called *The Ladykiller*, which he showed to the comedian. At first Chaplin loved it and said he would do it for Mercury, with Welles directing. Then he changed his mind. He couldn't bear to be directed by anyone else. So Welles sold him the project and, years later, Chaplin made *Monsieur Verdoux* with the credit "Based on an idea suggested by Orson Welles." (Chaplin's version was his own, but Welles's script had one great joke. His Landru is a lifelong teetotaler. But at the guillotine he is given a last, and first, drink of spirits. He responds in such a way as to suggest, "If only I'd known about this!")

So do not suppose that this man needed just rest and vitamins between such things as *Kane* and *The Magnificent Ambersons*. If he had made *Mexican Melodrama*, *The Pickwick Papers* and *Landru* . . . well, he might now be regarded as a very great man. He was already in the business of making unmade pictures—and he even dreamed of Chaplin and Garbo together as D'Annunzio and Eleonora Duse. Imagine this mind put in charge of a studio.

Not every idea withered. In the summer of 1941—as the sad news on *Kane* came in, and as Welles appeared at the state fair in Sacramento (an oven in summertime), making various delectable parts of Dolores Del Rio vanish—he set up three projects for RKO: *It's All True*, *The Magnificent Ambersons* and *Journey into Fear.*

To take the last, and least, first, *Journey into Fear,* from a novel by Eric Ambler, was an RKO project of some standing. David Hempstead was its assigned producer, and there were several treatments or scripts, one of them by Ben Hecht. Welles dumped that material, hired two new writers and planned to be closely involved himself. Robert Stevenson was the director RKO had in mind. Instead, Welles proposed the actor Thomas Mitchell—he never intended to direct it himself—with Joseph Cotten in the lead role, and Michèle Morgan and Ruth Warrick in support. "I wish to say also for your information," he told an RKO executive, "that as regards the story the chief direction which I am pursuing at this moment is increase in comedy and human interest value. The adventure and thrill part of it is already in the bag."

It's All True was a title registered on July 29, 1941—yet it was then a long way from the largely aborted project that goes by the same title, and that was revived and recovered in 1993 as the sketch of an uncompleted project. At first, it was intended as a very ambitious four-part movie, a collection of stories or pieces of material which all had a basis in fact. The pieces were as follows: a history of jazz, based on the lives of Louis Armstrong and/or Duke Ellington; *Love Story*, the novelist John Fante's account of how his parents had fallen in love; *My Friend Bonito*, about a Mexican boy and the bull he befriends, to be adapted by Fante and Norman Foster from a story by the great documentarian Robert Flaherty; and *The Captain's Chair,* another Flaherty story, set in the Arctic.

In July, Welles was seeking contracts at RKO for Ellington, Armstrong and Flaherty, and he was telling the studio that Gregg Toland had agreed to be his photographer, on a further leave of absence from Goldwyn. He also called for a regular budgeted position for his general assistant, Richard Wilson.

There had never been a Hollywood studio picture made in the form of this *It's All True*—there never has been yet. Still, early in September, Welles and his chosen director, Norman Foster, visited Mexico to look for locations for *My Friend Bonito*. By the end of the month, Foster had begun filming, with Alfred Gilks as his cameraman. There were many difficulties straightaway on what seemed a recklessly hasty venture. Foster found that easy promises were "now said to be impossible, with that peculiar shrug and smile that mean: 'Ya really didn't believe you could, did ya?' "

He had difficulty finding, and keeping, actors. The bullfighting authorities were very superstitious about allowing the major parts of their art to be photographed. There was too little film, and the cameras were slow in arriving. But the Mexican cameraman, Alex Phillips, had agreed to help Gilks, and Foster was as cheerful as possible: "I miss you very much, Orson, and wish you could be here to do this picture which I know will be very interesting, despite the grief."

Foster was not that far away. He was based in Aguascalientes and had been able to listen in on the radio to the second of a new series, *The Orson Welles Show*, which was also done as an almanac—a series of stories or items, with Welles and the voice of Jiminy Cricket as hosts. Foster was especially struck by "Golden Honeymoon," a Ring Lardner story in which Orson played opposite Ruth Gordon. The radio show was a weekly chore all through the winter of 1941–42, which means that Welles was supervising, directing and appearing in a show that ran from adapted stories and readings of the Song of Solomon and Poe's "Annabel Lee" by Welles himself to a complete play, *The Hitch Hiker*, written by Lucille Fletcher (then the wife of Bernard Herrmann), and another production of *A Farewell to Arms*, in which Welles was Frederic Henry and Ginger Rogers was Catherine Barkley.

It's a wonder that Dolores Del Rio ever saw him. Yet she said they would be married once her divorce was through. So they might have been but for the fact, late in the year, that on the *Orson Welles Show* production of a story called *There Are Frenchmen and Frenchmen* one of the other players was an eye-catching actress named Rita Hayworth.

And all of these sundries occurred as Welles made the most direct, realistic and tragic movie he would ever make, a movie some like more than *Kane*, and a project Welles surely aimed at the audience that preferred stories about families, romance, and mothers and sons—*The Magnificent Ambersons*.

14

In Spiritual Civilization

WELLES KNEW *The Magnificent Ambersons* as a book. He could believe that the novel described the midwestern social context that had made him. He was touched by the idea of a family's decline, of an age of elegance ruined by the automobile and of a spoiled young man who would not allow his widowed mother another chance at love.

There was a notion in Welles's scheme of the past that his father and Booth Tarkington had been acquaintances, and that Tarkington might even have remembered Richard Welles in creating the character of Eugene Morgan, a man who invents motorcars but feels foreboding about how they may destroy the grace of the world. A great deal of Welles's heart lies in *Ambersons*, and it is a heart that is conventional, nostalgic, romantic and innately conservative. He was, in his own life, famous and feared as an innovator, a man of new techniques and approaches, an example of startling youth sweeping aside the past. That view was widely held, but it was one he never understood. So he was bewildered that so few recognized his fondness for the spirit of the past. Indeed, that past— glowing, perhaps mythic and certainly impossible—was his best corrective to the despair he felt about progress and purpose. So, after *Kane* he backed off into the past. He was a little like the Kane who, on that night he met Susan Alexander, was planning to go to the Western Manhattan Warehouse, where his mother's possessions were stored—as he said, "in search of my youth."

Not that he believed there was solace or rescue there. On the contrary, the journey back served only to deepen and sustain despair. *Ambersons* would prove a killing wound, and its story is so dark and mournful that it would not be shown properly to the American public. If we compare *The Magnificent Ambersons* with a film made two years later, *Meet Me in St. Louis*, we can see how the Vincente Minnelli musical truly cherished the past, its style and the provincial fears that wanted to abide there forever. The Smith family in that St. Louis decide against the big adventure of New York, change and taking a chance. They are left in the false comfort that their treasured past will go on forever—always with a young, auburn-haired Judy Garland alive with song and hope. *Meet Me in St. Louis* is one of the loveliest American dreams ever filmed.

Ambersons does not have as many songs; it lacks color or children. Yet the two films are alike in period, in their midwestern setting, in the places romance and progress fill in their plots. There are enchanted occasions in *Ambersons*—the ball and the ride in the snow—but they pass. The family declines. People die. The values fade. There is no holding on to home. And the story's romantic hero, Eugene, is the inadvertent destroyer, the man who ushers in the drab future. He is, in the novel and the film, an insolubly divided man—like the two Kanes. But we may hear Welles's wistfulness about that calm past in Eugene's big speech at the dinner table after the callow, aggressive George has attacked automobiles. This is from the novel, but we can hear Joseph Cotten's sad, gracious kindness from the movie when it is a scene that lets us know, gently, how few American movies have bothered with the nation's history:

> I'm not sure he's wrong about automobiles. With all
> their speed forward they may be a step backward in
> civilization—that is, in spiritual civilization. It may be
> that they will not add to the beauty of the world, nor to
> the life of men's souls. I am not sure. But automobiles
> have come, and they bring a greater change in our life
> than most of us suspect. They are here, and almost all
> outward things are going to be different because of
> what they bring. They are going to alter war, and they
> are going to alter peace. I think men's minds are going
> to be changed in subtle ways because of automobiles;
> just how, though, I could hardly guess. But you can't
> have the immense outward changes that they will cause
> without some inward ones, and it may be that George is
> right, and that the spiritual alterations will be bad for
> us. Perhaps, ten or twenty years from now, if we can see
> the inward change in man by that time, I shouldn't be
> able to defend the gasoline engine, but would have to
> agree with him that automobiles "had no business to be
> invented."

The studio accepted *Ambersons* as a picture project in the summer of 1941. Welles persuaded George Schaefer by playing him the 1939 recording of the *Mercury Theatre on the Air* version (in which he had taken the part of George). Schaefer agreed, and the new contract (July 7, 1941) called for *Ambersons* and *Journey into Fear.* It was settled then and there that Welles could produce, direct and write *Ambersons.* In turn, RKO would have to approve the script, the cast and the budget; and it had the right of final cut. This picture would be made along regular industrial lines. Using King Vidor's yacht, Welles and his script assistant Amalia Kent sailed off to Catalina Island late in July. He fashioned a script— using the radio script as a basis and staying very faithful to the novel. Kent then turned that into a shooting script.

Some—Robert Carringer, for one—have argued that the movie of *Ambersons* had problems from the outset just because Welles was in sole charge of script decisions. Carringer says that the script develops into "a succession of dialogue set pieces." The scenes are of an unvaried emotional incandescence, yet they feel disconnected. There is some truth in those charges, and it is easy to conclude that Welles lacked the sinuous structural skills at which Mankiewicz excelled. This does feel less like a movie—but suppose Welles wanted the force of a novel, unrestricted by film's quickness, ease and charm. Of course, all we can now see is a film that was recut, against the letter and spirit of Welles's intent. But anyone should note that Welles's script added a lengthy final sequence that is not in Tarkington's novel. We have that scene in script form and in a few stills, and it may be among the finest passages ever filmed in America. It is not in the picture we have (or are ever likely to have). But it is possible to read the script Welles wanted and feel—or imagine—the power there might have been. So I would rather say that, yes, *Ambersons* is a less inventive and fluent script than *Kane;* and yes it may show the start of a significant handicap in Welles as a writer. But *Ambersons* had the script it needed, and sometimes a script is the better for lacking brilliance and dazzling structural virtuosity.

In other words, let us suppose that Welles knew what he was doing. It is in that light, I think, that we need to assess his decision not to play George. He was only twenty-six when the film was shot, and he could seem younger. His weight by then was a problem: this George could have seemed a hulk, a spoiled boy bloated by strawberry shortcake and close to a physical monster, too large or out of the ordinary for the house. Moreover, Welles could not have kept his charm and worldliness out of the picture. He would have seemed like the potential seducer not just of Lucy Morgan but of his own mother. How could that George stay quiet and rebuked by Eugene's speech about the automobile—when that George had so lately been the boss to Cotten's Leland? Welles as George would have been too much, too large for the real family life, and too dynamic to seem helpless in failure. Tim Holt was suitably blunt, brutish, limited, dense and ordinary. In absenting himself—and RKO always wanted him to do everything—Welles was making it clear that in *Ambersons* he preferred to keep faith with the novelistic affection for natural, humble, unexceptional people.

Schaefer was at pains to impress upon Welles the need for a hit, as well as a more conventional picture, this time. But, as so often in Hollywood, the boss seems to have been incapable of imagining the script on the screen. He trusted the popularity of the book and the effectiveness of the radio play. He saw a story that began at the beginning and advanced on to its conclusion. He felt the realities of love, society and family—and he could discover no one in power being attacked. He apparently never gauged the depth of tragedy in the script or the issue that had hurt *Kane*— that the audiences were not bound to identify with any character in particular. Rather, they were expected to observe the passage from dark to light, from magnificence to the grim. This was heresy for Hollywood, but still Schaefer gave his approval.

The one thing that troubled him was the potential cost. The budget was reckoned to be nearly $1 million for the basic reason that Welles was calling for large, very detailed sets—inside and outside. He wanted the scope and texture of the growing midwest town, and he wanted the claustrophobic density of the interiors. There were several sequences in which action moved from one room to another, and there was even a passage toward the end where George was meant to walk through most of the empty mansion, absorbing the family's decline. A whole city street had to be built. There was an elaborate ball sequence that called for a sense of deep focus and continuous action. Above all, Welles wanted the illusion of being a part of that time and place—and he wanted it real. That pressure on budget was likely to be exacerbated by the loss of Gregg Toland and Perry Ferguson.

There had been talk of Toland staying on, but he went back to Goldwyn and took Ferguson with him. Thus, at a stroke, Welles lost the team that had given him such power over physical reality. In their place, he was assigned Mark-Lee Kirk as art director. The Mercury unit was now based at premises RKO rented in Culver City on the Selznick lot. It was there that Welles saw material shot for tests by Stanley Cortez, who had so far photographed nothing but B pictures. Welles decided to take him on.

The picture was cast as well as any film Welles would ever make: Joseph Cotten, never better, as Eugene; Tim Holt, a superb piece of instinctive casting, as George; the faded, anxious-looking Dolores Costello as Isabel (she had been John Barrymore's wife); the eighteen-year-old Anne Baxter as Lucy (she had just done *Swamp Water* for Jean Renoir, and she had only narrowly lost the lead role to Joan Fontaine in the Selznick-Hitchcock *Rebecca*); Agnes Moorehead as Fanny; Ray Collins as Jack; Richard Bennett as Major Amberson. To make a good thing better, Welles assembled the cast early for several weeks of rehearsal—yet another sign of his wish to reach an ingrained familiarity in the group's playing, and of his realization that *Ambersons* depended on profound emotional reality.

The budget was reduced, on paper, to about $850,000—enough to win Schaefer's approval—though as events proved, the numbers were being played with. Not everyone at RKO was as generous as Schaefer or as convinced of Welles's dedication. The executive assistant, Reginald Ar-

The Magnificent Ambersons: Major Amberson (Richard Bennett), Aunt Fanny (Agnes Moorehead), George (Tim Holt) and Uncle Jack (Ray Collins)

mour, was suspicious. Early in October, he had to approve money for Welles and a replacement cameraman to go down to Mexico to visit the *Bonito* set. Al Gilks had been drafted for military service, so Floyd Crosby was his replacement. Welles was going down to approve some new locations and supervise some key sequences. What about the *Ambersons* rehearsals? asked Armour. Richard Wilson was to supervise them, according to Welles's instructions. Armour said that the most recent budget—$853,000—was very worrying. He hinted that this could prove a matter beyond Schaefer's decision.

Welles went to Mexico. Rehearsal continued under Wilson's guidance. *Ambersons* does not suffer for lack of rehearsal, though it was damned eventually for costing so much. *Bonito* was never finished. What survives of it is hardly worthy of Welles. The sidetrip to Mexico may have seemed at the time just one more proof of Welles's energy and his desire to be doing anything. But in hindsight it looks like an omen for enthusiasm smothering judgment.

15

Time for Everything?

S H O O T I N G O N *The Magnificent Ambersons* began on October 28. In the course of rehearsals, Welles had made a high-quality recording of all the dialogue—again, we can see the creative influence of radio in his approach. He even went so far as to play the recording as scenes were shot: he thought this would be a great economy, permitting more studio noise in the shooting of long, complicated takes. (The soundstages he was using at the Selznick lot had old floorboards that often creaked under the tracking camera he preferred.) But the actors were uncomfortable with this method; they found it at odds with the psychological intimacy Welles sought. So, in general, the playback sound was abandoned—though it was used in a few places (the ball scene and the drive in the snow) where the variety of noises was ruining clear dialogue recording.

Still, do not underestimate the effect on the actors—of living on those sets in the huge soundstages—as the voices of the story boomed and whispered in the darkness above them. *The Magnificent Ambersons* concerns a haunted house, after all.

The scene in which a sleigh ride in the snow gives way to the new automobile was done entirely on sets. But because Welles was determined on the feeling of real cold, all of it was shot at an icehouse in downtown Los Angeles. The temperature presented many problems: lights blew out; there was a disconcerting stink of fish; the icehouse had few other facilities suitable for cast and crew. But the actors' breath showed. That much seemed authentic, though the sequence as a whole has the enchanted, preserved air of a Christmas card landscape. Its deepest feeling is dreamlike. Ray Collins got pneumonia. Joseph Cotten made cocktails to warm everyone up toward the end of each day. And once Welles was so encouraged by the liquor that he begged a ride home with Anne Baxter and proceeded to maul her. At Sunset, she threw him and her torn bra out of the car.

No one was under more pressure than Stanley Cortez. He had been hired on at the last moment, without preparation, and he could only feel the burden of following Gregg Toland. Cortez never got on with Welles as Toland had. He had a lofty manner, and he chose to talk about scenes in painterly language, an attitude Welles found pretentious. Not that this gulf shows in the film. *The Magnificent Ambersons* has a textural beauty beyond even that of *Kane*, a kind of nostalgic gravity that embodies Tarkington's and Welles's attitude to the lost past. There is a dark, mourning look, like the black silk of funerals. In the big scenes in the house, where action flows from one room or level to another, Cortez did wonders with deep space and dark, embalming shadow. With the great test of the scene in which George wanders through the forsaken mansion, the camera tracking from room to room, he apparently came through a champion, as Welles gave orders for walls to be slipped away, allowing the camera entrance room. You have only to look at *Ambersons* to feel a cameraman of genius—and the same kind of work is evident in several later films by Cortez: Selznick's *Since You Went Away*; Fritz Lang's *Secret Beyond the Door*; Charles Laughton's *The Night of the Hunter*; *The Three Faces of Eve*; and *Shock Corridor* and *The Naked Kiss*, both by Samuel Fuller.

Cortez would earn an Academy Award nomination for *Ambersons*—as Toland had for *Kane*—but he never won Welles's affection. For Cortez labored after his effects. To Welles, he seemed horribly slow—whereas Toland had had the gift of getting what Welles wanted in no more time than it took to run the actors through a scene. *Ambersons* went fourteen days over schedule, and before the conclusion, Welles had dropped Cortez in frustration and was using Harry Wild in his place. When all was done, the costs on *Ambersons* had risen to $1.013 million. George Schaefer saw some footage a month into the shooting and was enthusiastic about it, but the budget had surpassed the level RKO had agreed to with their banks.

That said, the film that survives has moments of unsurpassed glory in which the inventiveness of *Kane* is given a more naturalistic grounding: the thundery night on which George stuffs himself with strawberry short-cake while Aunt Fanny quietly breaks down; the long dolly shot down the town's main street; its corollary, the tracking shot along built-up streets defaced by telegraph wires—apparently photographed by Welles himself in odd corners of Los Angeles; the varied moods and pacing of the opening montage, in which Welles's slumberous narrative voice hearkens back to a jeweled moment:

> The magnificence of the Ambersons began in 1873.*
> Their splendor lasted throughout all the years that saw
> their Midland town spread and darken into a city. . . .
>   In those days, they had time for everything—time
> for sleigh rides and balls, and assemblies and cotillions,
> and open house on New Year's and all-day picnics in the
> woods.

Then there is the enchanted moment at which the pace slows on a dissolve from day to night and the mansion becomes the site of a great ball. There is Ray Collins as Uncle Jack, a man in late middle age, running off into the immensity of a railway depot to catch a train and begin a working life; there is the sadness of Cotten, the weakness of Costello, the dogged limits of Holt, the electric youth of Baxter, everything that concerns Moorehead.

And Richard Bennett. Bennett was sixty-eight at the time, silver haired, his memory shot. He had been a matinee idol at the turn of the century, and he had made many movies. Welles said, "[He] had the greatest lyric power of any actor I ever saw." He found Bennett during the writing period, living in a little boardinghouse on Catalina Island, a has-been. He brought him back to be Major Amberson, treated him with love and respect, and gave him an epiphany, the scene in which the dying Major stares into the fire and tries to organize his scattered thoughts on what life is and where it comes from. This scene is in the book, but it is far more affecting in the movie because of its brevity, because of the image—the old white face, in darkness, illuminated by a flickering fire

---

* Eighteen seventy-three was just two years after Walter Thatcher went to Colorado to collect Charlie Kane—and it was the year that Welles's father was born, in St. Joseph, Missouri, when that town was the frontier and the stepping-off place for wagon trains going west.

that mimics the sun he talks about—and because of Bennett's face, and his bond with Welles. Bennett could never recollect the lines. So Welles read them to him, off camera, and Bennett repeated them. How Welles adored and worshiped old age and the somber luster of people at their own close. There is nothing more moving in American film than the face of the Major and his halting words:

> It must be the sun. . . . There wasn't anything here ex-
> cept the sun in the first place. . . . The sun. . . . Earth
> came out of the sun. We came out of the Earth. . . . So,
> whatever we are . . .

The picture was dark, but spirits were high. Mercury had a group of bungalows on the lot in Culver City. Welles had his own steam room, as well as a masseur. He had his private cook, who made lunches for everyone: hamburgers, several inches thick, made from fat-free sirloin, and homemade tapioca pudding. Then he would hold court, sitting at his ease, telling gorgeous stories about himself. He was like a prince, or some visitor from his own resplendent past, just passing through Hollywood. He never seemed like a resident.

While they were still shooting, on December 7, Japanese actions in Hawaii ensured America's entry into the war. Welles was on the radio that very evening, and he spoke out—as everyone was doing:

> Ladies and gentlemen, as we all know, our country has
> answered a vicious and an unprovoked attack by declar-
> ing war on Japan. This is a time for energetic and
> unashamed patriotism on the part of all of us: I know we
> all agree to that because I know that none of us will be
> satisfied with anything but complete victory.

War accelerated many energies, including that of the Office of Inter-American Affairs, a vaguely defined entity meant to foster feelings of allied goodwill in the Americas as war became more likely. Late in 1940, President Roosevelt had asked Nelson Rockefeller to head the office. In turn, Rockefeller had asked Jock Whitney to join him. Whitney, very rich, was a social figure whose partnership with David O. Selznick had led to the movie of *Gone With the Wind*. Together, Rockefeller and Whitney took an interest in the movie division of the office, promoting American films in South America and doing their best to establish as much mutual understanding as might help in the war effort.

It was diplomatic and bureaucratic hogwash that led to little more than the making at Disney of *Saludos Amigos*, in which Donald Duck visited Rio de Janeiro. The Office of Inter-American Affairs had one other coup, and disaster—*It's All True*. That background should be stressed as a corrective to Welles's subsequent plea that he was approached personally by Jock Whitney to donate himself to vital government work—so what could he have done? He could have refused. He could have discussed and finessed the matter until it went away. There was absolutely no compelling, external reason why he had to become involved with the office, or let it interfere with his other plans.

But Welles went much further. He took the initiative. Whitney and Rockefeller had thought of nothing more than a few broadcasts, and perhaps a lecture tour in South America—at his convenience. It was Welles who blew up the balloon. He began to talk about a film, a reappraised version of *It's All True*, in which the original four episodes would eventually come down to three. But one of the original four—*My Friend Bonito*, which was hanging over him, largely filmed and pretty bad—could become the first of the three, because of its Mexican setting. The three sections of the film were to be *My Friend Bonito*, a celebration of carnival and a re-creation of a famous event in recent Brazilian history: in 1941, four fishermen from Fortaleza, the *jangadeiros*, had sailed 1,600 miles south to Rio to demonstrate their wretched working conditions.

This bold, romantic plan came from no one but Welles. Though he would later protest that he loathed the idea of carnival, it was he who pledged that he would be in Rio by mid-February, when the carnival took place, for surely that had to be a set piece for the movie. The government put no money into the venture. RKO was to pay for *It's All True*. And when it ran into troubles, neither Rockefeller nor Whitney could do anything to help. The cause of duty was Welles's fabrication, covering his barely considered feeling that it might be fun to go to South America. He assumed he could finish *Ambersons* in time. He may have been happy to get away from a Dolores Del Rio who was talking of marriage, especially if the journey might avail him of more ladies as lovely as Del Rio but younger.

Let us add that he was moved by the state of war and wanted to do something. Welles admired FDR far more slavishly than the author of *Citizen Kane* had any right to esteem a political leader. He had avoided military service—and he had worked hard to avoid it. So as an excused soldier he may have felt guilty and all the more anxious to be of assistance. Grant also that he was bored where he was, and ready for something new. But then consider the rare quality of *The Magnificent Ambersons* and see how perilously he gambled with it.

By early January, as plans for Rio muddled along, it must have been clear to Welles how good *Ambersons* was; he said later that it was superior to *Kane*. But the schedule had gone over. Shooting did not end until January 22, and there was then another week of retakes. The editor, Robert Wise, and his assistant, Mark Robson, were already assembling the picture, but it was plain that Welles had to leave Los Angeles around February 1. The fine editing and the postproduction—vital to tone and atmosphere—would have to go on without him. He declared that he trusted Wise and his new manager, Jack Moss, to take care of things.

He must have been excited to take the chance; he needed an odd mixture of credulity and rebelliousness to trust a studio that had mounting reasons for doubting him. Above all, we should note that he was determined to go. The nominations were in for the Academy Awards: *Citizen Kane* was up for best picture; Welles for best director and best actor; Welles and Mankiewicz for best original screenplay; in addition, there were nominations for cinematography, music, art direction, editing and sound. The film had nine nominations, one fewer than John Ford's *How Green Was My Valley*. But *Kane* had already swept the New York critics' awards. The Oscars would be given out on February 26, and one would have thought that RKO would want Welles available for a big promotional campaign. But they let him go.

On the night of February 1, Welles signed off on his last radio show for some while: "Tomorrow night the Mercury Theatre starts for South America. The reason, put more or less officially, is that I've been asked by the Office of the Coordinator of Inter-American Affairs to do a motion picture especially for Americans in all the Americas."

He flew to Washington for instructions—no one there, or at RKO, had the least idea what he was going to do. Then he went on to Miami

and worked furiously with Wise for seventy-two hours in a hired cutting room to get as much of *Ambersons* edited as possible. The plan thereafter was that duplicate footage would be sent to Rio and that Wise would join him there for consultations. On that basis, Welles left a dark, immaculate, fatalistic film, but not before his bosses had insisted on two documents. He had to sign the new contract that gave the studio final cut. Also, while at Miami Airport on February 6, waiting for transport to Rio, he dictated a wire to the RKO authorities. It was sent off under the signature of his manager, Jack Moss, and it made clear that, in view of all the work still to be done on *Ambersons*, Welles was anxious that Wise be given "the final word." It was as if Welles believed he had the authority of Kane, that a wire would be honored. Whereas no one asked to sign those papers should have been rash enough to leave.

16

⟶ *Trouble Pictures* ⟵

R I O D E J A N E I R O and Los Angeles are about 3,500 miles apart as the crow flies—and any crow so inclined could make the journey going over land all the way. Aircraft were more considered and cautious. In America—despite the rhetoric of Nelson Rockefeller and Jock Whitney—it was believed that Rio de Janeiro was beyond simple distance. It was another kind of place. Communication might be achieved, by cable or by telephone, but with an uncertainty increased by the fact that, at 6:00 p.m., say, in Los Angeles, at the end of a working day, it was midnight in Rio. At midnight in that city—despite his declared aversion to music, dance, eating, drinking and beautiful women (the elements of carnival)—Orson Welles was not easily found. RKO believed he had gone on the lam; this was the last straw of irresponsibility. He came to the conclusion that they were cutting him out, plotting behind his back.

When Welles went from Los Angeles to Miami, the trip (with stops in Fort Worth and Nashville) took twenty-one hours. Then the Pan-American Clipper from Miami to Rio took another thirty-three hours. But eventually Welles came to rest at the Palace Hotel in Rio, in charge of a crew of twenty-five people, including camera and lighting men (for black-and-white and Technicolor), sound technicians, publicity people and Augusta Weissberger as his secretary. Tom Petty, an advance publicity man, found torrid weather and a Brazilian imagination avid for Welles. He reported, "This is an expensive town. New York prices on everything and much higher on imports. The English, she is not spoken very much. But my Spanish? She gets me by O.K." Welles on his Clipper flight was struggling to master traditional Portuguese.

Between February 13 and 17, with Joseph Biroc as camera operator but with insufficient lights (they had not all arrived yet), Welles did what he could to start and keep up with the carnival. At different times, he gave varying accounts of this experience. The footage he shot was voluminous and unorganized. There was nothing like a script and—until the experience itself—very little notion on any of the Americans' parts as to what carnival was or might become in a documentary film. Thus, the widespread RKO reaction at the time—that they were being deluged in endless footage of "jigaboos" jumping up and down—was as understandable as it was conventionally racist. The first footage had no synced sound, so

Welles arrives in
northeast Brazil.

there was not even the pulse of the music—something that had begun to make its impression on Welles. The studio was also seeing two things that may have come as news to Rockefeller and Whitney: that there were plenty of black people in Brazil, and that they often danced with whites. There was only so much Inter-American understanding the United States could take.

Whatever he had anticipated, Welles was having a very good time. Among Americans of his era, he was uncommonly relaxed with blacks and genuinely appreciative of black women, especially those who embraced the libertarian attitudes of carnival. Welles and the men on his crew— rather like the *Bounty*'s crew in Tahiti—discovered that lovely, young Brazilian women felt honored to have American attention.

Welles was active on all fronts, and at all times of day. He was seldom available or locatable after dark. But on February 25, he wrote to Rockefeller, thanking him "for this rare and beautiful opportunity." He was amazed at the friendliness everywhere; he was doing broadcasts in his inept Portuguese, and he was heavily into lectures and forums. He had also hobnobbed with Medare Vargas, the wife of the president, and, he had offered himself to her and her social circle as a versatile and willing entertainer with a secret weapon for the war effort: "magic speaks a universal language, it may prove useful for benefits and the like."

Rio had so taken his fancy that he cabled to George Schaefer suggesting that the world premiere of *Ambersons* be there. Schaefer still had no objection, though he was determined that the picture should open in America on Easter weekend. An answer print of the film—that is, its final form—was due in Rio on March 15, and Schaefer proposed that that print be used there.

But in Los Angeles, before then, the Oscars were awarded. There was a fierce atmosphere against Welles: in the early stages of the evening, mention of his name led to hisses. The business as a whole had been reassured by *Kane*'s commercial failure, and many regarded the film as so willfully dark and obscure as to be impenetrable. Welles had carried himself in town like an outsider and a figure of taunting superiority. He did not bother to honor the questionable myth of team spirit, and he had radically outstripped the notions of what kind of film could be made in Hollywood. How violently un-Hollywood it was to go off to Rio de Janeiro—as if he were Eleanor Roosevelt! He had no constituency in the town. He had paid no dues. He needed rebuke, if only because of that monstrous contract. It was always likely that the Oscars would crush his picture.

He lost as director and actor. Bernard Herrmann won for music, but for another film, *All That Money Can Buy*. Gregg Toland lost to Arthur Miller, who had photographed John Ford's *How Green Was My Valley*, which won for best picture and best director. It is an antique, sentimental picture, founded on emotional identification: it believes in order and reasoning and in pathos surviving hard times. It does not begin to understand the world or the despair of *Citizen Kane*. But there was one Oscar for Welles, to be shared with Herman Mankiewicz. Neither of them was there to receive it, but the award was read as an affirmation of Mankiewicz, the harshly treated professional—many had heard that Welles had sought to deny him credit.

Meanwhile, the editing on *Ambersons* was proceeding efficiently, and along the lines Welles had laid down in Miami. A print was sent to Rio, though it's not clear whether Welles was able to see it before he had a cable from Wise saying that George Schaefer had suddenly called for a screening for himself and Charles Koerner, another RKO executive. Wise ran the film for them on March 16, and Schaefer said he felt it was too long—it ran two hours and twelve minutes at that point, and, as far as can be established, it was the picture Welles wanted.

Cy Endfield attended that studio screening. He was a Yale graduate with some experience in the theater who had gone to Hollywood looking for movie work. Endfield happened to be an accomplished magician, and he'd used to haunt Wheeler's Magic Shop on Hollywood Boulevard. One day, Welles had come in, to see what was new, and Endfield had amazed him with a few card tricks. Welles had brandished hundred-dollar bills, trying to buy the secret to the tricks. Instead, Endfield bargained for a job. He was a huge admirer of *Kane*, though it galled him to find that he was six months older than Welles. But *Ambersons*, in that first cut, impressed him even more: "It was a picture done like music, so smooth, the choreography of camera and actors so beautiful. It was the best I'd ever seen. But I also knew it was boring other people. It didn't hold them. We came out, and Jack Moss said, 'We've got a problem.' "

Schaefer gave orders for a sneak preview the next day, March 17, at the Fox Theater in Pomona; it was shown after *The Fleet's In*, a Dorothy Lamour musical that had a number of good songs. The response was far too mixed for Schaefer's nerves (for surely he knew by then of moves within RKO to have him replaced—and Charles Koerner was a likely new man): seventy-two unfavorable cards and fifty-three positive. Hollywood previews are often a way of finding evidence to support opinions formed in advance. Some of the comments from Pomona are brutal and some touching: it was as if the Fox that night had gathered a cross section of all the opinions Orson Welles would ever inspire. Even the favorable responses felt themselves at odds with the crowd:

> We do not need trouble pictures, especially now. . . .
> Make pictures to make us forget, not remember.

> This picture is magnificent. The direction, acting, photography, and special effects are the best cinema has yet offered. It is unfortunate that the American public, as represented at this theatre, are unable to appreciate fine art.

> People like to laff, not be bored to death.

> The picture was a masterpiece with perfect photography, settings and acting. It seemed too deep for the average stupid person. I was disgusted with the way some people received this picture.

Two days later, RKO had another preview in Pasadena. By then, the picture was seventeen minutes shorter. Reactions were more favorable, but the studio elected to be more affected by the first reactions. The three people Welles most relied on—Wise, the editor; his manager, Jack Moss; and Joseph Cotten—all wrote to him to the effect that the picture was too slow and too dark. Moss sent a list of suggested cuts. Wise wrote a detailed, yet rather cool, report on audience reaction. He concluded,

> At Pomona we got a big hand and what seemed to be a sigh of relief on your line "That's the end of the story." At both previews there were too many people who walked out all during the show. This can be attributed, I think, to the great length and slow pace. The picture does seem to bear down on people.

Cotten's letter was warmer and more troubled. He admitted that Welles was his better in most matters of theatrical judgment. The screening had begun well, with an eager audience. But, "it happened gradually and awfully and the feeling in that theatre became disinterested, almost hostile and as cold as that icehouse they had just seen and my heart as heavy as the heart of Major Amberson who was playing wonderful scenes that nobody cared about."

Jack Moss said he was doing everything possible to have Wise sent to Rio so that he and Welles could work together. But the studio said there was a ban on civilian flying—so much for liaison with the government. Welles felt helpless without audience reactions. Suppose his friends were right, or close enough to be heeded? Suppose the studio had turned against him?

There were so many reasons for going back, for losing his temper and exerting his great skills in editing and retakes. After all, what was at stake was one of the greatest films ever made, even if it was his own second best. In Rio, the carnival was over; all he was doing was restaging parts of it for the camera, trying to discover a film, yet admitting—like Kane on the verge of the governorship—"If I attempt to outline to you my plans in detail, it will do nothing more than disclose how little I really know about what I'm doing."

In Culver City, Endfield asked Moss one day, "Why doesn't Orson come back?" "You want to know?" said Moss. He put some of the Rio footage on a Moviola: it was a scene shot live in a nightclub of chorus girls in skimpy clothes. Moss had visited Welles in Rio once, the day they filmed that scene. "So he took me aside," said Moss, "and he said, 'I've fucked that one . . . and that one . . . and that one.' He's not coming back. There's no place in the world he can do what he's doing there."

Welles had moved out of the Palace Hotel and into an apartment. He was spending more time in the small clubs in the favela district—the slums—listening to samba music. He had been on one research trip to the north of the country to choose locations for the *jangadeiro* story. But he was not really doing much except compose lengthy cables proposing and instructing on cuts and new scenes for *Ambersons*.

In Los Angeles, some new scenes were shot, with Wise or Freddie Fleck directing. Some of these were at Welles's suggestion, but others were taken out of his hands. The telephone was hopeless. Welles was often not by the phone when calls came. Moss had a line in the Mercury office that Welles could use for direct calls. And Moss would sit there hours on end, taking notes on recutting. The thirty- or forty-page cables would follow. Sometimes the phone would ring and ring, and Moss would ignore it. Some of the cables were thrown in the garbage, unread. The cutting went on, and there were battles over many scenes. Endfield fought tooth and nail one day to save the strawberry shortcake scene.

The Easter opening was missed. Schaefer's power was weakening. There were reports from some of the Rio crew—and RKO had always planted informers in Welles's crews—that the director was wasting time and money in Brazil and getting nowhere. Reginald Armour was beginning to impose limits on the Rio shooting. Welles had in mind a sequence at the Urca Casino that was stopped. He was also being criticized by Brazilian authorities for his enthusiasm for the favelas. The government did not want the slums shown. Gangs tried to break up the shooting in those areas.

By April 20, RKO had devised and shot an entirely different ending for *Ambersons*, the pale rose finish we have now. Welles was doing a radio tribute to President Vargas on his birthday and visiting Buenos Aires to receive an award for *Kane*.

Suppose he had gone back, in dudgeon and fury—modes in which he excelled—to be followed by charm and brilliance. The results on-screen could not have been as bad as they turned out. Welles was the Mercury, for good and ill; his presence gave others confidence. Many noted that Jack Moss—a squat, ugly man—did a poor job challenging the studio. *Ambersons* was very likely doomed as a commercial enterprise—Welles had infused it with a darkness nothing could remove. But so much might have been saved . . . if he had not been so drawn to doom. Instead, he tried to impress Schaefer by volunteering to give up color for the *jangadeiros* sequence. By mid-April, Schaefer had lost patience.

He had spent four days trying to reach Orson by phone. Once the operator had thought she heard the great Orsonian voice booming through the static. But there had been no contact. Schaefer was bewildered and horrified that Welles's plans were so grandiose. Color had never been an option! The plans to rebuild the Urcas Casino were likely to cost $25,000. "At that rate," groaned Schaefer, "we will have another *Ambersons* situation on our hands." He was at the end of his tether and his illusions over Orson—"You have no realization of money you spend and how difficult it is to recoup."

Welles had lost his movie, but he had won a reputation.

17

❦ *That's His Story* ❦

I N   R I O, Welles had few allies save for Richard Wilson, his American secretary, Shifra Haran (flown in, but with very little to do), and Augusta Weissberger, whose chief task was to keep Welles supplied with good cigars. Apart from that, he was besieged by editing memos on *Ambersons*, mistrusted by the RKO head office, treated with growing suspicion by the Brazilian authorities and the press, and regarded with degrees of fear, loathing and contempt by his own crew. The genius, the inspiration of his own people, had sunk very low.

The Brazilian press could make no better sense of what Welles was doing than could RKO. There were those rumors that he was concentrating on the poorest and least promotable aspects of life in Rio. There was also plenty of evidence that the same events were being filmed over and over again. For many of the RKO crew, the Rio shoot had become not much more than a chore keeping them from home and family.

Tom Petty, the publicity man, was doing all he could to generate favorable press—in Rio and the United States—but, he wrote, "Orson is so badly spoiled by the publicity breaks he has had without having to put himself out that it is virtually impossible to get him to do things that might make news." Afraid of informers in his own unit, Welles was becoming more secretive and arbitrary—all of which, his enemies said, was cover for his not knowing what he was up to.

Prodigious amounts of film were being exposed—but there was no script to let anyone know how it worked in the whole. "I have a feeling," Petty wrote home, "that if all the film was laid end to end it would reach to the States and there would be enough left over to serve as a marker for the equator." As for Welles, Petty was feeling more and more helpless. Like most of the crew, he had started off in awe of the big kid and this adventurous vocation. But, all too soon, the bullshit factor had set in. On April 7, they were still shooting—or restaging—carnival, with hired extras playing with balloons and confetti. No one knew what these scenes were for, but Orson was staging them with all the grand agony of a genius giving a master class. Then there was his uncertain temper:

He has a cane bottomed rocking chair which is liable to
turn over at any moment, loose bowels and the disposi-
tion of a teething baby—that's in the mornings. After a
lunch of spaghetti, black beans and fresh cheese his
humor improves and he's pretty good company. By
nightfall he's ready for the Urca Casino. After midnight
he likes to write. Anyhow, that's his story.

One of his chief assistants, Lynn Shores, was in rebellion. He voiced
his dismay that the same scenes were being done over and over again, and
he was incredulous at the amount of time spent shooting blacks. He also
prepared daily shooting reports—which went back to RKO—that were
very critical of Welles, observing his lateness, his days away from the set
and the wholesale extravagance of the venture. The loyal Richard Wilson
said these reports were fraudulent, but it's plain from the words of others
that Welles was unpredictable and often not to be found. A kind of warfare existed between Welles and Shores—but the assistant was not removed. Shores was especially critical of plans to go north to film the story
of the *jangadeiros:* "He said very often that he didn't think there was a
story in the 'whole God damn thing,' and that nobody wanted to look at
'a bunch of niggers.'" There were rumors in Rio that RKO had decided
not to proceed with that episode.

Welles did make efforts to repair morale, but by early May, Petty
reported,

Relations between Welles and the crew are still bad.
There are days when it looks like everything is going to
be happy and then he will pull some sudden stunt such
as picking up a gal and vanishing in his car for hours or
getting in a row with the person nearest to him and
everything is bad for the rest of the day.

In Los Angeles, under the supervision of Jack Moss and Robert Wise,
The Magnificent Ambersons had come down to an eighty-eight-minute picture—it had lost forty-four minutes. There were further previews in In-
glewood and Long Beach. They were not satisfactory, but no one could
see room for further improvement. It was in the second part of the movie
that the changes had been most drastic. Among the losses was a scene of
George, Isabel and Fanny on the porch of the Amberson mansion at
night, just talking in the summer heat—nothing happens really, which is

surely why it was cut, but in the script and the stills that survive one may feel a novelistic deepening as we see people who live together but without real contact. The scene aches with the daily pain of boredom.

There was a conversation between Fanny, the Major and Jack that went, a talk that is played against the buzz of passing cars and that notes the onset of decline in the family fortune. The Major's speech after Isabel's death was shortened; Isabel's burial was omitted; the scene at the depot between George and Jack was abridged.

The "happy ending" was shot, with Eugene and Fanny in the hospital corridor, looking up toward the serene music, obliged to hope that a desperate swish of good feeling could redeem the mounting darkness of the picture. That stood in for Welles's own ending—something he added to the book—a scene in which Eugene visits Fanny. He has to go by way of streets crowded with traffic—the theme of the automobile maintained until the end—and he finds her a shabbier, more downcast figure, living in a boardinghouse crowded with other families and near-derelicts. They have difficulty getting a private place to talk. The scene is merciless, as tough a closing as any Hollywood film had ever attempted. We can only guess how good Agnes Moorehead must have been in it.

Eugene reports on visiting the hospital. He reckons that George and Lucy will marry. He tells Fanny that George did ask for forgiveness, and he says the line used in the happy ending—"It seemed to me as if someone else was in that room down there at the hospital. And that through me she had brought her boy under shelter again . . . that I'd been true at last to my true love."

But that scene we cannot see is played bleakly. Fanny hears, but she is unmoved. Her isolation is complete. There are dark shadows in the grim boardinghouse. Her rocking chair squeaks throughout the scene. Eugene drives away in his car. Fanny is left behind, a lost soul, with the failure of all romance etched in Moorehead's eyes. The past is closed off, and, over black leader, we were meant to hear, "Ladies and gentlemen, that's the end of the story," as simple and potent a line as Welles ever gave himself.

That film is gone forever. We were judged unworthy of it, too eager for "laff"'s and forgetfulness. That is, in some part, our fault, as well as RKO's. But it was Orson Welles's fault, too. And surely he knew it and lived with it as a comeuppance of his own contriving. Years later, he told Peter Bogdanovich what that ending had meant:

> If only you'd seen how [Moorehead] wrapped up the
> whole story at the end. . . . Joe Cotten goes to see her
> after all those years in a cheap boarding house and

there's nothing left between them at all. Everything is
over—her feelings and her world and his world; everything is buried under the parking lots and the cars.
That's what it was all about—the deterioration of personality, the way people diminish with age, and particularly in those days. But without question it was much
the best scene in the movie.

One week after the Long Beach preview of the shortened *Ambersons*,
Welles and his crew began shooting the *jangadeiros* story in Rio harbor.
His *jangadeiros* were the four fishermen from the northern coast of Brazil,
Fortaleza, who had sailed a simple raft all the way to Rio and become na-
tional heroes. Welles went to film their story—he saw it as "a super West-
ern of the sea"—with the original heroes playing themselves.

On May 19, an assistant, Leo Reisler, accompanied the four fishermen to the Fluminense Yacht Club in Rio to put their raft in the water
and prepare to shoot the scene of their triumphant arrival in Rio harbor.

With Jacaré

Welles was on the shore, trying to supervise. A camera crew was ready to film. But there were problems in working out a signaling system to the *jangadeiros*. Jacaré, the leader of the four, brought the raft in closer to shore to see the signals better. A tremendous breaker flipped the raft over, and Jacaré was drowned.

In June, with very little film stock and less support or interest from RKO, Welles, Richard Wilson, a cameraman, George Fanto, and two others went to Fortaleza to film the rest of the *jangadeiro* story. They found a replacement for Jacaré. They wrote in a love story—one of the fishermen marries on the eve of the voyage. They did get some financial compensation out of RKO for Jacaré's family. And they obtained a great deal of spectacular footage of the raft and its triangular sail on the dark ocean. For close-ups, they shot from a low angle at the raft balanced on a set of pulleys but set up on the land, with someone splashing water on the sailors from a bucket to simulate the sea.

In Hollywood, George Schaefer gave final approval to the eighty-eight-minute *Ambersons* and was replaced by Charles Koerner. The *It's All True* project, so far, had cost about a million dollars. On July 1, the remaining Mercury staff at RKO were told to leave their offices.

18

Poor Bastard

THE STUDIO'S VERSION OF *The Magnificent Ambersons* did not open until the height of summer. On July 10, at eighty-eight minutes, it played at two theaters in Los Angeles on a double bill with *Mexican Spitfire Sees a Ghost*, a seventy-minute Lupe Velez picture. There was no sense of event for this opening, but RKO ran some ads, and they commissioned artwork from Norman Rockwell in an attempt to lay claim to heartland themes. Still, they took it for granted that the picture was a write-off, for the final budget was $1.118 million.

Ambersons was not suited to the moment. America was in the war, summoning men, munitions and a positive attitude—there was nothing in *Ambersons'* America to fight for (except, maybe, the capacity to see so deep into the soul and the hinterland). The successful movies of 1942 included *Casablanca* and *Yankee Doodle Dandy*, *Pride of the Yankees* and *Mrs. Miniver.*

There were a few who recognized what Welles had done (and when the movie opened, no one seemed to realize the studio intrusions). James Agee was sure of its greatness. But in *The New York Times*, Bosley Crowther hammered home the unwelcome severity of the film: "With a world inflamed, nations shattered, populations in rags, with massacres and bombings, Welles devotes 9,000 feet of film to a spoiled brat who grows up as a spoiled, spiteful young man."

Several months later, as the Academy Awards were made for 1942, the surprise was the extent to which *Ambersons* was noted. It was nominated for best picture; there were also nominations for Agnes Moorehead, for Stanley Cortez and for Al Fields for set decoration. It won nothing. *Mrs. Miniver* was declared best picture. Acting in that movie, Teresa Wright beat Moorehead for the supporting actress Oscar. *Mrs. Miniver* won six Oscars, yet it cannot be seen today without some mixture of revulsion, hilarity and disbelief. Still, in 1942 and '43, that film helped send Americans to war with faith, anger and confidence. It is dangerous to expect too much of movies. *Ambersons* did little more than challenge the reliability of American progress and sentiment, so it suffered.

In Rio, there had been dismay after the death of Jacaré—there were even stories that some people had threatened Welles. Lynn Shores was now plainly in better contact with RKO in Los Angeles than Welles was. He was also gathering a black file on the director in case the studio felt the need to sue. The starred event in that file was an incident in June when Welles was seen hurling furniture and household items from his sixth-floor rented apartment. Was he drunk? Was he reacting to a request for back rent on the apartment? Was he showing friends how he had played Kane in the destruction of Susan Alexander's room? Or was he yet again consumed by the terrible mortified temper that had led him to hurl hot plates at Houseman?

The new regime did allow the small crew to go to Fortaleza, and much more footage was shot there. But then Welles proposed a new scene to RKO—an enormous pageant, with an estimated cost of $150,000. It must have been provocation—a way of ending the movie. So it worked out. The studio closed him down. They put out notices in Rio that they were no longer responsible for any debts he might incur. Though no one knew for sure yet, there was 465,000 feet of exposed film, and a bill in excess of $1.2 million. Shores said there was no way of making the footage into anything, because there was no script.

It was all Welles could do to get out of Rio with so many unpaid bills. But more than ten years later, in a BBC television program, he had composed himself sufficiently to turn humiliation into an anecdote. He was in Rio at the eleventh hour, he said, with an authentic voodoo witch doctor hired for some scene. But then his funds were cut off. The witch doctor was anxious—he had paid for new costumes. Alas, said Welles, there was no money for them. At that point, he was called away to the telephone, to talk to RKO, to beg for mercy and money. It was useless. When he came back the witch doctor had gone, but he had left a long steel needle that spiked the script for *It's All True* to the desk. A length of red wool was attached to the needle: "This was the mark of the voodoo— and the end of that story is it was the end of the film. We were never allowed to finish it."

That story was told in 1955, with teasing relish, and with a certain ironic fatalism that entertained the thought of a voodoo curse that had settled on him that summer of '42. But by then, his urge to tell charming stories was the real curse, or that effortless way of reordering the past so that responsibility and real damage were glossed over. That kind of storytelling began right away in '42, for it had Welles making his way back to unkind civilization by way of the Amazonian jungle, where he met a Jesuit priest who, a week earlier, had seen the bowdlerized *Ambersons* in Washington. He had loved it—but clearly it wasn't quite the film Welles had intended. Ah, the horror—or is this story a little closer to Evelyn Waugh's *A Handful of Dust*?

He went home by way of Mexico and reencountered Dolores Del Rio, who had called off their marriage in his absence. He did his best to rewarm the friendship, but she must have heard many stories—Welles had grown a small mustache in Brazil to be closer to the local image of macho. It was on the same journey that he chanced upon a back issue of *Life* in which he saw a dazzling pinup picture of Rita Hayworth kneeling on a bed. "*That's* what I'm going to do!" he said. For Orson Welles, this was an ambition like yachting for George Amberson.

I sat down and watched The Magnificent Ambersons—*I thought you were probably going to expect it of me.*

More than that, I expected you to do it without being asked. What did you think?

I was amazed—it sometimes had the effect of making me think that Booth Tarkington was Henry James. Whereas, when someone like Henry James is filmed, they manage to seem like . . .

Booth Tarkington?

Yes, perhaps that's it. But why?

A film can only compete with literature if it understands the powers it has that are denied to the page. Or some such thing. The film of *Ambersons* is graver than the novel. Grander. It leaves the book feeling a little spelled out.

Yes, like the strange scene between Eugene and his daughter—the Indian talk.

All in the book, you know. So much of the film is so faithful, it makes the extra quality of the film harder to explain.

Did Welles mean to refer to himself in that scene?

A moment, I must make sure the reader knows what we are talking about. Late in the film, there is a scene with Eugene and Lucy walking in a garden—a strange, haunted sort of garden.

Yes, and Lucy says, "Ever hear the Indian name for that little grove of beech trees?"

By the way, there's a story that when the scene was shown in dailies, and Anne Baxter looked off toward the hypothetical grove, everyone in the audience looked—the suggestion was so persuasive. Anyway, she tells a story about the Indians who called the grove "Loma-Nashah" or "They couldn't help it." There was a very bad Indian, Vendonah (Rides-down-everything). She tells her father that Vendonah was

> unspeakable. He was so proud he wore iron shoes and walked over people's faces. So at last the tribe decided that it wasn't a good enough excuse for him that he was young and inexperienced. He'd have to go. So they took him down to the river, put him in a canoe and pushed him out from the shore. The current carried him on down to the ocean. And he never got back. They didn't want to get him back of course. They hated Vendonah, but they weren't able to discover any other warrior they wanted to make chief in his place. They couldn't help feeling that way.

Now, I was very struck by that as I read your last few chapters, with the crosscutting from Los Angeles to South America, with Welles's almost willful contrivance of his own disaster, the canoe and Jacaré's raft. It seemed . . . to fit!

But Tarkington wrote that passage when Welles was just two or so, and the scene was in the script before Welles went to Rio.

Even so, it seems so true, so sinister, so predictive.

Like a strand of red wool.

I know, it's reading things into the film. But I feel bound to do that by your urging. For the whole tragedy of Ambersons *and* It's All True *is hardly explicable except in terms of Welles's arrogance, his gambling with fate, somehow.*

Magic trusts such things—and Welles was not exactly uncomfortable with the figures of exotic Indians.

So he might have—?

He could read and understand, read and see himself—he was a master adapter, remember.

So he did engineer his own defeat, his own comeuppance?

I don't know. I doubt he knew. I think those forces were deep down, things he felt in the way a swimmer feels a current and wonders about the danger.

But he let the film be ruined?

There is a story of another great Indian, a man of great art and accomplishment. He was known far and wide for his brilliance, but he grew uneasy, for he thought the people would be bored with perfect things. So he designed and built a ruined city—more than that, a lost city, one that could never quite be found again.

All that was premeditated?

Ambersons *is known and treasured now as a lost thing; that is its special resonance, its character. Suppose it had been finished—at two hours and twelve minutes—lovely, sad, perfect—would we think of it so much? Or do we especially treasure the things lost?*

Like the prodigal? I don't know if I can believe that.

Try forgetting it.

It's so . . . vain, and so wretched. He did that? The poor bastard.

As soon as you said that, I knew Welles better—it is the cure to that mocking assurance of his. He becomes human.

I feel I am being used.

Never lose that feeling. Let me tell you another story that could easily be called "Poor Bastard." A scorpion and a frog—

I've heard this one somewhere.

—meet at a riverbank. The scorpion says to the frog, "Will you carry me across the water?" But the frog says, "Oh no, for if I do that you will sting me and I will die." Whereupon the scorpion says, "Now where is the sense in that? For if I sting you as we cross the river I will surely die, too." The frog considers, and he sees the sense of the argument. So he takes the scorpion on his back and sets off to swim to the other side. But halfway across he feels a terrible pain in his back, and he knows that the scorpion has stung him. "Scorpion!" he cries out. "Where is the sense in that? For now I will die. But you will die, too." And, as they sink together, the scorpion says, "I know, but it is in my character."

Poor bastards. Where do we go from here?

Into the rest of his life.

I begin to fear for all of us.

Take this comfort: the scorpion and the frog avoid at least one thing—loneliness. They have each other.

Welles on the set of *The Magnificent Ambersons*

Welles in *Return to Glennascaul*, a small ghost story filmed in Ireland in 1952

Part Three

COMEUPPANCE
1942 – 58

"... these unlucky deeds ..."

1

Alone in This Place

BIT BY BIT, in the late 1940s and early 1950s, Orson Welles gave up America and let the idea gather that it had dismissed him. There was an air of retribution and humiliation in the process. The spectacular youthful success of the years from 1936 to 1941 was answered by the long, slow arc of "decline." And Welles did little to alter that trajectory or its meaning. But there was another consequence, such as enemies could never have considered. By the middle fifties, he was available to be rediscovered. The story of Orson Welles can hardly be told without the emotional need of those who found Welles, and realized shortly thereafter that they had come upon the heart of movies, a most romantic model of genius, and even themselves.

It must have been in 1955, on what I still recall as an afternoon in early summer. That would fit, more or less. For I had read about *Citizen Kane* in what seemed then the *only* book available on film—*Film and the Public*, by Roger Manvell, which was published that year. And there was reason in 1955 for London to bestir itself over Orson Welles. He was in town. He was doing a series of short programs, *The Orson Welles Sketch Book*, for BBC television—that's where he told the story about the witch doctor in Rio; he was putting on an unprecedented play, *Moby Dick—Rehearsed*, at the Duke of York's Theatre. He was even married in London that spring in 1955, to Paola Mori, his third wife. I know, I know, we have missed the second wife. But, have no fear, we will find a way of fitting Rita Hayworth in—so long as you recognize in advance that tumultuous passions can come and go.

I knew nothing about the play—I did not follow theater yet—I was only fourteen. My family had no television set, so I never saw *Sketch Book*. And I cannot remember whether I ever saw in the *Daily Mail* any photograph of Welles coming out of Caxton Hall (the celebrity place for marrying) with the dark, lustrous Paola Mori on his arm. There must have been pictures, for she was some kind of a countess, too.

He was very likely lodged in a hotel only a few miles from where I lived in south London, with his bride, his half-eaten meals, his half-grasped projects and what was by then already the verdant, exuberant disorder of his life. But I never thought of him as there and then. Rather, I read Roger Manvell's claims for *Citizen Kane* and gathered that once, long ago, someone had made a film unlike all others, as if to leave hope or a warning that there was another way.

He had not vanished, of course. But Manvell left one to conclude that nothing else in his work had ever been as worthy. There was an air of loss or disgrace about the big man—yet whose loss, whose disgrace? I did realize that this Welles was the man who had eventually appeared in *The Third Man*. One of my grandmothers had taken me to see that film, predicting grimly that I would be too afraid to see it through. She had only three fingers on one hand. I can remember the splayed hand of those three, very cold and bony fingers on my hand in the dark—to reassure me, or to be more chilling? (she had been an actress)—though I cannot now recall on which hand some congenital damage had left her with just three perfect fingers. She was proud of that hand; she favored it. And she led me to believe that this Mr. Welles—or the Harry Lime he played (or both of them)—was a wicked fellow. But the black-market intrigue of *The Third Man* waited and prayed for Lime or Welles to appear, and from the moment he was there—so rich and fed in that gaunt Vienna—the film was his and he was riveting, a boy dressed up as a man, an act that appeals hugely to ten-year-olds. I had enough grasp of the film's story to know that he was wicked, but Welles's Lime disdained that verdict. He smiled at me, knowing that the Viennese pussycat sat on *his* polished shoes, and he talked the grand talk in the Ferris wheel, talk for which there was no rebuttal or answer. If he was going to die in the sewers, it seemed most probably because of his sheer, excessive, fatalistic intelligence.

This same Orson Welles had allegedly played an Oriental general—some khan or caliph—in another film I had seen, *The Black Rose*, a boys' adventure for which I did my best to identify with the hero, Tyrone Power, who falls into the hands of this vast, mocking, cruel lord of some indeterminate Asiatic hordes. His makeup there was total and consuming; there was no fit with the sugar bun face of Harry Lime. But it was apparently the same actor, and I had no deep grievance with the thought that actors were that sportive and volatile. I did not yet dream they might be so unstable or lost that they would take any excuse or opportunity to pop up in the "real," photographable world.

By 1955, I knew there were some actors I loved, and would follow—Montgomery Clift, James Stewart, Doris Day and an English actress, Virginia McKenna—and that was because they were usually the same, a mirrored pool in which I could swim. Welles was another kind of actor, one who played sinister and suspicious people. But I loved his voice, and I treasured the endearing way in which he said, "Free of income tax, old man," to Holly Martins, long before I understood income tax. But I also guessed that people made films, that they were shows that could be shaped and made for me. I had discovered already, by attending to the credits on films, that names like Howard Hawks and Anthony Mann were guarantees. These people told their kind of story, and I liked it. I knew that Alfred Hitchcock was a movie director—and thus, I learned that the director might have a defining power in the making of shows which always enthralled me. I mean by that all films: being in the dark with the light was enough of a sensation for me. Roger Manvell's *Film and the Public* talked about these directors, many of them foreign: Marcel Carné, Sergei Eisenstein, Vittorio De Sica, Fritz Lang, and Orson Welles.

Then I saw in the local papers that the Classic, in Tooting, was going to play *Citizen Kane* for three days. There were a few Classics in London. They were the only cinemas that revived old films. In those days, moviegoing was dominated by the new pictures, which came and went. You had to see them when you had the chance. Apart from the Classics, I knew no way of seeing old movies. If anyone had told me that most old movies were burned, or scrapped for the silver, I would have found nothing to quarrel with. The newness of movies was so much of their allure. Every week I wondered if the next week's film—the one in the trailer—wasn't more desirable than this week's. But Manvell's words determined me. He had said that *Kane* was "one of the richest mines of film technique yet created," but he'd stressed how moving the film was. The technical matters, he said, were only important "as part of Orson Welles's imaginative presentation of a subject which completely possessed him." I had to see *Citizen Kane*.

So I walked across Tooting Bec Common to see the first screening. I went on my own. The film must have been chosen because some manager in the Classic organization believed that Welles was "back" or "in," someone being talked about so that *Citizen Kane* was being referred to and ordinary citizens were asking, "What's that?" So the picture was brought back—I believe that it had hardly played in London since its debut in 1941, that bomb-heavy year in which I was born.

I was the only person in the theater, in the dark. That's how unknown and unique *Citizen Kane* was. For I had never seen any movie in less than a crowd. The theaters of south London those days were generally full. One would sit surrounded by strangers. It was often necessary to arrive half an hour early and stand in a queue. Even then, there were times when I was turned away because there were no seats left. Sometimes the last seat had been in the end place on the first row, with the screen like a great looming ship passing by, ready to suck me down. I had never been alone in that dark before, or guessed the terror it could hold. Nor could I really follow *Citizen Kane* very well. Come to that, I had never imagined that movies needed to be followed, or worked with. Most films were made to be effortless: it was a part of their beauty that the story was so clear.

But I struggled with *Kane* because I knew that its show was more intense than anything I had seen, because I felt aroused by the need to run a little faster, because the shining young Kane was so entrancing, so much made by Lime's light, and because the investigator in the film had my name. So being alone felt appointed—I had been called there. No one else was in the way. I can see now that my future was taken care of, and ruined maybe.

2

⟶ *Trying to Be Loyal* ⟵

IN 1955, the Welles I had just found seemed larger than all the garish size and dazzle he put on as an actor. He was only forty, I discovered; he should have been in his prime. For there in the dark place, *Citizen Kane* had not felt like a pastime or an entertainment. It was as if the medium had said, See, this is what I can be—or this is what you can find in me. It was like a treasure map, yet it was also as grave as a doctor's lucid map of my own life and death. I felt so very moved that someone, once, should have done this, and done it in part for me. That gratitude easily outweighed any difficulties I had understanding the "story." I knew this Orson Welles was a very great man—a race I wanted to believe in. And I was sure that movie, too, was great.

It is plainer now to me that Welles had been lost—for twelve or thirteen years—in the amalgam of fury, pathos and gallows humor that understood the very verdict that had been passed on him, I mean passed as something he could believe in his boyish way.

That much of his childhood was broken or ended, even if nothing like maturity replaced it. But what is most remarkable is how little he resisted the break, or struggled for a new wisdom. In the summer of 1942, Orson Welles did get a comeuppance—and he handled it not like the most energetic, eloquent, creative, bullshitting genius anyone had ever met but like an appointed victim.

His own people had foreseen the disaster with RKO—only Welles ever claimed to have been surprised by it. They had struggled to put the best face on the failure. Herb Drake had written to Welles in Rio, urging a demonstrative return: "You have got to come home the right way, hugely, not sneak in on a plane." As RKO began a campaign to discredit Welles, Drake worked at a plan that might outflank them. Go back to Washington and get acclaim there. Drake was all for involving Harry Hopkins, Nelson Rockefeller or Roosevelt himself: "If somebody in Washington will come out with a thank you statement to you, you will return a conquering hero." But no one in Washington ever came to the rescue—they regarded the whole Brazilian enterprise as typical Hollywood blue skying. If you want government help, you must first secure government money.

Instead, Welles delayed his return until all of RKO's damage was done. He made his inane tour of Latin American countries, kicking up minor stinks in Bolivia and Peru when he was not greeted by American embassy people of sufficient status. He behaved pettily, and in tones of hurt pride that made things worse for himself. Then, for the rest of his life, he told how the new regime at RKO had coined the slogan "Showmanship instead of genius": "So, in other words, they were selling their product on the basis that they no longer had me." That grievance shows how much genius meant to him, and how confused he was about his own glorious showmanship. After all, he loved showmanship—and why not? He took on an air of being wronged, or misunderstood, that ill befits a magician. It may have been the beginning of the great load of flesh he could never lose.

There is another way of putting it: he would not be reconciled with Hollywood. In all its history, that town has been a hard place for anyone seeking to make movies his or her way, with a little originality or danger. To get a movie made, one needs not just the ideas, the talent, the freshness—the integrity—but so many attributes that may seem to defy or compromise integrity: relentless perseverance; the air of being tireless and indefatigable; charm when dealing with reptiles; oceanic seductiveness for actors and actresses; salt-of-the-earthness toward crew members; a mixture of flattery, willing humiliation, cunning, bullying, playacting tantrums, deceit, bare- and handsome-faced lying and lawyer's teeth when treating the money people; demented ego; a readiness to admit no other attachment in life. And luck.

This list is not for laughs. Indeed, it is not really very funny when you think of it as the terrain our moviemakers, explorers of truth, delicacy and narrative line, must survive if they are to move us. The quantity of ordeals may even be enough to make one doubt whether real delicacy or truth can ever survive. Maybe the picture business *is* a place for brilliant scoundrels.

Still, the outstanding American figures in film, from Griffith to Hitchcock, from Selznick to Spielberg, have lived in that jungle. Orson Welles was not without the qualities I have listed (though he got all of his luck early). But he lacked one extra, call it lethal judgment, of knowing how and when to summon up every dark art without losing the knack of thinking well of himself. He was wretched and inept in the jungle. He would not ask, beseech or belittle himself—that was his fatal vanity—he would not be a performing Kong for the monkeys. Instead, he let them know that he regarded them as lesser creatures. Like God, he wanted to be asked. What vicious good fortune it was that, as a youth, he had got that carte blanche offer. It was the only way he would ever work in pictures. But by the age of twenty-seven, he had become the dreadful and living proof that Hollywood should not break its own rules.

He had come "home" in 1942, yet he was in no way "at home" in Hollywood. That strange tour of other countries showed how ready he was emotionally to stay in transit. He had a natural rootlessness that would only be fulfilled by becoming a kind of Flying Dutchman—or perhaps by political office. I'm sure he thought of staying in Rio—even of going up some dark river to be his own Kurtz.

Welles did make gestures toward finishing *It's All True*, and keeping the faith with those who had followed him blindly on the venture. But he had never known in his mind what that film could become, and he had never seen much of the footage, shot under difficult circumstances and with less than reliable craftsmen.

In the first few months back in America, he talked of buying up the mass of footage. From RKO's point of view, it was merely miles of film and a wasted investment. As he entered into negotiations with 20th Century–Fox to play Mr. Rochester in *Jane Eyre*, 20th Century raised the prospect of taking on *It's All True* instead of paying Welles any salary as an actor. He declined: such a deal would take away his independence, he said; and it would leave him without money. In that first year back home—as never before or after—Welles's hurt feelings were assuaged by getting money. So he gave up a chance to save the footage.

Instead, he said, he took the *Jane Eyre* salary to pay for processing the *jangadeiros* sequence. In February 1943 he wrote to a friend in Rio, saying that within a week he expected to know from that footage how good a film it could be. He never followed up on that promise; it may be that his heart sank when he ran all the picturesque but inconsequential material.

So RKO sent thirty-seven boxes of film to a storage vault in Salt Lake City. Then, late in 1944, rather than pursue the material, Welles used it as collateral in taking a loan of $197,500 from RKO. That loan was never repaid. As RKO prepared to foreclose, an attempt was made to run some of the footage to secure backers. A screening was announced, but Welles himself failed to appear. So he lost any rights. Some of the footage was dumped at sea. Some of it went by way of Paramount to the UCLA archive.* Then, decades later, it was used in the making of the documentary *It's All True*, which opened in 1993. That film gives a very sketchy, blindly heroic account of what had happened in Brazil, content to repeat Welles's self-portrait as victim and martyr. It also did what it could to reassemble the *jangadeiros* sequence in material that is often handsome yet lethargic and aimless, and not helped by poor music. It is a tribute of real (if incomplete) historic value, yet it inadvertently demonstrates the validity of decisions taken in the 1940s. There was never a movie there, only an extravagant, self-destructive gesture, and the aftermath of guilt.

As Welles wrote to Fernando Pinto in Rio, less than a year after the Brazil shooting, "The months roll by into years and the weight of my indebtedness to you and the Jangado Club grows heavier as the time goes by." Welles could be grand and solemn about his debt and obligations— everyone deserved a sincere show. "I well know my obligations and am deadly serious about the task of living up to them."

Maybe it would have been best to stick to the carnival. Welles guessed that the samba could have worked—Latin American music became very popular. He asked a few writers to come up with stories that the carnival footage might be hung on—simple love stories with crowds and music throbbing in the background. Eventually, this principle delivered in the 1959 French-Brazilian film *Black Orpheus*, an international hit for others.

---

* It was rescued only thanks to the studio archivist Hazel Marshall and an inquiring scholar, Charles Higham (later condemned by Welles for his two books on the director).

But Welles's carnival footage was disorganized, and the spirit to close was never there. Within a short space of time, *It's All True* became not so much a duty or an opportunity as a wound he could not leave alone.

By the early 1970s, the legend was an agony but one he could not quit on:

> It never worked. I tried everything. I was near it, near it, near it. And I wasted many years of my life. If I'd just forgotten it—turned my back on it the way the studio did—I would have been way ahead. But I kept trying to be loyal to it, trying to finish it. And I began a pattern of trying to finish pictures which has plagued me ever since.

3
His Word-carving Voice

THIS HAPPENED in September 1942. Welles had been back in America less than two months, but he was already haunting the radio studios of New York, doing this or that, being generally available. NBC had a series, *The Cavalcade of America*, produced by Homer Fickett. One of the writers Fickett kept around was the young and as yet unknown Arthur Miller—though Miller was only five months younger than Orson Welles.

Miller had been excited at the chance of doing a radio script on the life of Benito Juárez, the Mexican revolutionary and president. He had a handwritten script which he reckoned to deliver personally to Fickett before getting it typed. But as he entered the studio, he found himself in the echo chamber of a vaguely familiar voice of full oratorical fury roaring at Fickett and his alleged historical advisers—there was a professor from Yale there, taking the abuse on his scholarly chin—about the travesty and lies in the Juárez script they were rehearsing.

The young writer listened, entranced by the voice and its florid indignation. It seemed a voice right for his script. So he signaled to Fickett, and in a moment the tatty, rewritten pages were in Welles's trembling hands. He read them silently. He seemed to be mollified by the long speeches Miller had given Juárez. Before long, Welles was with microphone. Miller and everyone else "listened amazed at Welles's genius with the microphone; he seemed to climb into it, his word-carving voice winding into one's brain. No actor had such intimacy and sheer presence in a loudspeaker."

Welles was delighted. He embraced the scrawny Miller. The show was a great success. But Welles and Miller never worked together again.

4

⟶ *You Know Mr. Rochester?* ⟶

THE STORY BEGINS to fragment. There are exhilarating afternoons, like *Juárez*, that go nowhere; there are absences or waitings, such as afflict anyone who is chiefly an actor for hire; and there are failures, like *Jane Eyre*.

In the period after *Gone With the Wind* and *Rebecca*, David O. Selznick had mounted a production of *Jane Eyre*. He had hired Aldous Huxley to work on the script with the movie director Robert Stevenson and with Selznick's new associate producer, John Houseman. This was in 1940 and 1941, a year or so to make a script—whereas Houseman and Welles had together hacked a radio play out of the Charlotte Brontë novel in 1938 in a week. But Houseman had mentioned to Stevenson that Orson Welles might make a fine Mr. Rochester.

Then, late in 1942, Selznick had decided to sell the package to 20th Century–Fox—by then, the package included the Huxley script, Stevenson as director, set designs by William Pereira and Selznick's contract actress Joan Fontaine as Jane Eyre—too pretty by half, but what are the movies to do without prettiness?

Selznick had lunch with Welles at Romanoff's and tried to convince the actor to be Rochester. We tend to forget that, at this point, Welles was still theoretically close to stardom as an actor. Moreover, he was by then having to consider acting as—if only for the short term—his way of earning a living. (As it is, Edward Rochester was the first and last time he would ever take the male lead in a credible Hollywood love story.)*

---

* The Hollywood rendering of *Jane Eyre* was of a lovely orphan Jane, who becomes a governess and thus frees the benighted owner of a great house from tragedy, infernal marriage and even blindness for love.

Welles declared he was reluctant. He did not want to back away from the habit of doing everything. It might be close to losing face, to say nothing of going against his grain, to be other than producer-director-writer-actor. He meant this, from the heart, and he was being urged by his lawyers to relinquish as little as possible of that astonishing, inhuman eminence with which he had begun. He was to ask for a credit—"Production designed by Orson Welles"—if only to indicate how rare he still was. Selznick took this for haggling. Welles was getting $100,000 just for acting in the film. He held out for more: he would be billed above Joan Fontaine, who was certainly the stronger attraction after *Rebecca* and *Suspicion;* and he would have the power of associate producer (though not the credit).

Here was the seed for ugly growth. Welles was not much interested in *Jane Eyre* as a project. He was only unwilling to appear less potent. The movie had all too many godparents: Selznick, Houseman, Pereira—whose designs are at the heart of the picture—as well as executives Kenneth MacGowan and William Goetz (Selznick's brother-in-law) at 20th Century–Fox. But on the first day of shooting, Welles astounded and offended the cast and crew by arriving late—just as Rochester's eventual appearance is delayed and built up in the movie—with a retinue of manager, secretary and valet, and then ordering a reading of the script, preparatory to giving notes and instruction. He was fulsomely in charge, and the very courteous Stevenson (two years on the project by then) had to swallow the insult.

Fontaine said that this domineering attitude soon ran out of steam and stamina—so Welles took to taunting her about the comparative splendor of their sex lives. He also maintained that, whenever he was not needed, he was looking at *It's All True* footage—*It's All True* could sometimes sound like Bunbury in *The Importance of Being Earnest*. But Welles always held to the story that he simply produced the picture, that he rewrote the script with Huxley, discovered Elizabeth Taylor for the small but piercing role of the child who dies and "invented some of the shots. . . . Stevenson didn't mind that."

That he exerted influence is not in doubt. Welles did begin by ruling the roost—and a little of that goes a long way. He very likely cast Agnes Moorehead as Jane's aunt, and Moorehead has a good death scene, which may have been meant as something fit for Aunt Fanny. Further, *Jane Eyre* has a look—a use of shadow and deep blacks, as well as sets that reach out through the mist to lovely backdrops on painted glass—that could easily be the work of other people much impressed by *Kane*. Orson Welles was

Jane Eyre: Welles with Margaret O'Brien and Joan Fontaine

hardly welcome in Hollywood in the later 1940s, but his influence was all over the place.* *Jane Eyre* is often engraved in a Dickensian way, and very handsomely furnished. The feeling for Yorkshire is better done than in William Wyler's more celebrated *Wuthering Heights* or in the 1946 *Devotion*, in which Ida Lupino and Olivia de Havilland have a rare time pretending to be Emily and Charlotte Brontë.

Which is not to say that *Jane Eyre* flourishes—or that Welles is other than distressing as Mr. Rochester. He had worked hard on his looks for the picture. By dint of corsets, steam baths and dieting, as well as dark

---

* The look of *Kane* and its overall sense of entrapment, of meaningless death and futile accomplishment, are vital influences on film noir. Directors and craftsmen who joked about Welles's fall nevertheless copied many of his discoveries.

clothes, he did all he could to appear svelte. Yet this only succeeds some of the time. During moments when he has to move, the sheer bulk is painful. In one shot, the structure of his head is so adorned by the bay window of cheek and brow that we seem to see a figure eight lounging at the corner. His hair seems built up, his nose is aquiline—it actually reminds one of Barrymore, the friend who had died only months before the shooting of *Jane Eyre*. We need look no further for Welles's model. But his Rochester also sports a sultry tan—as if we are meant to believe in his time spent in Jamaica, or because Welles had a fancy to look darker than his current girlfriend, Lena Horne.

It is an odd assemblage of features, arresting sometimes but not attractive or wholesome. As with Barrymore on-screen, there is some sense of a defiance that will not scale down for the camera but that opts instead for the grand profilism of the Victorian stage. So no matter that this Rochester has glamorous accoutrements—a cloak, a Great Dane as his familiar and the moors of solitude to roam—somehow he seems a clod, a sham and a self-pitying phony. He could have been left behind by a traveling circus. Maybe it is just that Welles could not bring himself to believe in what must be an unequivocal love story. Rochester has no choice but to be Jane's dream, yet Welles was so averse to belonging to anyone.

Joan Fontaine disliked him: she thought that "Orson's concern was entirely for Orson." And we can feel how difficult he was to play with. He fidgets mentally, he seethes with his own scorn for what he is doing and the longing to take one half step aside to be the magician who might whisk Rochester's cloak away to reveal . . . a lion? Acting a large part in a film requires an innate awareness of level, so that a character seems consistent in these very basic, passive things: looking, watching, waiting, listening, breathing. Those ostensibly dull moments can be the passion of great stars—think of Dietrich, Garbo, Cooper, Cagney—but Welles had no patience with them. His boredom made him volatile and erratic. And so in *Jane Eyre* his Rochester is a man of shots and moments, never an aching romantic sensibility.

Welles's moments are frequently interesting—striking, quirky, potentially comic, parodistic, explosive, hints of other films that might exist in the wings of *Jane Eyre*—but not the inescapable romance the story demands. He is hardly ever moving—and Rochester is a role which requires ingenuity or true perversity not to hold an audience. So there is a feeling of Fontaine attempting the sturdy, earnest Ping-Pong of the story while Welles insists on playing chess in his head. There is no contact between them, and little reason to understand why this Jane is overwhelmed by him.

But for Welles, and Wellesians, there are surely moments, most of them in the vein of philosophical self-pity. "Would you say my life deserves saving?" he asks Jane, and it is easy to feel Welles's own suspense. He does grasp the plight of Rochester, the notion of a great man bowed down or warped by "some cruel cross of fate." And he is self-obsessed. There is a breathtaking moment in the studio moors, in the ground mist, when Jane first collides with Rochester on his horse. She does not yet know who this stranger is, but she tells him she works for Edward Rochester.

"You know Mr. Rochester?" he asks her, loaded with anxiety and curiosity—as if there could be no more pressing question in the world. The actor's own need burns through the persiflage. We hear the desperation that is still to come, of Gregory Arkadin dreading that his daughter might discover his secret. But there is also a note of longing in the question, that of a ruined actor who yearns to believe he has some secret soul worth discovering.

A loneliness looms up in such moments, the pit in the "large, brilliant and black eyes" Welles brought to Rochester, and the isolation of an actor who could not quite gain entry into his own play. This Rochester is a heartfelt outcast: this is why we never believe he needs Jane. He is described before he appears as "a wanderer on the face of the earth." Later on, when he holds a most implausible party, he takes Jane aside and asks her, "If all the people in this room spat on me, what would you do? If they left me, one by one, what then?" What a line for Welles the rejected.

She tells him she would comfort him, and in the story Jane and Edward are left together. But this is observed only in long shot. There is no great final embrace and no reliable prospect of this Rochester being rescued from his blindness. He needs it so much more than he wants a bride.

5

 *Sepia*

WELLES WAS DOING too much, yet not enough of it seemed worth the effort. Being so busy was a way of warding off the clear lesson that he was not properly occupied or tested. But was he also weary of that former concentration—or no longer suited to it? Had he risked losing his youth to it? Didn't he deserve a little bit of everything, taking life as a banquet?

RKO had no wish for *Journey into Fear* except to be rid of it. What they had was deemed lightweight, incoherent, a kind of pastiche. So, without paying him anything, they allowed Welles to come back to the studio in the fall of 1942 to do some editing and a Joseph Cotten voice-over, attempting to paper over the narrative cracks. The picture was released in February 1943, credited to Norman Foster, with Welles as the Stalinesque Colonel Haki—immense, authoritative, sinister, yet impassive, too, lest the makeup crack or the actor start laughing at the nonsense. It ended up a sixty-nine-minute program filler, not quite Welles but one more indication of his facetiousness.

On radio, he was reunited with CBS, and much of what he did reflected his affection for Latin America, the Caribbean and people of color. With Carmen Miranda and some of the Mercury people, he made a popular introduction to Brazil that let him go into raptures over the samba and launched a series on things generally south of the border. Whatever the fiasco of *It's All True*, Welles had a real love for those areas and people, and on the radio he did good work in his own vein of breezy liberalism.

"I'm queer for the Caribbean anyway," he admitted, "not as it exists, but as it was in my mind in the eighteenth and nineteenth centuries. The Caribbean is just great stuff. All of it. The whole idea of all those empires fighting over tiny little islands, and black independence and Spanish pride and the War of Jenkins's Ear and those great earthquakes."

He did programs on Simón Bolívar, Toussaint-L'Ouverture, slavery, Montezuma and Juárez again. He was always listening to Ellington, to Brazilian music or to Billie Holiday and Lena Horne on the radio. He still entertained whims of something bigger on the samba or jazz: in an odd way, in his head at least, this terrifically flat-footed genius had rhythm. And he was romantic enough to believe that women from Mexico and points south were "hotter," less constrained. There is sometimes a perilous proximity of old-fashioned racial stereotype and yearning sympathy.

He often drew black people. Welles was a doodling sketch artist, very quick and skilled in the way of a sensual cartoonist. His style was bold, violent, melodramatic—he drew in his best way of acting, going for the broad, emphatic effect, exploiting romantic cliché and swashbuckling energy. He could have played Long John Silver (or Othello) as quickly as he could have drawn them—and the results were sensational, so long as everyone was resolved to be in a hurry.

His own haste hardly distinguished between such things as radio plays, here today, forgotten next week, and overtures from Alexander Korda in England about doing a *War and Peace* with Korda's wife Merle Oberon as Natasha and Welles writing, directing and playing Pierre—or Napoleon, if he preferred. All the time, Welles was invited out. He might be humbled in Hollywood's eyes, but Hollywood regarded that as normal—and Orson had always needed more normalcy. Everyone ate someone's shit in that town; let Welles get a taste for it. Beyond that, he was such a jester, such a voice, such a knockout bad-temper man, everyone wanted him at parties. He was especially favored by moguls like Selznick and Zanuck.

One Sunday at the Selznick home on Summit Drive—Selznick liked to give Sunday parties, daylong open houses, with charades, hamburgers, gambling and movies, just to make sure he never got a rest—Welles the cartoonist noir had an odd opportunity. Selznick kept a book for his wife, Irene, in which visitors could put down *pensées*, poems and tributes to that lady. It was a standing joke that guests tried to duck. Irene loathed the book's vanity—she said. So the day came when Welles had to offer his piece. His page in the book was highly original—a calypso (Calyps. O. Welles) with a drawing of very full-lipped blacks beneath a sun and a palm frond. There is a snatch of music for the song, and the lyrics sprawling across the page and sometimes misspelled in Welles's own large hand.

Orson was a show; he was larger than life in a way meant to mask his fear or dread of that plain thing. He drew attention at social gatherings, and he hardly functioned, or existed, without that balancing circle, the audience. He was profusely spontaneous—it was a kind of danger. Those who had acted with him on stage knew the terror of adjusting to his plunging moods. They had seen the mad, challenging look in his eyes when he departed from the set text, daring others to follow him. Equally, they had known Welles step on their lines, impede their blocking or even barge them out of the spotlight when he wanted it more. Acting with him could be like playing squash with a brilliant cheat who kept talking all the time.

Yet the same man was prepared. Magicians have to be. Welles would do "impromptu" tricks. That meant he had cards up his sleeve, and sleeves specially tailored. Long before he adopted large, loose garments to hide his size, he had hidden places on him. This left a disconcerting clash of approaches—of natural actor and cunning director—and if anyone grew uneasy he had that wild laugh of his: fierce, demonic and somehow terribly lonely. He was famous for his laugh, but it was the spasm of an imprisoned creature, someone caught between being child and adult, a magician longing to be a shut-eye—that kind of fraud who comes to believe in his own tricks.

Kane: the life and soul of his party

The reason he was such a charmer, so welcome an entertainer at peril of wasting away more than his Sundays, was that he could do such tricks with the same glee and youthful intentness that he had turned on *Kane.* He was interested in so many things, and he relished every little show. There was something relentless and indiscriminate about the inventiveness, and something that dangerously depended on the awe and admiration that greeted it. He would also have had to chuckle gallantly at such things as his friend Selznick—an admirer, an employer he had declined and someone who had proposed sending *all* of *Ambersons* to the New York Museum of Modern Art, just in case, just to get it out of California—saying that Orson was a genius, you could tell because he had no movie! Schadenfreude, a relish for the dismay and defeat of rivals—enough to inspire thoughts of murder, or disappearance, in a lofty spirit. Their murder, his disappearance: this is the dynamic of *Mr. Arkadin*, a decade ahead of itself.

This assault on his confidence went on while he was twenty-seven and twenty-eight (three years younger than Quentin Tarantino in the year of *Pulp Fiction*). Welles loomed so large as an achiever; he had done so much, and so brilliantly, that it was far easier for rivals or approximate contemporaries to turn away from the spectacle, as if to say that Orson Welles was an aberration in nature, not real competition. He needed to be ignored. But Welles was tender, despite his accomplishments, just because he had hardly ever failed or been denied. He had never had to learn resilience; he had simply poured over his own brink, as astonishing as Niagara. Now he was unhired—invited everywhere but not considered on a picture. He was also gaining weight and being talked about behind his broad back. Why was such a hero not ready for war? The sound of his voice alone could have daunted enemies.

There was such talk—and such hostility—that he went for his army physical examination, courting public coverage. He failed grandly: he was 4-F, a danger to himself and anyone near him, so poised in talk, so inept physically. But on that occasion, he would claim later, he met a Mexican American, one Pete Vazquez, who told him what service meant to a humble Mexican:

> If the cops catch you on the street after eight o'clock,
> usually they run you in—or rough you up, anyway. If
> you look like a Mexican you just better stay off the
> street, that's all. And where can you go? It's real bad. I'm
> going into the Army, and it's all right with me. I'm glad
> to be going. Things'll be better in the Army, and I'm

glad of the chance to fight. It makes it hard, though, for
a lot of our fellas to see things that way. They want to
fight for their country, all right—but they want to feel
like it's their country.

Vazquez may well have been invented. But Welles felt warmly toward
Mexicans and all the other Pan-Americans. His own failure in the war effort, and his military incapacity, stirred him up on behalf of those underprivileged people. Which is a way of suggesting that, while his sentiments
were good and valid, they were carried on the energy of hurt feelings.

He lent himself to the cause of the accused in the Sleepy Lagoon
murder case. In August 1942, José Diaz, an ordinary Mexican American,
had been found killed. The press—especially the Hearst press—played up
the legend of Mexican gangs, the "zoot suiters," bent on violence and
mayhem. Racial paranoia built. A number of Mexicans were accused and
convicted on very flimsy evidence. Welles wrote the foreword to a pam-
phlet defending these men, and he served on the Committee for the Defense of Mexican American Youth. It was a situation in which he could
rediscover belief in himself, like that young Kane who turns on Mr.
Thatcher and all the forces of reaction with the rousing promise to defend the oppressed. Years later, in *Touch of Evil*, Welles still felt the pathos
of young, powerless, framed Mexicans, as well as the gravitational allure
of the dreadful, self-pitying hulk of a lawman who is framing them.

In 1943, the siding with insignificant Mexicans was a part of Welles's
rebelliousness, and of his being marked down for scrutiny by the FBI.
Some said it was also his taste for color—after all, wasn't he pursuing Lena
Horne, and looking to impress her?

That year, Helena or Lena Horne was twenty-six. She came from a
well-to-do black family, and she was so light in color that Louis B. Mayer
looked at her and wondered if he and MGM could let her pass. There
were advantages to such a ruse: she had a case for being the most beautiful, or attractive, woman in the country, as well as the best popular singer.
There was maybe too much of the lady in her, or too much anger at the
white world, for her to be an actress. But she had movies now, as well as
nights at the El Morocco on the Sunset Strip, where she leaned back
against a pillar—her favorite stance—and just let out in song: "You're My
Thrill," "The Man I Love," "Stormy Weather," which she did in a silly
film of the same name, or "Honey in the Honeycomb," which she sang in
Cabin in the Sky.

She had been married, though the union was on the rocks, and she
had two young children. She was being lauded in big magazines, like *Time*

and *Life*. She was a quarter inch from being white, and if she had crossed over she might have become one of the top entertainers in the world. Welles saw her and was besotted. She has never talked about him as a romance, and he sometimes suggested that his pursuit was beaten away. Horne's daughter wrote that Lena was fascinated by Orson, by his mind. But there must have been moments when even his clumsiness and her grace wearied of the life of the mind. And there were surely occasions when he pictured her in some movie that told the story of jazz, of song and the whole life America was denying itself in being so wary of things sepia. So it is not fanciful to wonder if, amid the foolishness of *Jane Eyre*, Welles didn't play with the notion of taking on the burnt glow of secret blackness and didn't turn a little dark for that great lady.

There was one radio show, *Something About Joe*, in which Welles and Horne played together. Could there have been more? She would soon marry the arranger Lennie Hayton, who was a calm and nurturing influence on her career. It is doubtful whether Welles and Horne could have helped each other; she may have been too grown-up for him. But he had the taste to know how remarkable she was, and he was romantic enough to fall in love for a month or so if the woman refused him. It is one more of those enticing projects that never came to fruition.

6

Rita

SO, INSTEAD, Welles married a bona fide war weapon, sleeker and more far-reaching than any artillery shell, and more persuasively attuned to damage, for Rita Hayworth's smile in all her pinup pictures was blatant indication of the rewards that must await the dutiful killer. (And of the girl at home that 4-Fs might enjoy? No, the dialectic of advertising then was simpler.) It must have been easy to be in love with Ms. Hayworth, and easier still to be seen with her glowing, redheaded willingness hooked on your arm, laughing and radiating for at least as long as anyone was watching and taking pictures.

This is not an attack on Rita Hayworth, rather it is a way of noting that her terrifically appealing and thoroughly American helplessness was hardly Wellesian—except as a token, a sort of testament to honorable, mainstream intentions. Marrying her was going Hollywood. That message outweighed all the mysteries of the coupling. The eighteen-year-old Gore Vidal, a Welles-gazer, first set eyes on the great man at the Beverly Hills Hotel:

> On his arm was Rita Hayworth, his wife. He has it all, I
> remember thinking in a state of perfect awe untouched
> by pity. Little did I know—did he know?—that just as I
> was observing him in triumph, the great career was
> already going off the rails while the Gilda of all our
> dreams was being supplanted by the even more beauti-
> ful Dolores del Rio.

Well, not quite. There was supplanting ahead, and maybe even current in an upstairs room at the same hotel, but it was not Del Rio, whose day had passed. Moreover, while academicians in the field might have argued that Del Rio was more beautiful than Hayworth, the general public had no doubts. To them, Del Rio was a somewhat vapid exotic, whereas Hayworth was as delectable as fudge sauce melting into French vanilla. She was the here and now, a phenomenon of stardom, and the certain albeit rather demented emblem of "it."

Hayworth was not quite what she seemed. Three years younger than Welles, she had been born Margarita Carmen Cansino, in Brooklyn. As a youth, she was very dark, with a low hairline and fearful eyes. From the age of twelve, she had been her father's partner in his Mexican dancing act. Her mother was an alcoholic, and the daughter was sometimes passed off as the father's wife as they toured. She had had very little proper schooling except for the seedier levels of show business. As father and daughter traveled and worked together, Rita would tell Orson—she had never told anyone else, she said—he had forced her to sleep with him.

Abused steadily, but smiling eternally in her father's arms while they danced, Rita was bereft, traumatized. She had sought escape by marrying Edward Judson, a man of mysterious business interests twice her age. Their wedding was in 1937, and he thereupon attempted to dominate and direct her career as an entertainer. She had just been signed up by Columbia. Along with the boss at Columbia, Harry Cohn, Judson changed her name, instigated a strenuous regime of electrolysis that raised her hairline and then dyed her hair to the famous burning auburn.

She was the creation of Judson and Cohn, with the husband offering her to the mogul as a bedmate. But her career flourished, for somehow, despite injury and indignity, Rita Hayworth had a smile people loved. On-screen, she was seen never as a victim but as a femme fatale or a gorgeous partner. She had made more films by 1940 than Welles would direct in his life, but her fame was built on *Only Angels Have Wings*, *The Strawberry Blonde*, *Blood and Sand* and *You'll Never Get Rich*, in 1941, in which she danced with Fred Astaire.

The marriage to Judson could not survive her success, or her susceptibility to hunks like Victor Mature. In 1942, they made *My Gal Sal*, in which he is a songwriter and she is the singer. Rita didn't sing; May Wynn did the songs for her. Mature didn't do much more than look pleased with himself—his vocation. But that seemed to suit her. It is a movie in which the two leads are having an unaccountably good time—compared with the audience. Between takes, and off the set, Mature was pitching his bravura woo to her. And she liked it: he made her laugh. Victor Mature may have been the ideal man for Rita Hayworth, a notion which conjures up images of Welles intruding like one more ogre with ways of making all his predecessors seem stupid.

Welles had aired the opinion—or the promise even—that he would marry her; just as Paris and the Philippines would be liberated. He must have seen something appropriate in her beyond the simple carnal desirability. She was offended when word of his guarantee got back to her: it was vulgar, patronizing and demeaning—and anyway she was a bigger star than he was, buster, no matter if he needed a couple of guys to carry his mind for him.

But he persevered. He said he would marry her: this was like a magician promising that the theater roof would vanish. He got her telephone number from another would-be lover, Anthony Quinn, and then, when they met, they got on. There was something restful in her drop-dead glamorousness. When Welles was with her, Hollywood felt bound to reappraise him. He had no difficulty in talking to her, and she loved to listen: the growing smile in attentive eyes was one of her fortes on-screen. He told her she was wonderful. She said she was no such thing, she was a mess. Not at all, he said, and he was wonderful, too, so if he said she was wonderful, it had to be. He read her mind, like a magic act, and once he saw she was insecure, hurt, certain of being misunderstood, there was not much trick to telling her about herself. Insecurity is *the* scar on the knee. She didn't like the movies, or the business. He told her she was exactly correct, and he gave her mountains of reasons for her feelings. All the men in her life had used her, she said. She was a victim, not a love goddess. Then Welles demurely outlined the sketch of a scenario in which he too was the plaything of Hollywood and its object of ridicule. They fucked a lot, and he may have been relieved and touched to find her shy,

With Rita

honest and plain at it. He was her star between the sheets, such a great talker, such a knowing man. And he liked her.

If only there were such a scene in an Orson Welles film.

What did she see in him? He was the gentlest, most intricate, inventive and amusing male intelligence she had ever encountered—only time would show how surely she would bore his wiles and depths. He talked to her, and had her talk to him in ways she had never managed before. He could explain to her, like a politician campaigning on a reform ticket, how dreadfully Hollywood had abused and humiliated her. He must have conjured up new scenarios for her every night—things she dreamed of as pictures. He would have known ways in the dark, murmuring about rosebuds, of freeing her from the history of sexual exploitation. And if, finally, that failed or was not miracle enough, maybe he was wit enough to give her the line she would use later that men went to bed with "Gilda" (her great role, not far away) or "Rita Hayworth" but woke up with the desolate, broken, humble her. He might have offered her that quip to mask his own disappointment—and he had married her to cheer himself up.

He sawed her in half. As they got better acquainted, as he substituted for Jack Benny on the radio, as he still saw Lena Horne and took his Sleepy Lagoon stand, as he entertained future projects and steadily worked on radio shows, captivating such passing colleagues as the young writer Richard Brooks (only three years his senior), so that Brooks treasured it all years later—"He had such a remarkable memory that if we'd get into a dispute about the way the story should go or not go, he'd say, 'Well, let's see now in *Lear* . . . ,' and then he would review the whole second act of *King Lear*, doing all the parts! Or he could quote from the New or Old Testament, by the yard. His wealth of information and background about story lines was inexhaustible. He was inventive. Fearless"—and, if we can just contain all this in one sentence, he was also putting together, ladies and gentlemen, The Mercury Wonder Show. Before your very eyes!

There were troops and munitions workers in Los Angeles, and show business did its bit for them, and for itself. There were stage door canteens as thick as gambling clubs. Welles put up a circus tent on Cahuenga Boulevard. Servicemen were admitted free, but seats—Sucker Seats— were held for celebrities, at thirty dollars each, so the stars could be available as stooges in the conjuring acts, having rabbits produced from their pants and generally being "demeaned and humiliated . . . in front of the servicemen." The iconoclast in Welles, the man ready to get his own back on Hollywood, loved the show and the authority it gave him. What magic always meant to Welles was the chance of instant superiority.

He reckoned they played eventually to over 50,000 people, and he said he was as proud of it as he was of anything he had ever done: he loved the rowdiness of the show, the sweating intimacy, the improvisation and the flap of the canvas. The company also included Rita, Joseph Cotten and Agnes Moorehead—she played the calliope outside the tent as the crowd came in. In a voodoo finale, Cotten reenacted "Interesting Experiences Among the Witch Doctors in Dark Africa." Rita was "The Girl with the X-ray Eyes" in one act in a demonstration of strange powers, "Recognized, but Unexplained by Science." There were feats of magic straight from "old Cathay"—Shanghaiism in the making. Dr. Welles presented his original experiments in animal magnetism—"All Nature Freezes at His Glance." And he sawed Rita in half, had the two halves walk around and then remade her. Had Rita Hayworth ever had such fun? Had anyone? The crowd roared and cheered for more every night. The greatest movie director in the world was in another element, but he loved it, and it helped persuade him that he might be a favorite of the masses.

One reason the show was such a hit, Welles thought, was the preponderance of men in the audience. His reasoning is not without interest: "Magic is directed almost entirely to men, you know. And it's a return for them to boyhood, childhood. It has nothing to do with women, who hate it—it irritates them. They don't like to be fooled. And men do."

Rita's happiness in being part of the act was sharpened when her proprietor, Harry Cohn, ordered her out of it. She was frantic, in case this might risk losing Orson. Cohn did not like this other influence in his star's life, and he had some point in wanting her to keep her evenings free as she shot *Cover Girl*, her biggest vehicle yet. But Rita could not be reassured. Orson was moved, and horrified, by her vulnerability. So they married; it was the only way of calming her, he said. The marriage took place on September 7, 1943, in Santa Monica. This was on an afternoon she had free from *Cover Girl*. The ceremony had press in attendance, but no one from Columbia and neither of Rita's parents. Welles had spirited the princess away from those old prisons.

The magic show went on as planned. Marlene Dietrich stepped in to be taken apart. You will wonder what that meant. Dietrich and Welles were friends and admirers. They had known each other since the days of Dolores Del Rio. Still, Dietrich then was very deeply involved with Jean Gabin, who—sharing your suspicions—offered himself free, and inescapable, to the show as a stage hand. There will be more Dietrich—

The marriage in Santa Monica, observed in his best Lelandish manner by Joseph Cotten

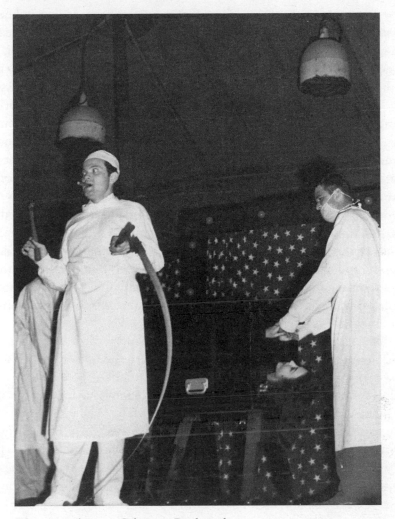

The magic show on Cahuenga Boulevard

have no fear. She and Welles were ships of a scale, luxury and romance that found fewer equipped ports as the years passed. They were bound to meet again. But in 1943 Marlene did the act, and in the throng of volunteers who stepped up every night to hold her legs in place for the saw, there was an eighteen-year-old from Corning, Iowa, who would also meet Welles again under studio lights—Johnny Carson. It was Dietrich who appeared with Welles, doing their act, in the anthology film *Follow the Boys*—Edward Sutherland was the overall director on the movie, but he stood aside to let Welles put the trick on film.

There was a moment in Orson and Rita's marriage when both parties reckoned on it as the "abracadabra" that would set them free from Hollywood. It was a strange mood of escapism, one that suggests two people equally adrift from reality. Rita said she would give up movies. Orson believed there was some sort of career for him in politics. He had been as thrilled as anyone by the tent show; he had felt useful and in touch with good, decent, ordinary Americans. If only they would understand and acclaim him, then he might convince himself that he was a straightforward hero. He came under the influence of Louis Dolivet, a Romanian who had founded the International Free World Association. Dolivet had married Beatrice Straight, a substantial heiress, so that he was able to run his organization, with a magazine, *Free World*, for which Welles began to write.

In the fall and early winter of 1943, Orson and Rita traveled extensively as he took on the life of a public speaker. They let it be known that show business was in the past. There will have to be more on this curious episode, and what it meant for Welles. But it was an important stage for the marriage, an illusion shared in equally, with Rita nursing Orson in Miami through a serious bout of hepatitis that made his subsequent drinking more dangerous.

They came back to Los Angeles in 1944 and settled for a while in a house on Carmelina Drive, which runs up into the hills. *Cover Girl* and *Jane Eyre* both opened that year, the first by far the greater success. Rita had never been more appreciated at Columbia, but Cohn had her "retirement" and Welles to contend with. Meanwhile, Welles plunged into a new regular radio show, *The Orson Welles Almanac*, for CBS, a helpless surrendering to money. His finances were in ruin still, and he had to take a loan from Rita to carry him. In the spring, Rita discovered that she was pregnant. Despite that, Cohn insisted that she work—she did a minor musical, *Tonight and Every Night*, set in London during the time of German bombing raids. They were slipping back into old ways, and Welles sometimes said he had been trapped into the pregnancy by sheer, old-fashioned lust.

That spring, *Life* magazine sent the photographer Peter Stackpole to their house for a shoot. The pictures are intriguing. Orson and Rita had two guests—his daughter, Christopher, and a young novice bullfighter from Mexico, a guy Welles was considering sponsoring. (Doesn't every house have one?) There is one picture of Orson sitting on a balcony of the house—with beard, mustache and commalike kiss curl—a pile of scripts in his lap. Rita, in shirt and dungarees, is stretched out on the diving board by the pool. The young toreador sits in the garden, watching them. And in the distance we can see the figure of Christopher, six years old, wondering how to play on her own. Then there is an interior shot, dominated by Rita and the bullfighter, who are rehearsing a pass, she the bull, he the fighter, while Orson looks on, plump and puffy. The lonely, wan-faced Christopher leans against him, her pinched gaze staring away at a corner of the room. Nothing really fits.

As Rita grew in pregnancy, Orson took off alone on oratorical travels, lending himself to the last campaign of Franklin Roosevelt. He met FDR; he traveled with him on the train sometimes, and sat up talking late at night. They got on: FDR said they were the two best, or most chronic, actors in America. Welles could believe that the president had personally encouraged him to have a political career. It was plain how sick FDR was, and how brave, yet how much he remained what Churchill would call him, "like a bottle of champagne just opened." There was enough wild, dreaming boy in Welles—and sufficient lack of the worldliness that struck others—to believe *he* might be president. After all, Roosevelt had blessed him, and Truman was such a small, boring man. Rita could be first lady.

But Rita worried in his absence. Once he was away she remembered how much smarter he was, how seductive. He was meeting people while she grew heavy. And in her helplessness, Columbia wheedled their way back—studio people who marveled at Welles deserting her. Nor was he fidelity itself. In New York, he met Gloria Vanderbilt—she was young and rich, very dark, and first lady material. They kissed and wanted more, but she held on to the thought that Rita existed.

Roosevelt telephoned Rita once to say how well her man was doing—Orson had fallen ill again with what may have been a recurrence of hep-atitis. The president told the wife not to fret if she didn't hear from her husband; he was on special missions. Rita was awed, then swiftly suspi-cious. Orson only came back to California after victory. He had the pres-ident's thanks—"It was a great show, in which you played a great part"—and on December 17 he had a daughter, Rebecca.

Almost immediately, he went away again, for more speeches in the East. He also began to write a weekly column for the New York *Post* in January 1945. Rebecca never held him for a moment, and Rita was crushed by the increasing absences. They talked less and less. They had bought a property together, a superb plot of land high on a cliff in the Big Sur section of the California coast. They planned a getaway house there, the ultimate love nest, but never went to see the work progress.

In the course of 1945, Welles had a passionate affair with Judy Gar-land that he hardly bothered to conceal. He was also seen with Lena Horne again, and there were reports that he was having prostitutes at the house of Sam Spiegel. (He was working with Spiegel on a picture project.) For the moment, politics seemed on the back burner. He was also en-

Tomorrow Is Forever: Welles with Claudette Colbert

gaged to act in a very silly movie, *Tomorrow Is Forever,* in which he played a husband who is thought dead. But he returns to find that his wife, Claudette Colbert, has married George Brent. Welles is shocking and shameless in the weepie, cynical and sentimental at the same time, but very good in a few scenes with Natalie Wood (playing his adopted daughter). It was easier to act with a child than to look after one.

Rita was drinking; so was Orson. They would fight. He would criticize her in public, and make fun of her. She snapped. "Goddamn it!" she yelled. "I'm not Mrs. Orson Welles. I'm Rita Hayworth!" Years later, while blaming himself, he said that she was both helpless and hopeless, someone beyond salvation. But he hardly made an honest attempt. Though they were unsuited, there was no question but that she adored him. He had grown bored and cruel. He had seen enough to hate clinging women.

7

⟶ *Overboard* ⟵

L A T E R I N L I F E , when he had found the manner of being wistful and rueful about his own past (though the seed was there in *Kane* in the line "If I hadn't been very rich, I might have been a really great man"), Welles would say of the years that followed *It's All True* that he was unable to get a film because of his soured reputation. But he would also declare how, in the very same period, he had given up pictures—indeed, had moved beyond being an entertainer. Just before and just after the end of the war, he often announced that there were more important things going on in the world than being an actor. But he never gave up anything—except wives, children and friends who "betrayed" him. He was always acting, always doing things for radio, always looking for new material.

Somerset Maugham's novel *The Razor's Edge* was published in 1944. Director George Cukor had what he thought was an early proof copy of the book. He read it and became very interested. That night, at a party at Darryl Zanuck's, he heard a voice spouting lines from the book in the form of ordinary conversation. A deep, sonorous voice: "I'm not really an educated man, and I wish I were. I'd love to read the *Odyssey* in the original Greek, and the Bible in the original Hebrew." It dawned on Cukor that the novel was all over town. "Orson Welles had read it and been struck by it and was becoming the character, using some of his expressions. It's an indicative, interesting thing about him."

Welles was among the great political speakers of his time—he had the voice as well as an imperial authority, and he was a superb writer of his own speeches; he even believed in what he was saying. But he sounded like the Chorus in *Henry V,* too awesome and final to leave real pols comfortable. Roosevelt liked him because the president loved acting; it was one of the inspiring tasks he had set himself. (Every great leader in that war was a movie fan.)

But Welles was so serious, so grave when he turned to politics, it shamed the professionals. Roosevelt always enjoyed the joke about his own image: that the rich man, the establishment figure, was tearing down the house; that the cripple was an icon of strength. In politics, Welles never found that humor. He could not tell Kane's jokes about wobbly

promises. Instead, he seemed to be on a Shakespearean stage. He was devout about great times needing great men. So he missed that drab, sly,
common touch that gets elected.

The things he wrote and uttered over loudspeakers in large arenas
were lovely and urgent, and they would have drawn attention to him even
if he hadn't usually been the largest man on the platform or the one smoking a cigar. Yet the message was as vague as it was soaring—or rather, it
was ahead of its time. His most concrete issue was race; his largest emotion was the need to keep vigilant after the peace: that there would be
greater dangers to come. He had a drama in his mind of a vast America,
imperiled by its own fears and weakness, a country that could easily sink
back into its racist past and the clutch of a few monopolists. Roosevelt, or
more pointedly the ghost of FDR, was his hero and savior; Welles seemed
strangely fulfilled by Roosevelt's passing, as if the country was then truly
exposed. Time and again, in Welles's imagination, the greatness of a figure is felt most deeply at death's threshold. Mourning made Welles electric and prophetic: it is a tone that surely carried over into his private
thinking on the sad, bereft world he would one day leave behind. But if
his drama seriously entertained a thought of his eminence, then it likely
had him and some Lena Horne as the ideal interracial couple, a lesson to
America.

"Race Hate Must Be Outlawed" was a July 1944 Welles article for
Free World. It is a stirring, nearly Lincolnesque speech, and hardly
grounded. For instance, it nowhere observes the quantity of black soldiers
fighting and dying. But it is rich and sonorous in a foreboding sense of
human nature. There is not a glimmer of cunning humor or fustian common sense. It is a lecture, addressed to the masses, and there is something
faintly sinister or menacing in its relentless measure and art:

> Race hate isn't human nature; race hate is the abandon-
> ment of human nature. But this is true: we hate whom
> we hurt and we mistrust whom we betray. There are
> minority problems simply because minority races are
> often wronged. Race hate, distilled from the suspicions
> of ignorance, takes its welcome from the impotent and
> the Godless, comforting those with hellish parodies of
> what they've lost. . . .

There's something not just solemn but melancholy to that, a vision of
nearly ineluctable human prejudice, a gulf of character such as divided the

scorpion and the frog in the famous story. Welles was not bracing or encouraging. He did not often convince readers or listeners of their ability
to overcome problems. In Welles's somber baritone voice, there was always the loneliness of imminent dismay.

This rhetoric could seem like helpless fodder for his orotund, bogus
voice. All too eerily, we can hear the hollow resonance of Kane the can-
didate. Yet Welles could be a dogged, brave campaigner for racial decency. In 1946, he would be caught up in the case of Isaac Woodward, a
black veteran who had been blinded in a mysterious altercation with the
police in the town of Aiken, South Carolina. There was a cover-up in the
town, but Welles would not back off. Though threatened personally and
daunted by official inquiries that cleared the police, Welles stood by
Woodward and helped in benefits that raised money for him. But ABC
was frightened by the case, because the town of Aiken had threatened suit
. . . and Welles had that habit of improvising on the air. They said he
would be terminated if he didn't keep to agreed scripts.

In the course of the 1944 election campaign, Welles was never more
striking than when summing up a picture of the opponents. The following extract is arresting, but it seems to describe timeless infidels or the
bearers of the plague instead of plain Republicans:

> You understand what I mean by "they." You know who
> they are. They are not essentially Republicans, but they
> have seized the Republican party as a vehicle for their
> ambitions. They are the partisans of privilege—the
> champions of monopoly—the opponents of liberty, the
> adversaries of the small business man, and the small
> farmer. They have been here a long time. They used to
> run the earth and run the world of men, but now—just
> now—they're losing out. They are making one of their
> last stands in this election. Must I name them? You
> know who they are. They have a long, long, weary,
> bloody history.

Sometimes this comes close to the cultivated fear of fear that Roosevelt warned about. It is also not far from the primal paranoia—"Must I
name them? You know who they are"—with which Joseph McCarthy
would make his name. That comparison is especially relevant since
Welles claimed later in life that he was approached to run against
McCarthy in the 1946 election, in which McCarthy was elected to the

Senate from Wisconsin. "So I've got him on my conscience," Welles joked, assuming the result had he decided to run. Of course, he did not run; in the fall of 1946, he would be making *The Stranger*, a film about a Nazi in the American bed.

Welles would later lament that he was warned that an actor with a divorce on his record would never get anywhere in politics (alluding to Ronald Reagan's later success, shrugging such things aside). But in the midforties those were handicaps, and by late 1946 Welles was close to having two divorces and two daughters to support. He was also besieged by income tax problems: the IRS was still diligently probing the cavities or deceits of 1941 and beginning to intuit that Welles had neither the records nor the patience to fend off claims.

That trait of character was a greater weakness in politics: he had no taste for detail, for boring things; he had no operation of his own—no money, no constituency, no real contacts. He knew Roosevelt, Truman and Henry Wallace, but hardly anyone else. He had paid no dues and gathered no favors. He was no more a part of politics than he was of Hollywood. Nor was he really Wisconsin's own. Think of the mockery McCarthy would have heaped on him. McCarthy had lived far longer in Wisconsin. He had been a lawyer, a judge, a farmer and a veteran of the air force. While Welles orated, the vulgar, purposely nasty McCarthy would have cut him up and made a stooge of him. Welles was a rival McCarthy might have prayed for.

So, in truth, politics quickly became another failed arena for Welles, and nothing indicates its tragedy so much as the death of FDR. Roosevelt had been in politics more than thirty years. He had carried heavy leg irons through the fight, and he had worn himself close to death. He was a real man, as well as a national actor, sapped by the daily strife and tedium of dealing. Welles hardly saw that. He responded to the symbolism and magic of the man, and he identified with his drama. The day after FDR's death, Welles contributed to the radio tribute—it is a heartbreaking piece, scarcely separable from the decline of Major Amberson. It is also, above all, the cry of loneliness and of an urge toward death. Welles's many regrets, his sense of loss, may have been crystallized in the death of the president. Whatever, this is great radio, and as emotional as Orson Welles ever managed to be:

> Something is on its way in a slow train from Georgia to
> the Capitol, the body of an American president is going
> home. . . .

Our last president was a member of my family. He
lived in our home as I know he lived in yours. My
home seems empty now as yours does. What a sadness
is played upon here, and it sings its song oblivious of
the fact that Welles in person was one of the more
absent heads of household that even Hollywood knew.
This is a remarkable eloquence so detached from actual experience as to be alarming—and it is *Kane*
again, that man who longed to be moved by the people, but who could not help moving, stirring and ma-
nipulating them. Even FDR, in death, resembled the
disappeared element in a grand emotional trick: "The
word for tonight is that he's here with us. He hasn't
gone. If it seems that way, it is because we've lagged
behind."

There were other areas in which Welles's touch proved too heavy. He
had been very excited about his column for the New York *Post*. He trained
himself to get up early in the morning to write it. And he needed the guaranteed $300 a week. But bit by bit the *Post* found that the other papers car-
rying the column lost interest. By May it was making only $125 a week.
Robert Hall, general manager of the *Post*, believed that Welles was writing too much on politics and world events. The syndicate had expected
inside showbiz material, gossip and anecdotes. Welles was deflated: "Of
course this would build an audience, but Bob, it wouldn't be the audience
I want to address. There is a serious public. I believe that time could teach
that public to take me seriously."

Ted Thackrey, editor of the *Post*, was drawn into the discussion. He
begged Welles to write spontaneously, free from advisers and accessible
to the ordinary reader. It is a very touching moment. A few years earlier,
Welles had been a phenomenon on the American landscape, an intellectual maybe but as "popular" as *The War of the Worlds*. Now, he felt himself
close to an outcast, an elitist and a kind of dead weight. He wrote to
Thackrey: "You are unhappy with my work . . . why not drop me quietly
overboard?"

The *Post* stuck it out. Thackrey liked Welles too much to lose him.
He had dined with him, and he still believed the flair and brilliance of
Welles's table talk—so funny, so knowing, so "in"—could reach the page.
But Welles the writer was too lofty. He gave up, no matter that he had
been paid in advance. As late as December 1946, Thackrey wrote to

Richard Wilson, Welles's devoted and nearly crazed assistant. He estimated that Welles was fifty-four columns behind in what he owed the *Post* and its syndicate. The money had been paid in advance. Thackrey could have been tough, but he stayed friendly—"we will be happy to receive them some time in the next century."

The *Post* is still waiting.

8

Not That Kind of Person

IN THE YEARS from 1944 through 1946, there was still more failure to endure, and to pay for. Increasingly in those years, Welles found that he could not make ends meet; he could not always pay his staff and his regular bills, much less remove the old RKO debt, buy back the *It's All True* footage or get away with the Wonder Show, the sheer fun of which was often financed out of his pocket, or on his credit. Worst of all, Welles lacked the patience, the humility or the skills to go out in the world and get funding. His solitude was never more apparent than when he either sat in silence with or began to berate and belittle rich men.

The *Almanac* radio show that began in 1944 for CBS was essentially live, intended as comedic. It had guest stars—Lucille Ball, Charles Laughton, George Jessel all appeared—it had comedy skits, and there was even what the ad agency behind the show called "the serious spot." At such moments, Welles might read from the Bible, do a scene from Shakespeare or recite poetry by John Donne. Welles was always tugging the show in that inspirational direction. He did an entire program on D day, for instance, which was, quite reasonably, judged to be more pressing than Jimmy Durante jokes.

But the ad agency was uneasy. They thought the *Almanac* lacked "architecture," their way of saying that Welles was forever altering the lineup and throwing in new pieces at the last moment. The biggest problem was Welles's uneasiness doing comedy. It surprised people that on the air Welles made jokes seem stiff, "read" and forced. They had been with the man in social situations; they knew how effortlessly he could keep a circle laughing. But on the air, even with a live audience, his comedy was flat-footed. "Does he feel that he can express himself adequately to the public in that form?" asked the agency. "Does he feel that he wishes deeply to study that form and put against it the same time and kind of effort which he has put against his undoubted mastery of other forms?"

At the close of its first season, the *Almanac* was not renewed. The next year, Welles was back, with a different sponsor and agency, but on CBS still, with *This Is My Best*. This was closer to the old Mercury shows, in that it generally ran full-length dramatizations: Norman Cousins's *The Plot to Overthrow Christmas*; a reprise of *Heart of Darkness*; *A Tale of Two Cities*, with Welles as Sydney Carton; a version of *Snow White* with Welles narrating, Jane Powell as Snow White and Jeanette Nolan as the wicked queen; Scott Fitzgerald's "The Diamond as Big as the Ritz"; *The Master of Ballantrae* and *Anything Can Happen*.

Then, in April 1945, the show ended. Welles and the studio director, Don Clark, had quarreled. The scripts were changed too much, and there had been excessive overtime. But when Welles said that he proposed to do (with Rita) a version of *Don't Catch Me*, a novel he had purchased with a view to filming it, the sponsor closed the show.

Welles was bewildered. He claimed that no one had objected along the way, that praise had turned suddenly into rejection. Welles had done a reading of *Don't Catch Me* and then decided that it didn't work: there was too much plot and not enough comedy. The agency found this unprofessional. *Don't Catch Me* had been announced. Don't worry, said Welles; he and Rita would instead do scenes from *The Taming of the Shrew*. That offer was refused. It was widely felt that Welles was doing too much, too many small things, that he had lost his old concentration, as well as people like Houseman and Howard Koch who could knock effective scripts together in a few days. The men from the agency could not handle Welles—that's why they were friendly to his face and then sent a dismissal notice. He said he had been conspired against, and then dismissed in a way worthy of a stenographer. He was accused of having behaved like a loudmouth, when he had been a model of tact and discretion. He was, after all, Orson Welles, capable of so much:

> Lies have been told. Somebody for his own purposes—
> in the interest of his own career—has treated me very,
> very shabbily. There may be two sides to every argu-
> ment—but here there wasn't an argument—I was sen-
> tenced without trial.
>   Speaking of trials, my lawyers assure me I'd win a
> suit if I brought it against you people, but I think you
> know that I'm not that kind of person.

Temperamentally averse to compromise, to getting along with the sharks and minnows in show business, Welles could move with awful speed from arrogance to wounded lament. This is akin to the child's way of dealing with the difficult or disobedient world—but Welles was now thirty. He was also in sharp need, and increasingly persuaded that there was no simple glory to be had in politics. So he made himself available to direct a movie. He would do it as nothing more than a job, just to show everyone that he could be professional.

The Stranger was put together by Sam Spiegel, a tough, charming Austrian who went under the American name S. P. Eagle. He was part hustler, part man of the world; he was a bon vivant, a talker, and he had a future—Spiegel would go on to produce *The African Queen, On the Waterfront, The Bridge on the River Kwai* and *Lawrence of Arabia*. But in 1945 he was ready to do anything he could. So he persuaded Bill Goetz and International Pictures to finance an Anthony Veiller script on the understanding that John Huston would do a doctoring job on it. Welles was hired as director and lead actor. He claimed to have been involved on rewrites, but in most respects he was under close orders to deliver the picture without frills or changes.

The story was not of Welles's choosing, though he did give it a personal note that clashes intriguingly with the sentiment of his politics. The time is just after the end of World War II. A fleeing Nazi, Meinike (well played by Konstantin Shayne, an actor Welles had used on radio and Akim Tamiroff's brother-in-law), comes by way of a spectacular, atmospheric Latin America to a small New England town. He is searching for Franz Kindler, a Nazi leader who has gone into hiding. In fact, Kindler is Charles Rankin, a professor at the college that dominates the town. Meinike arrives there on the very day that Rankin is to marry Mary Longstreet (Loretta Young), daughter of a Supreme Court justice. But Meinike was allowed to escape from prison so that he might lead a pursuer to the big fish, Kindler. That pursuer is Inspector Wilson (Edward G. Robinson). The unruly bundle of Kindler and Rankin (containing the name Kane as well as the dreamy threat of a Kain for kinder—the puzzle fiend cannot quite *not* notice these things) is played by Orson Welles in mustache and waved hair.

The pity of it is that this assignment sounds very promising. The notion of a Nazi mastermind who has insinuated himself into the Ivy League, and who has won the heart and body of Justice's daughter, is rich in menace and irony. The tranquil New England world could conceal great danger and ugly violence. The task that faces Wilson—to persuade Mary that her man is the devil—could be delicate and provocative. There

Fishing trip, 1947: John Huston, skipper, fish, Sam Spiegel, Jeffrey
Selznick (David O.'s son) and that sturdy seaman O. Welles (the left arm
is especially fine)

might be a remarkable contrast between the college's very white young
men and, say, the Nazi columns or the less solid groups in Dachau that we
see in newsreels. One might have thought that Welles the pamphleteer
would have leaped at the story.

Instead, the scheme succumbed to empty melodrama. Welles is both
very grand and very bad as Rankin. It's hard to resist the suspicion that he
was trying to be urbane, attractive and ambiguous, no matter that he
hammed up the wickedness in the man and helplessly glorified the malign
idea of a Nazi leader. I can only agree with Joseph McBride's reckoning

that Edward G. Robinson would have been much more effective in that role—restrained, stealthy, anxious, guilty (a little like the men Robinson played for Fritz Lang in *Scarlet Street* and *The Woman in the Window*). Done that way, Kindler could have been more frightening *and* more sympathetic. Then allow the possibility Welles himself wanted but was overruled on: that Agnes Moorehead could have played Wilson, the investigator. That stern woman could have been so much more subtle an inquirer, enough to do without the rather lurid marriage even, a plight that Loretta Young handled honorably but without much depth. Suppose the story had been worked out in such a way that we were unsure whether Rankin was Kindler, or that Wilson was a government agent. Suppose we had more chance to see Rankin's Nazism transposed into the reputable teaching methods of an Ivy League professor?

Still, for all Welles's assertion that "there is nothing of me in that picture," *The Stranger* does employ the odd, uneasy relationship between a somewhat hidden "great" man and an inquiring figure. Just as in *Mr. Arkadin*, the trapped beast must kill those sent to unearth him. And nothing in the movie has as much passion as the scene—crosscut with a paper chase amid fall leaves—in which Kindler embraces and then murders Meinike. Something in Welles felt the subject of the apostle who has become a helpless betrayer.

Welles spent a good deal of time building up the South American portion of the film. Twenty minutes of it was shot and then cut by Spiegel. Surely it was a reference to *It's All True*—and "much more interesting visually" as Welles put it—but truly we do not need that part of Meinike's story. Welles later defended those scenes as more interesting than the story—and thus emblematic of the clash between art and storytelling. But in *Kane* and *Ambersons*, there was no way of separating the look of the film from the movement of the story. In just a few years, Welles had become bored and arty, and scarcely interested in the rich story situation.

It was Welles's own opinion that *The Stranger* was his worst film. Most critics have gone along with that view. But *The Stranger* has a claim to fame. It was the only movie Welles ever made that showed a profit on first release. The picture opened in America in July 1946. Fifteen months later, the figures showed that against a negative cost of $1.034 million, it had gross receipts of $3.216 million. To all intents and purposes, Welles had proved himself a dutiful, efficient director—if that had really been the point.

9

Let's Have a Circus

IN THE OLD DAYS — and people were already remarking on an earlier Welles, more startling than the thirty-year-old—he had had extraordinary powers of concentration. He was doing so much, in a life also spilling over with incidents, dinners and liaisons, but when he came to a rehearsal, when he stepped up to the microphone or when he took the moments of *Kane* in hand, he was fixed, precise and accurate. Now, though, there was an air of blur, of haste while always being too late to get a thing right. He seemed irked by all the things he chose to do, and harassed by the quantity. Was he tired? Had he really expended some precious energy between twenty and twenty-seven that could not be renewed?

He could not quite discriminate, or judge the value of a project, much less see the practical way to proceed. It was as if he assumed that his great self, his genius, could marry up such diverse things as doing a parody of *Les Misérables* on the radio with Fred Allen and speaking out against the bomb tests on Bikini. He did not quite realize how, in some eyes, he had the knack of making comedy solemn while cheapening grave events and issues. He was no longer simply trusted, and this had as much to do with his growing reputation for unreliability as with the Promethean variety of his artistic character. He made people uneasy.

In the spring of 1946, between the completion of *The Stranger* and its opening, Welles plunged back into the theater, moving in nearly opposite directions at the same time. He sought to put on an immense musical extravaganza based upon Jules Verne's *Around the World in 80 Days* while also offering himself as the director for Bertolt Brecht's stark play about ideas and bigotry, *Galileo*. It was as if the capaciousness of repertory still possessed him, so that he would do *Macbeth* and *Horse Eats Hat* on alternate nights.

As far as anyone can tell now, out of a boy's love for the Verne book, Welles had the idea of a musical. It's not untypical of Welles that in the age of Americana musicals (*Annie Get Your Gun, Oklahoma! Carousel* and *On the Town* are all from the midforties), he chose a subject that is essentially European (though it has scenes in the Americas). Welles went to

Cole Porter to do the music, and it was Porter who recommended Mike Todd as a producer. Todd then was close to forty, an "inspired hustler" who had been involved on Broadway for several years without yet having a coup to make him famous.

Welles and Todd got on. Welles looked down on the producer but believed he was "touched with that particular grandeur which belongs to all the best of the circus showmen." Welles quickly wrote a script for the show, and with little more delay Porter penned a number of songs. With fatal speed, the enormous show came together, and never recovered from the impact. It was a story that ranged all over the world. It called for thirty-four sets, albeit ones meant as sketches. The cast was kept economical, with everyone playing several parts, but the show needed a wealth of exotic costumes. In addition, Welles wanted two proscenium arches so that, when the inner curtain closed to allow a set change, some characters could come out in front with patter and routines to cover the delay. He wanted it all to feel like the fantastical, silent movies of Georges Méliès. He called for a circus scene in which he would himself do magic tricks in blackamoor costume. There was a scene of a locomotive on a trestle bridge in the mountains. He even demanded a scene in which oil is discovered.

That's when the adroit Todd said he was broke and opted out. There were other sponsors: Alexander Korda, Toots Shor, Porter and Bill Goetz had some money in the show. But many of the paymasters' duties were taken up by Welles himself, and no one was quite sure where his money was coming from. On several occasions, he tried and failed to get more funding from the Schuberts in New York.

On April 27, the production began tryout performances at the Opera House in Boston. There was a good deal of exuberant chaos. Sets were not always put up in the right order. As well as directing (and now producing) the show, Welles found himself deputizing for other actors when they were ill—but he did not always know the lines.

On the last night of the Boston run, Welles appeared as himself when the curtain went up. "Ladies and gentlemen," he began. . . . Arthur Margetson, the show's Fogg, had lost his voice. He could not sing without putting his career and the show's future in jeopardy. Therefore, the audience was about to witness theater history: the seductive process turned on this allegedly rare opportunity. Welles would read Fogg's lines, and an understudy would sing the songs. And so—with the sympathetic support of yourselves, ladies and gentlemen—the show *might* work. For that night, it was like seeing a rehearsal. The audience felt blessed, and Welles had stumbled on the special appeal of seeming to enlist the audience in the workings of a trick. It was a spellbinding night, with Welles talking every-one—audience included—through their parts.

Reactions were very confused, but one visitor reckoned it was the most extraordinary American theater he had encountered. This was Bertolt Brecht, who immediately inquired if Welles would be interested in direct-ing *Galileo*, a play that was already promised to Charles Laughton. Despite the problems of a musical in progress, Welles jumped at the new opportu-nity and was hired.

By way of New Haven and Philadelphia, *Around the World* reached the Adelphi Theater in New York by May 31. By then, Welles was play-ing Dick Fix, the copper's nark who pursues Phileas Fogg. He had thrown more money into the mix—allegedly $320,000 of his own, cash or credit, by the time it was all over—and he had raised more funding from Harry Cohn of Columbia (and thereby hangs a story and a film). (In New York, crazed, he found time for a quick affair with Vivien Leigh.)

The reviews were very mixed. In the New York *Daily News*, John Chapman called it "wonderful, exciting and funny, and the most thorough and individual example of showmanship of the season." Everyone liked Mary Healy singing "Should I Tell You I Love You?" though generally the show was termed minor Porter—and very few of the songs have lasted in the popular repertoire. Worse, some critics found it both gimmicky and dull. The show had everything except good music, real comedy and a sense of direction. William Hawkins wrote, "One gets the feeling that Mr. Welles, the author, got his characters to a certain point and then said to himself in desperation, 'What must I do now?' Then he answered, 'Let's have a circus' or 'Let's have another reel of movie.' "

Hawkins lamented that the untidy giant of a frolic was all done in a "let's put on a play" spirit. And surely Welles had wanted to recapture some of the fun of the Wonder Show on Cahuenga Boulevard. But that had been close to improvised, and its riot had suited the mood of the ser-vicemen in the audience. There's no doubting Welles's love of amateur theater, but here he was offering it in a professional venue, and the jour-neying of the story had to seem contrived (as well as being very costly) on-stage. The show ran for seventy-five performances before expenses and slackening support finished it off. Yet on the way out, Welles thought to rekindle public interest by doing a cut-down *Lear* on alternate nights—a version set to music. In that summer, he took to the radio to deplore the current standards of dramatic criticism. After one critic had sneered that the show lacked only the kitchen sink, Welles appeared onstage with a sink. For himself, he loved the show, and said it was one of his best things.

There's no way of judging. But perhaps it did need a tent and kids in

the crowd—one London impresario tried to bring it in for the pantomime season. Then again, suppose that the book and the songs were
not good enough, so the production had to be the center of interest. The
story would wait. The persevering Mike Todd would later reclaim the
rights from Korda (after he and Welles had thought of filming it), and he
produced the movie—stately and dull, surely not as wild as Welles's
work—that somehow captivated the world in 1956, winning the best picture Oscar and ensuring Todd's fame the year before his death in a plane
crash. "Everyone" was in that movie, Welles noted—everyone except
him. Showmanship is a strange creature, but Todd had had an inspired, if
disordered, master to learn from. In *Around the World*, even in outline and
report, one can see Welles's astonishing taste for putting business, production, magic and amazement on the flimsiest of vehicles.

The same man was in genuine awe of the iron allegory and tough language of *Galileo*, a play sharpened in everyone's mind by the dilemma of
the scientist as exemplified in the new atomic age. In many ways, Brecht's
"epic" theater was not that far from the way Welles had done *Caesar*. But
Brecht and Laughton were very testing collaborators. Welles did not
much like Brecht, who could be abrasive and what Welles called "shitty."
Laughton was a tougher case altogether. He and Welles were not unalike
as actors, larger than life, prodigious but temperamental. Welles had a
penchant for thunderous outbursts. Laughton exercised his power in
more devious ways—by delay, indecision, insecurity and a creeping vulnerability that could turn anyone into his doctor. They were also two
imaginations that needed to be the center of attention, so they were
bound to clash. Could a way be found for Welles's mastery to fit
Laughton's complex needs? Could they sustain and satisfy each other?

The *Galileo* faction did not comprehend Welles's allegiance to *Around
the World*. And he could not extricate himself from that enough to sit
down and work with Laughton. So Laughton felt abandoned and neglected while Welles sought to delay *Galileo*. It fell to Richard Wilson to
keep in touch with Laughton, who was offended and disconcerted when
told that Welles would come when he was ready but that "when Orson
does a play . . . he really does it." That threatened Laughton: it did not
suggest a proper spirit of collaboration. So Laughton dropped Welles—
and picked up Mike Todd as a producer.

It was a nearly perfect picture of betrayal from Welles's point of view.
He had lost a major play as well as a fortune. He had felt people moving
in concert behind his back. But Welles was sweet and gentle in defeat (he
was the very man Laughton could have loved). He told the actor that

Mike Todd was a man of immense "charm," and that Laughton would know to convert that tricky commodity into Broadway expertise:

> He could take nothing from *Galileo* but me. This, for
> whatever it matters, he most assuredly has done. I'm the
> best man to stage the play, but I'm far—very far—from
> indispensable. I cannot but acknowledge that I need
> *Galileo* more than *Galileo* needs me.

Galileo would be stubborn yet. Todd did not last, and it was June 1947 before the play opened—in Los Angeles—with Joseph Losey as its director. One of his chief tasks then was to mediate between Brecht and Laughton. That was never likely as Welles's role. Nor was he exactly the director to match Brecht's instructions:

> The action must be presented calmly and with a wide
> sweep. Frequent changes of position and irrelevant
> movements should be avoided. The director must not
> for a moment forget that many of the actions and
> speeches are hard to understand and that it is therefore
> necessary to express the underlying idea of an episode
> by positioning.

The production was an enormous success, and it was delivered eventually by a producer who was at the same time making two remarkable films: Nicholas Ray's *They Live by Night* and Max Ophüls's *Letter from an Unknown Woman*. That model of efficiency was John Houseman.

10

I'm Aiming at You, Lover

THE STORY BEHIND *The Lady from Shanghai* is a good deal more interesting, and touching, than anything that appears in the film itself. For the rest of his life, Welles had a terrific yarn about the picture, enough to suggest that he could pluck a film out of the darkness as easily as he could a rabbit out of a hat. But conjurers do require a setup, and the rabbit has its needs. Welles also told a story about being invited to a party for Louis B. Mayer, assuming that he would be called upon to perform. So he wore clothes that had room for a rabbit. But his turn never came. As he sat listening to the vibrant acts of every musical star on the MGM payroll, the rabbit filled his deep pocket with shit and piss. *The Lady from Shanghai* has something of that smell about it.

According to Welles, it all began in Boston as he tried to put on *Around the World* while Mike Todd deserted him. There were costumes at the railway depot, or at the costumer's, and they could be released only on the payment of $25,000, or $50,000 or $55,000. Neither Welles nor the rabbit had this sort of lettuce. So Welles asked himself who in the world might come through in the pinch. There in the theater box office (or the hotel lobby—there are variants), he telephoned Harry Cohn (it must be April 26) and asked for the money to be wired to him. If you do that, Welles told Cohn, I'll do a picture for you from this terrific book. . . . He grabbed the paperback that the girl at the box office, or the hotel desk clerk, was reading and fired off the title: *If I Die Before I Wake*. On such stories rests the legend of Harry Cohn.

If I Die Before I Wake was a thriller, written by Sherwood King, published in 1938. Charles Higham, a Welles biographer, established that there had never been a paperback edition. That same April 26, Welles's assistant Richard Wilson tried to get a copy of the book to Cohn. But no one could find it. We are asked to suppose that neither the box-office girl nor the desk clerk would surrender hers. Instead, Wilson suggested to a Mercury employee, "Perhaps Franchot Tone has book." Here is a clue, for Welles was being hounded by lawyers acting for Tone, intent on enforcing a 1941 contract in which Welles had hired the actor for $75,000. It's not clear for what—it may or may not have involved the book that Tone had—but by late 1945, Welles had paid only $10,000 on the deal.

Still, something happened on April 26: a deal memo emerged, under that date, whereby Columbia would loan Welles $25,000 against $2,000 a week and $100,000 of possible profits for his services on *If I Die Before I Wake*, "or, in the event that you [Columbia] in your sole discretion do not like or cannot acquire said property on terms completely satisfactory to you, then I shall render my services in any other property which is mutually acceptable." By the end of May, somehow, Welles had acquired the movie rights to the book from Sherwood King. For a dollar, he sold them to Columbia.

But there is another complication. Years earlier, soon after the novel appeared, the B-movie producer William Castle had owned the rights to

If I Die Before I Wake and sold them to Columbia on the understanding that he would be involved if ever a picture materialized. With Welles's appearance on the scene, Castle produced a treatment for the story and sent it to Welles. The two men were acquaintances—they had even talked about working together. Welles responded, in friendly terms:

> About *If I Should Die* [*sic*]—I love it. . . . I have been searching for an idea for a film, but none presented itself until *If I Should Die* and I could play the lead and Rita Hayworth could play the girl. I won't present it to anybody without your O.K. The script should be written immediately. Can you start working on it at night?

I think we can let the box-office girl and the desk clerk go home—may they be happy together. What we have here is an intrigue in which a more or less familiar book, with some prompting from, and payoff to, William Castle and Franchot Tone, was floated as a studio picture, starring Welles and Hayworth. Tone's name never came up again, but Castle was associate producer on *The Lady from Shanghai* and present for most of the shooting. Perhaps he did do the first draft of the script.

Hayworth was in Welles's mind from the start, no matter that he would claim her presence came as a surprise, that she was Harry Cohn's idea, that he had had someone else ready but that, with Rita Hayworth as its star, the film's budget jumped up from $350,000 to $2 million. That spring of 1946, Welles and Hayworth were estranged. Lawyers were haggling over a property settlement, but divorce had not been set in motion. Rita had had an affair with the singer Tony Martin, but there's reason for believing that she wanted Orson back. He was romantically involved with Barbara Laage, a European actress in her early twenties. He would say later that the female lead in *If I Die Before I Wake* was meant for Laage. He would add that everything was over between him and Rita.

But there was a reconciliation. Orson moved back into the same house with Rita. If Cohn believed it was crazy not to put the couple together, Rita seemed anxious to give the marriage another try. From Welles's point of view, the project may have depended on Hayworth's starry presence. Her most recent film, *Gilda*, made during the separation from Orson, was her biggest hit yet: she had never looked more beautiful or played so overtly erotic and intelligent a woman. In *Gilda*, something seems to have educated Hayworth about the emotional dishonesty of men. For the first time in her life on-screen she had authority. Laage was set aside, though Welles was paying her a modest salary and reimbursing her for English lessons.

Suppose that Welles was not fully in charge—though this is the last possibility he ever allowed in talking about the picture. He did a script very hastily, holed up on Catalina Island, and working with a speed that showed some disdain for the story. He wasn't sure what to call it: *Black Irish* and *Take This Woman* were working titles, but they gave way to the star's thrust of *The Lady from Shanghai*. The novel's action had all taken place on Long Island—it was ideal material for an intricate, interior film noir about a strong but none-too-bright hero seduced and deceived by a femme fatale. But Welles opened it up to include a sea voyage from New York by way of the Panama Canal to Acapulco and San Francisco. That has to have been at Columbia's behest, for it altered the budget radically. But it allowed Welles to come within range of the look and light of *It's All True*—perhaps he could moonlight some footage to rescue that old project.

In October 1946, the picture began shooting in the Acapulco area, hiring Errol Flynn's yacht the *Zaca* (with Flynn as skipper) for the story's *Circe*. Everett Sloane was cast in the role of Hayworth's husband, Arthur Bannister, "the greatest trial lawyer in the world" but a cripple, a man who walks with two sticks. There were bit parts for old faithfuls Gus Schilling, Harry Shannon and Erskine Sanford. But no casting was more crucial than that of Glenn Anders as Bannister's partner, George Grisby. Anders had met Welles in radio, but he wasn't very active at the time. Then one day he got a call from Welles to be in Hollywood fast. As soon as he arrived, he had to play his own corpse—instead of a death certificate he was given a contract for $1,250 a week. So he started at his own end, and it would only suit the narrative fragmentation of the film if at this point Welles hardly knew what Grisby would be like alive.

The reconciliation with Rita Hayworth did not work. In later life, Welles would paint a picture of her as a tragic neurotic, a wretched creature, someone he had helplessly, and not unkindly, wronged. But was he always so much the protagonist and she the victim? There are stories that during their marriage he was not always sexually dynamic, that he was sometimes content to sit and watch her undress. On the *Zaca*, according to William Castle, there was a night when Hayworth openly flirted with Errol Flynn, as if to ask what a woman was to do if her husband "were unable to function."

This is speculation, but it grows out of the hatred one feels beneath the surface of *The Lady from Shanghai*. Welles later laughed off the idea that the picture was colored with thoughts of animosity or vengeance toward Hayworth. But he was too good a filmmaker to escape the charge. *The Lady from Shanghai* is very far from a good film. It suffers from boredom, laziness or impatience in its maker, so that he will not bother to develop or stick with the mood of intrigue. The courtroom scenes are absurdist humor from a different film altogether. And there is no handicap greater than that of Welles himself as the tough sailor hero, Mike O'Hara, "Black Irish," who is said to have killed a man in the Spanish Civil War and to be a typical rugged adventurer such as John Wayne or Gary Cooper might have played. But Welles looks boyish or even epicene—as a sailor, his walk makes us seasick. In his fight scenes, he is grotesquely unathletic. In his supposed love scenes with Elsa Bannister (Hayworth), he seems to be in another place. There is no contact or intimacy in the scenes. Welles's talk sounds postsynchronized, and we feel he is miles and months away, in a dubbing studio, observing his former wife with cold detachment.

The story needs to make us believe that Mike has been overwhelmed by Elsa, that an irrational sensuality leads him toward darkness. But Hayworth was shot with a fascinated loathing: Welles cut her hair and dyed it blond; he had her smiling very little; and he let her look older than she had ever done before. In *Gilda*, Hayworth had been intensely provocative, merry even, rich in hair, mouth, smile and body. But in *Lady from Shanghai* there is a grimness to her face and mouth, a severity in the eyes, that seems to be a response to the merciless absence of romance in the film.

In addition, the story is framed by O'Hara's voice-over narrative, done in a broad Irish accent that could only have prompted laughter in Welles's old Irish associates. The bogusness of the voice adds to his implausibility as a virile sailor. The narrative also encloses and distances the story as an example of O'Hara's benevolent foolishness. "When I start out to make a fool of myself," he tells us at the outset, "there's little enough can stop me." The tone is rueful, yet it has that edge of resigned self-glorification to be found in any Welles interview when he asks listeners to share in his disaster. The oil of self-regard has eased away pain, and it does not actually believe in its own stupidity. Rather, it offers it as a vouchsafe of warmth or humanity. As the film goes on, Hayworth's Elsa is variously set up, ogled, treated as a modern Circe, photographed in glowing but impassive close-ups in which she is lovely but baleful and reduced to viciousness and insanity. O'Hara leaves her on the floor, in agony and fear, dying from bullet wounds in the Crazy House. Welles's lumbering walk takes O'Hara away into the dawn and the deserted scene of San Francisco's Playland. As he goes, the voice-over knows that he will be found innocent—"But that's a big word, 'innocent'—stupid's more like it. Well,

A posed publicity shot for *The Lady from Shanghai*

everybody is somebody's fool.* The only way to stay out of trouble is to grow old, so I guess I'll concentrate on that. Maybe I'll live so long that I'll forget her—maybe I'll die trying."

It misunderstands Welles's profoundly solipsistic imagination not to see this, and the movie, as a verdict on himself and Rita Hayworth. Nothing else could better explain the facetious indifference of so much of the film, and the grinding misanthropy of certain scenes. The action is furious and empty. The set pieces—even the hall of mirrors conclusion, the aquarium scene, the trial—are camouflage for the lack of inner drive or conviction. But there are superb, nightmarish scenes in which we see the

* In *Touch of Evil*, the rhetoric is "He was some kind of a man. What does it matter what you say about people?"

Bannister marriage like a glass case of writhing reptiles in a zoo. In those moments, the revulsion for love and sex builds into a horror of human society and even a desperate belief that this world deserves atomic extinction. (In the Mexican sequences, especially, the brightness of the sun seems like a harbinger of nuclear explosions.)

There are two scenes—one on the *Circe*, one at a nocturnal beach picnic—in which Welles gives us composition and camera movement that treat Bannister, Grisby, Elsa and Mike as snakes all in one hole. The arrangement of bodies, the line of glances at the sharing of a cigarette and a light beautifully embody the loathsome human setup. Faces sweat. The cold beauty of Hayworth contrasts with the hooked or flabby gracelessness of Sloane and Anders. To touch a person here might risk contagion. Grisby and Bannister seem like the spent relics of some old homosexual past, and they both view O'Hara as a fleshy boy they are too jaded to take. There are potent hints of cruelty and humiliation—it is quite possible that Welles was alluding to Hayworth's ugly past and to her being a kind of slave to Harry Cohn, an imprisonment from which he had failed to rescue her.

Some critics have claimed to find *The Lady from Shanghai* one of Welles's most enjoyable films. On the contrary, I think it shows a degree of despair all the more unnerving in that it comes from a grown-up kid who is much less worldly than he wants us to think. Welles is giving up on his bread and butter, the Hollywood story film: he is too superior, or too bored, to make a genre mood consistent and constructive. Working at the height of film noir, Welles is interested only in deconstructing the atmosphere. He lurches from one set piece to the next. His style is showy and jittery, never trusting the script or the actors, and the film is full of close-ups that do not quite fit the situation. The mood is always being broken.

But the film's feeling for human horror is strong enough to grip us. In that vein, it has some of the greatest things Welles would ever do, things so black that they should never be forgotten or explained away. The available horrors of mass extermination in *The Stranger* cannot match the picnic scene in *Shanghai* in which O'Hara tells the others of something he saw in Brazil. This is the scene in which Bannister's arm comes up over his face—as protection, but also to mask his dark reverie, his sated communion with the slaughter:

> Do you know, once off the hump of Brazil, I saw the
> ocean so darkened with blood it was black, and the sun
> fadin' away over the lip of the sky. We put in at Fort-
> aleza. A few of us had lines out for a bit of idle fishin'.
> It was me had the first strike. A shark it was, and then

there was another and another shark again, till all about
the sea was made of sharks, and more sharks still, and
the water tall.* My shark had torn himself away from the
hook, and the scent, or maybe the stain it was, and him
bleedin' his life away, drove the rest of them mad. Then
the beasts took to eatin' each other; in their frenzy, they
ate at themselves. You could feel the lust of murder like
a wind stingin' your eyes, and you could smell the
death, reekin' up out of the sea. I never saw anything
worse, until this little picnic tonight. And you know,
there wasn't one of them sharks in the whole crazy pack
that survived.

The speech is stagy and literary. It is great radio, and Welles's Irish-
ness here has relaxed enough for it to sound as beautiful as a drug hitting
your senses. He looks fine—negroid even—surveying the bitter white
snakes. And the composition is as congested as a stalled subway car.

Such things were too much for Columbia and the public. There were
terrible difficulties making the plot comprehensible. The editor Viola
Lawrence had to take charge for the story to work. Music was added to
punch up scenes. Harry Cohn insisted on Hayworth's song, "Please Don't
Kill Me," which Welles shot like a death scene. The film was not released
until May 1948; it was 86 minutes, as opposed to Welles's cut of 155 minutes. By then Orson and Rita were divorced. The picture cost nearly $2.0
million, and it grossed a little less than $1.5 million.

11

The Winner Loses, Too

HOW DOES ANYONE live fifty years in the jungle of American
show business, meeting uncommon disappointment and humiliation (just
because he *is* afflicted by genius), and die with a boy's bright smile in his
eyes? This may be the most lovable thing about the Welles so many

---

* There was a story that when Jacaré was lost, off Rio, he was taken by a shark. (This
speech surely influenced Robert Shaw's memory of the *Indianapolis* disaster in *Jaws*.)

younger movie people revered in his last twenty years. Not that Welles liked his youthfulness to show. He laughed at himself, his naïveté, and so often disqualified it: Mike O'Hara never truly possesses it in *The Lady from Shanghai*, and even the young Kane seems too sardonic, too manipulative, to reveal his rapture at running a show. It suggests that Welles disliked, or feared, his own hopefulness. But he could never expunge it, or get control of it. His career became increasingly muddled, or inept, just because he would get drunk on hope and the dream of doing great things. He could hardly approve anything without believing in it and becoming excited.

He had been squeezed out of *Galileo* like an irritant pip; and there could have been murder if he'd stayed. But he was wounded. He had been eliminated from Chaplin's Landru project. A month after *Monsieur Verdoux* opened, another film went into wide release with a Wellesian contribution. This was David Selznick's production of *Duel in the Sun*, directed (for the most part) by King Vidor. It is a sultry melodrama in the Western genre, a film in which Selznick's mistress—Jennifer Jones—played a half-breed girl who is loved by the two sons, gentle and wicked (Joseph Cotten and Gregory Peck), of a cattle rancher. Selznick built the picture over a period of time into a burning colossus (it eventually cost $6.5 million, and it was in flaming Technicolor). Late in the day, he wanted to add a narrative that might cast the film's trashy story as some kind of prairie legend. So Orson Welles was hired—he hoped for a fat check—to lend a growling foreboding to this prose (Selznick apparently never detected Welles's elephant-large parody of the work):

> Deep among the lonely, sun-baked hills of Texas, the great and weather-beaten stone still stands. The Comanches call it "Squaw's Head Rock." Time cannot change its impassive face, nor dim the legend of the wild young lovers who found heaven, and hell, in the shadows of the rock. For when the sun is low and the cold wind blows across the desert, there are those who still speak of Pearl Chavez, the half-breed girl from down along the border, and of the laughing outlaw with whom she had kept a final rendezvous, never to be seen again. And this is what the legend says: "A flower, known nowhere else, grows from out of the desperate crags where Pearl vanished. . . . Pearl, who was herself a wild flower, sprung from the hard clay, quick to blossom . . . and early to die."

Unburdened of those rolling phrases—there is a sigh in the delivery as befits enormous evacuation—he waited for the money. For Welles already was as nakedly in need of immediate cash as he was incapable of sustaining serious, long-term plans for income or fiscal stability. He looked at money (or, rather, the bare table before it was put down) like a boy panting for lunch. But Selznick was a man of the world, someone who appreciated the fineness in Welles and his taste for splendid things, so he spared him money and gave him instead a pair of antique dueling pistols as a memento of the great experience. In respectful satire, Welles gave the mogul every subsequent Christmas two glass pistols filled with candy.

Then there were the several Korda projects—Welles had a special taste for attempting deals with such great independent moguls as Selznick and Korda. He liked them both; he enjoyed their automatic use of limousines, luxury hotels, gambling and lavish dinners. But he was sucker enough not to see that they had nearly as much trouble paying for the attributes of pomp as he would have had. There was the *War and Peace* with Korda, with Welles as Pierre, and Merle Oberon or Vivien Leigh as Natasha.

There was a *Salome* planned. Fletcher Markle was hired to write a script, and he tagged along on the *Lady from Shanghai* travels, hoping to consult with Welles, who wanted Vivien Leigh as Salome, with himself as both Oscar Wilde and Herod—but Korda was set on having Eileen Herlie (a lady who moved Welles not at all) as the veiled one. There was always talk of *The Master of Ballantrae*, for Welles was intrigued by that story of the antagonism between two brothers. But Korda could not get the rights. Korda had resuscitated an old script for *Cyrano de Bergerac*, written by Ben Hecht and Harry d'Abbadie d'Arrast in the 1930s. Welles reworked it. He longed to play the part, making Cyrano a real competitor with Christian for Roxane and imitating the great actor Coquelin, who had done the play with a nose that grew smaller in every act. *Cyrano* was to be designed by Alexander Trauner, with Jean Simmons as Roxane. It was one of the projects that eventually coaxed Welles to Europe—and it is a role in which one longs to see him, an ugly romantic, a wordsmith who is in a position to make light of his eloquence and a noble idiot. He could have been a wondrous, moving Cyrano, so much better than the José Ferrer who won an Oscar in the part in 1950, when the defeated Korda traded the rights to Stanley Kramer.

Salome ended up as something for Rita Hayworth, in the dire 1953 film, made for Harry Cohn and Columbia. Sooner than that, Cohn jumped on another Welles idea: he had suggested doing the *Carmen* story, murderous and hard-bitten, like a James M. Cain story, with Paulette

Goddard. It failed, but in 1948 Cohn starred Hayworth in *The Loves of Carmen*, one more of the anemic films that spelled out her decline. A time was coming soon when Welles could look at the films on view and see them as so many ghosts.

In the spring of 1947, he had not too much to be hopeful about. ABC had canceled the *Commentaries* on radio: he had no other regular outlet, and thus no steady source of income. The relationship with Rita was over, and *The Lady from Shanghai* had been both a very difficult film to cut coherently and a bloodcurdling expression of misanthropy. Welles's personal and business affairs were in ruin, and the loyal Richard Wilson was close to a breakdown trying to find order. In the years 1946–47 (and Welles noticed such things more than most people in Hollywood), there were atomic tests in Bikini, civil war in China and Greece, the slaughter of independence in India, violence in Palestine, the onset of Cold War and mounting paranoia about the red influence within America. On the movie screens, there was also the neurotic anguish of film noir. Against that background, he made an extraordinary return to form with a picture that delivers his most frightening and consistent portrait of evil.

Welles sometimes spoke as if he had been drawn into *Macbeth*, and had taken it on as just a job, or another way of proving his competence. That is belied by the film's power as well as by the narrative circumstances that produced it. For Welles, Shakespeare was a given*: it put him in his favorite role of adapter. Twice before, with the voodoo *Macbeth* and *Caesar*, he had seemed brilliantly innovative just because he had confidence in, and understanding of, the original material. He loved to take a Shakespeare text and revitalize it, because he believed that academia and the ages had lost contact with the barnstorming story value of Shakespeare. And this new *Macbeth* was all the more exciting in that it was conceived as a combination of film and theater, working quickly and cheaply in the spirit of the old Mercury Theatre and the Wonder Show on Cahuenga Boulevard. So often, Welles was at his best working swiftly and with the minimum of resources. So often, too, that success was prompted by a memory of how radio worked. Thus, his *Macbeth* is a radio film, a movie running inside a listening head in spirals of paranoia and ambition.

Having moved out of the house he and Rita Hayworth had lived in, Welles stayed for a while with Charlie Feldman, the agent and producer. Feldman had a deal at Republic, a studio owned by Herbert J. Yates and devoted largely to low-budget Westerns, to promoting Yates's wife, Vera

---

* With one, odd, exception: in all his years he seems never to have considered that very Wellesian venture—Prospero in *The Tempest*.

Ralston, and to occasional flights of fancy and pretension—like Ben
Hecht's *Specter of the Rose*, made in 1946. Feldman persuaded Yates to do
a *Macbeth* for $700,000, with $100,000 of that as Welles's fee. But in advance of the shooting, Welles would mount *Macbeth* onstage, using the
process to rehearse the actors. Thus, in May 1947, *Macbeth* ran for four
days at the University Theater in Salt Lake City (as part of the Utah Cen-
tennial Festival) before filming began in Hollywood on June 23 on a
twenty-three-day schedule.

He gathered one of his idiosyncratic casts made up of old associates
and newcomers: Edgar Barrier as Banquo, Dan O'Herlihy as Macduff,
Roddy McDowall as Malcolm, Erskine Sanford as Duncan, William Alland as dialogue director and one of the murderers, Brainerd Duffield
doubling as murderer and witch, Gus Schilling as the porter, his own
daughter, Christopher, as Macduff's son, Peggy Webber as Lady Macduff
and another witch. And for Lady Macbeth, he had Jeanette Nolan. She
was twenty-six then, the wife of actor John McIntire, and making her
movie debut. Over the years, Ms. Nolan has been criticized for her playing, and she won the part only after Welles had failed to get Vivien Leigh,
Mercedes McCambridge and Agnes Moorehead. But the complaints are
unjust. Together, she and Welles make the most passionate and tortured
couple in all of Welles's work. They make Arthur and Elsa Bannister seem
like an actors' sketch—yet they know that more modern, reptilian embrace, somewhere between devouring and destroying, like the lovemaking of scorpions.

For in *Macbeth*, Welles made a disturbing portrait of marriage (or
greedy sexual rapture) in which the having of children is replaced by the
murderous grasping of power. Of course, this is founded in Shakespeare.
But the brilliance of Welles's adaptation of the stage play for the screen itself testifies to his understanding of that. He was very drastic in cuts, re-
arrangements and even in a few soundalike additions. But the film is
faithful to the drama and poetry of the original—indeed, it is inspired by
the play.

Critics over the ages have wondered about where the Macbeths' children are. For, as she has to urge her husband into the murder of Duncan,
Lady Macbeth says to him,

> *What beast was 't then*
> *That made you break this enterprise to me?*
> *When you durst do it, then you were a man;*
> *And to be more than what you were, you would*
> *Be so much more the man. Nor time nor place*
> *Did then adhere, and yet you would make both.*

As Macbeth

They have made themselves, and that their fitness now
Does unmake you. I have given suck, and know
How tender 'tis to love the babe that milks me:
I would, while it was smiling in my face,
Have plucked my nipple from his boneless gums,
And dashed the brains out, had I so sworn as you
Have done to this.

These are fearful words: maybe the lady is mad already. Maybe she did murder her own babe so as not to permit a rival in her love affair with Macbeth. For there are no children in sight, and they would be vital to this story that hangs in so many ways on the matter of succession. Later on, as the threat of Banquo is considered (for the witches have told Macbeth that Banquo's progeny will be kings one day), Welles has Lady Macbeth turn vulpine and seductive. Her "come to bed" is not just a promise to bring him sleep at last but an invitation to fuck beneath the furs of bedding in what must be a damp, rock-walled chamber—for the castle of the play feels more like a cave in the movie. Would that love make a real human baby, or only the grisly clay doll that the witches pull from their caldron and that is seen under the main title "Macbeth"? Is Macbeth her child in the way that some spoiled children—even boy wonders—have to be the dominant child of a marriage?

The inner secret to Welles's *Macbeth* is that murder is their child, their true offspring. Mary McCarthy once observed about the play that Lady Macbeth "takes very little stock in the witches. She never pesters her husband, as most wives would, with questions about the weird sisters: 'What did they say, exactly?' 'How did they look?' 'Are you sure?' " Welles's film makes a strength, an answer even, out of that oddity. For it is as if the wife has whispered to the husband through the sisters. Welles has three sisters—haggish shapes silhouetted against the cyclorama—but his method leaves one wondering, Has a production of *Macbeth* ever had his wife as one of the witches? Or could the weird sisters be his dream, as she lies beside him, murmuring their spell? For Welles, the witches are a kind of stealthy marital sex that frees the deeper libido of ambition, murder and the horniness of power.

Nothing better illustrates this than our first sight of Lady Macbeth—dark, her hair lightly coiffed, in a skintight dress—reclining in a frame full of white fur, reading Macbeth's letter that describes the witches. (Jean Cocteau perceived that this was "almost a woman in modern dress . . . reclining on a fur-covered divan beside the telephone.") The tableau and the rolling action of her vivid body are very erotic, as is the suggestion

Macbeth: Welles with Jeanette Nolan

that she has dreamed the witches for Macbeth. They are her fondest gift to him, and the most tragic denial of nature, maternity and childbearing.

Welles, on the eve of making *Macbeth*, had just left his second child. There is no reason to think that he was stupid or self-centered enough never to reflect on this. In the long term of his life, he was not just an absent father but someone seen and felt as a stranger by his children. He was interested in himself, and smart enough to wonder how far this failure was a fruit of a career devoted to art, film, theater, performance, the show— call it what you will. And he was narcissist enough to make the failure a part of his art and work—horrifying, yet something he could not look away from. So it is relevant that his first daughter, Christopher, as Macduff's son, suffers a hideous death in the film.

This speculation might seem improper but for the integrity of the movie. Though made in a frantic hurry, with rented costumes and mysterious sets flung up out of papier-mâché, *Macbeth* works. No film since *Kane* had had so profoundly organized or expressive a photographic style. The black and white is very theatrical but beautifully harnessed to a world made of fog-laden noon and dank castles. The whites are as bright as bone, the blacks like holes of iniquity. Depth and height are consistently evocative as forms of moral hierarchy, and as measures of remoteness and intimacy in the psyche. With just a few set places—a window with spear-heads for bars, an open staircase, a warren of rocky passageways and a bare hall—Welles furnished the nightmare of *Macbeth* as somewhere ancient and primitive yet modern and eternal, too.

The dreamlike power was enhanced by sound. Several of the key so-liloquies are not shown in lip-synch but done as voice-overs. In other words, Welles seems to have feared a certain vulgarity or absurdity in hav-ing too much Shakespearean verse spoken by mouths we see moving—as if in life. It is easier "heard" inwardly: thus the great "Tomorrow" solilo-quy is done against rolling mist, while other inward speeches are played against the speaker's face. This method grew out of the way Welles shot *Macbeth*—with the actors miming to a prerecorded sound track (the way musicals are done)—but it came more seriously from radio and Welles's abiding respect for the listener's power to visualize. What works so well here is the constant sense of an unspoken rapport between Macbeth and his wife. They share thoughts the way a mother and a fetus share blood. And so the thoughts of murder mount with a magical stealth.

Mention "magic" and we see another way *Macbeth* spoke to Welles. For Macbeth is so spiritually ready to be visited by witches: their message voices his subconscious and gives him the perilous state of the "shut-eye," the sorcerer who sees his powers coming to life. When the ghost of Ban-quo appears, Welles handles the scene beautifully: in the crowded dining hall of Macbeth and the company, there is no ghost; but what Macbeth experiences is just himself and Banquo—only the occult exists.

Thus, there is not just terror but glee in Welles's Macbeth when Bir-nam Wood does come to Dunsinane: his defeat and death are clear, but magic is fulfilled. (And magic is a deadly supernatural force such that the restoration of proper kings will not remove.) Magic is the performance of wickedness and the kingdom of murder. It is also the theater of tyranny. In *Macbeth*, it becomes plain that Welles's way of photographing him-self—from very low angles, so that he seems huge but monstrous—is not simply ironic but a rapture of narcissism. And it makes clear the astonish-ing gulf between Welles the liberal, the defender of the helpless, and the imagination so drawn to dark greatness.

Welles is very good as an actor in *Macbeth*. As the triumphant warrior he is quite lean, with a slit of black mustache like a scar and dark curls be-neath helmets that are part Visigoth, part Tartar (no matter how cheap, the costuming is excellent). Then when he is murderer and king, he becomes drunker, much heavier and ponderous. But, at the end, "tied to a stake," waiting for Macduff and seemingly alone, he is vigorous, brave, defiant and inspired—he knows death cannot defeat the dread magic.

The playing is heartfelt, and liberated, as if Welles had found energy in the decision to be the black, roaring rogue, the genius who despises ordinary mortals. So often sheepish or overdone as an actor, Welles now cries out unfettered and free, a man of such power as to be unfit for company. James Naremore, in his book *The Magic World of Orson Welles*, makes the fine point that Welles cannot mask his exultation in this flourish. He also refers Macbeth's dying magnificence to a speech Welles had once written for Kurtz in *Heart of Darkness*. Read carefully, it shows how unshakably frightening *Macbeth* is and how much it reflects a creator giving up the ghost of ordinary life:

> I'm a great man, Marlow—really great. . . . The meek—
> you and the rest of the millions—the poor in spirit, I
> hate you—but I know you for my betters—without
> knowing why you are except that yours is the Kingdom
> of Heaven, except that you shall inherit the earth. Don't
> mistake me, I haven't gone moral on my deathbed. I'm
> above morality. No. I've climbed higher than other men
> and seen farther. I'm the first absolute dictator. The first
> complete success. I've known what many others try to
> get. . . . I won the game, but the winner loses too. He's
> alone and he goes mad.

12

In Italy, Under the Borgias

THEN, AS HAD happened before, Welles went away. He went to Europe, not with one plan but with so many that he quickly made a new disorder. In a general way, he did not come back to America for nine years. He did not foresee that long an absence. He never intended it, never meant to hurt America. Yet some sort of escape was predictable, or characteristic—and Europe (or, at least, its great hotels) was a place where men of the world with a reputation for genius and some dollars for many lire (or whatever) might be appreciated. He was weary of not being liked, and he was smart enough to know that Europe cherished Americans who despaired of their own brash, crude country. He might be understood in Europe. (After all, *Kane* only opened in Paris in the summer of 1946.)

So it proved. Jean Cocteau was not, perhaps, a typical European. But he met Welles in 1948, in Italy and France, and he identified the dynamic and elusive contrast he relied on:

> Orson Welles is a kind of giant with the look of a child,
> a tree filled with birds and shadow, a dog that has bro-
> ken its chain and lies down in the flower beds, an active
> idler, a wise madman, an island surrounded by people, a
> pupil asleep in class, a strategist who pretends to be
> drunk when he wants to be left in peace.

Only two years earlier, Welles had been busy addressing the state of America. He had had hopes of taking his show to Washington. No other actor talked as much about politics, or talked such sense. In 1945, as a reward, the FBI developed a file on him and labeled him a Communist. And it was in the fall of 1947—the very period in which Welles left the country—that the House Committee on Un-American Activities subpoenaed ten filmmakers. It would be easy, out of liberal loyalty, to suppose that Welles was in jeopardy. But the truth is that the FBI and others were losing interest in him as the red scare grew. There's no hint that he felt any need to flee, or that authorities were after him.

If such a case could have been made against Welles, he was doubly vulnerable, for the IRS had a very fat file on him and many grievances. That was a much more pressing reason for escape—just as it became a pressure to stay away. But in the immediate instance, Welles had left full of prospects. He had shot *Macbeth*, and he believed that Republic would, if necessary, send him the film and an editor wherever he might be in Europe. As he worked on new ventures there—in Italy, most likely—he could tidy up *Macbeth*. Just as he had left Jack Moss in charge when he went to Brazil for *It's All True*, Richard Wilson was expected to man the fort now. It nearly drove Wilson crazy.

Republic was outraged when Welles departed: it's not clear how thoroughly he had warned them. Then it turned out that the experimental approach to sound, and Welles's spreading around of Scottish accents as thick as porridge, left many problems in postproduction. Much of the verse was unintelligible. Studio executives were very reluctant to send the editor, Louis Lindsay, after Welles, and to pay for the trip. Wilson had to deal with "hysteria, snideness, sarcasm, threats," and he didn't always know where to find Welles. The studio was also promising to get Welles to pay insurance against any delays in the script. That alarmed Wilson, for he knew that the shell that remained of Mercury had no money. If they had, he would have been able to pay himself.

To solve Mercury's everlasting problem, Wilson was talking to Arnold Grant, an entertainment lawyer who reckoned himself a pillar of sanity for wayward artists. But Grant had a way of promising clarity and order and then moving on to other people's difficulties. Wilson wrote to Welles in February 1948,

> I'm therefore tantalized with the prospect that dangles
> right in front of our eyes—of your being out of debt—
> fully solvent—and even with a real bank account to back
> you up—if you'll consistently accept Arnold's advice for
> the rest of this one year. Yet Arnold, either because he's
> too busy or for other reasons, is advising the easiest way.

Grant never solved Welles's confusion (there are tangles too vital for relief), and he would have a history of not coming through: a decade later, he and David O. Selznick ended up suing each other after similarly sweeping promises.

So Wilson turned instead to Edward Small, an independent producer of consistently vulgar but profitable pictures (his logo involved such fanfare and building-size letters for "Edward Small Productions" that it seemed an oversight or a joke to leave his name "Small"). But Small and Welles had a brief business love affair, and the producer was eager to have Welles play Cagliostro, the eighteenth-century hypnotist, magician and scoundrel. It was perfect casting, with splendors of setting and costume such as Europe was known for. So as that picture developed, with Gregory Ratoff directing from a script by Charles Bennett, perhaps Small could pay for Lou Lindsay to go to Italy. You bet, said Small—he was "hot as a firecracker" on any Welles scheme and was already dreaming of an *Othello* and a *Moby Dick*. (You have to wonder if, somehow, Welles couldn't have contrived one work in which Othello was once a member of the *Pequod*'s crew.)

Othello was also attracting the interest of the Edinburgh Festival and the American National Theatre and Academy. Early in 1948, there was talk of doing a stage version at Edinburgh, and the movie right afterward, for under $800,000. How was Wilson to know that whereas *Macbeth* had been shot in three and a half weeks, *Othello* would drag on three years? "For Christ's sake, write," he begged Welles.

But in Europe Welles was forever on the move, so letters had to zigzag to catch up with him. He was busiest now on plans for *Cyrano* with Alex Korda, examining locations and clothes with the designer, Alexander Trauner, and practicing fake noses in some of the most lavish hotel bathrooms in Europe. He was on expenses in a Europe frantically open to the dollar. In spare moments, he was scripting another Korda project—Pirandello's play *Henry IV,* that magnificent study of delusions of grandeur. He would lament later that it had been a great script, fit to be published.

From time to time, as he and Lindsay found themselves in the same country and hotel, they would look at *Macbeth* on a Moviola. The Scottish sound track was largely replaced. Republic found the whole thing too long and too slow. In Los Angeles, Richard Wilson was trying to accommodate the fine musical score written by Jacques Ibert. From the hotels, Welles chopped twenty-one minutes out of the picture, without much complaint. It would be decades before the full-length version (the one praised in the last chapter) became available. Republic had taken against the picture and the difficulties it presented, but surely some of that reaction was prompted by Welles's own indifference.

Word spread in Hollywood that *Macbeth* was less than a breakthrough, and a lot less commercial than Olivier's *Henry V* (1945)—a considerable encouragement in the venture. So Edward Small cried off *Othello,* using political instability in Italy as his excuse. The Cagliostro project was sufficient. But the Edinburgh Festival still wanted a stage *Othello,* and Wilson found himself pledging Welles to dates that were never kept. Meanwhile, *Macbeth* was hell to finish, a hell made worse by promises from Welles that he would return, soon, to complete it himself. So Wilson fought the studio battles, with no support from Charlie Feldman, who only wanted the damned thing over. Then there was the distress of Welles's old chauffeur, Shorty, who had acted in *Macbeth* as Seyton but who was owed money so that he threatened to confiscate Welles materials he was storing in his garage.

Even granted hotel life and the parade of European women, this was more tumult than a boy wonder could easily handle. And Welles always wanted scenery to match his hopes, and people to like him. He wanted to be serene and assured. He wanted to give the great little boy's smile shyly to the camera and find a pigeon in the lady's brassiere—of course, after that surprise, more thorough searches would be done in the name of safety.

And late in the summer of 1948, just such a chance at bliss and ease came his way. He ran from it, for he was constitutionally on the run. But it caught up with him and gave him one of his greatest fifteen minutes.

Black Magic

By the midsummer of 1948, Alex Korda and Graham Greene had the script for a story they had cooked up together. It was called *The Third Man*, and Carol Reed was set to be the director. It concerned the trip a man makes to postwar Vienna to meet an old friend who lives there, named Harry Lime. From the outset, part of the appeal had been to film in Vienna itself. Greene added the central relationship of an old friendship so betrayed by Lime's wickedness that the visitor—a rather foolish writer of cowboy stories called Martins—trades him to the police. Korda had to have a partner in the picture—David O. Selznick, who fussed over the script and the title and had lots of ideas about the casting. Reed and Greene largely ignored the fuss, but they could not argue against Selznick's plan: Cary Grant for Martins and Noël Coward for Lime. But Grant wanted too much money, and as for Coward . . . well, Reed wanted

Orson Welles. He dined with Welles in London and sketched out the part, even if Lime wasn't much on-screen.

"I'd much rather come in two-thirds of the way through," said Welles, who had gathered from Reed that for most of the first two-thirds of the story the other characters talked about Lime. Welles knew the power of anticipation, and he saw that if the film was any good whoever played Lime would be acclaimed a great actor.

But then he went away again. Reed had to go to Hollywood to appease Selznick. Joseph Cotten emerged as the ideal Martins—Holly Martins it would be, for Cotten reckoned that Greene's name, Rollo Martins, sounded homosexual. Reed was happier still: Cotten and Welles were chemistry together, and they would be fun to work with. Selznick was wary: he said Cotten and Welles together might be worse than fun; they would play private jokes and make up their own dialogue; they were too close to being naughty boys. Korda said, Why not Orson? He owed him something after *Cyrano* and everything else had collapsed. But where was Orson? Korda's brother, Vincent, and Vincent's son, Michael, were given the challenge—find Welles in time for the shooting.

They had heard he was in Rome. When they got there, to the Grand Hotel, they learned that Welles had moved on to Florence. So they traveled on, only to find that Welles had just left for Venice. He had to be there, for the finally finished *Macbeth* was to be shown at the film festival. And he had another reason for Venice. He would shoot some footage for *Othello* there, for that project was said to be getting on its feet with Italian money. But then, for obscure reasons, *Macbeth* was withdrawn from the festival—it had something to do with European barriers to American film exhibition. So the Kordas found that cupboard bare. Welles had gone on to Naples. There they learned that he was on the isle of Capri. They took a boat over and were passed by another boat going back to the mainland—Welles waved to them across the water. He knew by now he was being tracked and could not resist the game. He went to Nice, to the Hotel Ruhl, and it was there that he allowed good fortune to catch up with him.

He felt like master of the hunt. But he was stupid when the deal was done. He was offered $100,000 up front for a few days' work, or 20 percent of the picture's profit. There was never a glimmer of the businessman in Welles, no real respect for profit. He took the cash, and never worked on a bigger hit.

Welles filmed a few days in Vienna and a few in London. He wore no makeup, and he might have been dressed in the very suit, draped overcoat and swaggering fedora in which he commanded Europe. Reed seemed happy to take the actor's suggestions, and Welles felt unhindered. Why not, for he was being taken at face value and encouraged to play himself. Greene's script and story called for this Lime: "his stocky legs apart, big shoulders a little hunched, a belly that has known too much good food for too long, on his face a look of cheerful rascality, a geniality, a recognition that his happiness will make the world's day." It's enough to make one wonder whether Greene himself hadn't had a notion of Welles all along.

When Lime at last appears, at night in a doorway, his face and existence suddenly caught in the light from an upstairs window, his plump boy's grin is ineffably sinister but sweet, and it goes into the camera like charm's knife. From this first glimpse, Lime's evil is complicated by the actor's self-regard and his confidence that we will play along, just like the cat that has to sit at his polished toes. "What a star entrance that was!" said Welles.

I argue with myself, more than thirty-four years later, about what Welles's beguiling look does to Lime. Greene wrote about a racketeer, a man who pollutes penicillin so that children die and suffer malformations. And even then Lime has glib excuses for himself that shade into the cynic's soothing policy of justification—superbly written, beautifully delivered:

> Look down there. Would you really feel any pity if one
> of those dots stopped moving for ever? If I said you can
> have twenty thousand pounds for every dot that stops,
> would you really, old man, tell me to keep my money—
> or would you calculate how many dots you could afford
> to spare? Free of income tax, old man. Free of income
> tax. It's the only way to save nowadays.

No direction could separate Welles from his own rueful contempt for income tax. Equally, Lime has an ambivalence that no other actor could have contributed. Noël Coward would have been nastier, crueler, more odious. Perhaps that is how Lime should be. Which of us wouldn't want to execute a real Lime? But movies teach us to enjoy wickedness. So, when I first saw the film as a child, I mourned Lime's death: he was too urbane, too smooth, too childish to perish, I thought. I must have missed a lot of what Greene intended. I was not alone: within a few years, as we will see, Harry Lime became a kind of raffish international hero.

But Welles did more than just be himself for the camera—and I don't think he ever gave a performance with so little ham or inflation. He had ideas. And Reed had the wisdom to let him go with some of them. Thus

On the Ferris wheel: Holly and Harry in *The Third Man*

it is that, at the end of the Ferris wheel sequence, Welles was allowed to add to Greene's script—there is no question about that. It was a little set piece speech, one that Welles would recite at dinner, one he was proud of and believed in: it was his new gloss on politics. It shows how slippery his brilliant mind could be, and how much Lime he had in him—enough to rot ordinary bodies:

> When you make up your mind, send me a message—I'll
> meet you any place, any time, and when we do meet,
> old man, it's you I want to see, not the police . . . and
> don't be so gloomy. . . . After all, it's not that awful—
> you know what the fellow said. . . . In Italy for thirty

years under the Borgias they had warfare, terror, murder, bloodshed—they produced Michelangelo,
Leonardo da Vinci and the Renaissance. In Switzerland
they had brotherly love, five hundred years of democracy and peace, and what did that produce . . . ? The
cuckoo clock. So long, Holly.

13

Chubby Tragedians

CHILDREN WERE CONCEIVED, carried, labored over, nursed, praised for first words and simple sentences, seen standing, walking and achieving bowel control in the time it took Orson Welles to make *Othello*. They mastered gum. This is not simply a mocking comparison. Rather, it is meant to draw attention to Welles's nurturing regard for the child in himself. *Othello* the movie began to be worked on in the summer of 1948. It did not have its world premiere until May 1952; and it did not open in America until the fall of 1955—as if to say, So what? to America and its less than complete acceptance of the prodigy. Think of the miles that distance runner Emil Zatopek accumulated between the Olympiads of 1948 and 1952 (he was a star at both), as Welles roamed around the old world *Othello*ing.

No film that Welles finished was more beset by obstacles or unlikelihood. Thus his greatest defenders speak of *Othello* as proof of his dedication, his perseverance—his professionalism, even. Surely he deserves praise for bringing the picture in, and for defying immense odds. But defiance was his forte. Beyond question, it was an achievement to make just one *Othello* with more or less the same cast, and with a spirited gesture at integrity of style and story, when he was compelled to stop and start again so often. He loved desperate spontaneity. Above all, there should be no fudging over the fact that Welles's *Othello* depended on his money just as its many delays were caused by his need to go off and earn more money. Effectively he paid for the picture—it would be too solemn to protest that the American people and treasury also paid for it as monies went to film, hotels, travels and dining, as opposed to the IRS. But money meant so little to Welles as a thing in itself; it was a negotiable, like charm or the script.

Still, we should be cautious of stooping to charges of professionalism. Rather, the caprices that assailed *Othello*, and that passed like storms, convinced Welles of a strolling, random and gaily amateur way of making films. He took immense chances with *Othello;* he inflicted that gamble on others, whether they liked it or not. He gave the exotic adventure every chance to escape. But somehow it survived, abided and grew—like a child a wayward parent sees too seldom—so he took heart at the vitality of survivors and the sheer unsinkability of some corks. *Othello* proved that dedication and professionalism were for the worriers of the world, cleric artists and the Jews in Hollywood. If *Othello* got made, despite everything, then either God or magic was on his side—or it was enough being Orson Welles.

In the beginning, it was to be a simple thing—though never as tight and studio-bound as *Macbeth*. As he made *Black Magic* in Rome at the Scalera Studio, Welles found himself talking to Montatori Scalera about the story of the Moor of Venice. It was a natural Italian production. Scalera said he would put up the money, so Welles began to talk to the designer Alexander Trauner: they wanted to do the story in the style of Carpaccio, the Renaissance painter. If there wasn't yet a script, there was an approach—to film in real palaces, in real costumes, and for Welles to be a full Berber. He did some shooting in Venice in the summer of 1948 with Lea Padovani as his Desdemona. She had handicaps—she was very dark, and she spoke no English; but she had the weight that can overwhelm stronger doubts—the director was infatuated with her.

For his Iago, Welles wanted Everett Sloane or James Mason. But Sloane had a complex: he was sick of being the ugly heavy to Welles's romantic lead. So he refused. Mason was not available, alas: he and Welles might have passed as brothers, or as men held by the same faintly mannered eloquence. Welles thought, instead, of Micheál MacLiammóir, whom he had not seen in fifteen years.

So Welles telephoned Dublin.

"I'm very ill," said MacLiammóir. He had had a breakdown.

"The trip and seeing me will cure you," Welles assured him.

"I'm very old."

"So am I."

"I've never played Iago."

"And I've never played Othello."

"I've put on weight," MacLiammóir admitted sadly.

"So have I. We'll be Chubby Tragedians together, and we'll be swathed in cheesecloth."

"Ah, but I don't think I'd be good in films."

"You're born for them!"

"But I don't see myself as a villain."

"You are patently villainous to all eyes except your own, Micheál!"

This was the first of many dueling talks between two old friends and rivals in the time of *Othello*. They loved to top each other, to tease and scold, and each always said the other one told shocking lies. This rapport was a good deal more important than any that might exist between Othello and his bride. And with MacLiammóir's casting, Welles's *Othello* tended to the view that the play works, or is driven by, Iago. There are scholarly disputes over this: there is a quantity of great love poetry within the play. But dramatically it hinges upon Iago's trap for his master and on Othello's jealousy and paranoia. The play can hardly be attempted without some of these questions arising—Why does Iago so hate the Moor? Why does Othello believe Iago? Does he even *need* that malicious voice to prompt his profound suspiciousness? And if so, how far is that because he is black, and married to a white woman? MacLiammóir wrote in his witty journal about the making of *Othello* that his Iago was to be impotent—"That's why he hates life so much—they always do." But MacLiammóir, as Welles knew, was homosexual, and in his looks and manner his Iago would be taut, vicious and snakelike in a play about two men in which loyalty cloaks betrayal.

There were meetings in Paris in the spring of 1949, with readings, rehearsals and terrific dinners. On one occasion, in white pajamas, Welles did a dance to a song he said he had written at the age of fourteen. It could have described the spirit of the man who keeps the company sweet when there is no money for tomorrow:

Everyone loves the fellow who is smiling
He brightens the day and lightens the way for you—
He's always making other people happy
Looking rosy when you're feeling awful blue.

Actresses came in and out for the parts of Desdemona and Emilia. One day, Cécile Aubry (fresh—or rather, soiled—from Clouzot's *Manon*) would be Desdemona. Then suddenly, *Othello* yielded as Welles caught the wind of a notion for a world tour of classic plays—himself, Micheál and Hilton Edwards from the Gate—*Moby Dick, Salome, Richard II, The Provok'd Wife, The Duchess of Malfi* and something modern to be cute. Then Betsy Blair came in sight as an ideal Desdemona. And all the while banquets—caviar and blintzes, champagne and brandy—with Welles speaking extempore on "the nineteenth century, the Fratellinis, war, America, infant prodigies, the Bhagavad Gita, Spanish cooking, the Ten Commandments and pistachio ice-cream." To be at the table was enter-

Othello: Welles with Micheál MacLiammóir

tainment enough, and it was always on to a cabaret later with the girls dancing in your lap.

They went to Morocco and shot for a month at Mogador and Safi. There are sumptuous scenes on old battlements by the sea, with the surf exploding against a dark sky—*Othello* has a richer sense of nature than most Welles films, and there is always the breath of a warm wind that serves the sensuality of the poetry as much as the glare of the sun. The work was often difficult because of that wind, and the limited range of local hotels. But Welles recalled it as a very happy time, until the money ran out. Scalera had gone bust.

And so began the intermittency of *Othello*, as Welles would depart to find quick fee-paying jobs while the cast and crew waited. They felt stranded; he told himself that they were at liberty in some of the world's great resorts and the best hotels money, or credit, could hold. In the next nine months, the shoot broke up, resumed in Venice and Rome, lapsed again before recovering in Tuscania and Viterbo. Then another lull before returning to Mogador and Safi. It was March 1950 before the footage was all obtained.

In that time, some of the players would travel a little in Europe to while away the days. Then, occasionally, they would see Welles, hurrying somewhere, assuring them that he was only weeks from resumption, and meanwhile had they tried *this* restaurant or seen *that* play? Whenever they reassembled, Welles would carry on the action of the film with miraculous confidence and enterprise, cutting together shots from Italy and Morocco, trusting that the whirl of action and the vitality of the cutting might conceal disparities of costume, weather and acting. Nevertheless, there are passages of general alarm, excursion and agitation in *Othello* when the collision of imagery has to make up for incomplete or cluttered coverage. At such times, the already melodramatic plot becomes a little more hallucinatory—and Iago's wickedness a little closer to the be all and end all. "I am not what I am," MacLiammóir hisses into the camera, so we are alerted to be ready for any juxtaposition or jump cut. And it more or less works: Iago's encompassing malice holds everything together in the way that Welles's hurry and insouciance kept the production in place.

He managed to fit the parts of his life together. In Italy, he was able to give a few weeks to the role of Cesare Borgia in *Prince of Foxes*, a Tyrone Power picture of intolerable slowness directed by Henry King. Still, Welles was made to play a Borgia, and it was bracing to *be* one of those Italian men of the world he had lauded in *The Third Man*. In addition, *Prince of Foxes* had gorgeous 20th Century–Fox costumes of a period close enough to *Othello*'s to justify—indeed, to require—a little judicious borrowing. Everett Sloane was in the picture, too, affording Welles the chance of admitting what a godsend it was that Sloane *hadn't* accepted Iago—in view of the rare and perverse brilliance of MacLiammóir. Similarly, when Fox filmed *The Black Rose*—another Ty Power vehicle, this one a little more engaging—in North Africa Welles was on hand to be General Bayan. The director on this venture, Henry Hathaway, was suspicious of Welles. He reckoned his actor was a scene-stealer and a cunning bastard who would do anything to evade direction and instruction. A little out of the social scene on *The Black Rose*—Hathaway tried to dine with Power away from their loud costar—Welles had a Berber mistress, a very tall and startlingly handsome woman. After all, a Moor in waiting owed it to himself to keep as much in cultural training as possible.

It was a time in which Welles was so forgiving and so forgivable that he sometimes entertained his first wife, Virginia, not to mention her second husband, Charles Lederer. There was even a day or two on *Othello*

The Black Rose

when Rita Hayworth sought him out before plunging into more marriage and notoriety with Aly Khan. With Lederer—the two had become buddies—Welles wrote a screenplay for a French movie that developed into *Portrait d'un assassin*, though the final film was cavalier enough not to use their script. And when Lederer was briefly afflicted, Welles wrote a scene or two for what would become *I Was a Male War Bride*. There was an imp and a genius in Welles that could probably have made a good job of any scene, so long as it had to be done before lunch, with lunch as the payment.

The meals were taken as seriously as the scenes from *Othello*—and that movie was often advanced with the strange mixture of gaiety, indulgence and bravura impromptu that attended the meals. Anecdotes kept happening. One day in Venice, waiting hopefully for production, MacLiammóir met Dearest Orson wandering like a thundercloud in voluminous indigo overalls. Fundless, they treated themselves to a superb paella lunch: "All chalked up. O. said wasn't it terrible having no money, and we agreed, but it doesn't really make much difference, we'll doubtless have some soon." Come to Torcello, he said, and let's talk about doing a movie of the *Odyssey*. Then there was money again! And a very beautiful French-Canadian girl, Suzanne Cloutier, for Desdemona. There they were on the canals, with Desdemona in a gondola and her father Brabantio (Hilton Edwards) at a window of his palace when Lady Diana Duff Cooper (aristocrat and actress once, in *The Miracle*) passed by in another gondola in a cyclamen and white mushroom hat with the cry, "Orson! All hard at work on *Othello!* And there's Desdemona's dad on the balcony! What fun!" You had to be there—and they were.

One day in Paris in 1949, a young Englishman came seeking Orson Welles. It was Kenneth Tynan, who had been an intense admirer since the day in March 1942 (close to the vulnerable age of fifteen) that he had seen *Citizen Kane* at a Birmingham cinema. The boy had written to Welles, and they were precocious letters. A correspondence had ensued. And now Tynan appeared—beautiful, insolent, stuttering, very smart and adoring. There would follow a real friendship—a state that Welles invariably resisted, refused or insulted. Tynan had the manuscript of a book, *He That Plays the King*, a full volume of dramatic criticism, and he wanted Welles to write a preface. It was the only way the book could get published.

Welles was stricken and confused: he craved admiration, yet so often he rebuked admirers. It was as if he was ashamed somehow to hear others repeat (and mangle) the lines he had written in his own head. Time and again, he avoided acolytes, cut them short in praise, was downright rude and surly. It was a peculiar but revealing trait, a dread of the thing most desired that involved vanity and its opposite, a need for glory and friendship and an insistence on isolation. There was an intimacy he understood but could never inhabit. Yes, he would do the damn preface—but he would not read the book or the pages of mash notes that Tynan had devoted to Welles, his ideal and father figure. Welles admitted that he could be "a total chameleon and hypocrite. If I like somebody, I pretend to be what I think they want me to be. I have no integrity in that respect. There was almost nothing Ken said to me on any subject that I didn't think, 'That's absolutely untrue. You're a nut.' "

So often, Welles elected to act out a relationship with someone rather than let it occur. So "scenes" attended him, and he was famous for both amiability and bad temper. Time and again, at the dinner table, he played to the crowd and to those who would repeat the story. At dinner one night in Viterbo, the not entirely unself-regarding and not wholly brilliant Suzanne Cloutier launched into a rhapsody of self-scrutiny in the soulful close-up mode. Orson (a rival, though one preferring the ironic fatalist close-up) exploded:

> Don't you realize, you great, big, cosmic mass of uncom-
> promising egocentricity, that if you are foolish enough
> to wish to impress an adult audience with the assump-
> tion of an attitude that has nothing whatever to do with
> the facts about yourself, you could conceivably find bet-
> ter models for style than stories from the Girls' Own
> Library or their probably inferior French equivalents?
> And another thing, if I were your Maman, I should be
> heartily glad to have you way over the other side of the
> Atlantic doing your proper work, which I now pay you
> the inestimable compliment of telling you is Movie-
> Acting, so shut up about your Maman and your every-
> thing else, for if you felt as you wish us to think you feel,
> you'd never talk about it so easily. What is more, you are
> conspicuously Failing to hold your Audience.

At least that's what MacLiammóir remembered him saying, and the Irish actor had an ear for lines as well as swelling invective. He was all the more essential to *Othello* in that he was keeping a diary. Cloutier digested the tirade, her ego as large and vacant as the moon. It seems never to have impaired the monotony of her performance. How could Welles have so hesitated over his Desdemona and picked this one? The answer, of course, is that the lady is a stooge in his *Othello*, not nearly as married to the Moor as Iago.

There is hardly an unspectacular shot in Welles's *Othello*, but there are seldom two or three in a row that make sense. As befits its circum-stances, the picture is forever beginning again, on a new, more stunning tack. Discrete passages of action rarely seem to possess sequence, real-ity—or pain; they are disparate shots cut together, often with a violence that is as swaggering as the boldness in every composition—the everlast-ing depth, the varieties of height, the way faces or profiles loom up out of velvet darkness. The deaths of Desdemona, Emilia and Othello are all a little surprising because of the simple lack of sequence.

The poetry hangs in the air, like sea mist or incense—how can it not with Welles, MacLiammóir and Fay Compton in the film (Cloutier sounds, looks and feels dubbed)? But people did not exactly speak to one another. As if to avoid the tedious discipline of synchronization, many big speeches are done in long shots, or they emanate from people whose backs are turned to the camera. There is little sense of contact, communion or even of characters looking at each other. Rather, they are figures who move and exist separately from their words—as if Welles had encouraged them to feel free and to conform to the very mannered photography. Was that designed early, or was it the only way such very fractured footage could be put together?

There are a few exceptions. There is a magnificent long tracking shot on a castle wall in Morocco, the sea behind it, with Othello hurrying along, Iago desperate to keep up so that he may drop rubies of poison in the Berber's ear. MacLiammóir noted that the shot was done "miraculously, in four goes. Infinitely easier than the short shots which pick out the middle of an emotion." That is not just good diary making, it is excellent criticism.

And it is in the scenes between Iago and Othello that the movie most escapes its flaws and mannerisms. The film begins with Othello dead, and with a funeral procession the stately line of which is crossed by the scampering Iago, in chains, being taken to prison or death. He is put in a small cage, which is then hauled up to dangle from a tower. Presumably he will perish there, like a scorpion with no meat or innocence to feed on. But the camera comes in for a close-up of Iago; his face jammed against the bars, in extremis, facing death yet triumphant. The provocateur of the story, its director, is shown at the outset, mortified (like the scorpion who ensured his own death) yet fulfilled. The film does not answer the question why Iago acts as he does, but it makes a monument of the mystery— is this not as Wellesian as *Kane*?

Note how far Welles loves this mystery. In the play, Iago has a grievance: Othello has disdained him as lieutenant and chosen Cassio instead. Welles drops that impulse. In the film, Iago's hatred has no other external provocation than that Othello has married Desdemona. But we do not perceive this as racial horror. The film of *Othello* gives Welles the chance to be a curly-headed, flat-nosed, burnished black man—and he has terrific close-ups of himself, like snaps from a joyous holiday adventure. But there is no exploitation of that special racial-sexual paranoia that Welles must have encountered with the voodoo *Macbeth*, by being in Brazil and in talks with Lena Horne. No, there is something else—unutterable— that animates Iago's sense of betrayal.

Othello never picks up on this. One of the great virtues of the movie is that, fleetingly, Welles manages to let the look of foolish slowness cross his face. So often he played masterminds, but his Othello is most noble in his innocence, his dullness. As Welles put it: "He's destroyed easily because of his simplicity, not his weakness. He really is the archetype of the simple man, and has never understood the complexity of the world or of human beings. He's a soldier; he's never known women."

All true, and a departure. Of course, we never feel he knows Desdemona either, so the chance of tragedy is nullified. But he trusts Iago, and there he is betrayed. And in Welles's moments of male betrayal, there is little to compare with the crosscut close-ups between Othello and Iago when the Moor realizes what has been done with him. Here at last, people look at each other, with stares to burn away flesh and life. There is horror in Othello's face, and cruel rapture in Iago's. Interviewing Welles, Peter Bogdanovich said, "The look between them is filled with ambiguity," and Welles slid away with "That's a very interesting moment in the play." Yet, in the play, Othello stabs Iago, seeking a physical release. The film's look is so much more wounded, and wounding.

So, in biographical terms, the movie of mishaps and rescues *was* shot. There would be further crises to get it finished. And then, at Cannes in 1952, when it was first seen, it shared the Palme d'Or (with *Two Cents*

Othello: Welles and Suzanne Cloutier

Worth of Hope, by Renato Castellani). That tribute shows how much of a reputation Welles had in Europe, and how ready smart Europeans were to rebuke America for not keeping him. For Welles, the prize was wondrous, comic vindication of the crazy way of working. For he knew that no one had ever made a film like *Othello*—or made it so interesting (it is nowhere near as good or powerful as *Macbeth*, but it is as fascinating as a sketchbook for a great movie).

Toward its close, Welles's *Othello* turns Othello's last great speech into the testament of a director who has survived his own storm. Though he supposedly holds the corpse of Desdemona, and is about to expire himself, this Welles is speaking to the camera, to 1952, to us. He looks up at a kind of skylight from which the world looks down on him (height is the secret to the film's great beauty), and he murmurs, most soulfully:

> *I pray you,*
> *When you shall these unlucky deeds relate,*
> *Speak of me as I am; nothing extenuate,*
> *Nor set down aught in malice: then must you speak*
> *Of one, that lov'd not wisely, but too well;*
> *Of one, not easily jealous, but, being wrought,*
> *Perplex'd in the extreme; of one, whose hand,*
> *Like the bare Indian, threw a pearl away,*
> *Richer than all his tribe.*
>   *Set you down this.*

It's enough to make a biographer know he is being addressed.

14

Citizen Coon

" T H E B E E is always making honey!" Welles must have said, for Kenneth Tynan attributed the remark to him in a profile published in 1953. If he hadn't said it already, he would have adopted it thereafter, for he was in a period of relishing enigmatic proverbs. In *Mr. Arkadin*, only a few years away, he will utter hardly anything but runic principles for the ages, daring us to giggle.

Still, the bee is a useful analogy: he buzzes, he stings and he stirs up his incongruous sweetness. He also moves hither and thither, without apparent radar or air traffic control, but seemingly bidden by some inner knowledge or ordering. That is what the bee experts say: it is their way of acknowledging that no one can *follow* a bee's inhuman and unpredictable moves.

Welles's honey making is of the same nature. The biographer is a clerk. He lives with growing archives of the materials of the life he studies. He goes out only to drag home the papers of another's life. At home, those papers crowd out the prospect of his own life. He reads, refers, compares, eliminates; he deals in proof, veracity, likelihood. He wants to make chronology of his subject's life so that he can properly narrate it as a life. So he tries to establish when, how and why this Orson Welles moved, say, from Munich to London to Barcelona to Marrakech . . . only to find that the maps and timetables do not fit. Welles does not travel coherently. He jumps like a knight; darting like a bee, he is in different places at the same time. He has no purpose except that of hoping to shrug off pursuit. He has no home, no archive, no library . . . this is anathema to the biographer. He has to recognize that he is dealing with an alien creature. Seeking a form to accommodate irrational and impossible journeys, he remembers how film cuts, dissolves and castles with time.

Several people observed in this time—in 1950, 1951 and 1952—that Welles was shabbier than usual. There was an air of being short of funds, no matter that Welles was steadily and cheerfully growing. Disappearances were more and more put down to an absence of cash—notes, bills, to drop on the table or press in a doorman's hand—that crisp savoir faire. This testifies to how thoroughly he had been struggling to pay for *Othello* himself; indeed, there were friends and colleagues he had not yet been able to pay. Thank God, he would reassure them, that you are *my* creditor, and not the forlorn seekers of payment from some drab, faceless "they" in Los Angeles, or wherever. The bee is always doing sweetness, and when he is so evidently nourished, so deep in a terrine as we speak, it seems churlish to call him a liar.

Who would want to dispute the story, or its dramatically reclaimed acceptability at the top table, of how Welles went some way to get finishing money for *Othello*? He was in Venice, at the Excelsior, endeavoring to secure money from a Russian. As Welles advanced across the hotel dining room on his quarry one day, he observed Winston Churchill and his wife at another table. Welles bowed, as one celebrity might to another: it is in the rhythm of things. Churchill then stood and bowed in return. The Russian saw this, and immediately closed the deal. He could not be deterred from giving money.

The very next day, on the beach, Welles had a chance to thank Churchill for his inadvertent cue. The former prime minister nodded sagely and then, for the rest of their stay at the Excelsior, rose in magnificent, silent respect whenever Welles passed by. He might have got *War and Peace* floated if only the right studio people had been there to behold such moments.

Instead, while editing *Othello* and always on the lookout for a little more money, Welles landed in Paris in the early summer of 1950 and put on an evening of theater, in English, with his survivors from Morocco and *Othello*. It was in two parts, the first a short play, written by Welles himself, *The Unthinking Lobster*, a satire on a Hollywood beset by religious movies involving miracles. (This was a jab at Italian neorealist director Roberto Rossellini, whose 1948 film *L'Amore* had been banned as sacrilegious in America because of its situation—a simple peasant woman, Anna Magnani, claims to have been seduced by Christ.) In Welles's play, a crass producer, Jake Behoovian, orders the lead role of a Bernadette-ish girl to be given to a studio typist, Miss Pratt (Suzanne Cloutier). Pratt begins to achieve miracles, and Hollywood becomes a shrine for the sick, insane and crippled—there had to be some explanation. At last, a weary archangel comes down to make a deal: if the business gives up on religious movies, he'll call a moratorium on miracles.

Under the heading *The Blessed and the Damned*, this skit played with a compendium version of the Faustus story called *Time Runs*. Welles played Faustus, and Hilton Edwards was Mephistopheles (Micheál MacLiammóir took over when Edwards had to go back to Dublin). Welles yoked these pieces together under a note in the program that declared, "They deal, respectively, with a lost soul and an inspired one, and are intended to develop, in contrasting styles, contrasting ideas regarding the state of Grace and the state of damnation." That seems a touch glib, but when in France. . . .

In fact, the French language was a problem, for Welles had insufficient knowledge of it to get what he wanted out of local technicians. He was diverted from greater wrath when Edwards told him he had seen a remarkable young woman who might make a fine Helen of Troy in *Time Runs*. This was Eartha Kitt, then twenty-two and a dancer with Katherine Dunham. Welles auditioned her in a tiny attic room at the Eduard VII Theatre, standing with his back to her. She read the lines and heard him mutter, "I don't know what I'm going to do. I have given the part to Suzanne Cloutier. But take the script and learn it. We open on Thursday."

There were those who thought that Mlle. Cloutier had no equal at standing still and looking beautiful, but she yielded graciously to Kitt,

Welles with the
manager of the
Carlton Hotel,
Cannes—
discussing the
bill?

who became part of a show that either impressed or befuddled French
critics with Welles's bluster, her jeweled inscrutability, the whim of the
whole thing, plus its being in English. Welles and Kitt dined out a lot—
at Bricktop's and Calabados—so that pictures of them together would stir
up controversy and sell tickets. One famous night onstage, when Faust
had to kiss Helen, Welles bit deep into her lip. Blood flowed, and it was
still there, vampiric, as she had to sing a little song, music by Duke Ellington and words by Welles:

> *Hungry little trouble, damned in a bubble*
> *Yearning to be, be or be free.*

(Listen, no one's perfect, not even a wonder.)

    Paris gossiped mightily about the couple, and Welles was heard to say
that Kitt was the most exciting woman in the world. She says that, while
she loved him, she protected that happy feeling by never going to bed
with him: she was petite and he was not, a clash that was more immediately problematic than being black and white. It may have been because
of her denial, but Kitt admits that as the summer went on and the curious

show traveled—to Germany and Belgium—Welles became stranger all the while, more lofty, more arbitrary in his teasing and his lies. The show also stretched to include more songs from Kitt, a magic act by Welles, a scene from *Henry IV* and conversation from *The Importance of Being Earnest* with Welles as Algernon and MacLiammóir as Jack. Those scenes adroitly appropriated some of Lady Bracknell's best speeches—for Algernon, of course—proof enough that Lady Bracknell is one of the most Wellesian roles he never got around to. (He had hoped to get Fay Compton to stay on for Lady B.)

What Eartha Kitt enjoyed most of all were four-hour, seven-course dinners with Welles, Edwards and MacLiammóir talking, and Welles not just eating his own food but raiding the others' plates. The previous October, in Rome, MacLiammóir had seen a "partial collapse" in Welles. Doctors had said his heart was "anything but satisfactory." Coffee and smoking had been outlawed. Yet how could an itinerant genius expect to win the loyalty of Churchills if he had no cigar in hand?

He crossed the Channel, shifting his base from Paris to London.

With Eartha Kitt

After all, in 1951, Churchill was returned to office. There was also a thriving radio system in Britain, and a widespread use of English. As he traveled, Welles took cases and cans of *Othello* with him, still editing the film, still looking for jobs to pay for that work. He moved, as so often, in nearly opposite directions at the same time. He gave himself to a series of half-hour radio shows, *The Adventures of Harry Lime*, an exploitation that had retained just three things from the original movie—the name Harry Lime, the voice of Welles and the sound of Anton Karas's zither music. It was enough. But Lime was now made into a raffish Robin Hood of Vienna (and other locales), a charming hero, a rogue by profession yet a righter of wrongs by taste. Harry Alan Towers produced the show, which was sold to America eventually as *The Third Man: The Lives of Harry Lime*. Welles was not just the star. He wrote some of the episodes, and he generally conducted himself as a veteran of radio whose experience and instincts were inviolate. I heard some of the shows as a boy, and they had no more appropriate audience. They were cheerful melodramas, rich in atmosphere and a sign of how much Orson Welles remained attached to the ethos of *The Shadow*. The Harry Lime shows invoked a world of evil geniuses, the European demimonde, Lime's insouciance, skulduggery, the bitter laughter of fading women of the world and the nocturnal hum of smart cities.

Such tales were in and out of Welles's head as he edited *Othello*, and we should be ready to hear Iago as a very modern rat. As if to enhance *Othello*ing, in the summer of 1951, Welles prepared a London stage production of the play. This was at the invitation of Laurence Olivier and Vivien Leigh. They had become managers of the St. James's Theatre, where they had won huge success with a 1951 Festival of Britain season that featured *Caesar and Cleopatra* and *Antony and Cleopatra*. As they took those shows to America in the fall, the St. James's was available. Welles would fill it with *Othello*.

He spent time with the Oliviers that summer, in London and at their country home, Notley Abbey. He was noticed there to be typing up a novel, a story about a great European tycoon who hires a man to investigate his own past. The novel had taken off from one of the Lime radio plays, "Greek Meets Greek," written by Welles himself, in which the great man had been named Arkadian, and Frédéric O'Brady—a friend—had played the part. This was a novel of which Welles would later deny having written a word.

Welles and Olivier talked. Olivier then had never played Othello, though he had done Iago to Ralph Richardson's Moor in a 1938 Old Vic production that had unnerved many people by stressing the homosexual bond between the two characters. They had sought advice from Ernest Jones, Freud's biographer. Olivier had been fascinated by the concept, while Richardson was horrified. As a result, the two actors were at odds, and the production was deemed a failure. But Olivier was still interested—there were strong homosexual yearnings in his own life. As Welles's *Othello* was being cut, this influence may have been potent.

Olivier talked of trying Othello, too (he would deliver a definitive performance in 1964). But Welles told him, No, it required a bass voice—such as he enjoyed. Really? said Olivier, noting that Welles planned to use as his Iago the Australian actor Peter Finch, the lover of Vivien Leigh. Welles's stage *Othello* ran at the St. James's from October 18 to December 15. He judged it a far finer performance than he had managed in the movie.

The production was tempestuous. One night, Welles nearly strangled his Desdemona, Gudrun Ure; on another, he threw coins in the face of Emilia (Maxine Audley), drawing blood. He was a dangerous actor to be with, a man who sometimes confused his own temper with the anger of characters. Olivier had a chance to see the performance, and he remarked tartly that Welles *could* have been a great Othello: "He had everything . . . except the breath. He didn't go into training." In Olivier's eyes, Welles was an amateur of genius, but not dedicated or focused. Kenneth Tynan was a good deal less kind. He wrote that Welles had "the courage of his restrictions," and he referred to the performance as "Citizen Coon." There is some real spite in this review from so intense an admirer, as if Welles had done something to hurt Tynan or provoke his envy. Welles chuckled at the taunt: it did not ruin the friendship.

As a London debut, this *Othello* was a disappointment. The general estimate was that Welles had let his potential as an actor be diverted by too many other projects. Was he doing *Othello* onstage for its own sake, or to make money for the movie? Could he concentrate on it when he was off doing the narration for another Harry Alan Towers radio series, *The Black Museum*, based on case histories from the files of Scotland Yard?

The bee was buzzing, but the activity seemed alien, and lonely. He took trips to Dublin to see his friends—he owed them money still, and he had endangered the stability of the Gate Theatre. While there, he appeared briefly in a little movie, the twenty-three-minute *Return to Glennascaul*, a charming ghost story directed by Hilton Edwards but under the load of Welles's influence.

And so the movie *Othello* was complete, and taken to Cannes in May 1952, where it was cheered loudly by the French. Welles had never won a real prize before (apart from the half share in the Oscar for *Kane*). And in France, above all, word began to circulate that he was a great movie director who had been cast aside by his own America.

A few years later, that very shrewd tourist Eloise arrived in Paris. She and Nanny went to the movies—thirty-seven times "and have seen Orson Welles 19 times." If only they had met: Orson and Eloise, two spoiled but neglected children. Think of their talk and their meals, the philosophy to go with a *bombe surprise!* Think of them as brother and sister in Cocteau's *Les Enfants terribles.* Think—ladies and gentlemen, you must be seated for this—but just picture them as Humbert and Lolita, skibbling from one motel to another.

15
Legends Grow

WELLES MANAGED to get everything wrong, even success. Winning the Cannes Palme d'Or in 1952 is tantamount to putting on an innovative *Peer Gynt* in northern British Columbia today. The event might be reported "at home," but only in terms to persuade homebodies of how vast the world is and how tiny the labors of man. A little more than forty years later, Quentin Tarantino won the Palme d'Or at Cannes with *Pulp Fiction* and contrived to become an American sensation, opening the New York Film Festival, brooding over his youth for television talk shows, seeing his picture a success at the box office and the winner of many critics' prizes. He was all moment. Yet *Othello* did not find a commercial opening in America until September 1955, by which time it was dismissed as an oddity, one more example of its maker's aimlessness. Is this all bad luck, or no head for business? Or did Welles himself begin to perceive that the very untidiness was his special thing?

These are years, coming up on forty, when his special lack of grounding, his homelessness, has its romantic allure—even if there are dark dawns when it fills him with terror. He has lost so much; that is a rueful joke when he keeps getting bigger. He has had such a downfall, yet there he is in some luxury hotel—if he reaches out across the sleeping beauty beside him he may find a matchbook that tells him which one, or which language their play is in. He is so large, so splendid, so filled with the plans of genius, but he is also like someone on the run. In a few hours, in daylight, he is going to have to discard the beauty somehow and walk out of the hotel, smiling, tipping, anecdoting, letting the desk clerk world know that everything is all right and that no account needs to be presented.

After all, he will be back. How do you know? My dear fellow, go upstairs, enter the suite quietly and see what I have left in the bed as a . . . deposit. You don't believe me? And then that building laugh, that audacious defiance of discretion— (I saw this Orson Welles at the Carlton yesterday, somebody will say, just standing there in the lobby, laughing. Such a laugh. You could hear the wickedness. Legends grow.)

While he laughs, and has people notice him, there is a growing army of those he needs to avoid. For he comes out of *Othello* with more debts than he cares to remember. Lou Lindsay, his editor, his friend, his loyalist inquirer after fresh funds, the man who cemented over so many cracks, is owed $30,000. Always will be: a souvenir. So new best friends will be in order, fresh saviors. Betrayals are like labels on old luggage. That laugh, by the way, is a sound recordist's dream: close up, it is warm, comradely, a hug, a knowing joke. But for anyone passing by, ten steps away, there is no doubting the emptiness, the menace, the nihilism.

He comes, more and more, to be a man known not just for his works but for the things not done, the plans announced. So soon it will be uncertain exactly what was done and what considered. Why not, then, put more of himself in some of the considerations than in the things done? Is filmography so flat-footed an art that it needs proof?

He writes a play—at least it is translated into French and published under his name as *A Bon Entendeur. Fair Warning.* It sounds delightful. It is a play, it seems, in which the actors begin to forget their lines. Everything comes to a halt. They speak to the audience, but only to ask, Who are you? What is this all for? Why are we here? It seems that some local weather effect involving an amnesiac gas has rendered all memories dead.

I've never seen the play—maybe it doesn't really exist except in commentaries like this—still, I feel bound to be stern with it, for this miracle of self-performed entropy, this magical invocation of calm, oblivion and near death in a live theater—can't you see Welles's cheeky grin searching the audience, restless but bemused, for a clue?—degenerates into a parable against using nuclear weapons. Sometimes one could imagine that Welles was driven to the point of daring and marvel in the nature of performance by the sheer banality of his ideas. That's another way of looking at *Kane:* how to make a superb show so as to *avoid* arriving at some drab meaning or settlement.

Large men of suspect power—vessels on the sea of café society—sooner or later attract each other. And so Welles fell into a brief comradeship with King Farouk of Egypt—another boy wonder become a pudding, a connoisseur of women, movies and his own boredom, and lately deposed as king by Colonel Nasser's coup. At a loose end, and weary of politics, he supposedly wants to pay for Welles to film *Julius Caesar* in an arresting modern style. Do they meet? Do they need to? Does some go-between make up the whole charade? (Now, that might make a nice movie—a hustler who tells Welles he has Farouk's ear, and even other fleshier parts. . . .)

Welles begins a script. Announcements are made. But in Culver City, at MGM, similar plans are afoot. One John Houseman is there preparing to produce a significant *Caesar*, with Joseph Mankiewicz directing a cast that will include Marlon Brando, John Gielgud, James Mason and Louis Calhern. A respectable *Julius Caesar*.

In July 1952, Welles wrote bonhomously to "Dearest Jack," hoping "some moderately happy solution will be found." He offered to buy MGM out. He allowed that they could do the same for him—I like the notion for *our* film that Welles sees the Faroukian *Caesar* as a way of getting hush money out of Metro. Or they could work together, as in the old days. MGM turned lawyerly in a solid way and told Welles to stop annoying them. They made a movie which is . . . unquestionably there, very definite, very well planned, a model for schoolchildren, but ruthlessly unmagical. Whereas Welles's *Caesar* movie, with Faroukian undertones (not to mention ours), *lives* in the imagination. After all, it takes a considerable humorlessness, a taste for plodding day-after-day work, a lack of faith in imagination, actually to *make* the movie—and Houseman's *Julius Caesar*, existence aside, has all those handicaps.

You're probably not going to believe this—that *is* the test—but in 1953, the year of Queen Elizabeth II's coronation, Orson Welles did the libretto for a ballet, *The Lady in the Ice*, about a prehistoric woman found in a block of ice. She is put on show in carnivals. A young man falls in love with her. His tears melt her ice. She comes to life, kisses him, and he is turned to ice. No nuclear weapons in sight, but somehow it doesn't seem gung ho on sex. This plays in London and Paris as a Roland Petit production.

Welles made a record of Walt Whitman's *Song of Myself*; he did *The Queen of Spades* for the BBC radio; he was doing new script ideas for Korda, and one of those turned into a French novel, *Une Grosse Légume*, translated and adapted by Maurice Bessy, an important aide in those days. It is set on a Mediterranean island, the scene of a power struggle between

Coca-Cola and Pepsi-Cola, and of the dance made by American aid and Communist influence. Yet again, Welles the political scientist goaded the satirical dramatist—and, plainly, this could have been a masterpiece. You can see it, can't you? With Anna Magnani as an island woman who oscillates between Mr. Coke (William Holden) and Mr. Pepsi (Gregory Peck). . . .

There was another dream, *Operation Cinderella*, about Hollywood movie companies occupying and dominating a small Italian town that has endured centuries of occupation. Welles would call this "the best comedy script I ever wrote," but I must admit to some skepticism. The Hollywood satire seems just a degree or two too forced—and too close to *The Unthinking Lobster* (can you remember what that was?). I prefer the island story, especially if we can get Billy Wilder to do it.

Undeterred, in that same 1953, the year of the British Coronation, *Roman Holiday*, the Houseman *Julius Caesar* and the deaths of Stalin and Beria, Orson Welles acted in three films. In Italy, for the director Steno, he appeared in an adaptation of the Pirandello play *Man, Beast and Virtue*. In France, for Sacha Guitry, he played Benjamin Franklin in *Si Versailles m'était conté*. And in England, he was the large, potent and murderous Sigsbee Manderson in Herbert Wilcox's *Trent's Last Case*. There is nothing more important to say about this threesome beyond their evident implausibility. But you can look them up, and track them down, and find three flavors of ham from this hulk who was sometimes hired and paid as a very grand actor.

We are advancing on the intrigue of *Mr. Arkadin*, but let me look around quickly in case there is something forgotten before we move on to that hallucinatory room. Would you believe that, in October 1953, Welles made a flying return to New York to do a drastically cut down version of *King Lear* for live TV, directed by Peter Brook, with Micheál MacLiammóir as his Edgar and that riveting English actor Alan Badel as the Fool? He was only allowed back because of a deal with the IRS whereby he got the best hotel accommodations, his fee went to the government and he was not arrested. And would you doubt but that from time to time in the very abbreviated *Lear* he was astounding, excited by the new medium and by Badel's icy humor? All he did was take the show over, redoing the script and throwing in lines from other Shakespeare plays as bridges. Then and there, with horror, he fell in love with TV— for there was a medium where, one day perhaps, he might just be allowed to exist, like a sunbather in the sun.

16
~~ Mr. Arkadin ~~

MR. ARKADIN is a bad film such as only a great and self-consciously wayward artist could make, and only then when he has achieved nihilism in which he needs to make decline his self-sufficient subject, and a warning to anyone who might entertain hope. There is something self-loathing in the picture, a feeling of murder undertaken for its own sake, without purpose or delight. There are loyalist arguments that no other project was more thoroughly stolen from Welles and re-worked by producers. For myself, I cannot escape a shiver of revulsion and contempt in the film, directed at the medium, at us and at its maker. *Mr. Arkadin* is tortured self-parody, the sure measure of how greatly, se-cretly, Welles was terrified at his own life and condition. Maybe the most disturbing thing about the picture is its celebration of Welles's third and least romantic marriage.

The picture grew out of Harry Lime and the radio exploitation of that character. Later on, in the comfort of brave melancholy, Welles said, "It was the best *popular* story I ever thought up for a movie, and really it should have been a roaring success." That cast upon it the forlorn light of abandoned genius, but the story was really one among many that Welles was cooking up. It was not much more than a trick, what Hitchcock called a Maguffin, but it had this extra bitter flavor—it was the structure and the idea of *Kane* done again. So it was self. But whereas, shall we say, *Kane* had been made with the delicacy and the aplomb of a Nabokov, *Mr. Arkadin* is a dispirited mess, with camp innuendos of greatness, such as Clare Quilty might have tossed off.

The radio show was "Greek Meets Greek," in which Harry Lime is hired by a certain Gregory Arkadian to investigate his past. Arkadian claims that loss of memory prevents him from knowing how he is so wealthy. This was a Lime episode written by Welles himself, and as he raked over the set elements of melodrama, he envisaged—"in a rush"—a deeper plot than a thirty-minute radio episode could contain. The Arka-dian figure has not really lost his memory. Rather, he wants to find out how easily anyone—the FBI, the IRS, the corps of biography—might be able to trace his guilty past. So he hires a jerk to private-eye his own history, and as this blunt fool discovers the various people who could testify against him, they are murdered.

I called this plot "deeper," but only in terms of intrigue. It is in truth no better a plot device than any of the lurid outlines of the Harry Lime show. For it is only *like Kane*. There, a man rounded up his old acquaintances in the desperate but very human urge to persuade himself that he had been loved, or that he had had some point in existing. In *Arkadin*, the process of revisiting is methodically bleak and formal, a way of erasing the past. It is about the act of vanishing—and so it is quite in keeping that Arkadin eventually exits in midair, like a soap bubble. Something in Welles was ready, eager even, for a turn in the world, or a fumbled button, whereby everything—the Italian Renaissance, old Chicago, *Citizen Kane* and even himself—would be gone as quick as a cut. There is so little hope for life or humanity in *Mr. Arkadin*.

Perhaps the scheme meant more to Welles once. Remember how, in the summer of 1951—very shortly after "Greek Meets Greek" was broadcast—Welles had stayed with the Oliviers at their country home in Buckinghamshire. While there, he had declared that he was writing a novel "about a rich and ruthless tycoon who employs a reporter to uncover his murky origins, then systematically eliminates all his associates." He was working at it intently, as if it meant something special.

A few years later, in 1955, a novel *was* published in France by Gallimard—*Mr. Arkadin*. Subsequently, it appeared in English in London and New York, credited to "Orson Welles," though without a copyright line. More or less, Welles denied that he had ever written that book. He said that his friend Maurice Bessy had done it—albeit with Welles's support—to help promote the movie (which opened in Madrid in March 1955). It had been intended at first as a newspaper serial. "I don't know *how* it got under hardcover, or who got paid for that," said Welles. But when Peter Bogdanovich observed that some critics had said the writing in the novel was often "beautiful," Welles growled and grinned. "Maybe I did write it at that."

The novel is not beautiful, or remarkable. But it is faithful to the movie, and it does contain most of the movie's scenes, even if the dialogue is usually a little different. It may be that, wearying of his own novel, Welles passed the job and some pages on to Bessy, who then worked from Welles's own script for the film—a piece called *Masquerade*, dated March 1953. (In all the hoteling of the year, if he awoke in the night, there could have been half a dozen scripts in progress around the suite.)

Masquerade and Gregory Arkadian became *Mr. Arkadin* toward the end of 1953—I prefer the extra syllable in the name, with its hint of the character as a long passage with many side entrances; and *Masquerade* could have helped the picture reach out for humor, or some admission of its own absurdity. The film came unsteadily into being as the work of several companies, including Mercury and Fontessa, the Paris base of Louis Dolivet. This is the Romanian liberal from America in the 1940s who had been one of Welles's political advisers. Dolivet had money, and access to more. Though he was without experience in movie production, for a season he became Welles's angel, the man who put together the funding for *Mr. Arkadin*. For many of these strange European years, Dolivet was Welles's patron.

Dolivet's education in the business was not pretty. The hope for democracy he had once encouraged had turned into an erratic dictator and a spoiled kid. Dolivet was disconcerted at finding Welles drunk so much of the time—and, as a result, so given to tantrums and sudden departures from his own script. Anyone more familiar with Welles at work might have been less shocked. Welles had always been an exponent of the expensive virtues of spur-of-the-moment ideas. But so often those ideas had been good. Now, they seemed the response to boredom. Robert Arden, the actor somewhat bewildered to be playing the key role of Van Stratten, the hired reporter, reckoned that Welles had shot his bolt on the script. Scenes that seemed promising in the writing now filled him with such dismay that he sought to change them. Arden thought that Welles had all the energy and the limits of a brilliant fourteen-year-old mind. Others thought the caprice was reckless and the temper malicious. Welles was furious if ever thwarted or opposed; sometimes this great man— revered by everyone—seemed to go out of his way to pick fights.

He could not even photograph his beloved with rapture. Dolivet was an amateur, but he had seen some movies. When he looked at the actress cast as Arkadin's daughter, Raina—the countess di Girfalco, or Paola Mori (her professional name)—he felt he was looking at the kind of placid café society beauty a man might dally with for a night. But Welles was involved in a serious affair with the countess: he said he could see no wrong in her. Other observers found her somewhere between passive and dull; they said her heavily accented English would not serve. No one could believe in the script's love affair between Van Stratten and Raina. Their faces, side by side, are a study in implausibility and lack of interest—and this from the man who had done those long conversations between George Amberson and Lucy Morgan. Where was love? Why should a movie risk its credibility by casting the director's mistress?

There was a little location shooting in Munich and Paris, but most of the picture was done in a Madrid studio or in nearby countryside. So much of the movie amounts to guest spots—character actors who came in for a few days' work, sometimes on a single set, encouraged to be extreme. Welles once said that he wanted them to be Dickensian characters "so dense that they appear as archetypes." But Dickens found the time and the literary need to love every one of his eccentrics. Welles seldom seems to have been more than the distracted organizer to a series of cameos—Mischa Auer with his flea circus and his magnifying glass; Michael Redgrave as a touchy junk shop owner; Katina Paxinou practicing jeweled and sardonic nostalgia as she recollects the past with the aid of a photo album; Patricia Medina (Joe Cotten's wife) as Van Stratten's showgirl lover. Only Akim Tamiroff offers more as Jakob Zouk, disgruntled, cold, hungry for goose liver and all too aware that his greatest asset—what he knows—endangers his existence.

These actors are all of them fine, granted that they simply do their scenes, in isolation. Welles observed that they were all very lonely people, but that is less a felt predicament than the film's failure to link them to Arkadin historically or emotionally. We know and want more of Bernstein, Jed Leland and Susan Alexander for themselves and for their mixed feelings about Charlie. But these exotics do not seem even to have known an Arkadin, much less felt his imprint. There is no mark of reality or circumstance in *Arkadin*, as there is in *Kane*. There is neither that script's care in making relationships palpable nor the filmmaker's craft in giving us an inhabited place. By 1954, Welles was vulnerable because he lacked the skill of Herman Mankiewicz. But he also missed the power of RKO to make places like Xanadu and the Amberson house. The sets and places in *Arkadin* are backdrops without texture or poetry. Budget surely accentuated the loss. Patricia Medina remembers that Welles asked her if there were props in her hotel room that she could bring along to the set to dress her scenes. She found nothing, so Welles raided his own Madrid hotel. In so many ways now, he was a hotel artist.

Such rootlessness is sad enough, but worse still is the ponderous pasteboard in the film's central trio: Arkadin, Raina and Van Stratten. There is so much potential in that triangle. Welles was playing a man who was meant to be infinitely rich and powerful, and inescapably guilty or suspicious. But does a man so potent need a reporter to find his past associates? And does he have enough reason to fear the past when the worst that is uncovered is the fact that he was once a pimp? Such questions are never answered, so these practicalities hobble the melodrama. Arden's Van Stratten has no skill, no charm, no magic—so why does Arkadin pick him, and how can Raina fall in love with him unless she is his mate in dullness?

Gregory Arkadin in the air

Raina Arkadin (Paola Mori) on the ground

Suppose instead that Arkadin loves Raina, even to the brink of an incestuous passion he cannot release. Suppose that he and the film had a Raina to gaze upon with awe and delight. Yet how seldom Welles's camera is excited by women. Suppose that Van Stratten is an investigative reporter (or even an FBI man close to freelancing), with enough class to appeal to Raina and her father. Suppose, in 1954, that the cast is Welles, Audrey Hepburn as Raina and Montgomery Clift as Van Stratten. No, better still, suppose that it is Ralph Richardson or Olivier as Arkadin.

For nothing is as fatal in *Mr. Arkadin* as Welles's own posturing performance, both arrogant and lazy. This is all the stranger in that he *had* nursed the idea, and he had always been fascinated by huge, celebrity figures whose power harbors some secret, or some emptiness. He had been impressed by Sir Basil Zaharoff, the arms tycoon. He made intriguing remarks about how far the look of Arkadin was based on Stalin, and he was positively mouthwatering on the man's Slav contradictions: "cold, calculating, cruel, but with that terrible Slavic capacity to run to sentiment and self-destruction at the same time."

Imagine an Arkadin who half-wants his own ruin, if only to reveal himself to Raina. Imagine that man hounded by a very clever Van Stratten. Imagine an Arkadin who cannot even quite remember his own past, who is vulnerable to frauds and pretenders, and then have that man virtually cuckolded by Van Stratten. But Welles could not write, or act that role.

Dolivet took the film away from Welles in the course of the editing because progress was so slow and the deadline of Christmas 1954 was missed. Still, Welles communicated with the editor, Renzo Lucidi, so that the picture might continue in his way. But Dolivet would not have it. Another editor was hired. Paola Mori's English proving something of a barrier, she was dubbed by the young Billie Whitelaw—no balm to marriage. Scenes were abandoned, and—according to Welles—an elaborate flashback structure was re-formed so that the film would run chronologically.

This is hard to fathom, for the picture already has a structure that confuses many viewers. As to the lost material, Welles said that one scene showed Arkadin as a sentimental, maudlin drunk. This is difficult to conceive, or to set within the large pattern of Welles's very hollow, ultrasinister overlord. How could he have made that reach or matched a true human figure with the Arkadin of fake wig, carpetlike beard and Alpine noses? Arkadin is all mask and tease, appearing when unexpected, his makeup showing, his looming size like a cut out tower wheeled in front of the camera. There was never a more drastic proof of his limitations, his humbug, as an actor.

The picture opened in Spain and England in 1955, and it received surprisingly sympathetic reviews even if it did no business. There was already a new wave rising that saw Welles as a hero. Welles attended the Paris opening (in June 1956), by which time Paola Mori was Mrs. Orson Welles. He said nothing to offend or to warn viewers that the film was less than what he wanted. But in time, he would be outraged: "It's terrible what they did to me on that. The film was snatched from my hands more brutally than one has ever snatched a film from anyone . . . it's as if they'd kidnapped my child!"

It was not until 1962—after *Touch of Evil* and just before *The Trial*—that *Mr. Arkadin* opened in New York. This was because of a lawsuit brought against Welles by the producers, complaining of the way he had undermined his own picture. The case was never brought to court, but it ensured delay. Welles and his supporters assert that the case was malicious and groundless. But I suspect it had merit. The Welles of this time believed in so little, and if he was to many a monstrous egotist, still he hated his own pride as much as anything. We should remember that this is the movie in which Arkadin delivers the speech—so much quoted afterward, and in better films, that it seems faintly spurious now in *Arkadin*—about the scorpion and the frog. It is a description of self-abuse and suicide. That Welles/Arkadin delivers it with a grandiose, shining relish only illustrates the theatricality of his most heartfelt moments. That Welles could not give the speech greater gravity or sadness surely helps us understand the man some often found odious. And so a speech full of terror became a cheap trick:

> And now I'm going to tell you about a scorpion. A scorpion wanted to cross a river, so he asked a frog to carry him. "No," said the frog. "No, thank you. If I let you on my back you may sting me, and the sting of the scorpion means death." "Now, where," asked the scorpion, "is the logic of that? No scorpion could be judged illogical. If I sting you, you will die—I will drown." The frog was convinced and allowed the scorpion on his back, but just in the middle of the river he felt a terrible pain and realized that after all the scorpion *had* stung him. "Logic!" cried the dying frog, as he started under, bearing the scorpion down with him. "There is no logic in this!" "I know," said the scorpion, "but I can't help it— it's my character." Let's drink to character!

17

∽ *Damned in Paradise* ∽

I T I S H A R D L Y possible to believe in Orson Welles's genius and not imagine him watching *Mr. Arkadin*—and himself in it—feeling the dismay. A more conscientious man might have been overwhelmed by depression. But it was a benefit of his rootlessness, his hoteling and his detachment from reality and responsibility that he could pass on and believe in beginning again. I am Orson Welles, the amazing Orson Welles; I will surprise myself. Thus, the elements in his nature that would so often fail at great work made him endlessly fertile and mercurial.

In Paris, early in 1955, he fell in with the English writer Wolf Mankowitz, who was scripting *Trapeze* for Carol Reed. This was a new friend and savior. Welles's head was filled with *Moby Dick*, but he had been unable to find a way of doing it in the French theater. So many people would wonder, How can the ocean and the *Pequod* be put on an ordinary stage—let alone Ahab and the whale? Mankowitz thought he could get Welles some TV work in London. Why not? The English had been very responsive to his broadcast of Walt Whitman. Welles was popular there as that lovable rascal Harry Lime. And in London he could speak his own voluminous English.

London had been the inspiration for *Moby Dick*, after all, so it was proper to go back there. For, in the autumn of 1954, Welles had deserted the editing of *Arkadin*—the kind of thing producers notice—to go to London to serve John Huston, who was beginning, God help him, a whole movie from the Melville story. He had it in mind that Welles should be his Father Mapple, and he had a five-minute sermon scene with Welles delivering the old-fashioned religion.

The actor was to get £6,000 for just two days' work. Welles was nervous: the sermon was a great and self-contained speech in what might be a very prestigious picture. He had reworked the script on the plane from Paris. Huston elected not to be offended by this—he and Welles immediately got on like old cronies and con men. They were filming at Shepperton, with a pulpit made from the bowsprit of a whaling ship. Welles wore a curly gray beard that jutted out like a spade, above a white shirt and a blue coat. Legend has it that Huston filmed the scene in a single

Father Mapple preaches in *Moby Dick*.

setup. But there are five setups in the film, enough to show Welles climb-
ing the rope ladder to the pulpit—it had to be sturdy for 300 pounds of
him—and then several angles, from long shots to close-ups, on the sermon itself.

Welles did his own text, and then, when gently pressed, he did Huston's. It is magnificent, thunderous and as incantatory as Melville's prose.
No actor could kill or waste the speech—but only someone of Welles's
grandeur could do it justice. Here is proof that on the grand scale of voice,
physique and imaginative reach he was a noble actor—a stage actor,
someone to fill a large hall. Yet there is more. As Mapple pursues the
Jonah story to its end, and Jonah speaks to God, Huston used the close-
up to cover Welles's heartrending "For what is man that he should live out
the lifetime of his God?" Suddenly, we see an old man, or one alert to

mortality. The last line is nearly a whisper; it was the most delicate thing Welles had done in forty years. Always uneasy with youth, he had some intimation of the grave, solitary splendor of old age. It is there in his Mapple. The crew gave him an ovation when he had finished. Huston chuckled at his own acute enterprise, and Welles bellowed with relief. If he had never done anything else, you would say, "Good God, what was that?" One touch of that Mapple might have made Arkadin alive and pitiable.

British television then was genteel and accommodating enough to make space for entertaining eccentrics. They held the air to talk about cooking, archaeology, household pets, astronomy or whatever took their fancy. It was a medium with the attitude of a library: not everyone could be expected to want everything, but that was no reason not to be as catholic as possible. So Welles was given a series of six "Sketch Book" shows by the BBC in which he chatted to the camera—treating it as an old chum*—about whatever he thought of: his own theatrical experiences, the adventure of *It's All True*, bullfighting, John Barrymore and the old *War of the Worlds* chestnut. He was relaxed, intimate, worldly and expansive.

He was writing a play, *Moby Dick—Rehearsed* it would be called, a brilliant solution to the difficulties of containing Melville's spectacle in the space of a theater. But first he had a duty to perform. Paola Mori had come with him to London, and she was pregnant. And so, two days after his fortieth birthday, he married her at Caxton Hall, in Westminster. She told the papers in London that she would not hear of him as "moody" or "difficult": "It is not that Orson is abnormal—he is supernormal. The secret is finding out how normal he is underneath the super." The third Mrs. Welles was lovely and elegant. Plainly Welles had been crazy about her, and he was sentimental over her history—a daughter of an opponent of Mussolini, she had spent part of her life in an internment camp. But she was no actress, as he had learned. Some of Welles's associates were also taken aback by her old-fashioned aristocratic ways, her arrogance and her single-minded shopping. So they married, whereupon she became nearly invisible in his life.

Welles never paused over *Moby Dick*. With Mankowitz's aid, a proper production was put together, with money from Oscar Lowenstein and Henry Margolis, set for the Duke of York's Theatre. The play Welles had

* He was, all along, on various TV shows laying down the basis for some kind of *My Dinner with Orson*. So many people longed to deliver that in-person wealth and gaiety.

made involves a traveling company of actors in nineteenth-century New England. They are about to put on a *King Lear,* but they quickly shift their energies to rehearse *Moby Dick*—it is entirely Wellesian that that kind of redirection is required, but it also affords a suggestion of affinity between the two plays in that the cabin boy on the *Pequod,* Pip, is played by the company's actress.

Because this is only a rehearsal, the ship, the sea and the whale are just "suggested." At times, Welles had the actors "on" the *Pequod* stand aslant and sway in unison, as if on the deck of a ship on a wild sea. At other times, with lighting and strobes, he made the whole cavern of the Duke of York's seem as if under the ocean. I cannot help but be enthusiastic for this audacious effort, all of which played six nights a week in June and July of 1955 only a few miles from where I lived. But I never saw it; I had not aspired to the theater then. So my anguish and reverence are intertwined and immense. I have been hard on Welles sometimes in this book—as if hardness had any effect—but I know that *Moby Dick* was genius, without ever having seen it. I tremble to think what would have become of this fourteen-year-old if he *had* seen it.

Welles gathered a remarkable cast for the show: Joan Plowright, already nearly twenty-six, was Pip, on her knees; Gordon Jackson was Ishmael, and Patrick McGoohan played Starbuck. Not that every report was favorable. That great comedian-to-be Kenneth Williams was also in the cast (in several small parts), for Welles picked up on his extraordinary, nearly unstable vocal versatility (like Welles, Williams would excel on radio). But by early June, as the *Rehearsal* was rehearsed, Williams was disillusioned: "I wish to God I had never *seen* this rotten play, and Orson Welles and the whole filthy tribe of sycophantic bastards connected with this bogus rubbish." Williams was very bitter. Welles might be "a brilliant personality," but he knew nothing about producing a play. Williams was a stickler for script, blocking and technical detail, but Welles was always changing such details. In turn, he was amused by the seriousness of his actors—one of Williams's roles was A Very Serious Actor. McGoohan was only A Serious Actor.

The play Welles had carved out of the book employs a philosophical battle between Ahab and Starbuck—it is one more of Welles's obsessive debates to the death between men whose antagonism never masks their deep-seated affinity or friendship. Nor is it hard to see the appeal of Ahab to the Welles of the 1950s, the self-aware, wounded outcast, the genius who had set himself in rivalry with God. Much of the language comes from Melville, but we can feel Welles's passion:

AHAB: Is then the crown too heavy that I wear? 'Tis iron, I know—not gold; split, too—the jagged edge is galling, and my brain beats against solid metal—! The diver sun, slow dived from noon goes down. My soul mounts up, yet wearies with her endless hill! Time was, when, as the sunset spurred me, so the sunset soothed. No more. No more. This lovely light it lights not me. Damned—most subtly and malignantly, damned in the midst of paradise!

STARBUCK (in a whisper): I think I see his end, but feel that I must help him to it.

First at the Hackney Empire in London, and then in Turin at the Fiat studio, Welles made attempts to film his *Moby Dick*. Perhaps American television would take it. But the money ran out—no one quite knew where the money came from, or whether it existed. Patrick McGoohan recalls long filmed dialogues between Ahab and Starbuck—that old Kane-Leland wrestling with ideas—that were very fine. McGoohan cherished Welles, even if he was horrified at the great man's irresponsibility, the drinking and the business folly. But in Italy, when the venture fell apart, McGoohan saw Welles weeping: "He was a very lonely man." Yet he was also a freshly married man with a new child on the way.

Few saw that nearness to despair. He was driven to stay proud, to be defiant, broad in gesture, to be the laughing devil—it *was* very apt that Arkadin, once penetrated, ceased to exist. He could not bear to be seen in regret or disgrace. But in London that summer of 1955, there was another incident that acted out defiance and tantrums as opposed to helplessness.

John Houseman came to town, to a great suite at the Savoy overlooking the river. He had had successes as a movie producer for MGM—*Julius Caesar, Executive Suite, Moonfleet, The Cobweb*—and now he was about to make his finest production in Europe—*Lust for Life*, with Kirk Douglas as van Gogh. He was at a nightclub, the Caprice, one evening when he heard that Welles would be coming over after final curtain on *Moby Dick*. Houseman felt wary and intimidated. But he waited, as if challenged. A little after one, quite literally, he *felt* Welles approaching: Houseman had always *had* Welles's aura.

Then Welles saw him and moved toward a Houseman who did not know whether to expect violence or embrace. "We were less than three

feet apart when the silence was shattered by a bellow of 'Jacko!' followed
by a loud moan and then a second and third 'Jacko!' as patrons of the
Caprice were treated to the surprising spectacle of two very large men,
locked in a frantic, clumsy embrace."

They sat down and reminisced over champagne. For an hour it was a
perfect reunion, with Houseman moved to see how "seductive and endearing" the wonder boy still was. Then Houseman said he was tired; he
had to go. He recalled too late that Orson preferred always to be the master of that curtain. They would see each other again, Houseman tried to
be reassuring. He wanted to see *Moby Dick*, but he had only a few days left
in England and he also wanted to go up to Stratford to see Olivier and
Leigh in *Macbeth*.

Welles slammed the table with his fist. Suddenly his face "had the
sweaty grey-whiteness of his great furies." "It is more difficult to get seats
for *Moby Dick* than it is for *Macbeth*!" he roared. This was a foolish lie, but
for Welles it was emotionally true. The old feelings burst out. He turned
on "Jacko": "For twenty years, you son of a bitch, you've been trying to
humiliate and destroy me! You've never stopped, have you? And you're
still at it!" Houseman led his wife away in a torrent of abuse. It would be
twenty-eight years before he met Welles again.

Of course, it was a "scene," fueled by drink and Ahab's adamantine
independence. But Welles believed what he said—paranoids are not making it up—even as he saw that the lost Houseman was the best professional ally he had ever had. He could not confide in Jack, or let him see
the tears; he could not ask for help, or be as meek as Jonah. All his energies relied on being wronged: that was what had left Arkadin as flat and
uninteresting as a paper mask.

18

⤙ *Pay the Devil* ⤚

IN THAT SUMMER of 1955, Welles was in transit, desperate to
get new ventures together—or chronically accumulating minor and incomplete projects. He spent time in France, Italy and Spain. He even lent
himself to a series of travelogues for Associated Rediffusion in London;

he said they were like home movies, and the series included pieces on pelota and bullfighting, Lime-ish thoughts on Vienna and the Dominici case (in which, it was alleged, an Italian farmer had killed a touring English nobleman and his family). He wondered about doing Hemingway's *The Sun Also Rises* onstage, with Marlene Dietrich as Brett Ashley! In Spain, he began to shoot some of what might be a *Don Quixote*, with Mischa Auer as the don and Akim Tamiroff as Sancho Panza. Very little was done with a finished script, nothing with a known budget.

Writers often wake up and rush out a page or two of something they will never resume. It keeps the habit going; it avoids boredom; and it takes only some pieces of paper. But Welles was acquiring a similar habit with film: shooting some scenes, like snapshots, and then forgetting where the footage was. A writer keeps files; he has a home. Film is so much trickier to store, and Welles was forever going from one world to another.

Ideas came and went, but Paola grew larger. With the baby due in November, she and Orson crossed the Atlantic on the *Andrea Doria*. He had an assignment enough to make him pack up and leave. As in the old days, he was going to revitalize classic theater for New York. The City Center Theater Company wanted him for a season: there would be a *Lear*, Ben Jonson's *Volpone*, and why not *Moby Dick—Rehearsed* and *Twelfth Night?* The details were not promising; his own money would not top $100 a week; the theater was a huge monstrosity on West Fifty-fifth Street; the funding was shaky and there would be union troubles all along the way. Against that, he had been asked and invited home to do what he and Houseman had done for New York . . . was it nearly twenty years before? It was the emotion in an offer that he could not resist, the implicit admiration.

Nothing went well, except for the birth of the child. When they arrived in New York, the couple went to the Volney Hotel, and Paola announced that she would have the baby there—in the Italian fashion. That was a little too much room service even for Orson. He had business all the time in their room, so Paola was prevailed upon to go to the Polyclinic Hospital. There, Beatrice Judith Welles was born on November 13, whereupon the family took a larger suite at the Sulgrave Hotel.

By then, the City Center "season" was having its problems. Welles had wanted to do *Volpone* with the TV comedian Jackie Gleason; he was, early on, alert to the great talent of some people on the small screen. He had told Gleason that he would leave the laughs to him. But Gleason was a suspicious man, and he heard that the short list of actors Welles had played straight man to was very short. He was also worried that Welles had one of Gleason's problems—he was drinking too much. So *Volpone* slipped away.

Soon there was nothing but *Lear,* and that so troubled it had to be done on its own. Welles had worked to import several English actors for the show, but Equity and the immigration authorities blocked the necessary visas. So, disgruntled, he was forced to cast locally: with Viveca Lindfors as Cordelia, Geraldine Fitzgerald as Goneril and Alvin Epstein as the Fool. The actors were left feeling they were not first choice. They were not always amenable to Welles's taste for night rehearsals, and they were troubled by the constant adjustments to the text. For Welles was determined to have a one-act *Lear,* the whole violent arc without an interval.

New York was not what it had been. Union regulations now got in the wonder's way wherever he turned. At one point, he wrote to his composer—Marc Blitzstein again: "This really has turned into a city entirely ruled over by lawyers. I would have thought my own name to say nothing of yours, and our mutual enthusiasm would have represented enough credit." Blitzstein had been charged to deliver an abstract, electronic score, and there were persistent difficulties in getting the sound cues right. Rehearsals went into the night, with numbing acrimony. Welles was seen to be drinking to keep himself going.

Between alcohol and paranoia, he took on more himself. The set—at $25,000—a mass of ramps and platforms, was his own design. Like earlier sets, it was tricky to work with and not always safe. He was hurrying, scared that the rehearsal time was inadequate. He was angry, too, for some of the company seemed to be resisting him, not living up to the notion that this was the greatest adventure in their lives. A few days before opening night, Welles slipped and fell on the set; his ankle was broken. Liquor and the excitement held off pain. He went on and was then, he said, devastated by a tremendous burst of applause from the audience to mark his return to New York. He lost concentration and reckoned he gave his worst performance as Lear.

The critics didn't bother to make comparisons, but they were dismayed. Or vengeful. The underground wisdom had been spreading that Welles was, within all his own splendor, an inept actor. Walter Kerr in the New York *Herald Tribune* harped on the absence of feeling or inner conviction: "He sounds a bass-note at regular intervals, pauses metronomically, varies from shout to whimper on a prearranged schedule. The result is an intelligent automaton at center stage." In *The New York Times,*

Brooks Atkinson said the evening showed "more genius than talent." Eric Bentley was more admiring in *The New Republic:* he thought the direction was remarkable, but as an actor Welles seemed to have no rapport with his fellows.

Overnight, the ankle changed this *Lear.* It was as if Welles had neither the confidence nor the strength for the real thing, especially in the face of disapproval. He came on in a wheelchair: quite obviously this was not Lear so much as Welles essaying Lear—my dinner with Lear. It was a plea for sympathy, and also a way of finding his own voice, as opposed to the burning music of Lear. He brought the houselights up. He apologized to the audience; he explained the situation as he sought forbearance. He used that favorite ploy that was at the same time self-glorifying and confessional: "Ladies and gentlemen, this is Orson Welles, and I am in trouble."

It didn't work. On the second night, as the lights came up, he saw his nemesis, John Houseman, in the third row, his head "tilted up in that disappointed tortoise expression." Some of the audience walked out; some of the cast members were furious that the play had been altered yet again. It was a short run, just twenty-one performances, and sometimes it was not much more than Welles being wheeled about by his Fool, reciting some speeches and generally chatting to the audience. The theater had over 2,500 seats, and Welles had reduced it to a talk show. That measure was brilliant and prophetic, but it seemed indecent to actors and audience alike. The show went into history as a travesty. It lost $60,000. Welles never acted on the New York stage again.

For his career, the damage was severe. And his broken confidence was never quite the same. No matter that he bullied, roared at and trampled on other people, he was easily hurt: he needed confidence the way he needed food. And he was huge now—that had helped crack the ankle. Nor could he quite reconcile that bulk and his best voice, the intimate, conversational tone, the rapturous anecdotalist. But he knew that theater could show him at his worst.

Almost immediately he retreated, with Paola and Beatrice, to Las Vegas and the Riviera Hotel. By March, he was doing a magic act at the hotel, mixed in with speeches from Shakespeare. He was rehearsing a large part of his professional future, a way of wowing the groundlings, doing *Lear* and whatever in the half-sung, half-recited manner Rex Harrison would perfect in *My Fair Lady.* He was a crowd pleaser again—the four-week job was extended to six—so he was euphoric. As for Las Vegas, it was as much the antithesis of being "at home" as anyone had yet invented. Oddly, Paola liked it.

For CBS Television, he played the great theatrical ham Oscar Jaffe opposite Betty Grable in a production of the Ben Hecht and Charles MacArthur play *Twentieth Century*. He guested on an episode of *I Love Lucy* and then persuaded Desilu to let him make a pilot for a projected series of half-hour shows. The pilot was never taken, but the show was filmed—"The Fountain of Youth," based on a John Collier story, with Welles as the on-camera narrator.

Finally, "The Fountain of Youth" is a slight piece, the TV equivalent of one of those quick Mercury radio shows in which Welles's saturnine voice guided listeners through a story with a twist. This time it is a tale of the older man, the bimbo he loves and the stud who cuckolds him—with the extra kicker that the older man is an endocrinologist who has got hold of a youth serum. But the Welles who had felt lost in *King Lear* radiated life, merriment and stylistic insight as he actually worked with TV. His narrator is in and out of the picture. The use of fake backdrops, theatrical lighting and flat-out trickiness is exhilarating and witty. The show resonates with the enthusiasm of a kid who has woken up to find a new kind of train set. Welles was young again. One has to wonder if he couldn't have revolutionized television.

But it was two years before this untaken pilot would get on the air. This disappointment was more crucial than *Lear*, for it blocked the director in Welles—though "Fountain of Youth" is modest, it helps reveal how bored Welles had been in *Mr. Arkadin*. There is some antic glee in "Fountain of Youth" that intuits the way television's true potency is as a kind of computer game handled by a teenager with a remote control and a sugar high. It was the new magic, but Welles grasped this with his customary, self-defeating haste.

He needed money—basic cash—for now that he was back in America the IRS was after him. So he sought jobs to give them something, but he preferred the jobs to be straight cash to avoid the garnishing. His agent put him up to the work of the heavy in a Jeff Chandler picture about to be made at Universal. *Pay the Devil* it was called, and it was $60,000. He never liked the script, but the film's producer, Albert Zugsmith, entertained him. All Welles asked for extra was a makeup man who knew how to mask his nose—this nose, he said, was a lifelong humiliation. Zug agreed. Then the word came that, as actors must at last, Welles *had* looked at the script and begun to rewrite his own scenes. Zug went down to the set to watch one of these scenes being filmed. "Excellent," he said. Really? said Welles. You mean it? Zug saw how much little boy there was behind the fake nose. Sure, he said, but if you're going to rewrite—and you are—why don't we do it properly?

A regime set in. Zugsmith and Welles sat up every night with vodka and cigars rewriting the next day's scenes. They got on the way boozy co-workers will when they know they're just giving garbage a shine. So it gets to be the last day on *Pay the Devil*, and Welles comes up to Zug a little ruefully and says, "I guess I can't come down tonight."

Why not? says Zug. So that night they really tie one on, and they are bosom buddies and Welles is saying how much he'd love to direct something for this freewheeling man. Zug waves at a shelf of scripts and says, "Take your pick."

"Which is the worst one?" says Welles.

"This one," says Zug, and he pulls out something called *Badge of Evil*. "You can have it."

Now, there are other versions of this. . . .

19

Touch of Evil

WELLES WOULD SAY later that he had been asked to play the heavy in what was called *Badge of Evil*, the part of a corrupt policeman named Quinlan in a southern California town. "I said, 'Maybe,' and I was still wondering whether I could afford *not* to make it when they called up Chuck Heston." Charlton Heston then was at his peak, having just finished *The Ten Commandments*. Universal sent him the script of *Badge of Evil*, offering him the lead role of Mitch Holt, the white assistant district attorney who brings the rogue cop to justice.

It's a good enough script, Heston said, but one that depends on the direction. Who had they got?

They told him they didn't know, but Orson Welles was lined up for the heavy.

"You know, Orson Welles is a pretty good director," said Heston, and they said, "Well, that's a very good idea."

So Universal got back to Welles and offered him the job. He said he would do it if he could rewrite the script. OK, they said, if you're quick, and if you'd settle for just your fee as an actor.

There's another angle. By then, Welles's old associate William Alland was an executive at Universal. He said he helped Welles get the job. It's not unnatural for several people to tell a story in a way that gives them the credit. But it's worth stressing that, all of a sudden, Welles got to be actor, director and writer on an American film. The doors were not that firmly closed to him. Moreover, whatever his reputation for irresponsibility and self-indulgence, the film that became *Touch of Evil* was clearly an attempt at a comeback—and one that might have caused a sensation ten years earlier, or ten years later.

Heston met Welles, who was wearing a black Moorish robe, serving malt whiskey and being mesmerizing. He was already rewriting the script, and Heston was delighted with the progress.

From the outset, Welles wanted to please and impress the studio. He would claim later that, in three and a half weeks and with four secretaries, he had done "an entirely new story and script." That is an exaggeration, and unfair to Paul Monash's first script from the novel. Indeed, Monash had defined the roles of Quinlan and Holt, and written them so that it was clear how far they were both ready to bend the law to get the conviction they believed in. Monash had also built up the gangster family, the Grandis, and given them a grudge against Holt. In addition, Monash had added scenes to the novel's story and written dialogue that Welles would embrace. As in the novel, Monash kept Mitch with a Mexican wife, Connie, who gets caught up in the intrigue.

This is not to doubt the value of what Welles brought to the script: he made the work his own; he shifted the focus of the film toward Quinlan, his role; and he envisaged a physical and social setting for the story more tawdry than anyone had dreamed of before. But he used what he had, kept much of it, and actually reduced the moral ambiguity of the Monash script. (That is worth emphasizing, for some admirers of *Touch of Evil* exult over the ambivalence of Quinlan being "a great detective . . . and a lousy cop"—Monash dialogue repeated by Welles.)

Welles reversed the gender of Mitch Holt's marriage. Now, "Mike" or Miguel Vargas (Heston) is a top Mexican narcotics cop actually on his honeymoon with Susan (as blond, American and ripe as Janet Leigh). The interracial marriage is a good deal more threatening to America when the other is the man—here was Welles pinching the kind of bigotry that had often fueled gossip about his taste for Mexican and black women. There was surely another kind of sly humor in persuading Heston—that very Aryan Moses, and a young conservative—to darken up and go Mexican. But there is something gloating and nasty in all the mishaps that interrupt the honeymoon. The Vargases *are* looking for a bed. They are about to have their first "American" kiss when the car bomb goes off. That killing separates man and wife, and subjects "Susie" to increasing indignities until—at the lurid motel—we are left to wonder whether she has been molested, raped or worse. The film's preying upon Susie's sexiness is lubricious but perverse; surely there is some horror of sex here—the impossibly bloated and impotent Quinlan could be seeing or directing the action.

Welles also elected to shift the action to the U.S.-Mexico border; and he opened the movie with a tour de force traveling shot, as if to dramatize juxtaposition and its explosive risk. This is also a film with two other mixed relationships: one between Marcia Linnekar, the murdered man's daughter, and Manolo Sanchez, the vain shoe store salesman who is suspected of having killed Linnekar; and another—if in retrospect—between Quinlan and the brothel keeper Tanya, the impassive judge of his decline. If one thinks of those three ties in concert, then the film seems to be nudging us toward some eventual American future of interracial marriage, even as it contemplates the actual intercourse with distaste and dismay. Quinlan is virulently racist, yet he had Tanya once. And now his candy bar vastness has put him out of action, so his view of the Vargases and of Marcia and Manolo is filled with loathing and the search for vengeance. This *is* a very disturbing film.

But its tarnished glory on-screen comes from the completeness with which Welles fleshed out this work. Not since *Ambersons* had he placed a film so surely that we feel we know both the town and the interior spaces involved in the story. In part this is because of the genius that saw how the decaying Venice—to the south of Los Angeles—could be made to serve as the twin border towns. (Welles had wanted to go to Mexico itself, but Universal insisted that he stay closer to home. Then he found Venice— much better than the real border.) Far more, it is because of a comprehensive cinematic vision, based on wide-angle lenses, moving camera shots and beautifully tacky sets that remind us of the Welles who commanded so many skills on *Kane* and *Ambersons*. The flashy nullity of *Mr. Arkadin* has gone. *Touch of Evil* is a continuous and consistent stylistic reverie on claustrophobia and corruption. The movie is a melodrama, and in many of the settings the sordidness is fondly piled on: for example, the motel, the canal finale and a real flophouse for the last murder, a place so ugly that Janet Leigh needed a guard—but Welles was working again with a confidence, a zeal and an absolute integrity of style and meaning that *is* movie. Heston and Leigh have both attested to the fact that he was alive and dynamic all through the shooting. It is as if his boredom with mastery had fallen away.

But here's the rub: the narrative and stylistic exhilaration are offset by a terrible solipsism. There is a black hole at the heart of the film that is not simply Quinlan but Welles's agonized feelings about him. For this Hank Quinlan is more than a crooked cop and a habitual manipulator of the law. He is a monstrous human hulk, waiting for ruin, even provoking it. In the novel and the first screenplay, Quinlan had been described as a large man—still, he was a highly efficient, if unscrupulous cop. But in *Touch of Evil* itself, he is gross, ponderous and immediately loathsome; and his first appearance is accentuated by a low, wide-angle shot so that Quinlan seems to lurch out of his car and into the camera, like a sagging balloon, obscuring balance and reason.

Welles was already large, yet he made himself far more unappealing for Quinlan, putting on padding and using a makeup that leaves the man feeling unwashed and half-cooked in chicken fat. Maurice Seiderman (the makeup man on *Kane*) was recalled: he created bags to go under Welles's eyes; he changed his hairline and did one more false nose more ungainly than Welles's own warped masterpiece. Welles exulted in this hideous exaggeration; he took pleasure in shocking friends by arriving at dinner parties made up as Quinlan still. Heston went along with what he saw was a none too subtle shift in the film—it had become the story of the decline and fall of Hank Quinlan.

Over 300 pounds already—and injured in another fall in Venice during the shooting—Welles was pouring added ignominy on himself. Then he found a way of pointing up the self-destructive urges in Quinlan. One of Welles's most exquisite and heartfelt additions to the script was the character of Tanya. She has no part in the action; she is an extra, a maudlin decoration. Allegedly, Welles thought of her overnight and then called up his old friend Marlene Dietrich (whose appearance in rushes amazed Universal). Would she be there next day?

"How should I look?" she asked.

"Be dark," he told her, so she revived a stylized gypsy look she had fashioned for *Golden Earrings* in 1947. Perhaps there was a little more planning: there was a simple cantina set, after all. As for the dialogue, that could have been learned on the day. Dietrich played it dead on, very straight-faced and unemotional—maybe to keep from laughing, for these lines ache with their relevance to Welles himself. Maybe it did shock Dietrich that Welles was determined to heap abuse on himself.

QUINLAN: Have you forgotten your old friend?

TANYA: I told you we were closed.

Touch of Evil: Welles with Marlene Dietrich

QUINLAN: I'm Hank Quinlan.

TANYA: I didn't recognize you. . . . You should lay off those candy bars.

QUINLAN: Uhh . . . it's either the candy or the hooch. I must say I wish it was your chili I was getting fat on. Anyway, you're sure looking good.

TANYA: You're a mess, honey.

And then later, as the world closes in on him, Quinlan asks Tanya to read his future. She is brief and decisive: "You haven't got any. . . . Your future's all used up."

Dietrich is riveting, in part because she is on for only a few moments, and she was always most effective in piercing flashes. But her past with Quinlan is sketched in, and the sadness is as crushing as the way Quinlan and Welles volunteer for humiliation. There has seldom been a mingling of narcissism and self-revulsion in scenes more complete or alarming. It suggests how far, even in a comeback that promises so much, Welles was ready to sink himself.

Yet for much of the shooting Welles was brilliant and dominant, his old self, collaborating with a master cameraman (Russell Metty) and prepared to work out very elaborate sequences in advance. On the first day of shooting, he had to do the intricate scene in which Quinlan is interrogating Sanchez in his apartment in the course of which the incriminating shoe box is "found," loaded with dynamite sticks. On the Sunday before shooting began, Welles asked the actors to his house to rehearse. Then he turned up at the set like a beginner. As Heston remembered: "He proceeded to lay out the scene in terms of *one* shot with a crab dolly, then encompassed all the eight or nine performers who had lines in the scene. The action ranged through two rooms, a closet and a bathroom, and as I said, thirteen pages of dialogue. It was quite a complex shot, with doors having to be pulled, walls having to be pulled aside—very intricate markings, inserts on the shoe box, and things like that."

As a set piece, it is less showy than the celebrated titles shot, but far more demanding, and far more dramatically important. The unbroken stream of time and space proves that Quinlan is a cheat; and the very cramped physical setting forces the antagonism between Quinlan and Vargas to the surface. You do not quite realize it is all one shot until later, because the dramatic reality is so intense. This is one of the greatest sequences in all of Welles's work, and it shows how far the beauty of *Ambersons*—maybe the most eloquent psychological narrative language in all American film—was still his to command. Welles finished the scene—scheduled for three days on the set—before 6:00 p.m. on the first day. "OK. That's a print," he said. "We're two days ahead of schedule." It was a boast to Universal but a lesson to himself that he could still make movies better than anyone else—if he could muster the concentration and had the material.

The details in *Touch of Evil* were and are breathtaking. Akim Tamiroff and a band of young Mexican hoodlums made the Grandi gang comic, yet never less than frightening. Janet Leigh got through the part despite having a broken arm in plaster. Joseph Calleia is very touching as Quinlan's

Touch of Evil: Welles with Charlton Heston

partner, Pete Menzies, admiring, a lapdog follower, a suppressed lover even, yet capable at last of standing back from the evil. The nearly constant nocturnal black-and-white photography is ravishing. The steadily delayed coitus is nagging, funny and neurotic until . . .

Until the motel sequence. This was Welles's most significant addition to the Monash script. Susie Vargas is "parked" while her husband does what he can to settle the Linnekar killing. She goes to the out-of-town motel, and there the Grandi gang plans to implicate her in unspeakably noxious things.* That motel is still one of the most frightening places in American film. One could argue that Dennis Weaver's night man—deranged by but terrified of the idea of sex—is an unrestrained, camp performance by a young actor egged on by a wicked, admiring director. "I felt in heaven working with him," said Welles. It is another set piece, de-

---

* That seems impossible in movies as we now know them. But *Touch of Evil* was made in the age of censorship, when a feeling of imprecise outrage and true horror was still possible. Of course, the Grandi gang make a cheerful stereotype of Mexican evil.

tachable, a grisly decoration. But very troubling. For Weaver shares his
dread with us, so we know this motel is a place of depravity and madness
before the gang shows up.

By then, Janet Leigh's Susie is sleepy, misty for her Miguel, stretched
out on the bed in her underwear, as voluptuous as the Sierras. The phone
goes dead, and she hears whispers in the walls: "You know what the boys
are trying to do, don't you?"

The boys are like rejects from the gang in *Rebel Without a Cause*, and
they are led by Mercedes McCambridge. She had known Welles from
radio days. He called her up out of the blue and asked her to come to the
set. She arrived, and everyone—including Janet Leigh and the boys—was
hanging around waiting for Welles to decide on the scene. He ruminated.
Then he decided McCambridge's hair should be cut. She was resistant.
He prevailed. Then he found black shoe polish and used it to heighten her
hair and her eyebrows. McCambridge later recalled,

> They brought a black leather jacket from nowhere, and
> I was "ready." Orson said he wanted a heavy, coarse
> Mexican accent. I said, "You've got it." He asked me to
> walk across the studio like a tough, masculine, hard-
> type broad. I said, "You've got it," and I did it. He said,
> in a statement terse and unadorned, that he wanted me
> to burst into Janet Leigh's motel room with all the
> other hoodlums. As their ringleader I was to give them
> the go-ahead to have their group pleasure with her, and
> I was to say in a gruff accent that I would hang around
> and watch.

In fact, the shoe-black woman says, "Lemme stay. I want to watch." A
guy says, of Susie, "Hold her legs," and a shadow falls across her terrified
face. She babbles, "Oh, no! Let me go," but nothing can be done. Nothing is really shown beyond terrible anticipation. It is enough; and it is
repellent.

Of course, the story ends well, or with the air of being well. Quinlan
is dead. Tanya has muttered, "He was some kind of a man. What does it
matter what you say about people?" Miguel and Susie are reunited . . . for
a lifetime of traumatic reaction? The little noir story has been no more
than a melodrama, a cop story, clouded by these rotting decorations and
by the fearful overcast of Quinlan's self-hatred.

Alas, there is no more. *Touch of Evil* is a kind of masterpiece, a terrific film, nine-tenths of a knockout comeback. But the redeemed fluency of Welles's style overwhelms the flaky, genre-bound content. There isn't a story as potent or as moving as that in *Kane* or *Ambersons*. Quinlan is ruined by self-pity and Welles's unstoppable combination of self-love and self-loathing. If only Quinlan were more ordinary, more amiable, more reasonable, more matter-of-fact (as well as corrupt) . . . if only he were like Nixon, say, *Touch of Evil* might be a great movie, a portrait of deranged duty and warped idealism. But Quinlan and the movie are unbalanced by Welles's chronic self-reference. It is a part of that weight that when Quinlan is incriminated by having left his "cane" at the scene of a crime, I fear that Welles is making a pun on "Kane," as if to say past greatness is now the burden of shame.* Nothing in the film, finally, is large and human enough for its stylistic wealth, so the beauty goes as crystalline and detachable as dry paint. It is as if Welles was lamenting that there can hardly be any more great films—the trick of doing it has taken over, the magic has turned sour. And so *Touch of Evil* is some kind of masterpiece, and an offense in the nostrils of the public. Welles had shut the door on himself.

He would never direct another film in Hollywood. He had dropped his Kane at the scene of the crime and successfully abandoned the kind of American future he only half-wanted.

20

Not Helpless at All

H E   S A I D   it had been heaven to work in the studio system again. He said that only with a camera operator like John Russell could he have done the several elaborate tracking and crane shots in *Touch of Evil*. He said Heston was a prince, Leigh a wonderful surprise and McCambridge,

---

* There is a collection of "canes" in Welles's work after *Kane*. The boy Georgie in *Ambersons* is seen in one tableau holding a smart stick. In *The Lady from Shanghai*, Arthur Bannister is a crippled puppet who lurches on two canes. And . . . well, you can find the others.

Tamiroff, Weaver, Calleia and Dietrich as good as actors could be: "Anything you think up, they'll just do." He said the studio people told him they were in love with the rushes. He said he thought he was back, with many more pictures to do at Universal. He would be wanted and admired again, above suspicion.

But it went wrong. *Touch of Evil* was macabre, perverse and unpleasant; its narrative moved in different directions; there were astonishing scenes—like those with Weaver and Dietrich—that hardly seemed *necessary*. When such astonishments and beauties hit the eyes of studio men, they sometimes produce bewilderment. Which should surprise no American filmmaker, much less catch him off guard.

In the spring of 1957, Welles produced his cut of *Touch of Evil*. Then he looked out at the rest of the world and wondered what to do. He went to New York to appear on *The Steve Allen Show*, and while he was away a studio editor was introduced. By the end of June, Welles had gone to Mexico to do some more shooting on his *Don Quixote*. In his absence, Universal reappraised the picture and sought to simplify it. Had this ever happened before?

It is never an excuse in Hollywood to say you've been betrayed. You have to take that possibility for granted, and plan accordingly. In fact, no one was more suspicious, or more certain of treachery, than Welles. It was because he came to the project with that expectation that he refused to deal with the studio people as human beings. Albert Zugsmith could see the studio's point of view: "Orson couldn't make up his mind on a lot of different ways in cutting. He cuts himself, you know, and he got into fights with an editor there." As Zugsmith saw it, Welles went off to Mexico in a huff and, "of course, the very fact that he had to talk to the studio was scary to him. He gets very nervous at times." William Alland saw that old haughty self-destructiveness again. The director who had moved and seduced the crew and the actors lost his temper with executives before they had opened their mouths—to shut them up. Heston, a very balanced observer, was somewhat startled to find that so brilliant a man was simply stupid with studio people:

> You can't leave a studio holding an unfinished film,
> surely not without talking to them. Orson had an odd
> blind spot. He was infinitely charming with his crew and
> actors, but I've seen him deliberately insult studio heads.
> Very dumb. Those are the guys with the *money*. If they
> won't give you any, you don't get to make many *movies*.

In the end, in November 1957 to be precise, when he was off at 20th Century playing a hammy Will Varner in the atrocious, fatuous and indefensible *The Long Hot Summer,* for the money, Universal cut about fifteen minutes out of the picture and got Harry Keller, a studio director, to film a few expository scenes intended to make the plot easier to follow. Universal had said that this work had to be carried out by someone other than Welles—but only because Welles had refused or evaded all prior requests. Welles was in contact with Heston and Leigh, and he urged them to be tough and, in effect, noncooperative.

Heston's contract gave him a piece of the picture. He believed he was legally obliged to help the studio get it in shape. Welles wrote to the actor, violent in capital letters:

UNLESS THE STUDIO IS STOPPED THEY ARE GOING TO WRECK OUR PICTURE— AND I MEAN WRECK IT, BECAUSE IT IS NOT THE KIND OF ONE-TWO-THREE, ABC VARIETY OF COMMERCIAL PRODUCT THAT CAN BE SLIGHTLY WRECKED. WITHOUT MY HELP THE RESULT WILL BE VERY MUCH LESS SATISFACTORY THAN THE MOST ORDINARY PROGRAM ITEM. THE RESULT WILL NOT SIMPLY BE SOMETHING LESS THAN YOU HOPED. THE RESULT WILL BE GENUINELY BAD.

This highly pressured complaint is nonsense and unfair. Time has allowed us to see both the Universal *Touch of Evil* and a version far closer to Welles's cut—though it is uncertain whether Welles ever actually arrived at a definitive version. The differences are not so great. The Keller scenes are flat. The Welles version is more intriguing, though not by so much as to make a decisive difference. For, in truth, *Touch of Evil* was always, in its meaning, a program item, a studio picture. The two versions do not make different statements about their own story or about life. Rather, Welles's version is a little more baroque in its decorative nastiness and its flights of fancy. There are very Wellesian things—but they are sidebars to the inescapable line of the film. For example, fifteen years earlier, RKO had altered the meaning of *The Magnificent Ambersons.* No one dreamed of that with *Touch of Evil.*

It is certain that Universal disliked their own film. Welles would later lament that "the picture was just too dark and black and strange to them. . . . Movies weren't nearly that black ten or twelve years ago," he said in the early 1970s. And yet, in 1958, the year *Touch of Evil* was released, Hollywood also produced—as well as *Gigi*—an absolutely nihilistic Western, *Man of the West*, the relentlessly antiheroic *Bitter Victory*, Douglas Sirk's tragic *The Tarnished Angels* (from Faulkner's *Pylon*) and one of the most baleful reflections on film itself ever done, Alfred Hitchcock's *Vertigo*. In other words, there *were* people in Hollywood with visions as dark as Welles's. Or darker. *Vertigo* is not a decorative film; its unease concerns the nature of fantasy in watching and making movies. The darkness in *Touch of Evil* was bravura, showy and unfelt next to, say, *Vertigo* or *The Magnificent Ambersons*. *Touch of Evil* has brilliance but in ways that make serious scrutiny a little queasy. The film's excellence is no more than the atmosphere of Quinlan's self-pity, and thus a cul-de-sac.

As Welles wrote to Heston, nagging the actor, urging him to be unprofessional, he came up with a construct that Heston could easily have returned to sender. For Welles could only work in Hollywood by clutching to himself the fatal reputation of forlorn, romantic intransigence. Just like Kane, he would not deal with the Jim Gettyses of the world but had to blow them away on the roar of his contempt. He could not deal with people. He was trapped in the narcissism of hurt feelings; so he wrote to "Dearest Chuck":

> If you are tempted to think of yourself as the helpless
> victim of sinister Hollywood forces over which you have
> no control, I must tell you that you're wrong. You aren't
> helpless at all, and it's well within your own power to
> save much of a rather large investment of time, money
> and—yes—love.

Universal opened *Touch of Evil* in February 1958 on a double bill, without previews. But American reviews caught up with it and were united in their commonsense response: the movie was terrific but oddly hollow. *Variety* said it proved that it took "more than good scenes to make a good picture." *The New York Times* said that the lasting impression was "effect rather than substance" and raised the legitimate question, Why would a villainous cop, having hoodwinked the taxpayers for some thirty years, suddenly buckle when a tourist calls his bluff? Perhaps it was because self-destruction was determined to die ignominiously in the trash of Americana.

Welles left America again, taking his family back to Europe. By January 1960, vast and magnificent in a midnight blue tuxedo and Chinese silk waistcoat, he would delight the Oxford Union with his sardonic intelligence and win victory (485 to 309) for the motion that "this House holds America responsible for spreading vulgarity in Western society." At the same time, in Oxford, he actually told admiring students that *Touch of Evil* was one of the pictures that had come out closest to his intentions.

The wind was changing. In the summer of 1958, in the magazine *Arts*, a young French critic, François Truffaut, lamented that *The Long Hot Summer*, and not *Touch of Evil*, had been an American entry at Cannes that year. This was part of a tirade of praise, for the film, for Welles and for the image of uncompromising poetic beauty in a movie director, the job to which Truffaut himself aspired:

> Welles adapted for the screen a woefully poor little detective novel and simplified the criminal intrigue to the point where he could match it to his favorite canvas— the portrait of a paradoxical monster, which he plays himself—under cover of which he designed the simplest of moralities: that of the absolute and the purity of absolutists.
>
> A capricious genius, Welles preaches to his parishioners and seems to be clearly telling us: I'm sorry I'm slovenly; it's not my fault if I'm a genius; I'm dying: love me.

This was extraordinary insight, and it was criticism that would be enhanced by Truffaut's own emergence as a director only a few years later. Welles could be very witty about the French—how he nodded sagely at their prolix and inscrutable questions and then meekly asserted, "Yes, of course, you're right." But he was self-adoring and smart enough to know that no one asked him questions like the French. In June 1958, back in Paris, he told *Cahiers du Cinéma* (rather like Kane considering retiring to Nice):

I'm seriously considering putting a complete stop to all
cinematic or theatrical activity, to end it once and for
all, because I've had too many disillusions. I've devoted
too much work, too much effort, for what has been
given me in return. I don't mean to say in money, but in
satisfaction. So I contemplate abandoning film and theater because in effect they have already abandoned me. I
have some films to complete: I'll finish *Don Quixote*, but
I'm no longer eager to throw myself into new enterprises . . . and while a little youth is still left to me, I
ought to try to find another area in which I'd be able to
work, to stop wasting my life trying to express myself
through cinema.

And so the scorpion waited on the riverbank, indulging in melancholy. And the new wind came up. In June, in Brussels at the World's
Fair, a competition declared that *Touch of Evil* had won the grand prix as
movie of the year. (Welles would joke that the idiot at Universal who
had let the film be submitted was fired.) And then in Brussels again,
in October, as the fair closed, a poll was undertaken to select the Best
Film of All Time—clearly the medium was beginning to die. One hundred seventeen film historians came up with twelve films. *Battleship
Potemkin* was the winner with one hundred votes. *The Gold Rush* and *The
Bicycle Thieves* got 85 each. In ninth place, with 50 votes, was *Citizen
Kane*.

Then a second jury of young filmmakers (it included Satyajit Ray,
Robert Aldrich and Alexander Mackendrick) had the inane task of pick-
ing a final six of "living and lasting value." They chose *Potemkin*, *The Gold
Rush*, *La Grande Illusion*, *The Bicycle Thieves*, Pudovkin's *Mother* and
Dreyer's *La Passion de Jeanne d'Arc*.

There was a din of cheers and boos from the audience, and one
voice—perhaps it was Truffaut's—cried out, "*Où est* Kane?"

It wasn't me; I have never been in Brussels. But *Kane* was everywhere in the late fifties. I had seen it in that empty suburban theater.
François Truffaut had dreams of being a boy out in the city at night, of
coming to a locked and barred theater that was playing *Citizen Kane* and
of using a walking stick—perhaps it was a cane?—to purloin stills from
the movie. There was a generation for whom *Kane* was being rereleased,
and in it they saw their futures as well as Orson Welles's past. Naturally,

they worshiped him and made him a kind of father. In the Winter 1961–62 issue of *Sight & Sound, Citizen Kane* was voted top of the top ten. Yet in 1952, it had not even placed in that elite group.* How were his spiritual children to know that Welles felt so wretched and lost? How were we to consider that fatherhood had never quite been his thing?

---

* Though Welles did volunteer his own top ten for that issue. His list was pious and loyal to academic notions of the moment: *City Lights, Intolerance, Shoeshine, The Baker's Wife, Stagecoach, Greed, Nanook of the North, Potemkin, La Grande Illusion, Our Daily Bread.*

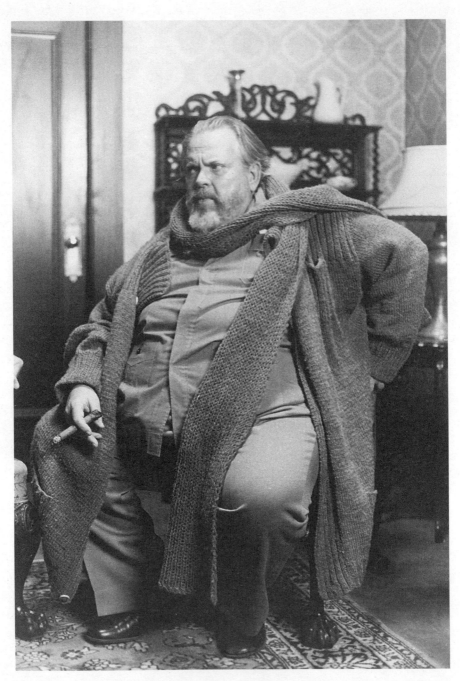

Portrait by Timothy Greenfield-Sanders, 1979

Part Four

XANADU
1 9 5 8 – 8 5

*"I want the story which I told you last night to
happen in real life . . ."*

KANE'S XANADU was built on the Gulf Coast of Florida. It entailed the creation of an artificial mountain as well as the deployment of 20,000 tons of marble and 100,000 trees. It was, of course, never finished, and at the end of the film its future is remarkably wrapped in smoke and darkness. Is the fire that burns the "Rosebud" sled eventually going to set free the buildings and the trees? Kane has no heir. There is nowhere for all his accumulated things to go. And, seemingly, in the mind of its movie and its America, there is no thought of the nation or Florida rescuing the place, making an attraction, or even a theme park for megalomaniacs, out of it. Xanadu seems determined to vanish.

Hearst's San Simeon worked out in so much less melodramatic a way. Its architect, Julia Morgan, estimated that, by 1945, the place had cost $4.7 million. Eventually, the estate passed from the family into the hands of the state of California, which has made a handsome exhibit of it. For a modest sum, any visitor can enjoy the Pacific views, the lofty, vain and graceful interiors, the enclosed pool and the superb exterior pool, so Roman that Stanley Kubrick and Kirk Douglas rented it for scenes in *Spartacus*. San Simeon is an institution now, one of the most eccentric and assured of preserved American homes, a model for every dreamer.

But Xanadus do not always need marble, stone, trees and severe chain-link fences. Some faces say "No Trespassing" as forcefully as signs. Xanadu in *Citizen Kane* is a state of mind, too: Jed Leland called it "a world . . . of his own, an absolute monarchy." Orson Welles found a similarly bizarre haven and prison in his last years, even if its props amounted to little more than a cloak, a chair and a bold face turned to the camera and the world. And Welles's Xanadu, it seems to me, is unexpectedly benign and forgiving. We can surely view his last decades as sad, overloaded and macabre: this *is* the age in which Welles became known as a shill for cheap wines, a genius without finished works. But the laugh never went away, and the burdened man never gave up his show. The poor bastard was magnificent to the end.

There are twenty-five years left to go in this life we are assisting, and I suspect that it would be neither reasonable nor kind—to Welles or to ourselves—to track them closely, as I have tried to do in the book so far. That might prove too grim and relentless; it would make too much of the lost chances, the wild hopes, the disappointment, the solitude and the humiliation of being Orson Welles and having to hear the question, Whatever *happened* to him? Not that those sadnesses can be omitted. But it was tough enough to live that life day by day while putting on the resilient air of appetite still—and him such a fake actor. Why could he never really lose weight? people ask. Because that would have begun to concede the regret, the melancholy and the horror. So he ate grandly, and often made a show of being seen at his food. At Ma Maison, sometimes, in Los Angeles, at his special table, he would order prime rib, and then an extra rib, but no potatoes: for he was on a diet, he said, like a pious little boy. And then that fearsome laugh, defying pity or salvation. Nearly twenty-seven years after *Touch of Evil*, he would die of a heart attack. He had meetings and a shoot set for later that day; there were plans still, always plans to contest the loneliness. But he may not have been entirely appalled at the shock of decisive pain, and he may have marveled that his corpse had taken that long to claim him. He was never a patient man.

As for the timing, alone in Los Angeles had its point: it would have the right ironic ring in obituaries. But the day before, he had visited *The Merv Griffin Show* for the umpteenth time, with Barbara Leaming, his biographer. He had done some light conjuring, nothing too strenuous, but enough to prompt the thought that he could have expired in and with a trick, subsiding as the two of clubs was discovered in Merv's handkerchief pocket: "How did you *do* that, Orson?" the loyal Merv would cry. But there would be no answer now, not even the smile or the sweet digestive chuckle.

There were those defenders of Welles who lamented—and some enemies who exulted in—his appearances on *Merv Griffin*, his commercials for jug wines and nursery foods, his playing of scenes with such allegedly unfit partners as Burt Reynolds, Kermit and Angie Dickinson. Such voices labored to explain Welles as someone obliged to humble himself in order to get a little further on with this or that lofty movie project. Enemies argued instead that happy meretriciousness had found its proper level.

My own feeling is that Welles enjoyed *The Merv Griffin Show*, and the instant, ghostly amiability of Merv himself. He liked to do gentle illusions for daytime audiences—they were routines he knew inside out, but he never tired of those gasps of wonder that greet proficient conjuring, or its brief air of mastery. And he reveled in the conceit that Lear and Kermit might be elements in one piece of magic, peas under the cups, his playthings. He cherished magic because it put him in charge, so he never regarded it as a cheap trick. To make people gasp with surprise is a noble calling. Any Lear he ever dreamed of would have had that aspiration. That's why his Lears and Othellos all seemed a little bogus, like player kings in Zenda, conned into taking the Big Part. Equally, he could sometimes make *The Merv Griffin Show* feel as if the cloak and staff of Prospero had enchanted the stale air and slick light.

Wherever he was, he was not quite at home; he carried the thrill of an invader. Yet he was in charge—Merv, Mike Douglas, David Frost, Johnny Carson, Dick Cavett, they all deferred to him, took it for granted that he was extraordinary and untouchable. They knew Kane, and overlooked Arkadin. They felt the rare, tragic energy in Welles. For decades, he played the role of a wandering genius, inexhaustible and seductive: it was his character. It was his work. Let us have the common sense and decency to see that it was his choice. Until the very end, waiting as patiently as he could manage, Orson Welles did exactly what he wanted to do. Spoiled children may live alone; they will die in their own solitude; but they do not pretend to be reformed, and they do not endure being thwarted.

He had foreseen the popular notion of his own awful, humiliating close. If only as an actor, he could make himself a kind of Falstaff for the honest, honorable and dignified life. In knowing how rotten he was as an actor, he surely measured the decay and the sheer waste in all acting. He had at least the shadow of one foot planted in the real world of behavior and sensation, where it was enough to dine on claret and good beef, with serious cigars and brandy to follow, to while away the hours with men of ideas and eloquence, taking remarkable women off to bed afterward. That sort of man might even have time and energy left over to run the world— to do serious things—or to wonder what might have been, if only Roosevelt had lived another year or two. . . .

Sometimes, dining with admirers, he could come very close to seeing his own dead end, and he was always ironic and wise in doing so. Something close to gentleness could settle on him, an amusement that knew how easy it would be just to talk for the next . . . twenty-five years:

> I project a certain aura of success, which encourages
> critics all over the world to think it's time to discourage
> me a little you know: "what would do him the most
> good would be to tell him that in the long run he's not
> so great as all that." But it's been twenty-five years now
> they've been saying that to me! No, I've really spent too
> many months, too many years, looking for work. And I
> have only one life. So for the moment, I write and paint.
> I throw away everything I do, but perhaps I'll eventually
> do something good enough to keep: it has to happen. I
> can't spend my whole existence at festivals or in restau-
> rants begging for money. I'm sure I can make good
> films only if I write the scripts. I could make thrillers,
> obviously, but I don't have any desire to. The only film
> I've ever written from the first word to the last and was
> able to bring to a proper conclusion was *Citizen Kane*.
> Well, too many years have gone by since I was given
> that opportunity. Can I wait another fifteen years for
> someone willing to place absolute trust in me again?
> No, I need to find another, cheaper means of expres-
> sion—like this tape recorder! . . .

That was Welles in 1958, in Brussels or Paris (it is not quite clear which), talking to André Bazin, Charles Bitsch and Jean Domarchi. At that time, he would never have found such warm or patient listeners in America. The French *cinéastes* were the first Mervs, and what a perfor-mance they got, what a man! "And I have only one life" is so much more than Quinlan or even Kane ever understood. Grant that Orson Welles could seem like that at the dinner table, round midnight, and it's easy to see how he won admirers who simply *knew* that he was the great man, criminally denied the picture business's trust. Few of those admirers ever realized that the business has never known such trust, let alone given it. Or that they were getting his greatest genius—the sad story of his fall, all done in that tone of voice that saw the darkening city with George Am-berson's awakened eyes. It was at the dinner table that he had his great un-ending play in which he was a noble actor. No wonder he grew large.

There were also professional performances, his concession to his most abiding, petty and unbecoming weakness—the belief that he had to work to live, to eat; and its accompanying vengeance—that, being so compelled, he would often take the worst work, or make the most transparent parody of it. In the late fifties and early sixties, he was "acting" for his living, drifting between the poles of contempt and sanctimoniousness; it is hard to know which is more painful to watch.

In *The Long Hot Summer*, released in 1957, his Will Varner—extravagantly chuckling and cunning—is a patriarch, and a rubber nose bubbling on a stew of swooping, simpering, often unintelligible "accent," akin to one piece of glossy meat in a pot of gumbo. Welles's unstoppable overdoing of everything was grimly beheld by a circle of more or less Methodist actors (Paul Newman, Joanne Woodward, Anthony Franciosa, Lee Remick), none of whom had the wit or experience to know that the only way of doing this kind of nonsense was overdoing it.

The Long Hot Summer, made just after *Touch of Evil*, must have helped an outsider believe that Hollywood had given up its own ghost. Though nominally drawn from William Faulkner stories (Paul Newman plays a spiffed-up version of Flem Snopes, renamed Ben Quick to go with those blue eyes), *Summer* is a Hollywood attempt to cash in on the sweaty emotionalism it associated with Tennessee Williams and "the South." The movie comes with its gluey theme song (a 20th Century–Fox device), sung by Jimmie Rodgers, which warns, "The long hot summer seems to know every time you're near." Not that reticence or shyness is the mode in this film. The best that can be said for Welles's landowner— with a face the color of a tobacco leaf, in a straw hat and an orange robe—is that he seems determined to give the impression of having a good time.

He looks awful, and acts worse. Producer Jerry Wald suggested sarcastically that Welles's accent might require subtitles. Not at all, said Welles. Encourage people to go back to the book. There is no such risk, but there are scenes in the script that edge diffidently toward emotional truth—one, in particular, has Welles reconciling with his daughter, played by Woodward. She seems ready for something more searching, but then he sweeps the scene off its feet with fraudulent gusto. There is but one quiet, enjoyable moment. Varner is talking to his mistress (Angela Lansbury), and he soulfully laments that at sixty-one he's not much good for anything. We are not talking about golf.

"Don't tell *me* you're too old," she chides him. "I happen to be in a position to know."

This is not plausible, much less pretty to picture. But Welles lets a little burp of satisfaction escape Varner's lips, and one eyebrow arches like a salute to his own ego.

He went briefly to the Cameroons, in French Equatorial Africa, to be a bombastic American in *The Roots of Heaven* for John Huston. But the picture they were doing proved less interesting than seeing how the dying Errol Flynn handled his considerable heroin habit in the heat while servicing a quite beautiful teenager he had with him, at the same time writing love letters home to another teenager, Beverly Aadland, the more famous Lolita of his last years. There was great drinking in Africa, too, and—inevitably—a little filming on an entirely forlorn venture. Darryl Zanuck, the producer, was there as well, having cast his mistress, Juliette Greco, in the film, his face all the more pinched to see that she was spreading her affections around—even as far as the crew! As everyone agreed, the studio system was crumbling.

Elia Kazan recalled a Paris dinner, with Welles and Zanuck, at which Welles "strained to amuse" the mogul as a way of getting a loan that would send him on to his next harassed destination. Kazan heard Welles laugh in "an explosion of impatience and pain." Years later, as Orson died, Kazan wondered if death wasn't "the last of a series of small 'deaths,' none of them visible to the eye but all demoralizing something essential within him and leading to the final collapse."

Welles went to Hong Kong, a dull stopping place on his childhood trips, and found that now, "Shanghai has moved here, with a little bit of London, Paris and Chicago thrown in." He was playing the skipper of a ferryboat, and he gave the man an English accent—"an attempt to be upper drawer on the part of a bottom drawer Englishman—reformed Cockney." He had another false nose—common and low class—for the occasion. "I enjoy not recognizing myself," he told an interviewer. His character was broad, the film was *Ferry to Hong Kong*, and Welles had a falling out with his costar, Curt Jurgens, because Jurgens believed the story was serious, while Welles knew it had no chance except as a farce.

He played Benjamin Franklin again in the French movie *Lafayette*, and steamship inventor Robert Fulton in Abel Gance's *Austerlitz*. He was the enthroned chieftain Burundai in *The Tartars*, in which he and that old rival Victor Mature flashed wide-screen sneers at each other and—thanks to crosscutting—fought with swords the size of cabers. He took two roles in Richard Fleischer's seminally wretched *Crack in the Mirror*—he and Fleischer were chums then. He was Saul in an international coproduction of *David and Goliath*. (Consider the noses of antiquity that he had fashioned—somewhere there ought to be a great shelf of Wellesian noses, like the elbows of ordinary men.) For Fleischer, again, he narrated *The Vikings*, his voice like Thor's horn. He also narrated *King of Kings*, Nicholas Ray's Christ story (or "Christ!" movie), without credit, only because he had demanded a rank on-screen to match that of Jeffrey Hunter, the unfortunate Jesus.

In Spain, for producer Samuel Bronston, who had done *King of Kings*, he found Charlton Heston again at the premiere of *El Cid*, another Bronston picture. So Welles took the actor to a distinguished dinner at Horcher's. Then he outlined a new project for Heston which Welles could see in his head: the epic of Cortés and his conquest of Montezuma's Mexico. With Heston signed up, the necessary $15 million would surely follow. A script? asked Heston. By all means, said Welles, offering brandy, we'll do that, too.

Heston regretted. He was weary of epics and work itself. But he did what he could to persuade Bronston to let Welles have $2 million and the run of the sets left over from *55 Days at Peking*. "He'll improvise the damnedest spy story you ever saw," said Heston. But Bronston was going broke, Heston was going home and Welles was left to look elsewhere. Cortés would have been Mexico again, that old Latin American dream.

I have held back two roles that span the extremes of his desperate acting. In 1959, for the same Richard Fleischer, he had played the Clarence Darrow character in *Compulsion*, a movie about the Leopold-Loeb murder case. That story was a part of Welles's own childhood, for the two rich kids had murdered the teenage Bobby Franks in Chicago in 1924, when Welles himself was nine. The movie was written, with crime and trial, to be a treatise against capital punishment. That was the message that its producer, Darryl Zanuck's son, Richard, wanted, and it was something that appealed to Welles, too. Welles let it be known that he liked the theme enough to entertain the thought of being the director. But Fox feared his extravagance, and they hired him for just ten days to play the lawyer Jonathan Wilk (the Darrow role), who was defending Leopold and Loeb (played by Dean Stockwell and Bradford Dillman).

So Fleischer had reason to be apprehensive when Welles arrived. Years later, the director told Barbara Leaming, "You don't know how to handle him. You don't know what way he's going to jump. He's got this overpowering voice and presence. You really have to feel your way for a while to see whether you can direct him or whether he's going to direct you. He knows so damn much. He knows what you're doing before you think of it yourself."

Inevitably, there came a clash, or a testing moment. Welles had to make an exit one way. He stopped and puzzled over it. Somehow, he wanted to go in the opposite direction. Fleischer explained that there was no set built to cover that way. Again, Welles ruminated. "You know what *I'd* do if I were directing this picture?" he said.

Compulsion: with Dean Stockwell and Bradford Dillman

Fleischer fed him the next line.

"I would wait until they built the wall for me," said Welles.

"Orson," said Fleischer, "this is the reason why I am directing this picture and you are not."

Welles chuckled and swallowed graciously. It was easier to give Fleischer credit for nerve and timing than to admit the profound truth of the observation.

As the defense lawyer, Welles had an immense speech to deliver, the one that seeks mercy for the convicted youths. It is a stirring if solemn address, Darrowesque if not quite what Darrow had said. On-screen, it runs over ten minutes. Welles had wanted to do it all in a single setup—years later he claimed that Fleischer had shot it that way but then edited it with many reaction cutaways. In fact, because he had Welles for only ten days,

Fleischer broke the speech down into several pieces and then shot it bit by bit, for the convenience of camera and set. That made the momentum of the great speech harder to achieve. Welles had no shame about demanding all the text on cue cards: he said that was meant as a reassurance, but he was by then well into the habit of declining to learn lines. It was a way of telling himself he was above all of it.

His makeup was simpler and more carefully done than Will Varner's. It did not detract from the character and what he said. But Fleischer was especially surprised to see that Welles did not enjoy playing *with* other actors. He did not like to look them in the eye. In crosscut conversation scenes, he preferred to have the other actor *not* present. That is very uncommon. Most actors want to feel the human response. They like to have the "other" lines fed back to them in the character's voice. It is a code of courtesy among good actors to stay to give that off-camera support. But Welles preferred to be alone.

He did the speech, and did it beautifully. Of course, he had many of the attributes of a great, showboating lawyer—a Father Mapple beseeching the good in every juror's heart. The grisly and contemptuous acting in so many of his films of this era should be set against the whispered gravity and genuine intensity with which he speaks for his clients:

> Your Honor, if you hang these boys, you turn back to
> the past. I'm pleading for the future. Not merely for
> these boys but for all boys, for all the young. I'm plead-
> ing not for these two lives but for life itself, for a time
> when we can learn to overcome hatred with love, when
> we can learn that all life is worth living and that mercy
> is the highest attribute of man. Yes, I'm pleading for the
> future in this court of law—I'm pleading for love.

That big scene was an event at the Fox lot. There were many visitors. One day, a Fox executive, Sid Rogell, came along with some friends. Rogell was a Welles enemy from RKO days and *It's All True*. It was Rogell who had enforced the eviction order, pushing the Mercury people out of their offices. Welles spied him on the *Compulsion* set, stopped shooting and ordered him out. Rogell thought it was a joke, but Welles pushed the humiliation all the way home, and for a moment he had the power. The unit depended on him working. So Rogell went away. There may have been no retaliation. But months later, the picture was being looped and Welles was back to redo the lawyer's speech in those parts where camera noises or the creaking of a large, crowded set had spoiled the live track.

He then discovered that the IRS was garnishing his fee for the film, a matter in which the studio could have taken a prompting hand. He lost his temper and, irked at the nagging detail of looping, walked out with some work undone. The whole thing was a model of his relations with the big studios.

Compulsion was a deserved success. Fleischer and cameraman William C. Mellor had given the black-and-white imagery a look of *Ambersons*. It had very good reviews. In Cannes, Welles, Stockwell and Dillman shared the acting prize. But there was no recognition from the Academy. Those nominated for best supporting actor that year were Arthur O'Connell and George C. Scott in *Anatomy of a Murder*, Robert Vaughn in *The Young Philadelphians*, Ed Wynn in *The Diary of Anne Frank* and—the winner—Hugh Griffith in *Ben-Hur*.

Then, in 1966, Welles played a supporting role in *Is Paris Burning?* the movie about the Allied advance on a city that the Germans threatened to destroy. Though made by René Clément, a good director and a member of the French Resistance, the picture was ruined by a wretched script (pinned on Gore Vidal and Francis Ford Coppola) and the scheme of putting star actors in every role. Welles was Raoul Nordling, the Swedish consul who acts as a go-between for the Resistance and the German general (Gert Fröbe).

He was hideously overweight at the time (he shot it right after *Chimes at Midnight*). This is not just another assault on his lack of discipline but a point that mars the film. Paris in 1944 was not well fed. The actors who inhabit the Resistance are lean and hungry. But Nordling is like a food dump. Nor does the movie leave this evidence of our eyes alone. Early on, Nordling is enlisted to aid Leslie Caron's husband. They go to a railyard where people are being shipped to a concentration camp. This was, apparently, a very uncomfortable scene, set in the historic railyard, with many extras who had been there during the Nazi era. Welles would say that he found the shadow of truth oppressive. But that unease was surely added to by a prior scene in which the gourmet consul recollects Caron and her husband from a prewar lunch and the excellent mousse she served—what flavor was it?—yes, of course, trout mousse. The shadow of Welles's gourmandise here is worse than history.

Later, Welles had a scene with Fröbe as Nordling tries to persuade the general to spare Paris. They seek a small room to talk in confidence and find a pantry filled with food for a party. As they talk, Welles's eye drifts off to the rich desserts, and he cannot restrain a pudgy finger from reaching out for a fragment of chocolate, or whatever. *Is Paris Burning?* is a mess of a film, and maybe that was evident while it was being made. But the "joke" is ghoulish, and it leads to subversive thoughts, such as, How many French freedom fighters could there be hiding in Nordling's block-wide lounge suit?

There was a nightmare and a constant mockery in this restless life of the supporting actor, as well as odd moments of glory. Consider the contrast between the almost depressively purposeful liberal humanitarianism of Clarence Darrow and the black comedy of Welles doing a Darrow for the money and having the IRS come up from out of the floorboards at the last moment to pick his pocket. Then recall another of his cameos, the rotund movie producer with Tyrolean hat, slit mustache and Elsa Martinelli as luggage, in the wretched *The V.I.P.s.* Max Buda the man is called, Kordaesque, grandiloquent, fragrantly bogus, sincerely bogus, and always pursued by tax laws. The sparklingly young David Frost sees Buda at the airport and sly-whines at him, "Aren't you overweight?" (a luggage joke applied to the man himself). Welles was trading on himself as a figure of fun: the jokes and the movies were equally grotesque. It seems like a willing torture, his acceptance being the height of mortification. It's a wonder he didn't appear, nearly naked, as a has-been wrestler. A few years later, in London, he shot a fragment, "Tailors," in which he and his size are steadily humiliated by Charles Gray and Jonathan Lind.

And yet, in the early sixties, there was an underground Welles, as merry, active and sometimes comically serious as he would ever be. Amid the debris of all the inane acting-for-hire movies, he was challenging the loftiest projects of his life. One can only reconcile the split levels of his life by arguing that, Quixote-like, he could keep the spirit of ideas and hopes intact against terrible travails and indignity.

He was always doing his own *Don Quixote*, and always saying that the dross and the shit were tolerated for its sake. It had begun in 1957—or was it '55?—in Mexico, Spain and Italy, and it had had Mischa Auer and then Francisco Reiguera as the Don, Akim Tamiroff as Sancho Panza and Patty McCormack as the child to whom Welles tells the story. It went on and on. *When Are You Going to Finish Don Quixote?* said Welles, roaring with laughter—*that* would be its title. Auer was dropped. Reiguera died. Tamiroff died. McCormack lived past her childhood. And as the decades elapsed, so Welles grew into quite new and different visions of what the film would be.

Some say there was a finished version, a cut or even a work print in

Los Angeles when he died. In 1986, in an inventory of Welles's unfinished or unreleased projects, Jonathan Rosenbaum said it was "currently in the process of being restored." Perhaps, one day, something called Welles's *Quixote* will emerge. Yet I wonder if it should. For good and ill, it was during his *Quixote* that Welles discovered the nature of a film that never was, would be or should be. Its legend is tattered and complete enough. Actual screenings would be so deflating, so much less than the thought of existence. The magic has been achieved; I hope that flat-footed completion will never spoil it.

As if that was not enough, in early 1960, Welles returned to another obsession, Falstaff. The old debacle *Five Kings* saw fresh life—in Belfast, for five performances, at the rickety Grand Opera House—as *Chimes at Midnight*, with Welles as Falstaff, Hilton Edwards the narrator and a young English actor, Keith Baxter, as Hal. It had been meant as the start of a tour that would go by way of Dublin, Paris, Amsterdam, Brussels, Athens, Cairo and so to London. It did reach Dublin, but it faltered there. "Orson got bored," said Baxter, "and decided he didn't like the company. But on the last night, coming back to England, he said to me on the ship, 'This is only a rehearsal for the movie, Keith, and I'll never make it unless you play Hal in that, too.'" So capricious, so persistent.

But Welles was hurrying to London with the chance of directing Laurence Olivier in Eugène Ionesco's *Rhinoceros*. Along with Samuel Beckett, Ionesco was then the epitome of the chic experimental playwright. In the play, everyone gradually turns into a rhinoceros—all except an Everyman figure, Berenger, who resists. To adopt the blurb for the published play, which says it all with foreboding clarity, "It shows us the struggle of the individual to maintain his integrity and identity alone in a world where all others have succumbed to the 'beauty' of brute force, natural energy, and mindlessness."

In short, it was just a little Kafkaesque, ending with Berenger alone in the world:

> Now I'll never become a rhinoceros, never, never! I've
> gone past changing. I want to, I really do, but I can't, I
> just can't. I can't stand the sight of me. I'm too
> ashamed! I'm so ugly. People who try to hang on to
> their individuality always come to a bad end! Oh well,
> too bad! I'll take on the whole of them! I'll put up a
> fight against the lot of them, the whole lot of them! I'm
> the last man left, and I'm staying that way until the end.
> I'm not capitulating!

The play proved a hit, and an embarrassment. Later on, Welles said he fell out of love with the work as rehearsals went on. Others felt that he was so enthusiastic for it he was always adding interpretations and bits of business. Welles and Olivier did not get on. The actor was in a crisis: his marriage to Vivien Leigh was over, and he was in love with Joan Plowright (who was also in *Rhinoceros*). During rehearsal, from New York, Leigh announced that Olivier and Plowright were lovers. As work went on, Olivier first ignored and then barred Welles. But the play did well, moving from the Royal Court to the Strand, acquiring Maggie Smith when Plowright stepped down to avoid publicity. Noël Coward went to see it and judged that "Larry" had narrowly survived Welles who "directed into the ground. . . . I am sick of these amateur pseudo-intellectual scribblings—Ionesco in my opinion is *not* a playwright and not a particularly original thinker. He merely tries to be, which is fatal."

Welles was rueful, and wounded. He believed that Olivier had sensed rivalry from the start and then outmaneuvered him: "He behaved terribly during the show. He's always very sinister and does strange things." As Welles saw it, Olivier led a conspiracy against the director so that he was compelled to give up on rehearsals. Olivier could not stand equals: "He doesn't want anybody else up there. He's like Chaplin, you know. He's a real fighting star." Perhaps Olivier just recalled 1946, when Orson had snatched his Vivien while he acted in Shakespeare.

How many people must have asked him, "Why do you get involved in these forlorn ventures?" There is an answer—that only the disasters and mishaps can lead you to treasure. Why don't "they" just ask me to make films? he would say, but with a look of wicked innocence that warned most of them off. Then sometimes someone asked, and sometimes, despite every misadventure and unlikelihood, the film was made and it was more than anything ever seen before.

When he did his little bit for *Austerlitz*—the inventor of the submarine—he met Alexander Salkind and his son, Ilya. Alexander was Welles's age, an engaging Russian; the son was in his early twenties. They wanted to do a Welles picture based on the Gogol story "Taras Bulba." Welles agreed, on condition that he could do the script. But when the script was done, the Salkinds said, Alas, how can we compete with the big Hollywood *Taras Bulba* that is coming, the one with Yul Brynner and Tony Curtis? They were correct; that *Taras Bulba*—released in 1962—was so bad as to be beyond competition.

But the Salkinds persevered. They offered Welles a list of books he could choose from for another picture. Can't I do an original? he begged.

No, they said, look at the list. It had many Russian classics, all out of copyright, and Franz Kafka's *The Trial*. I'd rather do *The Castle*, said Welles. Don't be difficult, they replied, do *The Trial*. Oh, very well, he sighed.

It should have been impossible. At the time, the Salkinds had no money, just their list and a warm regard for Welles. The plans to film in Zagreb went horribly astray—though there would be one Yugoslavian discovery. Still, money was acquired from here and there, and from a few places never quite revealed. Welles did the script. He was allowed to make the film in liberty—or rather, he was left alone to overcome the enormous physical obstacles that arose. He had a cast as good as any since *The Magnificent Ambersons*. And if the result isn't quite Kafka, and not entirely Kafkaesque, Kafka can live with that. Welles's *The Trial* is also an astonishing work, and a revelation of the man.

In the course of 1961, Welles worked on his adaptation and also designed elaborate sets that were to be built in a Paris studio. Then, shortly before the unit set out for Zagreb to shoot exteriors and one vast office interior, the Salkinds reported, Alas, no money for sets. Welles was briefly overwhelmed. He had done all this work on sets, and he believed that Kafka's world needed to be made solid. It was night, and he was in his hotel room, pacing, worrying—this is a restless dolly shot back and forth, and him with his weak ankles—when he saw two moons through the window: the illumined clock faces above the old Gare d'Orsay. Eureka! At 4:00 a.m. he went down to the abandoned railway depot and found in it all the settings he needed, *plus* a "kind of sorrow that accumulates in a railway station where people wait."

Truly, there is a dolorous unity, a sense of the afflicted and worn-out parts of a city, in his *Trial*. This is not quite Kafka. Alan Bennett, who wrote a television play about Kafka, observed that Welles had inflated the setting, stressing the bureaucratic infinity, while Kafka had written about small, cramped interiors. But Welles had a passion for blighted cities; he could see the beauty in spoilage and desolation. It is there in the spreading city that chokes the life of the Ambersons, and in the border town of *Touch of Evil*. It is even there in the clammy corridors of the castle in *Macbeth*. And it is there in the odd air of makeshift and macabre in *The Trial*. That sense of place is vital to the movie's beauty, and to its nearly suffocating melancholy.

Welles never claimed to be Kafkan. He felt bound to make Joseph K less passive—"to interest me, the characters must do something." He also proposed that, had Kafka been writing after the Holocaust, he could not have endured his own book's ending and the resignation with which Joseph accepts his fate and his death. That seems not just poor literary criticism but a sign that Welles was never a searching reader. For Kafka's sense of inescapable destiny was not vulgar enough to be outraged or empowered by a new ending. Indeed, if Kafka had been less certain about fate, he would not be as funny. And Welles missed Kafka's humor, like a man who never saw the moon because the sun was shining.

Which is not to dismiss Welles's *The Trial* as solemn. Despite his own famous laughter, Welles the filmmaker was seldom funny. There is no doubt about how gravely he regarded the matter of self-expression. Though Charlie Kane was possessed of a wink and a grin, whenever he felt a responsibility to himself he turned dour, grim and rather nasty. And so right up to the end of *Touch of Evil*—"He was some kind of a man"—Welles could be deaf to irony or absurdity when passing judgment on himself.

The Trial breaks that rather sterile pattern, thanks to the trembling, jittery volatility of Anthony Perkins as Joseph K. Of course, it is an advantage (and a clarification) to have anyone else at the center of a Welles film, for the director's vanity could only be exposed in the several battles between the inspired director and his obdurate performances. (*Mr. Arkadin*, say, might begin to relax and expand with anyone else in the title role.) But Perkins, then at his peak and crisis, brought a tormented delicacy to the part that filled Welles with excitement and a kind of erotic attentiveness. He was as greedy for Joseph as he was for himself in *Kane*.

So Welles's *The Trial* has Kafka's structure: of Joseph K being indicted for some unspecified crime and led on a futile search for justice when all that awaits him is the absolute congruity of his own inner instincts about guilt and the system's stupid complacency about the individual being extinguished. But what the camera *sees* is a rare physical story: of the sprightly, repressed dancer in Perkins being forced into awkward postures, and of his closeted sexual nature being teased by rapaciously attractive women. The half-buried guilt in Joseph K is that he is unfit for women: his trial is being exposed to the lascivious invitation of Jeanne Moreau, Elsa Martinelli and Romy Schneider—Welles's greatest witches, and the sexiest women in all his work. For, somehow, he is able at last to set women free to prey on this querulously, denying, gay Joseph. It is as if, finally, the slender man has escaped from Welles's bulk.

The Trial is often marginalized by Welles admirers; they look on it as a tour de force but a bit of a dead end, an assignment rather against the current of Welles's true interests. I disagree, and I would quote Welles as evidence. He said that he was never happier than when making the film. He ranked it very high. And once—in startling language, for the habitual interviewee was not always candid—he owned up to the picture:

The Trial: Anthony Perkins and Romy Schneider

What made it possible for me to make the picture is
that I've had recurring nightmares of guilt all my life:
I'm in prison and I don't know why—going to be tried
and I don't know why. It's very personal for me. A very
personal experience, and it's not at all true that I'm off
in some foreign world that has no application to myself;
it's the most autobiographical movie that I've ever
made, the *only* one that's really close to me. And just
because it doesn't speak in a Middle Western accent
doesn't mean a damn thing. It's much closer to my own
feelings about everything than any other picture I've
ever made.

As a moviemaker, Welles could seem very isolated. He hardly seems to have watched other films, let alone taken on their influence. But *The Trial* is surely enriched by one other movie: I doubt it would be as good and unnerving without Perkins's extraordinary performance in Hitchcock's *Psycho*, released in 1960. For it was in that film that we first saw the potential in the very sensitive, gangling, ready-to-stammer mother's boy, in the secret gay soul so threatened by the spied-on nakedness of Janet Leigh in the bathroom. And just as Hitchcock gave Norman Bates a kinky ear for wordplay, Welles wrote scenes—stunning passages of verbal betrayal—for Joseph:

> K (*to the police inspector searching his room*): Don't touch those record albums.
>
> INSPECTOR: What's this thing?
>
> K: That's my pornograph . . . my phonograph.
>
> INSPECTOR 2: What's this?
>
> K: What's what?
>
> INSPECTOR 2: A circular line with four holes.
>
> INSPECTOR 1 (*writing*): Circular . . .
>
> INSPECTOR 2: No, it's not really circular, it's more ovular.
>
> K: Don't write that down, for heaven's sake!
>
> INSPECTOR 1: Ovular. Why not?
>
> K (*ironically*): Ovular?
>
> INSPECTOR 1: We can't not write it down just because you say we shouldn't.
>
> K: Ovular isn't even a word.
>
> INSPECTOR 2: You deny that there's an ovular shape concealed under this rug?
>
> INSPECTOR 1: He denies everything.

There's the comedy: Joseph is in emotional denial. He is plainly drawn to the haggard beauty of Miss Bürstner (Moreau), who undresses in front of him, stretches out on the bed before him—while he is apologizing all the time for being there. Then there is Hilda (Martinelli), telling him suggestive stories, showing him her stockings and promising, "I'll come back soon and then I'll go with you wherever you like and you can do with me whatever you want." Finally, there is Leni (Schneider), ward to the advocate, princess-whore aide to the very large figure of the law, but itching to screw Joseph in a sea of legal papers and prepared to show him her fascinating physical flaw—her webbed hand. And all the time Joseph is the horrified, beguiled voyeur child, the boy who wants but cannot take.

Which brings us to the Advocate, the modest yet supreme role Welles took for himself (though he said that he picked up that job only late in the day, when he couldn't get Jackie Gleason). "I really didn't want to be in *The Trial*," he said. Yet he substantially enhanced the role of the Advocate by giving him the speech about the law and the supplicant which belongs to another character in the novel and which is nowhere near as resonant or decisive there as it is in the film. For Welles the writer-director begins his film with a version of that parable—so that the ensuing drama seems like its enactment—then appears near the end to reprise the parable. He stands there, large, commanding, himself, owning the screen where the parable unfolds like a movie. In Kafka, there is never any ultimate authority. But Welles cannot resist the egotistical gratification of awarding himself that role. The Advocate seems like the master of the dark, decrepit labyrinth, and his confrontation with Joseph K is the culmination of the lesson. It is also the fat man and the thin man face to face. And it is another version of the glib fatalism of the scorpion and the frog, delivered with unpleasant self-satisfaction by the master of the apparatus:

> ADVOCATE: Before the law there stands a Guard. A Man comes from the country, seeking admittance to the Law. But the Guard cannot admit him. Can the Man hope to enter at a later time? . . .

> K: I've heard it all before. We've all heard it. The Man is dying of old age, still waiting there, and just at the end the Guard tells him that the door was meant for him, only for him.

> ADVOCATE: The Guard tells him no one could enter this door. And now, I'm going to close it.

As the Advocate in *The Trial*

And so the master, confronted, turns into the invulnerable magician, the master of ceremonies, not a real, ordinary man. Still, in *The Trial*, so much reality has been admitted—Joseph K is Orson Welles's greatest stricken hero. It is a stunning film, less than Kafka, but more.

There had been a time when Welles had seemed uncommonly a man of the moment. One of the ways he stung and intimidated Hollywood was in that attitude that told them, for God's sake, remember there's a world beyond Los Angeles, consider these times! Welles could make powerful men feel provincial and stupid—it was irresistible. *Citizen Kane* would not close its own eyes to the nature of political power and the way it had been commandeered by showmen no longer content with show business. *It's*

All True had rested shakily on the claim that there were higher causes than finishing a picture in Hollywood. And there had been the Welles who chatted with Roosevelt, as an equal, the public speaker who sometimes supposed in his own mind that he might have been king, for surely he understood the larger cares of kingship. Then, his own languid worldliness had exactly coincided with the Harry Lime panache that reckons to know the dark world for what it is. By instinct and observation, in timing and timbre, Welles understood the sickening equation of insignificant dots and huge tyrants in the world. Hadn't he once done a *Caesar* that helped wake New York up to what fascism meant? He read the papers; he sometimes wrote the papers; he had talked with the responsible leaders of the great powers—hadn't he? Seen Hitler as a child, looked like Stalin for *Journey into Fear* and done that dainty money-raising con with Churchill—the discreet salutation of big gun cigars.

And yet, he was rootless, homeless and forever out of his time. This began to be inescapable in the early sixties. He was not fifty yet. He was only two years older than John F. Kennedy, but here was a president whose youthful rhythms, and that odd aura of being Cary Grant, left Welles seeming large, slow and ancient. JFK was hip, cool and never hammy; in contrast, Welles suddenly began to seem archaic, florid and rhetorical. And in the sixties America made reckless, savage excursions in ideology and lifestyle that were beyond the curiously chaste, conservative Welles. He had been thought red once, but now he turned a watery pink, the fate of color movies that fade. He was not drawn to drugs; he was upstaged in a world where men tried looking like women; and he had no sympathy for any kind of anarchy. Black rights—the cause over which Welles had once been ahead of his time, burningly eloquent, if rather safe from action—were established. Did he ever go on marches now? Did he ever utter significant opinions about Vietnam? Or did he just observe a Nixon with that bereft sense of his own surpassed age and history, just as Falstaff beholds King Hal and sees a future so bleak and pragmatic there is no talking to it?

Even in his own field, the movies, he had a chance to be modern again. It was in 1962, for the first time, that *Sight & Sound* had elevated *Citizen Kane*. Moreover, Europe was witnessing so many new ways of making films—modern, economical, daring in subject: in France the New Wave (Truffaut, Godard, Chabrol and so on); in Italy, Fellini, Antonioni, Pasolini, with Bertolucci to come; in Britain, Lindsay Anderson, Tony Richardson, Karel Reisz. Nearly all of those men were admirers of Welles's work. Some of them said they might not have started without his example. For no one else had done so much to make a way for a cinema that is personal, audacious and beautiful. The Europe Welles retreated to was suddenly alive with what he could easily have called his own tradition.

But he could not get a grip on the new age. His passionate isolation—his ego—had ways of ignoring it, or letting it slip past like the rush of water. He did not welcome or encourage rescue.

He came to live more and more, with Paola and Beatrice, in Spain, Franco's Spain, the subtlest and most progressive fascist state in the world, where the crippled victims of the civil war were beginning to be the figures in tourist photographs. That Spain was oddly stable, growingly prosperous, and it was a world of great plains, castles, cathedrals and bullfights— if that was how you wanted to perceive it. This was the man who had once done a commentary for *This Spanish Earth*, only to be told by the then unimpeachably authentic Ernest Hemingway that he rather sucked. He did not approve of the new Spain, which was being brought up to speed on an Anglo-American model. He was as sentimental about Quixote, the old España and the bulls as Hemingway.

By the late 1950s, Hemingway and Welles were sometimes to be seen in the same parts of Spain, like voluminous Packards masquerading as brave bulls. There was in those years a spectacular rivalry between two matadors—Luis Miguel Dominguin and Antonio Ordóñez—considerably built up by Hemingway's assertion of the classic status of the confrontation and his contract to cover it for *Life* magazine. Both Hemingway and Welles favored Ordóñez; so they rivaled each other in lofty claims of *afición's* insight into the beauty of Ordóñez's art. The writer Peter Viertel knew both Americans—who strove not to meet, let alone talk (how do clouds convene?). But Viertel could talk to both of them. Welles told him that he had a screenplay in mind, "about an old man's obsessive admiration for a young torero; the protagonist of this story was an aging movie director intent on recapturing the magic of his youth by following a young bullfighter around Spain."

Nothing would come of it, of course. But here is the start of themes that fascinated Welles in his last years: lost youth; the betrayal of a fond, old admirer; the homosexual undertone—and all held in place by the gloating self-reference. Viertel asked Welles whether it would be based on himself, or on Papa: " 'About both of us,' he bellowed before succumbing once again to uproarious laughter."

Another person was there, Anatole Litvak, the movie director. He laughed at Welles and Viertel and told them they were both in love with the young Ordóñez. This hero worship was a sign of retarded manhood.

"No," said Welles, "premature senility in my case." That was a scheme he had flirted with all his life.

Still, in that atmosphere, he revisited his past, and maybe fleshed it out a little. He would recall that season he had had in Spain, after the Gate Theatre, when he had written pulp thrillers, enjoyed the good rough wine, living in an apartment in a Seville brothel, and . . . well, here it is, as told to Peter Bogdanovich a few years later, an exquisite anecdote:

> Well, in the corner of Spain—and in that corner of that town—the bulls are the whole meaning and purpose of life. If you were seventeen and a rich young prince of a pulp writer like me, you could get to be a bullfighter by the simple expedient of buying the bulls. So that was how I worked it. All on a very small, provincial scale, you understand, but towards the end, for a couple of times, I got paid myself. Almost nothing, but, still, for a few minutes there I was a pro—scared to death, of course, but having the time of my life.

Now that latter paradise, the time of one's life, is frequently to be found only years later, as memory warms the facts. His pulps have not survived; nor are there snapshots of Welles the bursting boy in a suit of lights. Bullshit might be sufficient verdict, but for the sheer loveliness of the above recital. For Welles never had an equal at the hushed reverie to describe old glories—nor, I suspect, did he ever need the glories themselves. He was a spellbinder who made himself his first sucker. He believed he had been there; the desire could not be denied. And he lived so much of the time in the romance of great pasts—it never hurt that he had a real past of his own busy enough to fill many lives.

In Welles's telling tall stories to susceptible interviewers, or in yarning away at a late dinner table, the bullshit can seem harmless and entertaining. If one had to hear him lying over the years and decades, then surely it was possible to see the fabrication as chronic and self-destructive, even the secret to his own disaster. Yet there was another way of hearing it. For Welles's art, his poetry, could turn on the great romance (and its self-deception) of conjuring up a lost elysian time.

That is surely the emotion that guides *Kane* and *Ambersons*, the feeling of some lost grace trampled by modernity's dark indifference. (Amid all else, *Kane* is a tribute to a gorgeous, adventurous past—to the lost glory of youth.) Equally, it is the wonder that could lift up Welles's deep-dyed cynicism in the course of a single sentence. For the myth was a tonic; the past could become as bright as future in a boy's eyes. I speak in that way because of the extraordinary incongruity, the surpassing sleight of camera, that was about to find "Merrie England" in Spain as Welles came at last to put Falstaff on film.

He had loved thinking about Falstaff for decades. He had worked and reworked the story of Falstaff and his cronies, of the friendship with Prince Hal, estranged from his real father, Henry IV, and of Hal's sudden abandonment of the old friend when it is his turn to be king. He loved history's England. In a conversation conducted near the end of his life in merrie Las Vegas, he gave some sign of what the character meant to him. He was talking to the BBC, at a time when it was hard to believe there would be more films. His beard was gray; his bulk was enclosed in a dark suit with a floppy polka-dot cravat. His voice was often cracked and weak. And there he was, patient and obliging for the film crew, in the suave gloom of a suite at the Riviera in Las Vegas. Available for interview. He did not seem well; reflection was making him sad. Yet what else did he have to do?

The conversation turned to Falstaff, and Welles called the great, fat blowhard "almost entirely a good man." He remarked on the cleverness of the theory that Falstaff was a Hamlet who had grown old and fat in England. But then he rejected it, for Hamlet, he said, is not a good man: there is wordiness, cruelty, coldness and too much modern cleverness in Hamlet, perhaps. And as he delved deeper into the subject, he leaned forward a little, drawn by his own feeling. His voice lowered. He was alive with earnestness. It is one of his gentlest and most affecting moments on-screen:

> Falstaff is, I think, Merrie England. I think Shakespeare
> was greatly preoccupied, as I am in my humble way,
> with the loss of innocence and I think there has always
> been in England an older England, which was sweeter
> and purer, where the hay smelled better and the weather
> was always springlike and the daffodils blew in the gen-
> tle warm breezes. And it's the nostalgia. You feel it in
> Chaucer and all through Shakespeare. And I think he
> was profoundly against the modern age—as I am.

What does that mean, besides the yearning? England's living in the past is in fact a handicap, nearly a disease—as Welles knew, for he had tried to work there. The ancient history of England, as of any old country, includes startling cruelties, implacable tyrannies and fearful ordeals narrowly escaped. For thirty-four years in England, I hardly saw daffodils without there being a chill in the air. And yet . . . England adores the pipe dream of itself, and sometimes finds more sentiment in nostalgia than in anything else. "Merrie England" is a tourist trap for gentle, foolish minds maybe. The past may be no more than regret, dismay and an excuse for the present. But Welles was, in many ways, a sentimental old fool—or a cold, lonely man who longed to be foolish. And Falstaff was his god and his way back. The fat old Englishman was his hope for goodness, and the best emblem of his longing to be so ancient and beaten nothing else mattered.

"We have heard the chimes at midnight," he would say, so eager, so weary, only on the eve of his fiftieth birthday, but exulting in all the used up time and the chilly proximity of death, on a snowy Spanish plain that purported to be a scene from old, if not olde, England. All that magic requires is belief—and a dread of life without such lies.

Chimes at Midnight was shot in fragments in various parts of Spain in the winter of 1964–65. It was, in Welles's mind at any rate, a cheerful, muddled enterprise in which he worked valiantly to avoid the disasters of too little money, his own illness, the restricted availability of many of his leading players, the winter, the obdurate Spanishness of Spain, the impossibility of getting decent live sound and the way his own producer had to be kidded into thinking they were filming *Treasure Island* for as long as possible. It might end up a superb trick, but it was also a con, a scheme, something like the desperate attempt of Falstaff and his gang to survive in a tough world. For despite the elegiac regard for the putative smell of sweet hay, once upon a time, Welles knew that Falstaff was a version of himself, the scrambled buffoon, saint and rogue, wondering where the next banquet was coming from—your average embarrassed entertainer: "He is a kind of refugee from this world [the legend of Camelot]. He has to live by his wits and be fun. He hasn't a place to sleep if he doesn't get a laugh out of his patron." For Falstaff *is* more than just the good man of Welles's reverie: he is a drunk, a liar, a braggart, a coward, a bad influence and a thoroughgoing failure. He is someone that Hal has to be rid of. Like Hank Quinlan, he's a mess. Falstaff was the Welles who owed money all over the world, who had abandoned and exploited associates, who had lied, tricked and feasted away the years endeavoring to protect his own quality, his legendary goodness. He was an embarrassment to himself and to others—there is no decent escape from this, not even in the hay, the daffodils and the excitement of a new film. So *Chimes at Midnight* is often wondrous and nearly always chaotic.

The money was always elusive, and subject to rumor. When the film was at last done, Welles would sigh and say that this entire Shakespearean

chronicle, with battles, horses, armor and the antique accoutrements of Merrie England, had cost only $1.1 million—this was virtually what had been paid to Elizabeth Taylor for *Cleopatra* a few years before. But the bewildered producer, Emiliano Piedra, only there because he was mesmerized by Welles, said, No, not so, it cost very little over $800,000—what *Kane* had cost nearly twenty-five years earlier.

And at the outset, Piedra had wanted *Treasure Island*, which seemed surefire with Welles as Long John Silver. So Welles had concocted a nonsensical plan to do the Stevenson and the Shakespeare, as it were, simultaneously. The quickness of the hand defies the eye, and obviates the need for sanity. The only set ever built for the film, Mistress Quickly's tavern—built and decorated largely by Welles himself—was also intended as the Admiral Benbow Inn, the eighteenth-century establishment owned by the Hawkins family to which Billy Bones retires in *Treasure Island*. A ship was hired in from the *Billy Budd* production to be the old *Hispaniola*, and Keith Baxter (the Belfast Hal) was contracted to be not just Hal but Dr. Livesey, too, while John Gielgud's gaunt Henry IV plays over the subtext of a savagely dieting Squire Trelawney. Perhaps that extra two or three hundred thousand was regarded as legitimate plunder—and is a treasure buried somewhere. The craft of getting pictures made can be so brutal and devious that there is constant need of romancing, liquor and encouraging anecdotes.

Prodigies of subterfuge and barefaced cheek were required to get the film made: the rolling plains of central Spain with mountains in the distance were somehow meant to be the misty, wooded English countryside. Some actors were available for only a few days—Jeanne Moreau (Doll Tearsheet) for five; Gielgud for ten—so their scenes had to be done very quickly and sometimes without time to include the actors they were playing with. So Gielgud did his speeches looking at a stand-in whose shoulder was all the camera saw. He had to do cutaway close-ups, with timing and expression dictated by Welles. He felt at a loss, with only his magnificent technique, his trust of the language and his fearful certainty that Welles was not to be negotiated with carrying him through. The great battle sequence, shot in one of Madrid's parks, had its big shots with lines of horses. But then, day after day, Welles went back to the park with just a few men, some weapons and water to make mud to obtain the terrible scenes of close slaughter that make the sequence so powerful and such a feat of montage.

The fragmentation was not easy, and there were players in the movie—Marina Vlady and Fernando Rey, Jeanne Moreau and Walter Chiari—who were not English or even English speaking. Moreau was compelled to do some love scenes with Falstaff with a double, because Welles seemed timid about putting on the makeup and becoming the fictional wreck in front of her. But Welles was inspiring. He told actors to trust him: glance off in that direction, in this mood, and the shot will fit. He willed it so and told everyone he had the movie in his head from the start. Just because the live sound was going to be unusable, he often gave audible coaching to the actors. "It was very larky making the film," said Keith Baxter. "We all had a lot of fun; it was wonderful, hilarious."

Welles held the unit together, yet few others knew what was happening or how the film would function. Time and again, he would interrupt one scene by jumping away to another—it seemed volatile, dangerous, disordered even. To work that way, everyone, himself included, had to believe in Welles's genius, and he had a theory about it that sounds precarious and self-serving, and that only helps explain the final air of discontinuity in the movie. For there is very seldom the magnificent, mortal unity of time and place such as dominated *Ambersons* and much of *Kane*. That concentration is gone. In turn, a series of spectacular shots or movie events seem isolated, even edited at random. The drama and the pathos suffer badly in consequence. Yet Welles was headed down a very dangerous stylistic street of believing he could do anything so long as it was done his way, the scorpion's way:

> Sometimes what seems disorderly has a perfectly logistic purpose. But in order to explain why I'm changing the scene would take ten minutes of conference. So I don't explain, and it looks as though I am being capricious. When I'm outside, the position of the sun determines everything: I'll suddenly jump from one sequence to another, even go into a sequence that wasn't planned for that day, if the light suddenly becomes right for it. The sun is the most beautiful light in the world, and the way to make it beautiful is to film it at its moment; so that means jumping. Those are the technical reasons for the orderly disorder. Then sometimes the actors aren't right on that day, you see that they need another day, another mood. The thing isn't working. Then you must change, and the change does everybody good. Sometimes, when all the lights are in one position, in order to move logically to the next scene as planned creates an enormous waste of time. And rather than lose time in moving the lights, I confuse everybody else by jumping to the next thing I know we can shoot. I think you will agree that the disorder doesn't mean that we work slowly. I think it is terribly necessary to work quickly.

In the same interview, Welles started talking about the liberation of improvisation, something that suggests he felt some urge to imitate the rhetoric of the French New Wave. But Welles was never a sound manager of his own affairs. And that freewheeling, improvisational approach—especially when geared to conservative, if not old-fashioned dramatic ideas—needed someone in charge. So the Welles who would cheerfully boast of eliminating clerical attention to sound, continuity and makeup was engaged in making a *Chimes at Midnight* that failed commercially exactly because of shortcomings in sound and continuity.

The self-consciously hectic approach had many causes: uncertain funds; terrible scheduling problems; the difficulties of working in English, Spanish and French (at least) all at the same time; and his own failing health, which did intrude on the *Chimes* schedule that winter. And there were other causes that existed only in Welles's personality: impa-

tience; the dread of boredom; the increasing megalomania that places itself above conventional, dull order—and the need to turn Falstaff into a
surrogate of himself.

Keith Baxter was there for most of the production: Welles was plainly
fond of him; Baxter felt that the director had a fatherly regard for him.
(He saw the same feeling for Anthony Perkins, who had come to Madrid
hoping to be Orson's Hal.) Baxter won the role because Welles was loyal
to the stage production. He said later, "At that time, Orson was very possessive about me—I don't mean it in any restrictive way at all, but I was
very much pulled into the family."

As it seemed to Baxter, *Chimes at Midnight* altered as it went along as
a movie. Falstaff became a good deal less comic, "but that's because Orson
was never a good clown. He could be a buffoon, but he was not a great
clown. The early comedic scenes are rather uneasy, and don't really come
off well, but that's because Welles himself never felt that kind of gaiety.
He wasn't that sort of person." It's a shrewd point: Welles could and often
did make fun of his characters, to prove his knowingness, but he could
never let himself shine forth as weak, dishonest or stupid, as someone to
be laughed at. And that is the secret to Falstaff: he is *not* simply a good
man but a fellow whose good instincts are clouded by failure and sheer
ordinariness.

Moreover, the frequent use of stand-ins (supposedly to focus on the
stars) also sheltered Welles from his own trepidations. He was very nervous about being Falstaff. Baxter believed the resemblance between the
role and the actor was the source of that fear:

> You felt that there was a great deal of him in Falstaff—
> this sort of trimming one's sails, always short of money,
> having to lie, perhaps, and to cheat. He obviously felt
> there was a lot of himself there in the character. But
> when you suddenly have the chance of your dreams
> coming true, of doing what you've always wanted, you
> get a terrible attack of jitters. Also he'd seen Ralph
> Richardson play Falstaff and I think that frightened him
> a bit, too.

In Richardson's Falstaff there had been such an immense quietness, a
vacancy almost, in which one might feel the common man naked in his
lies and shortcomings. Welles knew that pathos of Falstaff all too well:
that was what brought gloom to the film, a chasing away of the comedy,
or—as Baxter felt—too heavy a foreboding of how it must end. But for

Welles, Falstaff had a load to bear so much greater than padded stomach: he was the turning point between Merrie England and grim modernism. So Welles's anxiety made for too portentous and hollow a performance. But when was Welles ever naked or plain as an actor? He could not get to that place.

I am being tough on the film because of all it meant to Welles and his life, and because it has come in for much praise. At the time, of course, it was damned. Bosley Crowther, in *The New York Times*, delivered a crushing but not unfair rebuke:

> This difficulty [the sound quality] of understanding Mr. Welles's *basso profundo* speech, which he seems to direct towards his innards instead of out through his lips, makes it all the more difficult to catch the drift of this great, bearded, untidy man who waddles and cocks his hairy eyebrows and generally bluffs his way through the film.
>
> Is this Falstaff a truly jovial person? Does he have a genuine wit and a tavern-companion's grand affection

Chimes at Midnight: Welles with Jeanne Moreau

for the fun-loving scapegrace, Prince Hal? Has he, deep
down, a spirit of rebellion against shifting authority? Or
is he merely what he looks like—a dissolute, bumbling,
street-corner Santa Claus?

Even Pauline Kael, who, ironically, was one of the film's early defenders, felt that it was ruined by the atrocious sound. She also remarked
on the lack of comedy and made a brilliant observation about Welles's
voice: "It was too much and it was unexpressive; there was no warmth in
it, no sense of a life lived." The bogusness of the man and actor was glar-
ing—and Falstaff is a great creation of dishonesty—but Welles could not
simply put his feet in the man's warm, battered shoes. He wanted red
shoes.

The film has great things, of course: the battle; Falstaff and Shallow
coming in out of the snow, old men crooning to themselves about the
past, with Falstaff's rubicund cheeks in the firelight recalling Major Amberson—though that recollection cannot help but make the *Chimes at
Midnight* ring false. Baxter and Gielgud are very good. Moreau and Margaret Rutherford as Mistress Quickly are more than adequate. Occasionally, a piece of Spanish Gothic brings medieval England to life.

And it is a very somber work, a tragedy, no matter that Shakespeare
meant something less fateful and more complicated. The great moment
comes when the newly crowned Hal spurns Falstaff. Baxter felt Welles's
emotion while that scene was shot, with Falstaff on his knees, being dismissed. For once, the complementary angles were shot in the same
breath. "It says a great deal for Orson that, although he felt so strongly
that Hal was a monster, the shot of Falstaff looking at me—proud of me
for being so magnificent—is terribly moving," said Baxter.

That's true, and remarkable. Hal and Falstaff count among the greatest conflicts of loving men Welles ever did. And there is in Welles's eyes
in the shot something more than pride—it is satisfaction, the realization
that prophecies of betrayal have been fulfilled, leaving a serene ruin that
waits only for death. There is also some wistfulness for a love that cannot
be uttered, and that may only be identified in the instant of rapture. Hal
is a monster in Welles's eyes, and Baxter plays him cruelly. He is the
model producer pragmatist Welles could never be, or endure, the master
Machiavelli. But he is also the beloved that Welles could never quite
admit. There was too much turmoil in the man, too yeasty and deceitful
an ego, for him to be the great, simple actor he needed for *Chimes at
Midnight*.

* * *

And yet, ladies and gentlemen . . . it is hard to criticize *Chimes at Midnight* without recognizing the inevitability of some layered Wellesian challenge in any attempt to write about the man. Sooner rather than later the biographer and the man become like Leland or Kane, or Hal or Falstaff. The argument has to be joined; Welles's enveloping attempt to be seductive cannot be shrugged off. So, no matter the dreadful sound, the inappropriateness of Spanish landscapes, no matter the untidiness that wants to masquerade as poetry, still *it was done. Chimes at Midnight* is so unlikely, such an epiphany; it bespeaks an extraordinary act of will, not to mention the idealism that saw such a thing might be. So what if Falstaff *is* "wrong"? Welles's Joseph K was not Kafka's man. And in that case the substitution was fruitful. The Falstaff may be less so, but who can ignore the turbulent innocence of the egotism that has made it? The film—like so many things Welles did—is monstrous, arbitrary, like a child's tantrum, so immature and yet so passionate, mistaken and yet radiant. And he, nearly as dropsical as his hero, dragged it into being. There are extremes at which selfishness is so vast and deformed, it is beside the point to moralize over it. If Welles had been a better man, he would never have done *Kane:* that film is driven by remorse. And if he had made only *Chimes at Midnight*— emerging out of obscurity to do it—no matter the faults I find in it, I suspect that I would *know* it as a footprint of genius. Am I being too difficult in objecting? Am I a Leland, or a Hal, bound to betray the man who gave me a life and so much to love?

Then again, there are stalwart Wellesians who put *Chimes at Midnight* above everything: Peter Cowie, who wrote a book about the man; Jonathan Rosenbaum, who has done more than anyone to track down the details of the life and the films, and Joseph McBride, who has written (and who makes me wish that what he said was correct):

> *Chimes at Midnight* is Welles's masterpiece, the fullest most completely realized expression of everything he had been working towards since *Citizen Kane*, which itself was more an end than a beginning. The younger Welles was obsessed with the problem of construction, and solved it perfectly with a style which locked the apparently powerful hero into an ironic vise of which he was almost totally unaware. We could not be farther from the characters, and perhaps this distancing, however suited to the telling of a story of futile omnipo-

tence, was an acknowledgement of artistic immaturity
on Welles' part: faced with the problem of defining
himself, he contrived a style to prove that definition is
illusory. In *Chimes at Midnight*, Welles has fused his own
viewpoint and that of his hero into a direct communication of emotion.

Emotion cannot be defended or denied. I can only repeat that, for me,
in *Chimes at Midnight*, the attempt to deliver it is too deliberate, too sentimental and too much at odds with the given material. There is a moment that is shattering—yet it hardly draws upon the whole film. Much
less does it exhale the last sigh of Merrie England. But maybe the Welles
who signals feeling is the coldest Welles of all.

Let me, instead, propose his next film, *The Immortal Story*, as a complete yet simple achievement, as filled with emotion as the empty chair
left behind at the end of Dennis Potter's last television interview, made in
the compelling shadow of his pancreatic cancer. *The Immortal Story* is not
well known. It runs only fifty-eight minutes, and it was shot in 1966 for
French TV, released two years later and played at the New York and London film festivals of 1968.

"The Immortal Story" is a seventy-five-page novella, written by Isak
Dinesen in 1951 and published two years later as one of her *Anecdotes of
Destiny*. Welles told a story of how he had loved Dinesen (or Karen Blixen)
from afar and had once even traveled to Denmark to see her. But he had
been afraid to risk meeting her and so he stayed in his hotel for three days
and then went away. For years thereafter—nothing is too precise in this
story—he had worked on a letter to her, a very long love letter. But she
had died in 1962, while he was still engaged on the letter. Stories are easier to believe than to authenticate. What is more far-fetched is that Welles
did not even appreciate the astonishing, ravaged, syphilitic beauty of the
elderly Dinesen. But he felt kinship with her lofty, lucid prose, as well as
her unyielding sense of destiny and commitment. He shared her "certain
love of greatness," the thing she called "my daimon."

The story she called immortal was the story of all stories. In the
1860s, in Canton, there lived "an immensely rich tea-trader," Mr. Clay.
Welles quietly shifted the action to Macao, whose legend he had already
appropriated. Clay is a capitalist, an accumulator, a man blind to anything
that is not a matter of fact. He has a clerk, Elishama Levinsky, who reads
to him at night the litany of business accounts. Then, one night, with
nothing else to read, Levinsky finds in his pocket some words by the
prophet Isaiah. Clay is perplexed: has this prophecy happened? No, says

the clerk, who reads the prophecy again. Clay is shaken, for this recounting of something beyond fact has reminded him of a story he heard maybe fifty years earlier.

It is the story of a sailor who comes ashore and is invited to a rich man's house to make the man's young wife pregnant. Of course, says Levinsky, I know that story. Everyone has heard it. That story is always there: "All sailors know it. All sailors tell it, and each of them, because he wishes that it had happened to him himself, tells it as if it was so. But it is not so."

Clay broods on this, and he cannot abide the potency of a fiction that has no support in fact. He tells the clerk: "I want the story which I told you last night to happen in real life, to real people."

"I shall see to it, Mr. Clay," says Levinsky.

The Immortal Story won its modest money because Jeanne Moreau agreed to play the woman Levinsky hires to be the daughter. A sailor is found. Welles is Mr. Clay, the impotent old man.

In later years, Welles was often bad-tempered about the project. It had to be done in color; television would hear of nothing else by 1966, yet Welles did not admire color. It was too modern, too industrial. He had insisted on black and white for *Chimes at Midnight*, and that had become another of its handicaps. The color in *Immortal Story* is not clear, resonant or consistent. The sound is bad again. The picture was made without flourish—thank God—and it would have had to go out of its way to mar the inevitability of Dinesen's own narrative. The movie has the kind of fidelity to the novella that a lover like Welles found most easily if he had never met the beloved. Peter Bogdanovich once tried to have Welles elaborate on the story's possible references to filmmaking, but Welles was bitter:

> PB: Someone commented that the idea of *Immortal Story* relates to the whole notion of a director making things actually happen. Is there anything to that? Do you think that's part of what interested you?

> OW: No.

> PB: Because a director basically does what Charlie Clay tries to do in the movie.

> OW: "Charlie Clay"—the name's *Charles*. Certainly no one ever called him "Charlie" in his life; it was "Mr. Clay." No—he was trying to be God, not a director.

But in neither the novella nor the movie is Clay's first name ever mentioned. Somehow, however, he is Charles, no matter that Welles preferred to see no allusion to himself. As if he had ever had a choice. He could not make a movie, or speak for more than a few minutes, without polishing his own legend. There was no need to drop Canton for Macao, and it makes no real difference. But Welles went further: he took up a seashell that figures in the Dinesen story and turned it into a souvenir of the glass snow ball in *Kane*. He knew all too well how far *Immortal Story* reassessed *Kane*, and he heard the scorpion's wry confessional in a line from Dinesen which is taken as the climax of the movie, Levinsky's reflection as he sees Clay dead, with the story come to life:

> It was hard, he reflected, as he had often done before, it
> was very hard on people who wanted things so badly
> that they could not do without them. If they could not
> get these things it was hard, and when they did get
> them, surely it was very hard.

For there was a demon in being a blessed, spoiled child, and in rising to so much so young; and there is a demon in every storyteller and every great seeker after glory, in getting there and telling the story perfectly. It is like eating from the tree of knowledge, or being immortal while still alive. This is a fate that only a rare kind of ego can conceive, yet it is also one accessible only to those who are hooked on the enchantment of stories and story making. *The Immortal Story* concerns approaching a threshold, one akin to Faust's pact with the Devil—of yearning for story and seeing it come alive. That power is not quite decent: it must kill the god, the director and the storyteller. And so again in *The Immortal Story*, Welles reenacts his own blazing extinction, the fire first ignited in *Kane* to consume Xanadu.

But the film is so simple as to survive its "faults" in making. There are no stylistic excursions; there is no showing off. It is enough for the fable to be unfolded, with just Erik Satie's piano music as accompaniment. Norman Eshley did not act as the sailor, Paul; he merely presented the figure from myth. As Virginia, his bride, Moreau is time-worn until a healing light settles on her at her bridal bed and fiction makes her young again. As Levinsky, Roger Coggio is benighted, resigned and another, infinitely defeated Thompson. And as Clay, usually seated in enveloping wing chairs, nearly moribund, static, stagnant, on the lip of death, Welles consented to play without smile, pathos or seductiveness. For once, he took no more than his assigned role in a ritual.

And there is never any doubt about how close this Charles is to cold clay, or how ready he is to become it. This is a small, great picture—and it was the last story film Orson Welles ever completed.

Chimes at Midnight had its world premiere at Cannes in 1966. Welles celebrated his birthday there, the picture was well enough received and he was given a special award for his contribution to world cinema. But the film received no prizes—how odd, for it is so much better than *Othello*, which had taken the Palme d'Or. Maybe Europe was accustomed to Welles. He had done the circle of hotels and interviews. *Chimes at Midnight* would not open commercially in America until nearly a year later, and then it did badly. Welles was as little known in his native country now as at any time since before his going to New York in the late 1930s. Very few Americans as yet recognized that his trio of works in the sixties—*The Trial*, *Chimes at Midnight* and *The Immortal Story*—far surpassed the things he had done from *The Stranger* to *Touch of Evil*. The three literary adaptations, whatever their limits, are challenging, mature and heartfelt. It seems perverse now that so few saw their worth: if they had been first films, every one would have been seen as a masterpiece.

But many people regarded Welles as a big bore, and out-of-date—largely true, yet in his latest films he seems to have been aware of such burdens. The islands of finished work were still lashed by stormy seas of inconsequence and incompletion. He had thought of doing *Lord Jim*, but Richard Brooks stepped in, with studio money and Peter O'Toole, and murdered Conrad. In Italy, he did a TV series about Spain—*Nella Terra di Don Chisciotte*—home movies on themes, places and stories of a Spanish nature, and all done to aid the ailing, faltering *Quixote*, the project he was asked about in every interview.

Dino De Laurentiis announced that Welles would make *The Bible*, along with Federico Fellini and Robert Bresson. Welles wrote some script for the stories of Abraham and Jacob, and more or less they were used when the whole book fell on John Huston's insouciant shoulders. Welles begged not to be given a credit.

There was talk of a *Crime and Punishment* with Maximilian Schell as Raskolnikov; there were once to have been other Isak Dinesen stories; *King Lear* was never out of mind, and there was a thing called *The King of Paris* with Welles as Alexandre Dumas. He was doing television commercials, in England especially, and he was on the box there, being interviewed by Bernard Levin and doing the narration on a documentary about Jane Goodall and primates.

Welles was always reading, and seeking projects. But he was no longer trusted, for so many ventures had come to nothing. In the midsixties,

Fielder Cook, a TV and movie director, read and loved a novel, *The World in Winter*, by John Christopher. He went to London, where the rights were held, and made an offer. The agent told him that someone else was also bidding for the film rights. But the author chose Cook's bid.

So Cook, who was staying at the Ritz, was in a celebratory mood, and dreaming already of how to do a story about a world overtaken by constant winter. Then the phone rang in his room.

"Fielder Cook, this is Orson Welles."

"Oh, sure it is," said Cook, certain he was being teased. "So who's calling?"

The great voice was patient. "No one's calling. It is me. I've just been told that they've accepted your offer instead of mine."

Cook was amazed. He was one of those whose life had been changed by seeing *Kane*. He had followed the Welles career. He said he had had no idea Welles was the other interested party. "Can't we do something with it together?" he asked.

"Together! You've stolen my book—*and* you're living in my hotel!"

As Cook would discover, Welles was calling not from Paris, Los Angeles or Casablanca. He was in a tiny room a few floors above—economizing, but still at the Ritz, and, like Gregory Arkadin, goosing someone by phoning from very close at hand. Welles would not entertain so much as a meeting. And *The World in Winter* has never been made.

With Peter Viertel, he wrote a script for *The Survivors*, a play written by Viertel and Irwin Shaw. They worked at Welles's house in Aravaca, in Spain, arguing, fighting, dining and getting it done, with Welles often excusing himself to go to the basement, where he was editing *Quixote*. As they wrote, the money for *The Survivors* vanished. But Fred Zinnemann called Viertel. He was setting up the movie of *A Man for All Seasons*, and he was thinking of Welles as Cardinal Wolsey. Should he offer Welles the role? Zinnemann asked Viertel. Of course, said the writer, he'll be brilliant.

"But will he be difficult?" asked the director.

"Sure, he'll be impossible, but it will be one of the highlights of your picture."

So Zinnemann and his designer, John Box, put the enormous Welles in red robes in a tiny office that was then painted in cardinal colors. Zinnemann noted that "Welles filled it with his presence until there was no oxygen left to breathe." It took a day, Welles remembered, and it is an extraordinary scene of hubris, like a great diseased plum ready to burst, or die.

As Wolsey in *A Man for All Seasons*

He did a cameo in the rather silly James Bond movie *Casino Royale*. He was fatuous in a disaster, *The Sailor from Gibraltar*, an adaptation from Marguerite Duras which Tony Richardson was making out of love for Jeanne Moreau. The production was a grinding confusion, none of it helped by Welles, who—as Richardson saw it—was "nervous, drunk, and irresponsible."

As he shot *Casino Royale* in London, living on the picture at an apartment above the Mirabella restaurant, surrounded by empty caviar pots and bottles of Dom Pérignon, Welles gave an interview to Kenneth Tynan which would appear as the *Playboy* interview in March 1967 (an attempt to help launch *Chimes at Midnight*—or *Falstaff* as it was called there—in America). The interview ranged all over his world and life, and Tynan was a friend, yet it was little more candid than any other talk. He could be deprecating and modest, but only in the subtly glorifying way of the self-imagined legend. He worked hard to furnish the image of the self-confident bon viveur. Why did he live in Spain or Italy? "The Mediterranean culture is more generous, less guilt ridden. Any society that exists without natural gaiety, without some sense of ease in the presence of death, is one in which I am not immensely comfortable."

Asked about his vices, he admitted to melancholy and sloth: "I don't give way to it for long, but it still comes lurching at me out of the shadows." Gluttony, too, he had to accept, and with mixed feelings:

> It certainly shows on me. But I feel that gluttony must
> be a good deal less deadly than some of the other sins.
> Because it's affirmative, isn't it? At least it celebrates
> some of the good things in life. Gluttony may be a sin,
> but an awful lot of fun goes into committing it. On the
> other hand, it's wrong for a man to make a mess of himself. I'm fat, and people shouldn't be fat.

Tynan also asked Welles about women—if in a very general way. The interviewer knew more about Welles than he ever asked; he knew that the extrovert legend was also very sensitive about his privacy. Tynan wondered if there were limits on what women could do in the world. "It's improbable that they will ever be as numerous as men in the arts," said Welles. "I believe that if there had never been men there would never have been art—but if there had never been women, men would never have made art." It was a pious homily, already out of keeping with the times. It did not begin to address the minor parts women played in his movies, and it did not come close to the mounting complexity of his life.

Welles had always had affairs; they tended to be with exotic, dark women, often those he was working with. "Years of my life have been given up to it," he told Tynan. And nobody ever got the impression that it mattered much. Welles liked to seduce, but he seldom had lasting ties to women. Of his three daughters, only Beatrice had captured his imagination or lived with him very much. She had been touching as the page in *Chimes at Midnight*, and it may even be Beatrice in toy armor in the scenes where we see Falstaff scampering on the battlefield. There is such youthfulness in the running, it cannot be Welles.

But Welles's third marriage, though it had lasted, was not much more than a formality. No woman had forced herself on Welles as an intellectual presence or challenge. As he worked on *The Survivors*, Peter Viertel learned that Paola was herself having an affair—with an airline pilot. She was anxious whenever this man was away, and Welles saw the strain. She should probably have an affair, he confided to Viertel, they're so relaxing.

But on and off throughout the sixties, Welles was himself engaged in the most significant love affair of his life. On his trip to Yugoslavia while making *The Trial*, in March 1962, he had met a young woman named Olga Palinkas. She was dark, very beautiful, warm, funny and smart, and at least twenty years his junior. She worked on TV in Zagreb, but it was said that she was also an actress, a writer and a sculptress. One observer remarked on the deep impact Palinkas made on Welles: "He's very impressed that she doesn't need him to exist. He worships her . . . because it's the first intelligent woman he has had in his life."

They talked of collaborations to come, and gradually something of Welles's mythmaking began to add to the young woman's considerable personality. She was, he said, half Hungarian, and so another name was fashioned for her—Oja Kodar. And as a sculptress, knowing that women's work was so often slighted, she assumed—or was it just that Welles invented this?—the name of Vladimir Zagdrov. He enjoyed the tradition of a creative woman masquerading as a man—after all, Isak Dinesen was really Karen Blixen—but he enjoyed the fakery, too.

By the late 1960s, Welles and Kodar were seen openly together. In 1967, onboard a yacht off Hvar on the coast of Yugoslavia, he filmed parts of a movie called *The Deep* or *Dead Reckoning*, which he and she had adapted from a Charles Williams novel, *Dead Calm*. It was a thriller, and it starred Welles, Kodar, Jeanne Moreau, Michael Bryant and Laurence Harvey. Moreau was apparently not pleased at having Kodar around. The picture was seemingly financed by Welles and Kodar themselves. In the space of two years, with several trips to Eastern Europe, much of the film—or most of a film—was shot. But there were gaps, and when Harvey died in 1973, there was still material involving him left to be done. Those who have seen passages of the film suggest that it is conventional at best. There is the possibility that *The Deep* was always a front for the developing affair with Kodar.

At the very least, their bond helps explain a number of Wellesian acting jobs in pictures that employed Yugoslavia or that eastern edge of Europe: *The Last Roman* (in which he played Justinian); *Sutjeska* (in which he played Churchill); *The Battle of Neretva* and *Orson's Bag*, an attempted miscellany for CBS Television.

Paola made no attempt to interfere. Not that her husband was an easy man to trace or discipline. There seemed, once again, very little chance of a decent commission to direct in the late sixties, but Welles's life was teeming with actual projects and tempting prospects. He began to be in America more, if only to appear on *The Dean Martin Show:* his debut there was in September 1967, singing "Brush Up Your Shakespeare" with Dean while doing one of Shylock's speeches from *The Merchant of Venice*. He played Tiresias in a movie of *Oedipus the King;* he played a lead role in

Hurried departure from a hotel? No, as the magician in Henry Jaglom's *A Safe Place*.

Michael Winner's *I'll Never Forget What's 'is Name*. He acted in *House of Cards*, *The Southern Star*, *The Kremlin Letter* and *Start the Revolution Without Me*. Twice he helped novice directors by playing magicians in their first pictures—Brian De Palma's *Get to Know Your Rabbit* and Henry Jaglom's *A Safe Place*. This latter was the start of an important friendship that lasted until Welles's death. He played General Dreedle in Mike Nichols's film of *Catch-22*, one of many projects he had wanted to do himself.

And in November 1968, Welles at last met Peter Bogdanovich. Seven years earlier, the young critic had compiled a monograph on Welles to go with a season of films at the New York Museum of Modern Art. They had never met then; Welles had not even acknowledged the monograph. Then one afternoon, with Bogdanovich now living in Los Angeles, his phone rang: it was Welles, wanting to thank him and asking for a meeting at the Polo Lounge in the Beverly Hills Hotel.

They got on. Welles wanted the friendship. Bogdanovich admitted that the one film of Welles's that he didn't like was *The Trial*. "I don't *either!*" lied Welles. Talk got around to "a nice little book" they might do, with Bogdanovich interviewing Welles. There's no doubt but that this was Welles's plan, but Bogdanovich was flattered and happy to be involved. A publisher and an advance were arranged. Bogdanovich, who was making his own way in Hollywood, volunteered to help agent for Welles, so he got the older man—often—on *The David Frost Show*, *The Dick Cavett Show*, *The Merv Griffin Show*. Before long, Welles was on *The Tonight Show* with Johnny Carson. Perhaps there was a chance of rehabilitation—even a new life as a television personality?

The friendship deepened, yet Bogdanovich sometimes stumbled upon a hidden Welles, someone achingly lonely and sensitive beneath the panache of the great diner and the anecdotal host. Within a year of their first meeting, Bogdanovich made a passing remark about that film *The Trial*, the one neither of them liked.

"I wish you wouldn't keep on *saying* that," said Welles.

"Oh, I thought you didn't like the picture either."

"No, I only said it to please you, I like it very much. But I have a much poorer opinion of my life's work than you possibly could guess, and every negative thing that I hear from a friend, or read from a person that I vaguely respect, reduces the little treasure that I have."

Bogdanovich was taken aback. But neither he nor Welles knew how soon there would be a very sharp attack on the centerpiece of the little treasure. And no one could have guessed how far the attack would establish and define Welles for the rest of his life.

* * *

The American movie was doing very well in the late sixties and the early seventies. In the gradual breakup (or metamorphosis) of control in the picture business, there were young, willful and maverick directors having their own way and making fresh, dangerous pictures that entertained millions while whispering to them about the true, troubled state of the nation: Arthur Penn did *Bonnie and Clyde* and *Little Big Man;* John Boorman made *Point Blank;* Sam Peckinpah made *The Wild Bunch;* Robert Altman was at his first peak with *M*A*S*H, McCabe and Mrs. Miller* and *The Long Goodbye;* Martin Scorsese would soon deliver *Mean Streets;* Steven Spielberg was beginning—*Duel* had played on television; Bogdanovich had turned in three winners in a row, all different in genre: *The Last Picture Show, What's Up Doc?* and *Paper Moon.* There had also been *The Graduate, Patton, Harold and Maude, The French Connection.* Francis Ford Coppola was making *The Godfather* in 1971–72.

Welles wanted the role of Vito Corleone. "I would have sold my soul to have done it," he would say later. Coppola seems never to have considered the possibility—imagine the sunken Vito Welles would have been, self-pitying, grandiloquent, hammy and altogether archaic. Then recollect the human liveliness of Brando in the part and feel the continental divide between their acting styles. We were spared; the project was saved. But that mercy is minor next to the way all the filmmakers in the previous paragraph worshiped Welles and took it for granted that he had forged their path and made the status of the movie director something to be honored. For Welles had said that directors make pictures. They might be artists—even if that sometimes meant the director had to be fired, had to go into exile and had to abide in his own wilderness.

From Bogdanovich to Coppola, the new directors had no great taste for wilderness, and for a moment at least they lived and worked in a climate where they might thrive without challenge or rebuke. But they esteemed Welles not just for the particular films: nearly all of them remembered the impact of *Kane* when they had been kids. They had felt and aspired to its terrible authority and ambition. And they regarded Welles as a kind of necessary martyr for them and later glory: he had opposed the system. They saw that as courage and integrity—it was not yet possible for them to know the helpless rebellion that had taken Welles away. More or less, these directors believed they were working in a self-image Welles had laid down. There was a picture business, still, and no one was above making money. But that dangerous drug art was alive—as it had never been, say, for John Ford, Howard Hawks, Ernst Lubitsch, King Vidor and so on.

In the tens of thousands of new film courses in American academia, Welles and *Kane* were passwords. There was an art house cinema in Cambridge, Massachusetts, called the Orson Welles—he had graced it sometimes with his presence. With so many luminaries in film aware of Welles's legacy, and anxious to redeem the past, it was no wonder that in 1970 the Academy decided to grant him a special honorary Oscar "for superlative artistry and versatility in the creation of motion pictures." He was very touched, but he chose not to attend: he said he would feel foolish. So John Huston accepted on his behalf, and Welles sent a clip of film "from Madrid." "Good night, Orson, wherever you are," said Huston at the Oscars, pretty sure that Welles was only a few miles away, watching on television.

For he reckoned to be magnanimous yet withdrawn as the establishment of film begged his pardon for neglect. He would blush, bow, smile and sigh—he had the act beautifully timed: it was gentle, yet impatient and subtly tortured—pained to hear the very words he had dreamed of, humiliated by his own need for glory. And the glory did not abate. In the winter of 1971–72, *Sight & Sound* polled critics and found not just that *Kane* was still the top film of all time, and Orson Welles the most esteemed of directors, but that *The Magnificent Ambersons* now placed eighth in the top ten. The time was not very far away when in *Day for Night* the director (played by François Truffaut) would have his recurring dream in which as a child out on the city streets at night he comes upon a locked and barred theater playing *Citizen Kane*. It was an *hommage*, and audiences everywhere understood it . . . even if they didn't quite fathom the symbol of *Kane*'s theater being locked and barred, like Xanadu, an unbreachable place. The kids might steal, but they couldn't trespass.

Then people began to think for themselves, and to ask questions. In 1970, Charles Higham published *The Films of Orson Welles*. This was not a biography, though it raised the call for a good one. It was a study of the work, and it was far better than the series of showbiz biographies Higham would write later. The book was full of admiration, yet it saw the self-destructiveness in Welles, the coldness and the boredom. It provoked ire in Wellesians—in Bogdanovich and Richard Wilson—by suggesting that Welles needed to abandon some projects, to leave them unfinished. It was a thoughtful, well-written inquiry, full of sympathy and pained insight. Higham deserves credit for the first significant piece of writing to break past Welles's own guidelines for how he should be perceived. Let me quote one passage to suggest the quality:

I have only seen Welles in person once: in the theater of
the County Museum of Art in Los Angeles, where he
was directing a magic show—re-creating his celebrated
stage performance of the past thirty years for a television spectacular. In one unforgettable hour he emerged
in all his colors. He was grotesque as he forced an unhappy duck over and over again into a brass bowl for a
trick, saying jokingly to a notably unsettled hand-
maiden, "I had 2,000 pigeons with me in the South Pacific in World War II and not one of them died." He
was tragic as he brooded alone, pushing back his assistants, his face knotted in grief and despair, lost, totally
isolated, upset by their slowness. He was terrifying in
his anger at the incompetence of his young assistant
magicians; a thunderous oppressive force seemed about
to break from him and destroy all concerned. He would
laugh bravely in the face of destiny as he guffawed over
his own jokes through a Churchillian cigar. He would
be momentarily affectionate and understanding to a
confused girl. Yet, especially in brief moments of pause,
I sensed the face of a man at once anguished by all that
had been lost and afraid that beyond the gargantuan
meals and wine-bibbing, the anecdotes and the back-
slapping, the raucous laughter and the assembly of famous friends, there would only be silence and loneliness
and invalid rugs: the cold truth of dissolution.

Then in 1971, first in *The New Yorker* and later in expanded book
form, Pauline Kael published a 50,000-word essay, "Raising Kane." She
was not evidently an enemy to Welles. In her review of *Chimes at Midnight*
(highly favorable and against the general trend), she was in no doubt
about his eminence or his lost powers:

> At fifty-one, Welles seems already the grand old master
> of film, because, of course, everybody knows that he'll
> never get in the position to do what he might have
> done. Governments and foundations will prattle on
> about excellence and American film companies will rush
> to sign up Englishmen and Europeans who have had a
> hit, hoping to snare that moneymaking gift. And tired
> transplanted Europeans will go on making big, lousy

American movies, getting financed because they once
had a hit and maybe the magic will come back. And
Welles—the one great creative force in American films
in our time, the man who might have redeemed our
movies from the general contempt in which they are
(and for the most part, rightly) held—is, ironically, an
expatriate director whose work thus reaches only the
art-house audience.

But in the years since that 1967 review for *The New Republic*, Kael's
own position had changed. She had become a film critic at *The New Yorker*;
she had played an important part in the recognition of *Bonnie and Clyde*;
and she had sensed the new vitality of movies around 1970—for they
helped make her the most dynamic and influential American movie critic
of the time. "Raising Kane" had a thesis that easily concealed her admiration for Welles: it was that Herman J. Mankiewicz had really written *Kane*,
that Welles had striven over the years to steal credit for the picture and that
he had always been someone who needed writers and other brilliant collaborators. Kael had talked to selected sources: the Mankiewicz family, the
old RKO boss George Schaefer and John Houseman. It emerged that she
had also resisted talking to Welles, or his other close collaborators. So the
appearance of research behind "Raising Kane" was misleading. Yet it
helped give substance to the belligerent tone and the air of exposure.

There was a germ of truth to it all—Mankiewicz was a smart writer,
with shrewd insights into Welles and especially into his crafty vanity,
which wanted to be seen as the master of everything. But the bias in Kael's
approach blinded her to the ample evidence (later detailed by Bogdanovich and others) of how much Welles had contributed to the scenario. More important than that, Kael the screen hound seemed to have
set aside her acute response to the sniff and excitement of movie itself and
to the roots of authorship that rested in how the whole thing was done in
terms of light, space, movement, sound and atmosphere. "Raising Kane"
was not generous to that broad area of genius and control, and it did not
pay much attention to how modestly Mankiewicz and Gregg Toland had
fared without Welles. The essay seemed calculated and mean-spirited, as
well as less than thorough or conclusively accurate. After all, the real Kael
of 1971 knew that writers do not make movies—she knew it, for instance,
when she saw *McCabe and Mrs. Miller.*

Because Kael wanted to praise the Hollywood screenwriter, she labored to place *Kane* as the culmination of the witty, spiky, wisecracking
comedies of manners, so enriched by the self-conscious bitterness of ex-

newspapermen. There's something in that argument, I suppose, but much less than in the notion that *Kane*'s spatial suffocation, its melancholy and its inward certainty about futility was the beginning of film noir. So in large as well as small respects, the essay was misguided.

Still, it was written by a remarkable critic who had recently had warm feelings for Welles. So the biggest pity about the essay's gratuitous and acerbic slant was that it canceled out some telling observations about Welles and the movie, not least this: "It is a shallow work, a *shallow* masterpiece." Kael meant by that that all the fun and sizzle of the picture was geared to essentially trashy urges: "what makes it such an American triumph—that it manages to create something aesthetically exciting and durable out of the playfulness of American muckraking satire."

Of course, that misses entirely the somber (though not unamused) nut of nihilism in the film, of that self-centeredness which vanishes like a large, iridescent bubble. Kael has never felt the innerness of *Kane*, the place where Welles and Kane become the same creature, or its hapless yearning. Nor does she begin to recognize that Welles—at the moment of his glory—had seen the shallowness inherent in the medium and begun to be bored. That is how his great work seemed to him like a dead end, and all the more melancholy for that reason.

But Kael had stumbled upon something that could be very disconcerting to the best film critic in the world, just as it appalled the man who was increasingly the idol of young directors: that the movies were not and never would be good enough, deep enough, to hold his interest. He had gone deep—no one yet has gone deeper. But it was not enough, not compared with literature, music, painting or just watching life go by. The movies, in other words, are the art of a culture prepared to settle for the shallow. The artistic status of the filmmaker was not actually substantiated by the work. *Citizen Kane* was the first movie to reveal that—and Welles, for a long time, was the only man who noticed it.

"Raising Kane" was a prolonged controversy. It brought out many defenders and only multiplied the number of times *Kane* was shown. In academia, it helped bring respectability to the study of Welles—for academics have always preferred comparing film with some kind of writing to exploring film itself. Welles was injured, but that was good for him, for it pierced the somber dignity that was a larger wrap than cloaks. The controversy removed that archaic edge so palpable if you think of him as Vito Corleone. He was "relevant" again, according to the more stupid usage of that word. And he had a new angle: he could lament that the attack had damaged him in his alleged and daily effort to get new work. As if Merv Griffin took any notice of Pauline Kael!

* * *

By 1971, Welles was no longer living in Spain. But he had his home there still, in an expensive, protected suburb of Madrid. Rather than let it sit empty, he had leased it for a year to the English actor and writer Robert Shaw, the man who had played Henry VIII in *A Man for All Seasons* and who had just finished shooting *Young Winston*, in which he played Lord Randolph Churchill. Shaw moved to Madrid, in part to escape taxes, with his wife Mary Ure and their many children. Both the Shaws were by then dangerous drunks. In the early hours of the morning of November 17, 1971, the fire brigade was called to the house—it was called Fincha mi Gusto. The fire seemed to be located in Shaw's (and Welles's) study. It was all attributed to bad electrical wiring, though there were darker stories of Shaw's drunkenness being to blame. But a great deal of Welles's personal archive—never too thorough or tidy—was destroyed.

The fire, and Kael's onslaught, might have been regarded as heavy blows. And Welles responded to Kael's essay with great wrath or sadness, depending on his mood. Still, there was also something liberating in what happened. His business affairs had always been disordered to a point that defied those eager to help him. He was dismayed by the confusion, so fire seemed providential and cleansing. He was not his own record keeper; he preferred the myth and the fun of making up stories. He said often that he loathed possessions; he vigorously resisted the idea of writing his autobiography; he had never been much impressed by the aura of "home." He had resolutely begun the burning of Charles Foster Kane's habitual disorder—that image of the veritable city of forgotten possessions in Xanadu is still among the movie's most troubling pictures of futility.

And if Higham and Kael had begun to show something beyond the image of the Great Master, that was not really an offense. He did not like to be praised. His ego had always flinched from naked public stroking: he was shy enough to want to conceal his greatest weakness. But he knew, too, how little mileage there is in being a great master. People expect their masters to be dead. How much more glamour and magic might there be in extra hints of fraud, misanthropy, charlatanism and melancholy? In middle age, Welles's smile had been very grim, as if he was fighting his bulk, his failure and his tragedy. But from the midseventies onward, the smile came back, quite serene at times, merry and floating, and seeming very free. There is no proof for such things, but in his last ten or twelve years, Orson Welles seems to have been lighter in spirit, and somewhere closer to gaiety than at any time since, say, 1942.

There was another blow—if that's how you care to read it. Welles had always suspected John Houseman behind Kael's attack—and his old colleague *had* talked to her. But in 1972, something more substantial appeared from Houseman: *Run-Through*, a volume of autobiography. That book was structured as overture and three acts. The overture was dedicated to his mother. Act One to Virgil Thomson, Act Two to Welles and Act Three to the memory of Herman Mankiewicz. Act Two—159 pages—is likely to remain the most intimate piece of writing ever done on Welles. It was penetrating, to be sure; it saw and stated many faults in Welles. And in Act Three, Houseman clearly presented Mankiewicz as the man who rescued Welles from his indecision before *Kane*. But what any reader—and surely Welles is to be included in that number—must feel is the stricken love Houseman felt for Welles, not just in the late thirties but as he was writing the book. That does not mean that *Run-Through* would have been cozy reading for Welles—and I am assuming an instinctive nature in Welles, no matter how devious, complex or self-regarding, one that could not analyze himself in the way Houseman managed. But not even Welles could have mistaken the love. Indeed, the book is like those moments in *Kane* in which even the most antagonistic survivors—Leland and Susan—are bound to admit some warmth and wondering still for Charlie. *Run-Through* was oddly close to a premature obituary—and nothing is more beguiling to anyone aiming at eternity.

Welles sometimes conceded the extra ease of being, if not quite old, at least beyond middle age. He told Merv Griffin once, "I think the only absolutely fatal age is middle age. I spent my youth pretending to be old and I'm getting to the time of my life when I'm going to start pretending to be young. But never be middle-aged. I'm leaping nimbly out of it."

And nimbly he moved from Dean Martin's show to David Frost's and back again, with increasingly minor, yet gross and seated acting roles all over the world. For instance, he was Louis XVIII in *Waterloo*, a king in costume, stagnant in a fauteuil, his legs splayed out, his eyes blinking against the face's flesh, waiting for Bonaparte's return and then slowly descending a staircase (with a cane to support his load). There were all manner of those bits and pieces, done without shame, and for the largest fees he could negotiate.

The one thing he knew he lacked was power—the authority that commands an enterprise and its crew, the opportunity that keeps orchestral conductors so long-lived (he might have noted the exercise they take on the job, too). Power for Welles had its last hurrah in a venture that was in part a movie and in part a rambling, ongoing party that could have lasted out the years. This was called *The Other Side of the Wind*, an invocation of the ineffable that hints at the elusiveness of the film.

"I never believe anything I read in the *Inquirer*": the king in *Waterloo*

It had begun years earlier, in Spain, as Welles watched from a safe distance the progress of the elderly Hemingway following the bulls. The great man was surrounded by his cult and the clutter of lunches that lasted until dinner. Welles was amused, and even touched, for he was not entirely averse to that kind of entourage himself. He was also tickled by the notion of the old artist who may be repeating the lines of characters from his own books of yesterday, books he can no longer match. There was a script, *The Sacred Beasts*, in which the beasts were the bulls, the titans of art and the bullshit brigade.

Oja Kodar had then added to the stew—for in her sharp but sympathetic way, she may have had a clearer eye for the subject. Welles elected to make the Hemingway figure a movie director of a certain age, named Jake Hannaford. But Kodar had another slant on the figure, which Welles admiringly let in to his script. She described it thus:

> My story is that there is a man who is still potent—it's
> not that he is impotent—but gets a real kick from the
> idea of sleeping with his leading man, sleeping really
> with the woman of his leading man. So he is not a clas-
> sic homosexual, but somewhere in his mind he is pos-
> sessing that man by possessing his woman. And at the
> same time, he is very rough on open homosexuals.

So there were two scripts packed into one (and the notion of Hemingway men encountering Kodar's more modern sensibility is an intriguing reflection on her life with Welles). But there was another take on the whole thing that said there was not really what you'd call a script so much as the idea of the film. When Welles had made *The Kremlin Letter* for John Huston, in 1969, he had asked Huston to play Hannaford, and the director had agreed in his easygoing way.* But nothing happened, and no script was delivered.

Then one day in July 1970, in Los Angeles, a young cameraman, Gary Graver, fresh out of the Vietnam War and with the experience of just a few exploitation movies, heard that Welles was at the Beverly Hills Hotel. So he called him up and was told that Welles had left. Graver went home to his apartment, where the phone was ringing. It was Welles.

"Get over to the Beverly Hills Hotel right away," said the familiar voice. "You're only the second cameraman who has ever called me up. The first was Gregg Toland." At the hotel, Graver was required to shoot some tests for *The Other Side of the Wind*. The chance call was hired. Within days, charitably, Welles was calling him "Rembrandt." Graver would be Welles's close associate for the rest of his life, a modest talent inexplicably plucked out of nowhere by the great man, or taken as a dare, or a whim. Graver was devoted, loyal, obliging, self-sacrificing. He was a kind of slave who also let Welles do much of his own lighting. But he was no Gregg Toland.

---

* Welles probably knew Huston's very marked and often cruel aversion to homosexuals.

By 1971, *The Other Side of the Wind* was being shot, much of it in Carefree, Arizona—close to Welles's new house. John Huston duly arrived and was magnificently unfazed to find that there was no script, only speeches on pieces of paper. But he did not have to learn these, Welles said, it was enough to read them and then come up with talk of his own that approximated them.

So Huston, who had been acting like a character most of his life, stood there in the light and did his best, assured by Welles that he was in no way playing anyone who might be deemed to be a version of Huston or Welles. When Huston had a conversation scene to do, he was told that the other person in the scene would be, or had been already, played by Lilli Palmer. Huston was amazed at this, but valiantly he did as he was told.

There was a crew in Carefree—in a house with a pool wedged up in a cliffside—for several months. There were kids doing elaborate catering, and there was Welles, often to be seen in a purple robe, alternately sitting amid the turmoil of the set in thought or striding around bellowing that he was to be trusted and obeyed. There were huge tantrums and large meals. All manner of talent came and went: Susan Strasberg, who appeared to be playing a spiteful film critic based on Ms. Kael, Bogdanovich, Rich Little, Edmond O'Brien, Cameron Mitchell, Paul Stewart, Mercedes McCambridge and Oja Kodar, who somehow managed to have better clothes, more makeup and more provocative scenes than anyone else.

There was filming in Los Angeles later, in the San Fernando Valley— McCambridge recalled a scene in a yellow school bus inhabited by dummies, herself, O'Brien, Mitchell and Stewart—the point of which she could never grasp. "I don't see how [the film] can ever be finished," she said. "Those of us who began the film when it began are either dead or unrecognizably older. People change over a span of a decade or more."

On another occasion, at sunset, on the roof of a home in Arizona, McCambridge and Little were to stand side by side against the brilliant sky. It was a shot of their heads and shoulders, but Welles wanted the sense of agitation beneath them.

"Why?" asked Little, striving to be professional.

"Why must I be challenged in such things?" Welles roared to the heavens. "I need your shoulders to be still, your hips to sway ever so slightly, a rocking on your heels that is barely noticeable . . . all of this will give me the effect I need with the midgets that will be milling around your feet."

"What midgets, Orson?" asked Little.

Welles was too weary to answer, but a crew member quietly confided to the actor: "Mr. Welles says he's going to be shooting them in Spain next month."

This was filmmaking out of any control, subject only to the director's will and whims. Who knows if there was ever anything like a script? Who knows how much of what was done was just the spur of the Wellesian moment? But much footage was shot. Welles was even seen to be editing the material. The project acquired a producer. It stretched into the late 1970s. Welles and Kodar are said to have put $750,000 of their own money into the picture.

Then other investors were found—a Spaniard and a French-Iranian group headed by Medhi Bruscheri, brother-in-law to the shah. But this money failed to come through, because the Spaniard was pocketing it. That calamity was averted when a French company, L'Astrophore, stepped in. When Welles was given the American Film Institute's Life Achievement Award in 1975, a couple of scenes were shown, and the director used the occasion to beg for completion money. There were offers, but L'Astrophore turned them down, confident that better offers would follow. Chaos ensued and reached stability only when the shah's regime in Iran ended and all foreign assets—including the picture negative—became subject to another whim, that of the Ayatollah Khomeini. Welles would die with the footage, its rights and prospects subject to that medieval tyranny. The party had turned into a complete travesty.

One day, it may be freed. I hope not. *The Other Side of the Wind* should stay beyond reach. The enterprise, as Kodar saw it, may have had great points and insight—and Welles sometimes said that the sexuality in the picture was her doing. It even shocked him. But for him it was essentially a terrible but superb fantasy inflicted on reality, an outrage, an imposition on friends and followers, a test of his authority. It was a Xanadu—a place no one can go to but which no one should forget. *The Other Side of the Wind* was always, in Welles's mind, a monstrous, ruined film, an impossibility such as only greatness could command.

That makes it sound odious, as well as capricious and irresponsible. But no one was hurt. And who can really deplore a million or so dollars of someone else's money going to waste? There are creations, works and wonders that are more significant in their nonexistence, their disappearance and their shadow than in being there. For those who have to believe in Welles beyond a reasonable doubt, and for those—like the man himself—who would like to, *The Other Side of the Wind* is a paradise of possibility we can hope to arrive at one day. I can think of one comparison: with the suitcase of manuscripts that Hemingway's first wife, Hadley, once lost. They both make the idea of lost property offices fertile and romantic.

* * *

Amid the wantonness of *The Other Side of the Wind*—indeed, at the very same time (but in a good deal less of the same time), and with the backing of L'Astrophore and some Iranians—Welles delivered a small, unruly yet fabulously organized picture of the utmost originality, delicacy and sly, personal insight. It was almost as if, with the exercising of all his worst personal habits and whims, a man might also discover the best of himself; it was a vindication of something Welles had always attempted, and often been faulted for, doing everything at once. *F for Fake* is flawless; it is unlike anything anyone had ever done before; it was unexpected, and astonishing—and Welles was hardly satisfied if he couldn't be that; it is a mere eighty-five minutes (though the length is relevant) of adroitly juggled essay, reportage, fiction, movie and unadulterated charm. It is the lightest, wittiest film he would ever make—it reaches the child in all of us and confirms the unmediated boy in its maker. It is also a confession that warns us to trust nothing. But tongue in cheek was always Welles's most testing form—and, God knows, he had the cheeks for it.

What prompted this marvel? Well, there are several possible answers, my dear ladies and gentlemen, several different strands in the montage of the film, and if I call them "possible" that is as a courtesy to you—they are all essential. This book is drawing to its close, so it is time for us to be in earnest, to think of summings-up and answers. Let us hope to avoid solemnity without shirking the proper seriousness. So where does it come from, this *F for Fake*?

First, Welles had seen and been entertained by a BBC documentary done by the Frenchman François Reichenbach on a certain Elmir (or is it Elmyr?) de Hory, an art forger. Except that "art forger" is unduly crude. De Hory was also a painter of sensitivity and refinement. He did do "copies," or we might even think of them as "tributes" or "homages," of such skill and sympathy that some museums, galleries and collectors were deceived. Except that *deceived* is altogether too blunt a word. If the beholder looks at a canvas, *sees* and *feels* its beauty, and *knows* its truth (for him- or herself), where is the deception in all those italicized and profound abstractions? After all, weren't there weary days for any Degas or Picasso when the artist did his best (a bored, disgruntled, depressed best) to copy or *be* himself? Well, Elmir (or Elmyr) did that without the depression or the resistance: he was a passionate, heartfelt copier, as good as Xerox but warmer. (And Orson Welles was someone who, for decades, had been admonished for not being himself always.)

There was also the case of Clifford Michael Irving, an American who lived on the Spanish island of Ibiza (a haunt of de Hory, too). In

New York, in December 1971, McGraw-Hill announced that they would be publishing the autobiography of Howard Hughes. The manuscript—close to a quarter of a million words—had been coaxed out of the reticent Hughes by Irving, a novelist. McGraw-Hill issued a statement from Hughes himself to promote the book: "I believe that more lies have been printed and told about me than about any living man— therefore it was my purpose to write a book which would set the record straight."

But is there ever, with anything interesting, any hope of having the record straight? The record, I would like to suggest, is like our memories of sex and love—unforgettable and unreliable. And Hughes, a dour but romantic man, had often behaved as if anxious to be less alive than a suspect in a pulp novel. The Irving book was not authentic—which is not to say that it is less than a good read or short on insights into Howard Hughes. The walls that separate biography, autobiography and romance are not as distinct as the areas in a bookstore, and you should not put complete faith in them. No matter the amount of research that has been gathered and digested for the work of nonfiction, still the story has to be told. Readers want story: they want the thing to hang together. Readers love rosebuds. And when, from start to finish, we know that we are reading a work of fiction, nevertheless we read to believe in the detail, the background, the *stuff*. If someone in Graham Greene's London takes a 49 bus, it better be the one that went from Crystal Palace to Shepherds Bush. Don't try the excuse, This is Greeneland.

The case of Clifford Irving had prompted all of those thoughts anew, and surely it had also added luster and fun to the legend of Hughes. Irving had appealed to Welles, who in his own turn had always seen Hughes as—as it were—random, humdrum casting for Charlie Kane. Hughes certainly did that part, and he had invented the daily life of Xanaduism, but without the panache or the enthusiasm that Welles had envisaged. So Hughes was begging to be taken: so anxious to vanish, he was ready for magic. And Irving had pulled off the great trick. That he had to spend a little time in prison was a small price to pay for the very instructive hoax. There are also moments in *F for Fake* that suggest that Welles, de Hory and Irving were friends of a sort, or had been at some of the same parties. But editing can suggest anything. And film as a whole is so damnably suggestive, ladies and gentlemen, that perhaps our grandparents should have stomped it out, banned it once and for all, seeing the confusion and the confusionists that were likely. Ah, the errors of our grandparents, and the fun we have had as a result. The days that we have seen.

Then there is editing. Welles had always relished this aspect of filmmaking. It is done sitting down: there is less risk of weak ankles snapping, and Welles had for years been advancing on some magnificent enthronement (*Welles and the Chair* is a thesis of infinite promise—I am disappointed that it has not been pursued).* In his later years, there are stories and tableaux of him in basements and hotel suites, seated at, or surrounded by, Moviolas—like the circus maestro with his semicircle of adoring lions. In the editing room, in its windowless gloom, he could work forever, with meals called in and the debris of food heaped on the film cans. It was a situation he loved, where he could talk back to the images, make them the obedient stooges for magic. That pose is evident in *F for Fake* and the far less happy *The Making of Othello*, and it marks a transition in Welles the movie stylist.

In his early work, and as late as the famous opening of *Touch of Evil*, he had loved extended takes and their unbroken venturing through space and time. The very long takes in *Ambersons* are what build its naturalism, its psychological delving into character and its achievement of social depth and texture in terms of the real dimensions of the house. *Kane* has similar passages, and an uncanny feeling for oppressive space and the sheer beauty of real time passing and of real moments observed.

Yet even in the early days, Welles delighted in set pieces of montage: the tumultuous obituary in *Kane* brimming with life, the parade of passing fashions that comes early in *Ambersons*. Then there is the funhouse and the hall of mirrors in *The Lady from Shanghai*, where the stylist seems to come alive with the chance to make madness manifest in the cutting.[1] And so, by the time of *Touch of Evil*, the famous opening is not too far from a camp version of the long take, more show off than show us.[††] The battle in *Chimes at Midnight* is positively Russian in being based—for both energy and violence—in the cutting.

But in *F for Fake*, the entire mise-en-scène is dictated by montage; it is a pattern of fragments (essentially unreliable) put together in the lovely and persuasive rhythms of fabrication. What I think I am seeing here, or saying here, is that Welles had experienced and taken on a growing awareness of film as a means of manipulation, a fraud, and not a poignant rendering of reality. To that extent, the stylistic change is both the natural

---

* It would have to include, for NBC-TV and the *Hallmark Hall of Fame*, his Sheridan Whiteside in "The Man Who Came to Dinner" (done in November 1972). He had been considered for the 1941 movie (the role then went to Monty Woolley). But in '72, at last, he got his chance at the role based on Alexander Woollcott—in a specially designed wheelchair.
† Susan Sontag once observed that it seemed to come from another film.
†† The camp version came along eventually, in Robert Altman's *The Player*.

resort of an increasingly chair-bound man and an expression of cynicism, nihilism and futility. Remember Welles as the disastrous organizer of his own affairs, and the very mannered editing of those later films becomes an intriguing mockery of his real-life failings. He was only ever organized on-screen. That is a very bitter joke, and magnificent defiance of life, reality and his own nature. Artists do not meekly express themselves—they often make a monument that will mislead those who come in search of the truth.

Which brings me to the next impulse. *F for Fake* was made in the immediate aftermath of Pauline Kael's "Raising Kane," as was the first attempt at *The Other Side of the Wind*. But if that misbegotten venture is helpless proof of all Kael's worst suspicions (and there *is* a prosecuting attorney in her), *F for Fake* is the hand behind the back, the droll retort and alibi, that yes, my dear, but you only guessed the half of it.

That does not mean we, and Welles, owe Kael's spite less than gratitude. For her attack had freed him. He had been as guilty, as pent up, as any concealed party fearing discovery. But once exposed, he flowered. Yes, he was a trickster, a rather nasty operator, a credit thief, a bully, a manipulator, a shallow genius (the release! in not having to be deep!), a less than wholesome great man . . . oh, very well, a habitual liar, a liar of genius.

He had invented his childhood and the character of his parents—better that than live in their shadow like someone waiting in hunched dismay for Freud's couch to be vacant. (And may I say here, ladies and gentlemen, that Orson Welles seems to me all his life to have been someone both arguably, vividly disturbed and hysterically well, beyond treatment, so knowing that no doctor ever had a chance with him. Manic-depressive? I daresay. The victim of hideous mood changes? To be sure. But implacably opposed to cure, treatment or even diagnosis. For he exulted in the illness, as a true egotist knows that everything about him is extraordinary and precious.)

He had lied his way into the Gate, and dared his listeners to address the lie. He had lied with *The War of the Worlds*. He had wondrously confused fact and fiction in *Kane*. He had never been to the South Seas in World War II, except in his sleep. He had . . . oh, what's the point, *you* have been here all the time, following along.

It comes to this: Welles had read Kael and seen the light at the end of his own tunnel, that lovely dawn in which he was, yes, indeed, a fraud. Nothing else redeemed the futility he had seen and felt since *Kane*. F for Fate, for Futility, and F for Fuck Off. The happiness in *F for Fake*, the exhilaration, comes from that discovery and the jubilation that knows there is no higher calling than being a magician, a storyteller, a fake who passes the time. This is the work in which Welles finally reconciled the lofty, European, intellectual aspect of himself and the tent show demon who sawed cute dames and wild dreams in half. For it can be very hard to live with the belief that nothing matters in life, that nothing is solid or real, that everything is a show in the egotist's head. It loses friends, trust, children, home, money, security and maybe reason. So it is comforting indeed, late in life, to come upon a proof that the emptiness and the trickery are valid and sufficient. A very sweet, shallow serenity is left.

After the film came out, Welles regathered himself. He said that the admission of fakery, the devout self-description of charlatan, was just a ploy to make the trick work. He had to do it—the scorpion has to sting, doesn't he? "In *F for Fake* I said I was a charlatan and didn't mean it . . . because I didn't want to sound superior to Elmyr, so I emphasized that I was a magician and called it a charlatan, which isn't the same thing. And so I was faking even then. Everything was a lie. There wasn't anything that wasn't."

And never was or could be, ladies and gentlemen. This Orson Welles of ours—I hope he is ours, now—would have vanished if one unequivocally sincere remark had escaped his shameless lips. Even "Rosebud." He trusted nothing, and was never to be trusted. But sometimes in the leaping assertion, the sheer ballet, of his lies, truths could be glimpsed. There are Welles loyalists who agree with him, who say that, yes of course, the confession was a necessary masquerade. Ladies and gentlemen, see *F for Fake*, feel its exultation, enjoy its simple trick (I will not spoil it for you with analysis) and know the boy who was always Orson Welles pretending to be a very wise and wicked wizard. *F for Fake* is a blissful, idyllic comedy—made by a man too often engulfed in his own humorlessness, so that every hearty laugh left you more depressed.

And—here is the last spur—if the film is happy it is because of Oja Kodar, too. She made the film with him, and she was with him when it was made. She is the naked lady who makes a monkey out of Picasso in its climax. She is more than Welles's accomplice and model, though. She seems to be his friend, too. Early on at the railway station, as Welles, in black cloak and black Spanish hat, does elementary magic for a little boy, she is there, in furs, to say, "Up to your old tricks again, I see." It is a sweet, generous moment—I don't think a woman in his work was ever so natural, so kind or so life enhancing. Kodar relaxed Welles, took the edge off his misogyny and made his gazing eyes innocent, sexual and unashamed. We see bits and pieces of her naked in the Picasso period and, again, the mood is that of paradise. We feel happy for him.

Oja Kodar in *F for Fake*

F for Fake blows Welles's cover, for a world smart enough to see. He knew it was a new kind of film, an essay if you like, ideally suited to television. It could have secured a new future, the sort of thing he had always excelled in on radio—bits and pieces held together by his voice, and his offer of himself. He might even then—in the moment of Watergate, don't forget—have become a droll commentator on the grotesque newsreel of our times. (Suppose that he had been Cronkite—how better prepared we would have been for a world out of our control.) But the world missed that. *F for Fake* hardly played. No one much noticed the warmth, the fun or the sexiness. He was safe; he was still that famous failure "Orson Welles."

There is also a passage in *F for Fake* in which the movie goes to Chartres, reflects upon the beauty of the cathedral and considers both the anonymity and the transience of that greatness. The carved stone is surely proof against fakery just because its artists are not known. We see details of the Gothic stone and glass, then we move to faraway views of the cathedral on the flat Eure-et-Loir horizon. Then the image slips from day to night, and the cathedral is only the ghost of a ship at sea. Welles's voice speaks of time moving on, at last, erasing the moment of great art. It is the voice that saw the onset of urban blight and the fading of magnificence in *Ambersons*. And it is a voice that makes gentle, wistful mockery of itself, and himself.

F for Fake opened in 1974 at the film festivals of San Sebastian, New York and London. It was appreciated, but it had only modest commercial runs. Apparently, the film was too odd, too personal and too unreliable to be liked. Welles's hope, that he would be invited to do more things in the same manner, never materialized. There would be no rescue that worked—yet maybe he would have dragged any helping hand down into his own ocean.

But Spain was given up. He came back to America, for good, and ill, the better to be on call for the Los Angeles TV talk shows that wanted

The magician and the world: *F for Fake*

him. In 1974, he bought a house done in an Oriental style on the edge of Las Vegas, and there he parked Paola and Beatrice. For himself, he also lived in Los Angeles, in the hills, more or less with Oja Kodar, though she was definite about maintaining her independence. The state of two households was observed in hurt silence by Paola. But it added to the mystery and confusion of his life, for though Welles was, allegedly, all those years waiting for the big call, he was also hard to find, and regularly in transit.

In Los Angeles, returned, he became a famous public figure, the inescapable monument to himself. He got into the habit of lunching at Patrick Terrail's restaurant, Ma Maison, on Melrose. Indeed, he became a fixture there and even a reason for going to the place. He had his own table, and he could be beheld there, drooping over a chair, often in the company of a small dog, Kiki. And so, somehow, a world-famous sophisticate was reduced to having a home in Las Vegas and keeping company with a poodle.

There were macabre stories—of how Welles had once, literally, been trapped in a car, too large to get out of it, so that the vehicle had to be cut open. There is never a way to disprove such stories, and there was no escaping the cruel jokes about his size—sometimes offered in his very presence, on talk shows. That's how Burt Reynolds once treated a gibe from Welles. The fat man was mortified. He wore robes, caftans and, finally, black cloaks as well as the soft, enveloping dark suits and black silk shirts specially made for him. He was, he had to know, an object of ridicule, on show in the city that prizes leanness above most things. He did his very best.

He might be comped at Ma Maison to boost custom, but he fed from its simplest menu: fish, fresh fruit and mineral water. He was, increasingly, under doctors' orders. He was far too large for anyone's comfort. Like anyone weighing 350 pounds, he had back trouble and high blood pressure. He saw a doctor once a week for checkups. There would be diabetes and heart trouble very soon. He stopped drinking—and drink had been energy for him. The laugh became thinner and creakier without booze. The cigars were more and more just props instead of pleasure. For fifty years, at least, he had been a reckless hedonist, a man whose attitude to life and work could not be separated from the display of self-indulgence. "Are you still eating?" "I'm still hungry." But now the hunger was like a dream and a torment. He had once tried to diet, using pills, and now he researched the surgical procedures that simply cut away embarrassing fat. But such work was an assault on the system, and he was no longer strong. So he had to stay cheerful and seem robust—that is the nature of public appearance and putting yourself up for work. He had to laugh at Reynolds's mean joke, and he had to smile on that insecure actor so that Burt would not give up on him. Reynolds was then "big," and even a meal ticket for Welles. A poodle, Las Vegas and being polite to Burt Reynolds: is this hell?

He was very busy, yet sometimes it was like a parody of being busy, of public performance and private dreams. There was always *The Other Side of the Wind*—new stuff to be shot, old stuff to be edited and the growing legal tangles to be studied. He was doing commercials for just about any product that asked; he was "always" on *The Tonight Show* and *Merv Griffin*; he would do the narration for documentaries—so long as his contract made clear he never had to look at the picture, just read the text. He was an actor still: at last, in 1972, the *Treasure Island* he had started years earlier came out; he would be in *Voyage of the Damned*, with Pia Zadora in *Butterfly* and in some of the Muppet movies, talking to the animals. But he was no longer so mobile, so there were fewer movies that could employ him. He sometimes said that the only movies he acted in now were foregone failures to which he was supposed to bring a touch of class. More and more, he did his work seated. It was far from clear that those dainty ankles could sustain 350 pounds.

There was another ongoing project, *The Magic Show*, current for at least the last twelve years of his life. With Gary Graver shooting, and the magician Ab Dickson involved, Welles was collecting all his old tricks, making reflections on the nature of magic and throwing in as many other fragments, recollections and ideas as he could think of. Burt Reynolds and Angie Dickinson were, from time to time, participants in *The Magic Show*, pieces of which were filmed over the years as money and studio space became available. On one of those occasions, Welles and Dickinson posed for a photograph that is touchingly comic and forlorn. Welles—in a dark suit and black shirt not tucked into his pants—is sitting in a chair that seems to be a type of electric chair. There is a cigar in his right hand. Ms. Dickinson is doing her diligent best to stay on his lap. But the Wellesian stomach is so far-reaching that there is not enough lap. So the slender actress leans back against him, perched on one knee, and throws her arm around his neck to avoid falling over.

It is a precarious position, one not easy for either party. But if a man can no longer have a pretty woman locate his lap, there are so many other physical rites brought into question. The whispering about Welles by then—and certainly whenever he was seen with the gorgeous Oja Kodar, and when she urged him into filming her as a naked beauty such as might have driven Picasso crazy—was along the line, How does he do it? or does he do it any longer? For example, Welles *was* very fond of Angie Dickinson—an entirely understandable feeling—but to see them together was to recognize how far sexual congress of nearly any kind would have depended on engineering, or equipment, and an extensive kindness in the partner. As hard as the thing may have been to do, it is very difficult to write about. I am reminded of how I saw a scrap of a man once, in a cancer ward, waiting for some kind of humiliating treatment that had no chance of success. He was half naked on a gurney, and there were plenty of people around to notice or to consider how not to notice. The man was masturbating furiously—as if in a hurry because of all he had to do.

> "Nay, I speak from my heart," said Mira. "I have been trying for a long time to understand God. Now I have made friends with him. To love him truly you must love change, and you must love a joke, those being the true inclinations of his own heart. Soon I shall take to doing a joke so well that I, who once turned the blood of all the world to ice, shall become a teller of funny tales, to make people laugh."
>
> —Isak Dinesen, *The Dreamers*

> When I say there's a dead end, I don't mean that the young people aren't up to making the films that were made earlier. I mean the medium has exhausted itself in a way. All we can do is repeat ourselves. This may be sour grapes, justifying my own difficulties in making movies; I see that as a possibility. But if it is sour grapes, it still counts for me, and it still makes sense. I have to say that I have doubted, since the first movie I made, that I could do anything except show that I can still do it. Now, who wants to show that you can still do it? Maybe you do when you are forty and you begin worrying about middle age, but when you start worrying about old age, showing you can still do it is a concern that should be behind you.
>
> —Orson Welles, to Merv Griffin

* * *

Loneliness dominated; it had always been pervasive, no matter that Welles was so often at the head of the table or in the chair in a talk show to which all others were turned. He knew "everyone," yet he kept only a very few friends. Roger Hill—his old teacher, his colleague and a person from whom Welles still sought approval—was still one of them. They were still talking, still making plans. Hill, the older man by more than twenty years, would outlive Welles.

Other ties fluctuated. The great friendship with Peter Bogdanovich had produced rich, entertaining interviews, conducted in the early seventies. But then mistrust developed. Bogdanovich had become so successful that he felt more like a Hal in Welles's life. There was a movie—*Nickelodeon*—that Welles thought he was to direct but that ended up Bog-

Welles, speaking at the Directors' Guild, with Roger Hill and Peter Bogdanovich (photo by Florence Dauman)

danovich's. For his part, Bogdanovich reckoned it a little too devious in Welles that he had gone and sold his autobiography to *McCall's* for a large sum of money. That book was never written, but it left their already contracted interview book with Atheneum stranded. It had always been one part of Welles's business confusion that he could seldom resist up-front money. He had never been an easy partner or a straightforward man. Bogdanovich returned the full advance himself.

Robert Kensinger was a young movie enthusiast who went to work for Welles in 1978. He was a great admirer, and he was startled to discover the gulf between the performer and the private man. Welles lived then on Wonderland Avenue, off Laurel Canyon, "renting a crummy little tract house, one of those early sixties sloped hard-edged buildings. It was such a shabby, unemotional piece of architecture." The interiors were cramped. The garden was littered with thrown-away Macanudo cigar butts—this is a terrible image, a blindness to nature.

But Welles had few friends and fewer callers. The place was barely decorated: "It felt almost like a hotel room. He didn't do anything to leave a personal mark." Welles often sat in the gloom on a lounger watching television—but rarely seeing movies. When out in public, he didn't drink and ate carefully. But at home there were binge feasts, and he was still drinking heavily in the evenings. His bathtub was full of old books. His closet had maybe thirty identical black silk shirts.

Oja Kodar kept a room in the house. They did a lot together, but she wasn't always there. Kensinger could see their fondness, and he believed there was no other woman in Welles's life, but he said, "I think his sex life was essentially over."

Kensinger would often drive Welles to television studios for his appearances, or to studios where commercials were shot—for Paul Masson wine. There was another young man, a valet, a kid Welles hated but endured. Once Kensinger observed Welles asking the kid to get him a pair of scissors.

"Why?" asked the kid insolently.

"So I can stab you with them," said Welles.

On another occasion, when Kensinger collected Welles from the studio, they put together the little cash they had for dinner. (Welles's operation was always done with cash—no checks or credit cards.) They ended up at a restaurant and watched a family eating happily together. "Look at them," said Welles. "They all love each other, they're all together—what lucky, lucky people." As Kensinger observed, Welles saw or heard little of his three daughters.

Bogdanovich's place in Welles's life was largely filled by Henry

Jaglom, who had cast Welles in *A Safe Place*. Jaglom was an independent filmmaker: he made films on his own, usually with his own money, then sold them himself—very shrewdly. He adored Welles, and treasured his sweetness. They often lunched together, and Jaglom began to keep sound recordings of those occasions—for use someday in a book. Jaglom did all he could to encourage the older man and to help his career. In return, Welles gave Jaglom advice: "Never need Hollywood. Don't let anybody tell you what to do. And never make a movie for anyone else, or on some idea of what other people will like." Jaglom had good connections: he had been part of the group that made *Easy Rider*. It was Jaglom who facilitated a meeting between Welles and Barbara Leaming, who would become his official and very generous biographer. And it was Jaglom who urged Welles into a project called *The Big Brass Ring*.

> Posterity is a whim. A shapeless litter of old bones: the midden of a vulgar beast: the most capricious and immense mass-public of them all—the dead.
> —Kim Menaker in *The Big Brass Ring*

> I've set myself against being concerned with any more worldly success than I need to function with. That's an honest statement and not a piece of attitudinizing. Up to a point, I have to be successful in order to operate. But I think it's corrupting to care about success; and nothing could be more vulgar than to worry about posterity.
> —Orson Welles, the *Playboy* interview

The Big Brass Ring has never been made, and if the shades of Orson Welles have any luck, it won't be. That will make it so much easier for good men and true to assure us of what has been lost. Four years after Welles's death, for instance, Gore Vidal—a friendly acquaintance to the great man, one who often invited him to dinner, only for some last-minute problems (Welles needed an early night before tomorrow's dog-food commercial) to intervene—wrote an appreciation of Welles for *The New York Review of Books*, of his humor, his effortless storytelling and self-dramatization, and of their running Rudy Vallee jokes. The piece is fond and merry and given flavor by a few majestic inaccuracies. It is full of nice anecdotes.

At one Ma Maison lunch (*avec* Kiki to keep them honest), Welles thanked Vidal for having put in a good word for him with Johnny Carson. Carson, it seemed, had gone a touch cold on Orson as a *Tonight Show* guest. Vidal had talked to Carson, who had been "astonished. There was no problem that he knew of."

Welles sighed at Vidal's naïveté (there is a key to his social superiority): "There's more to this than Johnny will ever tell you," he rumbled. "Much, much more." Is there clearer demonstration of the man's taste for his own melodrama?

Anyway, Vidal concluded his belated obituary—it's plain how much he missed Welles, and his voice on the phone—with a tribute to the script for *The Big Brass Ring*, which, he wrote, is "plainly [Welles] at the top of his glittering form."

That script had been published, modestly, in 1987, as a work by Orson Welles "with Oja Kodar," which to me conveys collaboration and not just that she was in the room, or his life, at the time. The published version contains enormous but not unexpected respect from Jonathan Rosenbaum, whose valiant efforts for Welles scholarship sometimes obscure the plain fact that an OW shopping list is just that, and not a holy text. And the afterword to the script recounts the efforts made by Welles and Jaglom to get the picture made. Allegedly there was $8 million ready for it with Arnon Milchan to produce. All that was needed was a big star to play the lead, Sen. Blake Pellarin, a man of presidential timber—or perhaps it is just that he is made of wood. Six actors were offered the chance, for $2 million: Warren Beatty, Clint Eastwood, Paul Newman, Jack Nicholson, Robert Redford and Burt Reynolds. All six declined. Jaglom and Rosenbaum take that as the last straw of evidence of the hideous crassness of the Hollywood system, and the virtual conspiracy to ensure the "failure" of Orson Welles.

On the other hand, decisions not to be Blake Pellarin seem to me evidence that one can be an international icon without losing all reason. I have seen no point in this book in praising everything Welles touched. It seems more helpful in reaching an understanding of him to say that there was much work that was reckless and wretched. And that sometimes it not only coincided with the very good and the great but in intriguing ways resembled it. *The Big Brass Ring* is as bad as anything Welles ever did or attempted. The script is deficient as suspense story—and it is one more lame try at the thriller genre. Its structure and unfolding are cockamamie: for instance, very early on Pellarin comes upon a young woman stealing his wife's jewels and—on impulse—aids and encourages her. It is the one arresting moment in the script, but it is never developed. The characters are cardboard filled with literary talk of the most wearying pretension. The women are facades. The sense of politics is not just archaic but fanciful—one marvels that Vidal was taken in. Yet the sentiments are riveting for the biographer.

Senator Pellarin has just lost a presidential election—he has lost to Ronald Reagan, the actor, divorcé and professional nonentity often held up by Welles to mock his own earlier decision not to throw his hat in the ring. Thus, at the outset, the scenario is less autobiographical than a kind of wistful fantasizing over lost chances—call it Merrie Welles. But the nakedness of the romantic preoccupation is breathtaking. Pellarin is only a figment and a gesture toward courage, integrity and charisma. Those six stars surely knew how little there was to hold on to in the role. Let's face it, Pellarin is not much more than a gay wet dream. Yet Welles had so numbing a sense of the man's greatness, we may be embarrassed by the confessional:

> He is a great man—like all great men he is never satisfied
> that he has chosen the right path in life. Even being
> President, he feels, may somehow not be right. He is a
> man who has within him the devil of self-destruction that
> lives in every genius. You know that you're absolutely
> great, there is no question of that, but have you chosen
> the right road? Should I be a monk? Should I jerk off in
> the park? Should I just fuck everybody and forget about
> everything else? Should I be President? It is not self-
> doubt; it is *cosmic* doubt! What am I going to do—I am
> the best, I know that, now what do I do with it?

This sounds like a role that required an American Olivier, Spencer Tracy at his greatest, or the Brando who gave up on difficult work and blamed everything else in the world. Yet the part as actually written is made for . . . George Hamilton, or Oliver North.

Quite swiftly, though without dramatic logic, the action of *The Big Brass Ring* confronts Pellarin and Kim Menaker (do you see "Kane" in the mirror there?). Menaker is a disgraced Rooseveltian aide, and he has some of Welles's very fanciful history, too:

> I was one of the young people who started under Roo-
> sevelt. Some few of us got close enough to catch his

interest; and it pleased him to encourage Presidential
dreams. It was absurd, of course, but there was one of us
who actually made it: Lyndon Johnson.

Menaker is . . . *homosexual:* at last, that pondering about the self is out
of its closet, like a yeti blinking in the sunlight, but given to boozy, sentimental speeches and calling Pellarin "Boysie." This emerging from the
closet settles the biographical question: no matter the dreams and wondering, no matter the fascination, Welles was *not* gay. Why? He couldn't
conceive of loving any other person in the world. So Menaker's love for
Pellarin is an odious, smarmy parody of affection. Welles was gay in a way
uniquely his: he loved himself. But love was the least thing his great work
could ever deliver or make us believe.

So we are left with just the romance he felt for himself, and the ba-
thetic discovery—not rendered as drama but described by another character—that Menaker has kept a handkerchief, starchy now with the
ejaculate of his own jerkings off over Pellarin. Even Vidal finds this device somewhat . . . icky. When Pellarin learns of it, the script asks him to
utter "a sudden, terrible groan." That was not what Beatty, Redford,
Newman, Nicholson, Eastwood or even Reynolds had been waiting and
searching for.

Of course, Welles was to have played Menaker, hurrying in the inane
"action" from Africa to Europe, engaging in long, doleful and very windy
dialogues with Pellarin that are grotesque versions of the great male battles in Welles's earlier work. There is one scene to conjure with. We are
in Madrid, and it is fiesta time. Pellarin has at last found his own long lost
true love—a lady, though she is not really seen or heard in the film;
women, as so often, are neglected. Don't ask how she fits in to the action—she is *there*, what does it matter what you say about people? Pellarin
couples with her: "The scene is strange, almost surreal. . . . (The action
must be given in synopsis. . . . The climax of this sequence is strongly
erotic: to spell out its specific details would be to risk pornography.)"

The discretion is lunatic. But one thing is spelled out. Menaker is outside the room, yet he has a rare view. The very large Welles-Menaker was
here to be "like a great child rocking in its cradle" on a Ferris wheel and
no doubt aching to be in that room, living it up as one of those dots. This
is among the great comic images never risked.

So it is absurd, a folly, something to laugh over, and an astonishing revelation of innocence, adolescence and rank melodrama. It is also very
Welles, and the work of someone who was no longer well or strong

enough to keep up the mask of worldliness. Never made, *The Big Brass Ring* should never be forgotten—or abandoned as a vital, illuminating footnote to the egotistical drama and despair of Kane.

We are near the end, and maybe that is a good thing. But Welles was not still, even if he now needed a wheelchair at airports, or some excuse if a job needed serious walking. He narrated a Jacques-Yves Cousteau documentary; he did TV specials with Dom De Luise; he was there on camera as jocular host and master of mystery in a dire NBC series, *Scene of the Crime*.

He was approached to direct another man's script: Ring Lardner, Jr., had written *Rocking the Cradle* about the 1937 production of Marc Blitzstein's *The Cradle Will Rock*. He said he would direct if he could rewrite the script—so there is another scenario, published now, and very well done (so well that maybe the expert Lardner felt a little twinge for Mankiewicz in the reading). Rupert Everett was going to play Welles; Amy Irving would have been Virginia Nicholson Welles. But at the last moment it failed to happen.

He was working on other things—a script of *Lear* and a script from Isak Dinesen's *The Dreamers*. The *Lear* was to have been for French television, a scaled down version, just the human story. Jack Lang was supporting it. But Welles believed that he was being used by the French, so he backed out. He played a significant and charming role as a wise old man at the back of the theater in Henry Jaglom's *Someone to Love*: it would prove a gracious farewell. There was so much not finished. *Don Quixote, The Deep, The Other Side of the Wind, The Big Brass Ring, The Dreamers, Ambersons . . .* even *It's All True*. But in 1985, it was reported that over 300 cans of that film had been found.

He was doing more work on *The Magic Show* in early October. Barbara Leaming's book, *Orson Welles: A Biography*, had just been published. He liked it, and why not? The book was broadly accurate and very fond. He had beguiled the author, of course, in the nicest possible way. They had had good times together, and the book benefited enormously from his easy, flowing talk. It would have been mean-spirited to check everything he said.

On October 9 he was on *The Merv Griffin Show* with Ms. Leaming, doing some light magic and helping promote the book. He did not look well—but he had not really ever looked well, exactly. Beautiful sometimes, yes, magnificent and glorious. But well?

He went to Ma Maison for dinner, and then he went home. He seems to have done some work on the script for *The Magic Show*. But he was there in the house, alone, with no one to hear or report on any word, when a substantial heart attack killed him. October 10, 1985.

Well . . .

I had nearly forgotten you.

There were other books I had to attend to. And the O'Toole lawyers!

My readers may think I invented you.

Like this Orson Welles of ours?

The story has to be told. You can't give people a life without making a story out of it.

And how does it end? Not just the date of death, surely?

We could perhaps summon up the ending he had intended for *The Magnificent Ambersons*. Just his own very quiet and gentle voice over black leader, saying, "Ladies and gentlemen, that's the end of the story."

Must we be so sad? And is it the end?

Not at all—Welles goes on. The books about him do begin to accumulate. There are those laboring to complete the unfinished pictures. And I think he is as current as ever. There are young people still, seeing *Kane* and feeling its wonder. But I'm not sure they are any longer inspired to make movies. The medium as a whole is too forlorn.

And Welles?

The undefeated champion. It's becoming clearer, year by year, that no one else will surpass him or *Kane*. He plumbed the depths even if it is a shallow medium. He stole perfection.

And he is well thought of still?

In 1992, when *Sight & Sound* did its poll again, *Kane* was still on top—the fourth decade in a row, with nearly twice as many votes as the next film.

But your book—and some others, perhaps—treat him as someone more complex than just a hero.

I hope my Welles may be more compelling than a hero—grander, sadder, tougher. After all, it's one thing to be a magnificent piece of work but quite another to be magnificent *and* a poor bastard at the same time. He was very brave, I think. And sometimes it takes great courage to be imperfect.

You don't think you've been hard on him? I mean, people like to feel good about their heroes.

I've done my best by him. I'd like the readers to go away as muddled in their feelings as everyone left behind after Kane's death. But, in general, film fans should be careful about wanting to love their idols. It is a very tough business for staying decent in. Do not forget the scorpion: he will kill you as he warns. In the end, if this Welles is not likable enough, not sweet or amiable, I'll take the responsibility. I feel too close to him to shrug him off.

You like him?

Worse than that: I fear I'm like him. That Orson Welles took my life. By the time I realized it, it was too late to go back.

I had a question. You say sometimes that he didn't really see many movies?

Indeed, he said once that it is very harmful for moviemakers to see movies. He wanted to stay innocent. But I think he was bored by other people's films. Egotism is shameless. Time and again, asked about other directors—Bergman, Resnais, Rossellini, Bresson, Antonioni—he said he had walked out. He cannot have been comfortable in theater seats. He said he liked John Ford and Jean Renoir. But I'm not sure how many of their films he ever saw.

You see, it's the same as with people. He went through people, like light going through film. You could say his parents marked him for life—by spoiling, neglecting and dying. But I doubt it. I'm not sure he really noticed them that much—or anyone else who came close to him. And selfishness is very hard. So many people weaken with it. Not Welles.

The view from Nepenthe (photo by Lucy Gray)

So how do we close?

There's a line Jeanne Moreau said once, about Orson being "so much like a destitute king . . . because there was no kingdom that was good enough for Orson Welles."

There's something else. The day he died—October 10, 1985—I drove down to the site of Nepenthe. It's that place on the Big Sur coast where he and Rita Hayworth were to build their dream hideaway. It's as lovely a spot as any I've seen. And think of that dream, that rapture—the two of them above the Pacific.

But it never happened?

That's right. They never lived in the place. I thought of a panoramic view from there—the trees and the ocean. That might work. And it would remind us that the world is very large and the greatest films so small.

So film perhaps had made a wasted life?

One has to do something.

FILMOGRAPHY

ARCHIVES

BIBLIOGRAPHY

ACKNOWLEDGMENTS

INDEX

FILMOGRAPHY

CHIMES AT MIDNIGHT (1966, 119 MIN.)
dir. and scr. OW; exec. prod. Alessandro Tasca di Cuto and Harry Saltzman; with OW, Keith Baxter, John Gielgud, Norman Rodway, Jeanne Moreau, Margaret Rutherford, Alan Webb, Marina Vlady, Walter Chiari, Fernando Rey, Michael Aldridge.

CITIZEN KANE (1941, 119 MIN.)
dir. and prod. OW; scr. OW and Herman J. Mankiewicz; with OW, Joseph Cotten, Everett Sloane, Agnes Moorehead, Ruth Warrick, Dorothy Comingore, Erskine Sanford, George Coulouris, Paul Stewart, William Alland, Fortunio Bonanova, Gus Schilling, Harry Shannon, Buddy Swan. Of course, it is available on video and on a fine laser disc; but there are always those who have never seen it, or never seen it as a movie, so *Kane* should be seen as a high-quality 35-mm print, in an otherwise empty theater (this is not just a sentimental touch; unlike many great movies, Welles's are often most themselves when playing to an audience of one).

F FOR FAKE (1973, 85 MIN.)
dir. OW; scr. OW and Oja Kodar; prod. Dominique Antoine; with OW, Oja Kodar, Elmyr de Hory, Clifford Irving, Edith Irving, François Reichenbach, Laurence Harvey, Nina Van Pallandt.

FILMING OTHELLO (1979, 84 MIN.)
dir. and scr. OW; prod. Klaus and Jurgen Hellwig; with OW, Hilton Edwards, Micheál MacLiammóir.

THE FOUNTAIN OF YOUTH (1958, 25 MIN.)
dir. and scr. OW, from John Collier's story "Youth from Vienna"; exec. prod. Desi Arnaz for Desilu; with OW, Dan Tobin, Joi Lansing, Rick Jason, Billy House, Nancy Kulp.

THE IMMORTAL STORY (1968, 58 MIN.)
dir. and scr. OW, from the novella by Isak Dinesen; prod. Micheline Rozan for ORTF;

with OW, Jeanne Moreau, Roger Coggio, Norman Eshley, Fernando Rey. The most difficult to see of all the released films at present, and in great need of rescue.

IT'S ALL TRUE (1993, 89 MIN.)
dir. and scr. Myron Meisel and Bill Krohn, with Richard Wilson. A somewhat loyal documentary on Welles in Brazil but a more successful attempt to give a flavor of what *It's All True* might have been like.

JOURNEY INTO FEAR (1943, 69 MIN.)
dir. Norman Foster; scr. Joseph Cotten and OW (uncredited), from the novel by Eric Ambler; with OW, Joseph Cotten, Dolores Del Rio, Everett Sloane, Ruth Warrick, Agnes Moorehead, Jack Moss, Edgar Barrier, Richard Bennett.

THE LADY FROM SHANGHAI (1948, 86 MIN.)
dir. and scr. OW, based on Sherwood King's novel *If I Die Before I Wake;* with OW, Rita Hayworth, Everett Sloane, Glenn Anders, Ted de Corsia, Erskine Sanford, Gus Schilling.

MACBETH (1948, 107 MIN.)
dir., prod. and scr. OW; exec. prod. Charles K. Feldman; with OW, Jeanette Nolan, Dan O'Herlihy, Roddy McDowall, Edgar Barrier, John Dierkes, Erskine Sanford, Peggy Webber, Lurene Tuttle, Brainerd Duffield, William Alland. Note that for a time this was available only in an 86-minute version, but the full original has been restored on video.

THE MAGNIFICENT AMBERSONS (1942, 88 MIN.)
dir. and scr. OW, from the novel by Booth Tarkington; with Joseph Cotten, Tim Holt, Dolores Costello, Agnes Moorehead, Anne Baxter, Ray Collins, Richard Bennett, Erskine Sanford. Ideally seen in a superb print, projected in the hall of an empty mansion; the best way of grasping the "original" 132-minute version is in a reconstruction by Jonathan Rosenbaum in *This Is Orson Welles;* the laser-disc version by Voyager includes the October 29, 1938, radio version performed by Mercury, with Welles as George, and without Fanny at all.

THE MAKING OF CITIZEN KANE (1992, 90 MIN.)
dir. Leslie Megahey; BBC television documentary.

MR. ARKADIN (1955, 95 MIN.)
dir. and scr. OW; exec. prod. Louis Dolivet; with OW, Paola Mori, Robert Arden, Akim Tamiroff, Katina Paxinou, Michael Redgrave, Mischa Auer, Patricia Medina, Jack Watling, Suzanne Flon, Frédéric O'Brady. There are several versions of this; some are called *Confidential Report.*

THE ORSON WELLES SKETCH BOOK (1955)
BBC television episodic series.

THE ORSON WELLES STORY (1980, 210 MIN.)
dir. and prod. Alan Yentob and Leslie Megahey. The most exhaustive and interesting interview OW ever gave to television; a shorter version eventually played on American TV, on TNT, in 1990.

ORSON WELLES: THE ONE-MAN BAND (1995, 90 MIN.)
dir. Vassili Silovic; scr. Silovic and Roland Zag; made possible by Oja Kodar. Contains fragments or extracts, as follows: "Churchill"; "*The Deep*"; "*The Dreamers*"; "*F for Fake, Trailer*"; "Filming *The Trial*"; "Magic Show"; "*The Merchant of Venice*"; "*Moby Dick*"; "*The Orson Welles Show*"; "*The Other Side of the Wind*"; "Stately Homes"; "Swinging London"; "Tailors"; "Vienna."

OTHELLO (1952, 91 MIN.)
dir, prod. and scr. OW; with OW, Micheál MacLiammóir, Suzanne Cloutier, Fay Compton, Robert Coote, Hilton Edwards, Doris Dowling, Nicholas Bruce, Michael Laurence.

THE STRANGER (1946, 95 MIN.)
dir. OW; prod. Sam Spiegel; scr. Anthony Veiller and John Huston (uncredited); with OW, Edward G. Robinson, Loretta Young, Philip Merivale, Richard Long, Byron Keith, Billy House, Konstantin Shayne.

TOUCH OF EVIL (1958, 108 MIN.)
dir. and scr. OW, from Paul Monash script and Whit Masterson novel, *Badge of Evil*; prod. Albert Zugsmith; with OW, Charlton Heston, Janet Leigh, Akim Tamiroff, Joseph Calleia, Joanna Moore, Valentin De Vargas, Ray Collins, Marlene Dietrich, Dennis Weaver, Mercedes McCambridge, Mort Mills, Joi Lansing, Zsa Zsa Gabor.

THE TRIAL (1962, 120 MIN.)
dir. and scr. OW, from the novel by Franz Kafka; exec. prod. Alexander and Michael Salkind; with OW, Anthony Perkins, Jeanne Moreau, Elsa Martinelli, Romy Schneider, Suzanne Flon, Madeleine Robinson, Akim Tamiroff, Arnoldo Foa, Fernand Ledoux, William Chappell.

ARCHIVES

The most substantial Welles archive consists of papers cared for by Richard Wilson, after Welles had left Hollywood. It is at the Lilly Library, Bloomington, Indiana. This book quotes from that archive as indicated. Numbers in parentheses refer to pages in this text:

"Dadda" Bernstein, letter to OW, May 21, 1930 (28)
Diana Bourbon to Ernest Chappell, Oct. 9, 1939 (131–2)
Hadley Cantril to OW, Apr. 6 and 11, 1940 (108)
Herb Drake to William Schneider, Jan. 15, 1941 (180, 181)
Herb Drake to OW, June 1, 1942 (235)
Norman Foster to OW, Sept. 25, 1941 (198)
Jane Eyre contract, Loyd Wright to James Morris, Dec. 24, 1942 (240)
Herman Mankiewicz to OW as quoted in Herb Drake to OW, Aug. 26 and Sept. 5, 1940 (154)
"The New Actor" tour, memo itinerary, Oct. 11, 1940 (179)
Tom Petty to Herb Drake, Jan. 27, Apr. 7 and May 5, 1942 (212, 218–19)
George Schaefer to OW, Sept. 15, 1939, and Apr. 13, 1942 (128, 217)
Lynn Shores matter, memo, Apr. 1942 (219)
Ted Thackrey to Richard Wilson, Dec. 26, 1946 (264)
Arnold Weissberger to Richard Baer, Dec. 18, 1939 (133)
Arnold Weissberger to Herb Drake, Jan. 2, 1940 (157)
Arnold Weissberger to OW, Oct. 1, 1940, and Jan. 17, 1941 (quoting Morris Ernst) (154–5, 188)
OW to Diana Bourbon, Oct. 12, 1939 (132)
OW to Joe Breen, July 10, 1941 (197)
OW to Hadley Cantril, Mar. 26 and Apr. 6, 1940 (107, 108)
OW to Columbia Pictures, Apr. 26, 1946 (274)
OW to Eleanor Goldsmith, July 5, 1938 (95)
OW to Bob Hall, May 30, 1945 (265)
OW to Charles Laughton, July 27, 1946 (273)

OW to Fernando Pinto, Feb. 26, 1943 (237)
OW to Arthur Pryor, May 30, 1945 (265)
OW to RKO, Feb. 6, 1942 (197, 211)
OW to Nelson Rockefeller, Feb. 25, 1942 (213)
OW to David O. Selznick, May 19, 1937 (90)
OW to George Schaefer, Sept. ?, 1939, and Mar. 6, 1941 (129, 190)
OW to Ted Thackrey, July 1945 (263)
OW to Sidney Whipple, Apr. 15, 1939 (118)
OW, notes on script for Roosevelt obituary (263)
OW, "You understand what I mean by 'they,' " undated (261)
Virginia Welles to Arnold Weissberger, June 21, 1940 (155)
Ward Wheelock to OW, July 28, 1939 (129)
Richard Wilson to OW, Nov. 20, 1947, and Feb. 10, 1948 (291)
Robert Wise to OW, Mar. 31, 1942 (215)

BIBLIOGRAPHY

BY WELLES

(with Oja Kodar), *The Big Brass Ring*, film script (Santa Barbara, CA, Black Spring Press, 1987). (417, 419, 419–20)

Bright Lucifer, play (?1933), typescript in Wisconsin State Historical Society, Madison, WI. (42)

Chimes at Midnight, film script, ed. Bridget Gellert Lyons (New Brunswick, NJ, Rutgers University Press, 1988). Also contains excellent interview with actor Keith Baxter. (364, 378, 380, 382)

(with Herman J. Mankiewicz), *Citizen Kane: The Shooting Script and Cutting Continuity of the Completed Film*, in *The Citizen Kane Book* (New York, Little Brown, 1971).

The Cradle Will Rock, film script (Santa Barbara, CA, Santa Teresa Press, 1994).

(with Roger Hill), *Everybody's Shakespeare* (Woodstock, IL, Todd Press, 1934).

Une Grosse Légume, novel, trans. Maurice Bessy (Paris, Gallimard, 1953).

Heart of Darkness, 1939 typescript (Lilly Library, Bloomington, IN). (128, 289)

His Honor the Mayor, play for radio (New York, Dodd Mead, 1941). (191)

Interviews: with André Bazin, Charles Bitsch and Jean Domarchi, *Cahiers du Cinéma*, June and Sept. 1958 (trans. in script for *Touch of Evil*—see page 435). (347, 356)

with Juan Cobos and Miguel Rubio, *Sight & Sound*, Autumn 1966. (379)

with J. A. Pruned, *Cahiers du Cinéma in English*, no. 5, 1966. (366, 376, 379)

with Kenneth Tynan, *Playboy*, Mar. 1967. (8, 10–11, 390, 417)

La Santa de Orson Welles, film script, ed. David Ramon (Mexico City, Cineteca Nacional, 1991).

Letter to *The Times* (London), Nov. 17, 1971 (on the making of *Kane*).

Memo to Edward Muhl on *Touch of Evil*, *Film Quarterly*, Fall 1992.

Mr. Arkadin, novel (Paris, Gallimard, 1955; London, W. H. Allen, 1956). Authorship uncertain, but a valuable backup to the film. (319)

Moby Dick—Rehearsed, play (New York, Samuel French, 1965) (329).

"Orson Welles Writing About Orson Welles," *Stage*, Feb. 1941; rep. *Hollywood Directors 1941–1976*, ed. Richard Koszarski (New York, Oxford University Press, 1971).

"Pete Vazquez," in Citizens' Committee for the Defense of Mexican American Youth, *The Sleepy Lagoon Case* (Los Angeles, 1942). (247–8)

"Race Hate Must Be Outlawed," *Free World Forum*, July 1944. (260–1)

Jean Renoir obituary, *Los Angeles Times*, Feb. 18, 1979.

This Is Orson Welles, interviews with Peter Bogdanovich (New York, HarperCollins, 1992). The indispensable book, not just because of the depth and sympathy of the conversations, but because of the magnificent editorial work by Jonathan Rosenbaum, which includes the fullest Welles chronology ever published. (10, 19, 57, 147, 148, 182, 206, 220–1, 238, 240, 309, 323, 374, 393)

Touch of Evil, film script, ed. Terry Comito (Brunswick, NJ, Rutgers University Press, 1985). (338–9)

The Trial, film script (London, Lorrimer, 1976). (369, 370–1)

(with Howard Koch), *The War of the Worlds*, radio script, in Koch, *The Panic Broadcast*. (12–13, 103, 104, 105)

Vogue par Orson Welles, Dec. 1982 (the Christmas issue of the French fashion magazine, with a large section selected, written and illustrated by OW). (7, 17, 19, 20, 23–4, 32)

ON WELLES

Brooks Atkinson, "Plans for a New Theatre," *New York Times*, Aug. 29, 1937. (83)

Anne Baxter, *Intermission: A True Story* (New York, Putnam, 1976).

André Bazin, *Orson Welles: A Critical View* (Paris, Editions du Cerf, 1972; New York, Harper & Row, 1978). Includes foreword by François Truffaut and profile by Jean Cocteau.

Laurence Bergreen, *James Agee: A Life* (New York, Dutton, 1984).

John Berry, interviewed by Patrick McGilligan, *Film Comment*, May–June 1995. (91, 110)

Maurice Bessy, *Orson Welles* (Paris, Seghers, 1963; New York, Crown, 1971).

Pierre Billard, "Chimes at Midnight," *Sight & Sound*, Spring 1965.

Marc Blitzstein, *The Cradle Will Rock* (1936). (81)

Peter Bogdanovich, *The Cinema of Orson Welles* (New York, 1961).

———, "Is It True What They Say About Orson?" *New York Times*, Aug. 30, 1970.

———, "The *Kane* Mutiny," *Esquire*, Oct. 1972.

———, *Pieces of Time* (New York, 1973).

———, see also *This Is Orson Welles*.

Jorge Luis Borges, "An Overwhelming Film," *Sur*, 1941; repr. *Borges In/And/On Film*, ed. Edgardo Cozarinsky (New York, Lumen Books, 1988). (77)

Patricia Bosworth, *Montgomery Clift: A Biography* (New York, Harcourt Brace & Jovanovich, 1978).

Sara Holmes Boutelle, *Julia Morgan: Architect* (New York, Abbeville Press, 1988).

Frank Brady, *Citizen Welles: A Biography of Orson Welles* (New York, Scribner's, 1989). A major and valuable book.

Richard Brooks, interviewed by Patrick McGilligan, *Backstory 2* (Berkeley, CA, University of California Press, 1991). (253)

Kay Brown, letter to David O. Selznick, July 20, 1938 (Selznick Archive, Humanities Research Center, Austin, TX). (90)

Felix Bucher and Peter Cowie, "Welles and Chabrol," *Sight & Sound*, Autumn 1971.

Gail Lumet Buckley, *The Hornes: An American Family* (New York, Knopf, 1986). (249)

Simon Callow, *Charles Laughton: A Difficult Actor* (London, Methuen, 1987).

————, *Orson Welles: The Road to Xanadu* (London, Jonathan Cape, 1995). Immense, thorough, enthusiastic yet skeptical, this is the first of two (or three?) volumes by a man who is also an actor and a director. Why are so many Welles books by Englishmen?

Hadley Cantril, *Invasion from Mars* (Princeton, NJ, Princeton University Press, 1940). (108)

Robert L. Carringer, "*Citizen Kane, The Great Gatsby* and Some Conventions of American Narrative," *Critical Inquiry*, Winter 1975.

————, *The Making of Citizen Kane* (Berkeley, CA, University of California Press, 1985). (145–6, 201)

————, "Rosebud, Dead or Alive: Narrative and Symbolic Structure in *Citizen Kane*," *PMLA*, Mar. 1976.

William Castle, *Step Right Up! I'm Gonna Scare the Pants Off America* (New York, Putnam, 1976). (275, 276)

Raymond Chandler, *Selected Letters*, ed. Frank MacShane (New York, Columbia University Press, 1981).

Charles Chaplin, *My Autobiography* (New York, Simon & Schuster, 1964).

Michel Ciment, *Conversations with* [Joseph] *Losey* (New York, Methuen, 1985). (59–60, 65)

Harold Clurman, *The Fervent Years* (New York, Harcourt Brace, 1945). (118)

Jean Cocteau, "Orson Welles," *Cinemonde*, Mar. 6, 1950. (62, 286, 290)

Richard Combs, "Burning Masterwork: From *Kane* to *F for Fake*," *Film Comment*, Jan.–Feb. 1994.

Aaron Copland and Vivian Perlis, *Copland: 1900 Through 1942* (New York, St. Martin's Press, 1984). (116)

Joseph Cotten, *Vanity Will Get You Somewhere: An Autobiography* (New York, Mercury House, 1987). Slender and discreet, but fond and merry. On Welles: "Exasperating, yes. Sometimes eruptive, unreasonable, ferocious, and convulsive, yes. Eloquent, penetrating, exciting, and always—never failingly even at the sacrifice of accuracy and at times his own vanity—witty. Never, never, *never* dull." (55)

Peter Cowie, *The Cinema of Orson Welles* (Cranbury, NJ, A. S. Barnes, 1973).

Marion Davies, *The Time We Had with William Randolph Hearst* (New York, Bobbs-Merrill, 1975).

Otis Ferguson, *New Republic*, June 2, 1941 (on *Kane*). (193)

Perry Ferguson, "More Realism from 'Rationed' Sets," *American Cinematographer*, Sept. 1942. (166)

Hallie Flanagan, *Arena: The Story of the Federal Theatre* (New York, Duell, Sloan & Pearce, 1940). (70, 78)

Richard Fleischer, *Just Tell Me When to Cry: A Memoir* (New York, Carroll & Graf, 1993). (359–60)

Joan Fontaine, *No Bed of Roses* (New York, Morrow, 1978). (240, 242)

Roy Alexander Fowler, *Orson Welles: A First Biography* (London, Pendulum, 1946). Not just the first but written by a teenager (English, of course).

Richard France, ed., *Orson Welles on Shakespeare: The WPA and Mercury Theatre Playscripts* (Westport, CT, Greenwood Press, 1990).

————, *The Theatre of Orson Welles* (Cranbury, NJ, Associated University Press, 1977).

Ted Gilling, "Interview with Bernard Herrmann," *Sight & Sound*, Winter 1971–72. (100, 164)

————, "Interviews with George Coulouris and Bernard Herrmann," *Sight & Sound*, Spring 1972.

Patricia Goldstone, "MacLiammóir," *Sight & Sound,* Summer 1978.

Eric A. Gordon, *Mark the Music: The Life and Work of Marc Blitzstein* (New York, St. Martin's Press, 1989). (332)

Ronald Gottesman, ed., *Focus on "Citizen Kane"* (Englewood Cliffs, NJ, Prentice-Hall, 1971).

———, *Focus on Orson Welles* (Englewood Cliffs, NJ, Prentice-Hall, 1976).

Graham Greene, *The Third Man,* screenplay (London, Lorrimer, 1968). (295, 296–7)

Merv Griffin and Peter Barsocchini, *From Where I Sit: Merv Griffin's Book of People* (New York, Arbor House, 1982). (400, 414)

Derick Grigs, "Orson Welles: Conversation at Oxford," *Sight & Sound,* Spring 1960. (347)

Lawrence Grobel, *The Hustons* (New York, Scribner's, 1989).

Gilbert A. Harrison, *The Enthusiast: A Life of Thornton Wilder* (New York, Ticknor & Fields, 1983).

Ron Haver, "The RKO Years: Orson Welles and Howard Hughes," *American Film,* Dec. 1977–Jan. 1978.

William Randolph Hearst, "The Snow Melts on the Mountain," *San Francisco Examiner,* July 4, 1994. (156)

Ben Hecht, *A Child of the Century* (New York, Simon & Schuster, 1954). (22)

Ernest Hemingway, *Death in the Afternoon* (New York, Scribner's, 1932).

William A. Henry III, *The Great One: The Life and Legend of Jackie Gleason* (New York, Doubleday, 1992).

Charlton Heston, *The Actor's Life: Journals 1956–76,* ed. Hollis Alpert (New York, Dutton, 1976). (345, 346)

———, interview with James Delson, *Take One,* July–Aug. 1971. (335, 340)

———, *In the Arena* (New York, Simon & Schuster, 1995). (335, 344, 359)

Charles Higham, *The Films of Orson Welles* (Berkeley, CA, University of California Press, 1971). (396)

———, *Orson Welles: The Rise and Fall of an American Genius* (New York, St. Martin's Press, 1985).

Roger Hill, *One Man's Time and Chance* (private, 1977).

Peter Hogue, "The Friends of Kane," *Film Comment,* Nov.–Dec. 1991.

John Houseman, *Front & Center* (New York, Simon & Schuster, 1979). The second volume of an outstanding autobiography. (316, 329–30)

———, interview with Penelope Houston, *Sight & Sound,* Autumn 1962. (119)

———, *Run-Through: A Memoir* (New York, Simon & Schuster, 1972). The essential first volume of the autobiography and a superb wounded tribute. (50, 52, 66, 67, 69, 82, 85, 109, 111–12, 134, 139, 145, 189)

John Huston, *An Open Book* (New York, Knopf, 1980). (326, 358)

Eugène Ionesco, *Rhinoceros* (London, Calder, 1960). (364)

Alva Johnston and Fred Smith, "How to Raise a Child," *Saturday Evening Post,* January 20, 27 and February 3, 1940.

Nigel Jones, *Through a Glass Darkly: The Life of Patrick Hamilton* (London, Scribner's, 1991).

Pauline Kael, *Kiss Kiss Bang Bang* (Boston, Atlantic–Little, Brown, 1968). Contains her warm review of *Chimes at Midnight.* (382, 396–7)

———, "Raising Kane," in *The Citizen Kane Book* (Boston, Little, Brown, 1971). The inflammatory article, reprinted from *The New Yorker,* not fair or kind but fascinating and vital. (137, 158, 398)

Elia Kazan, *A Life* (New York, Knopf, 1988). (74, 358)

Robert Kensinger and Kristine McKenna, "Orson on Wonderland," *Grand Street*, no. 49, 1994. (416)

Eartha Kitt, *Confessions of a Sex Kitten* (London, Sidgwick & Jackson, 1989). (309)

Howard Koch, *The Panic Broadcast* (Boston, Little, Brown, 1970). Contains the broadcast script for *The War of the Worlds*. (102, 103, 104)

Gavin Lambert, *Cukor on Cukor* (New York, Putnam, 1972). (259)

Barbara Leaming, *If This Was Happiness: A Biography of Rita Hayworth* (New York, Viking, 1989).

———, *Orson Welles: A Biography* (New York, Viking, 1985). A very valuable biography in that it sustained Welles's final years and evidently entertained him; appropriately, the best parts are just Welles in conversation. (26, 48, 78, 143, 333, 359, 365)

Janet Leigh, interview with Rui Noguiera, "Psycho, Rosie and a Touch of Orson," *Sight & Sound*, Spring 1970.

———, *There Really Was a Hollywood* (New York, Doubleday, 1984).

Robert Lewis, *Slings and Arrows: Theater in My Life* (New York, Stein & Day, 1984).

Archibald MacLeish, *The Fall of the City* (Boston, Houghton Mifflin, 1937). (76)

———, *Panic* (Boston, Houghton Mifflin, 1935). (53)

Joseph McBride, "The Lost Kingdom of Orson Welles," *New York Review of Books*, May 13, 1993.

———, *Orson Welles* (London, Secker & Warburg, 1972). (383–4)

———, "The Other Side of Orson Welles," *American Film*, July–Aug. 1976.

Mercedes McCambridge, *The Quality of Mercy: An Autobiography* (New York, Times Books, 1981). (342, 403–4)

Mary McCarthy, "General Macbeth," *Harper's*, June 1962. (286)

Micheál MacLiammóir, *All for Hecuba* (London, Methuen, 1946). (36, 38, 40, 47)

———, *Put Money in Thy Purse* (London, Methuen, 1952). (298–9, 301, 303, 304, 305)

Roger Manvell, *Film and the Public* (Harmondsworth, Middlesex, Penguin, 1955). (233)

Burgess Meredith, *So Far, So Good: A Memoir* (Boston, Little, Brown, 1994). (115–16)

Richard Meryman, *Mank* (New York, Morrow, 1978).

Arthur Miller, *Timebends* (New York, Grove Press, 1987). (239)

Jeanne Moreau, interview, *American Film*, May 1976.

James Naremore, *The Magic World of Orson Welles* (New York, Oxford University Press, 1978). A fine, searching book, beautifully illustrated. (289)

———, "The Trial: The FBI vs. Orson Welles," *Film Comment*, Jan.–Feb. 1991.

Peter Noble, *The Fabulous Orson Welles* (London, Hutchinson, 1956).

Clifford Odets, *The Time Is Ripe: 1940 Journals* (New York, Grove Press, 1940). (179)

Laurence Olivier, *Confessions of an Actor: An Autobiography* (London, Weidenfeld & Nicolson, 1982).

Tim Page and Vanessa Weeks Page, eds., *Selected Letters of Virgil Thomson* (New York, Summit, 1988).

William S. Pechter, "Trials," *Sight & Sound*, Winter 1963–64.

Guy Peellaert and Michael Herr, *The Big Room* (London, Picador, 1986).

Tony Richardson, *The Long-Distance Runner: A Memoir* (New York, Morrow, 1993). (389)

RKO, "Citizen Kane: Souvenir Program" (New York, 1941).

Howard Rodman, "The Western Manhattan Warehouse," draft for an article published in truncated form, *American Film*, January 1986.

Jonathan Rosenbaum, "The Invisible Orson Welles," *Sight & Sound*, Summer 1986. (364, 402)

———, "Pages from the Endfield File," *Film Comment*, Nov.–Dec. 1993.

———, "The Seven *Arkadins*," *Film Comment*, Jan.–Feb. 1992.

———, "The Voice and the Eye," *Film Comment*, Nov.–Dec. 1972. On *Heart of Darkness*.

———, see also *This Is Orson Welles*.

Henry Sheehan, "TV as Snowglobe," *Film Comment*, Jan.–Feb. 1992.

David Shipman, *Judy Garland: The Secret Life of an American Legend* (New York, Hyperion, 1992).

Peter Stackpole, *Life in Hollywood, 1936–1952* (Livingston, Montana, Clark City Press, 1992).

Audrey Stainton, "*Don Quixote: Orson Welles's Secret*," *Sight & Sound*, Autumn 1988.

Robert Stam, "Orson Welles, Brazil and the Power of Blackness," *Persistence of Vision*, no. 7, 1989.

James G. Stewart, "Development of Sound Techniques," American Film Institute Oral History, Los Angeles, 1976.

Susan Strasberg, *Bitter Sweet* (New York, Putnam, 1980).

W. A. Swanberg, *Citizen Hearst* (New York, Scribner's, 1961).

Booth Tarkington, *The Magnificent Ambersons* (New York, Doubleday, Page, 1918). (201)

Howard Teichmann, *Smart Aleck: The Wit, World and Life of Alexander Woollcott* (New York, Morrow, 1976).

Dorothy Thompson, *New York Herald Tribune*, Nov. 2, 1938. On *The War of the Worlds*. (105–6)

Kay Thompson, *Eloise in Paris* (New York, Simon & Schuster, 1957). (314)

Virgil Thomson, *Virgil Thomson* (New York, Knopf, 1966).

Gregg Toland, "How I Broke the Rules in *Citizen Kane*," *Popular Photography*, June 1941.

———, "Realism for *Citizen Kane*," *American Cinematographer*, Feb. 1941.

———, "Using Arcs for Lighting Monochrome," *American Cinematographer*, Dec. 1941.

François Truffaut, *The Films in My Life* (New York, Simon & Schuster, 1975). (347)

Kathleen Tynan, *The Life of Kenneth Tynan* (New York, Morrow, 1987). (303)

Kenneth Tynan, *Profiles* (London, Nick Hern Books, 1989). Contains three essays on Welles, written in 1943, 1953 and 1967. (307)

Gloria Vanderbilt, *Black Knight, White Knight* (New York, Knopf, 1987). (257)

Gore Vidal, "Remembering Orson Welles," *New York Review of Books*, June 1, 1989; repr. *United States: Essays 1952–1992* (New York, Random House, 1993). (138, 250, 418)

Peter Viertel, *Dangerous Friends: At Large with Huston and Hemingway in the Fifties* (New York, Doubleday, 1992). (58, 373)

Nicholas Wapshott, *Carol Reed: A Biography* (London, Chatto & Windus, 1990; New York, Knopf, 1994).

Ruth Warrick, *The Confessions of Phoebe Tyler* (Englewood Cliffs, NJ, Prentice-Hall, 1980).

Armond White, "Wishing Welles," *Film Comment*, Oct. 1988.

Kenneth Williams, *The Kenneth Williams Diaries*, ed. Russell Davies (London, Harper-Collins, 1993). (328)

Robert Wise, "Dialogue on Film," *American Film*, Nov. 1975. (164)

Bret Wood, *Orson Welles: A Bio-Bibliography* (Westport, CT, Greenwood Press, 1990).

————, "Recognizing *The Stranger*" and "Kiss Hollywood Goodbye: Orson Welles and *The Lady from Shanghai*," *Video Watchdog*, May–July 1994. Remarks on material cut from the two films.

Fred Zinnemann, *A Life in the Movies* (London, Scribner's, 1992). (388)

Vera Zorina, *Zorina* (New York, Farrar, Straus & Giroux, 1986). (89)

Albert Zugsmith, interview with Todd McCarthy and Charles Flynn, *Kings of the Bs* (New York, Dutton, 1975). (334–5, 344)

ACKNOWLEDGMENTS

I thank Orson Welles—though I never met him.

I thank Tony Safford, who read part of the manuscript and suggested that it be presented as a novel. I thank Jonathan Segal, who said that would be too simple.

There are people who knew Welles with whom I have talked—some of them years before the occasion for doing this book: John Houseman, Virgil Thomson, Henry Jaglom, William Alland, Cy Endfield, Patrick McGoohan, Loretta Young, Michael Aldridge, Peter Bogdanovich, Fay Wray, Gary Graver, Kay Brown, Cecil Brock, William Herrick, Stanley Cortez, Irene Selznick, Jeffrey Selznick, Fielder Cook, Alan Badel, Cynthia Lindsay, Janet Leigh, Roddy McDowall, Howard Koch.

There are people who helped with the research and the work: Dale Kutzera, who researched in the Welles collection at the Lilly Library in Bloomington; Leslie Felperin, who hunted for pictures in London; Lorraine Latorraca, who turned the manuscript into type.

Then there are friends and colleagues who helped with talk, suggestions, discoveries and argument: Quentin Curtis, Patrick McGilligan, Chris Walters, Kieran Hickey, Brian Gordon, Tom Luddy, Mark Feeney, Bob Gottlieb, Peter Scarlet, Nick Scudamore, Todd McCarthy, Virginia Campbell, Nigel Jones, Charles Bell, Richard and Mary Corliss, Charles Higham, Richard Jameson, Stephen Schiff, Steven Bach, James Toback, Pierre Rissient, Andy Olstein.

I owe a great deal to my publishers, especially to Sonny Mehta, Jonathan Segal, Carol Janeway, Ida Giragossian, Elise Solomon, and Katherine Hourigan in New York, my copyeditor, Susan Brown, and Alan Samson, Philippa Harrison and Richard Beswick in London. I am especially grateful to my agent, Melanie Jackson.

I also thank a "rival," a man of great generosity and kindness, as well as the author of fine books—Simon Callow.

And I thank Lucy, Kate, Mathew, Nicholas, Zachary and Rachel, to whom the book is dedicated, and who has always had too romantic a view of Mr. Welles.

The author and publisher also wish to thank the following for permission to reprint materials in this book:

The Lilly Library, Indiana University, Bloomington, Indiana, for materials in its Welles archive.

The estate of John Houseman for extracts from his book *Run-Through*.

HarperCollins Publishers for extracts from *This Is Orson Welles*, edited by Peter Bogdanovich and Jonathan Rosenbaum.

The Hearst Corporation and the San Francisco *Examiner* for an extract from the poem "Song of the River" by William Randolph Hearst.

Ms. Joanne Styles for lyrics by Roger Hill.

INDEX

Italicized page numbers indicate photographs.

Photographic Credits

The author and the publisher are grateful to the following for the provision of and permission to publish the following photographs:

Permissions Acknowledgments

Grateful acknowledgment is made to the following for permission to reprint previously published and unpublished material:

Cahiers du Cinema: Excerpts from an interview with Orson Welles (*Cahiers du Cinema*, No. 84, June 1958, and No. 87, September 1958). Reprinted by permission of *Cahiers du Cinema*.

French Vogue: Excerpts from the December 1982 French *Vogue*, chosen and written by Orson Welles. Reprinted by permission of French *Vogue*.

HarperCollins Publishers, Inc.: Excerpts from *This Is Orson Welles*, edited by Jonathan Rosenbaum, copyright © 1992 by Oja Kodar, Jonathan Rosenbaum and Peter Bogdanovich. Reprinted by permission of HarperCollins Publishers, Inc.

Joan Houseman: Excerpts from *Run-Through* by John Houseman (New York: Simon & Schuster), copyright © 1972 by John Houseman. Reprinted by permission of Joan Houseman.

The New Republic: Excerpt from film review by Pauline Kael of *Chimes at Midnight*. Copyright © 1966 by The New Republic, Inc. Reprinted by permission of *The New Republic*.

Reed Books: Excerpts from *All for Hecuba* by Micheál MacLiammóir (London: Methuen & Co., 1946), and from *Put Money in Thy Purse* by Micheál MacLiammóir (London: Methuen & Co., 1952). Reprinted by permission of Reed Books.

San Francisco Examiner: Excerpt from the poem "Song of the River" by William Randolph Hearst. Reprinted by permission of the San Francisco *Examiner*.

Turner Entertainment Co.: Excerpts from screenplay *Citizen Kane* by Orson Welles and Herman J. Mankiewicz, copyright © 1941 by RKO Pictures, Inc.; excerpts from screenplay *Magnificent Ambersons* by Orson Welles, copyright © 1942 by RKO Pictures, Inc. All rights reserved. Reprinted by permission of Turner Entertainment Co.